SEEING JUSTICE DONE

From the early Middle Ages to the twentieth century, capital punishment in France, as in many other countries, was staged before large crowds of spectators. Paul Friedland traces the theory and practice of public executions over time, both from the perspective of those who staged these punishments as well as from the vantage point of the many thousands who came to 'see justice done'. While penal theorists often stressed that the fundamental purpose of public punishment was to strike fear in the hearts of spectators, the eagerness with which crowds flocked to executions, and the extent to which spectators actually enjoyed the spectacle of suffering suggests that there was a wide gulf between theoretical intentions and actual experiences. Moreover, public executions of animals, effigies, and corpses point to an enduring ritual function that had little to do with exemplary deterrence. In the eighteenth century, when a revolution in sensibilities made it unseemly for individuals to take pleasure in or even witness the suffering of others, capital punishment became the target of reformers. From the invention of the guillotine, which reduced the moment of death to the blink of an eye, to the 1939 decree which moved executions behind prison walls, capital punishment in France was systematically stripped of its spectacular elements.

Partly a history of penal theory, partly an anthropologically-inspired study of the penal ritual, *Seeing Justice Done* traces the historical roots of modern capital punishment, and sheds light on the fundamental 'disconnect' between the theory and practice of punishment which endures to this day, not only in France but in the Western penal tradition more generally.

Paul Friedland is Professor of History at Cornell University. His first book, *Political Actors: Representative Bodies and Theatricality in the Age of the French Revolution* (2002), was awarded the Pinkney Prize for the best book of the year by the Society for French Historical Studies.

Seeing Justice Done

The Age of Spectacular Capital Punishment in France

PAUL FRIEDLAND

OXFORD
UNIVERSITY PRESS

Great Clarendon Street, Oxford OX2 6DP,
United Kingdom

Oxford University Press is a department of the University of Oxford.
It furthers the University's objective of excellence in research, scholarship,
and education by publishing worldwide. Oxford is a registered trade mark of
Oxford University Press in the UK and in certain other countries

© Paul Friedland 2012

The moral rights of the author have been asserted

First Edition published in 2012
First published in paperback 2014

All rights reserved. No part of this publication may be reproduced, stored in
a retrieval system, or transmitted, in any form or by any means, without the
prior permission in writing of Oxford University Press, or as expressly permitted
by law, or under terms agreed with the appropriate reprographics
rights organization. Enquiries concerning reproduction outside the scope of the
above should be sent to the Rights Department, Oxford University Press,
at the address above

You must not circulate this work in any other form
and you must impose this same condition on any acquirer

Published in the United States of America by Oxford University Press
198 Madison Avenue, New York, NY 10016, United States of America

British Library Cataloguing in Publication Data
Data available

Library of Congress Cataloging in Publication Data
Friedland, Paul
Seeing justice done : the age of spectacular capital punishment
in France / Paul Friedland.
p.   cm.
Includes bibliographical references and index.
ISBN 978–0–19–959269–2 (hardback)
1. Capital punishment—France—History. 2. Executions and executioners—
France—History. 3. Guillotine—France—History. I. Title.
HV8699.F8F75 2012
364.660944—dc23   2012002449

ISBN 978–0–19–959269–2 (Hbk)
ISBN 978–0–19–871599–3 (Pbk)

Contents

List of illustrations	viii
Acknowledgments	ix
Introduction: Reading and Writing a History of Punishment	1
The Sow of Falaise: The Making of an Historical Legend	2
A Distant Mirror? Reading Historical Narratives of the Sow of Falaise	10
From the Barbarians' Point of View: Narratives of Punishment as Historical Anthropology	11

I. THE ROOTS OF MODERN PUNISHMENT IN PRE-MODERN EUROPE

1. The Fall and Rise of Rome: Compensation, Atonement, and Deterrence in the Early Middle Ages	23
Roman Law after the Fall of Rome: Deterrence Decontextualized	26
The Laws of the Salian Franks: Punishment as Payback	29
Christian Penance and Atonement	32
The Renaissance of Roman Legal Studies in Medieval Europe	38
2. Criminal Intent and Spectacular Punishment: The Infiltration of Roman Legal Theory and Practice into French Customary Law	46
Intentionality and Customary Law	49
Lèse-Majesté and Treason in Customary Law	52
High Justice, Low Justice, and the Spectacularization of Punishment	56
The Homogenization of Justice	65

II. EXECUTIONERS AND THE RITUAL OF EXECUTION

3. Extraordinary Beings: The Life and Work of Executioners	71
A Race of Outcasts	71
A People Apart: Duties, Privileges, and Restrictions	76
The End of an Era: The Abolition of Havage	85
4. The Execution of Justice: The Ritual of Punishment in Medieval and Early Modern France	89
The First Stage: Display and Shame	91
The Second Stage: Expulsion and Liminality	98
The Third Stage: Death as Reintegration or as the Ultimate Exile	101

Beyond Deterrence: The Execution of Inanimate and Non-Human Bodies   107
Reconciling the Irreconcilable: Sixteenth-Century Jurists on
Customary Practice and Deterrence Theory   112

III. SPECTATORS AND SPECTACLE

5. From Ritual to Spectacle: The Rise of the Penal Voyeur in Early Modern France   119
Watching Executions before the Sixteenth Century   120
Spectacular Novelties   124
A New Spectacularity: Anatomy Theaters, Executions, and the Diary of Felix Platter   128
Markers of a Shift in Viewing Habits: L'Estoile's Journals and the Rise of Canards   132
Executions as Tragic Spectacle: Rosset's *Histoires tragiques*   136

6. Executions, Spectator Emotions, and the Naturalization of Sympathy   143
A Rising Spectacularity   144
Sentimental Journey: From Stoic Insensitivity to *Sensibilité*   150
"Neither shame, nor horror in attending"   155
The Naturalization of Sympathy: Sensibility as Human Nature   158

7. A Spectacular Crisis: Watching Executions in the Age of *Sensibilité*   165
Penal Spectators and the First Glimmerings of Self-Consciousness   166
Collision Course: Spectacularity, Sentimentality, and Exemplary Deterrence   168
The Execution of Damiens: "The most horrible and disgusting punishment that justice has ever dared to imagine"   176
The 1750s: A Watershed of Sensibilities   183
In the Wake of Damiens: A "Horror" of the Penal Spectacle   186

IV. A DEATH PENALTY FOR THE MODERN AGE

8. Theorizing a New Death Penalty: Penal Reform on the Eve of the Revolution   195
Utopian Penal Reform   196
The End of Utopia: Montesquieu's *L'Esprit des Lois*   199
Beccaria's *On Crimes and Punishments*   205
Beccaria's Reception and Legacy   208
The Great (non-)Debate on Capital Punishment from Beccaria to the Penal Code of 1791   209

9. **Legislating the New Death Penalty: The Simple
   Deprivation of Life** — 218
   Guillotin's Proposals for Reform — 218
   The Naturalization of the Executioner — 224
   A New Penal Code? — 226
   Debates on Capital Punishment — 230
   A Spectacular Death vs. the Simple Deprivation of Life — 233
   Killing Humanely — 235

10. **Executing the New Death Penalty: The Invisible Spectacle
    of the Guillotine** — 239
    The Search for a Humane Killing Machine — 240
    Inventing the Guillotine — 243
    The Guillotine in Action — 247
    Gauging the Guillotine's Popularity — 252
    The Industrialization of Capital Punishment? — 260

Epilogue: The Play Over, the Actors (Slowly) Leave the Stage — 266
The Guillotine: A Disappearing Act — 266

Conclusion: Punishment Past and Present — 280

Notes — 285
Index — 325

List of illustrations

1. The Execution of the Sow of Falaise. Frontispiece to Arthur Mangin, *L'Homme et la Bête* (Paris, 1872).   8
2. Fourches patibulaires. Eugène Viollet-le-Duc, *Dictionnaire raisonné de l'architecture française du XIe au XVIe siècle* (Paris, 1868), 5:561.   61
3. The Wheel, from *Les Grandes Misères de la Guerre* by Jacques Callot (Paris, 1633). University of Michigan Museum of Art.   64
4. Gruet au pilori des Halles. Facsimile of the original illustration, in Paul Lacroix, *XVIIIe siècle, Institutions, usages et costumes* (Paris, 1875), 305.   96
5. Antoine François Derues faisant amende-honorable devant Notre Dame, 1777. Bibliothèque Nationale de France.   97
6. Les pénitents de Limoges (retrospective exhibition at the Palace of Industry, *Histoire du costume*), *Le Monde illustré* (10 October 1874), no. 913.   105
7. Execution of Anne du Bourg, 1559, reproduced in Alfred Franklin, ed., *Les Grandes Scènes historiques du XVIe siècle, reproduction fac-similé du recueil de J. Tortorel et J. Perrissin* (Paris, 1886).   132
8. Cartouche à l'Hôtel de Ville avant son supplice, reproduced in Paul Lacroix, *XVIIIe siècle, Institutions, usages et costumes* (Paris, 1875), 311.   171
9. Thomas Artur de Lally, condamné par Arest du Parlement d'avoir la tête tranchée en Place de Grève, le 8 May 1766 . . . . Bibliothèque Nationale de France.   187
10. Ecce Custine, 1794. Carnavalet Museum/Snark Archives. © Photo12/The Image Works.   237
11. Machine proposée à l'Assemblée nationale pour le supplice des criminels par Mr. Guillotin, 1789. The Getty Research Institute, Los Angeles, CA (2682-320).   245
12. Matière à réflection pour les jongleurs couronnées, 1793. Bibliothèque Nationale de France.   251
13. Jacques-Louis David's sketch of Marie-Antoinette on her way to the scaffold, from a facsimile of the original in Hector Fleischmann, *La Guillotine en 1793* (Paris, 1908), 215.   261
14. Illustration accompanying the guillotine in each department, with assembly instructions, from a facsimile of the original in Philippe Maréchal, *La Révolution dans la Haute-Saône* (Paris, 1903), 406.   263
15. Execution of Eugène Weidmann. © Roger-Viollet/The Image Works.   278

Acknowledgments

This book has been a very long time in the making, and I have incurred many debts. I am especially grateful to the National Endowment for the Humanities, and to the American Council of Learned Societies, which helped to make this book possible through year-long fellowships. I owe thanks as well to the Minda de Gunzburg Center for European Studies at Harvard University, which has provided me with an academic "home" for the past few years.

Early drafts of chapters were presented to colleagues at several institutions. I am enormously appreciative of the many individuals who participated in the following workshops, who took the time to offer me advice and criticism: "The Seminar" of the History Department at Johns Hopkins University, the MIT History/Literature Workshop, the Annual Speakers Series at Penn State University, the Harvard Colloquium for Intellectual and Cultural History, the Bloomington Eighteenth–Century Workshop, and the Stanford University Humanities Center. While it would be impossible to thank everyone who contributed to this project, I owe particular thanks to the following individuals who, whether in person or by email, shared texts or offered advice, suggestions, and criticism: Keith Baker, David Bates, Antonella Bettoni, Tom Conlan, Dallas Denery, Michel and Danielle Demorest, Guy Dupont, Dan Edelstein, Garrett Fagan, Benoit Garnot, Art Goldhammer, Joan Landes, Tyler Lange, Judith Miller, Jeff Ravel, Robert Schneider, Carol Steiker, Danielle Trudeau, and Dror Wahrman. I would also like to express my gratitude to the staff at Oxford University Press, especially to Christopher Wheeler and Stephanie Ireland, and to Richard Mason, my copy-editor.

To the special few on whom I have inflicted a good portion of the manuscript, I am especially grateful. David Bell pushed me to think more deeply about sentimentality, when I was still resisting the idea. Joan Scott challenged me, as always, to rethink my own assumptions. As I began to stray outside my chronological comfort zone, I benefited from the much-needed encouragement of Dan Smail, and from the sage advice of Barbara Rosenwein, who saved me not only from making many errors but also from falling under the sway of an outdated historiography of the Middle Ages. (As is perhaps inevitable in a book that attempts to tell a story over such a long period of time, errors no doubt still remain, and the responsibility, of course, lies squarely with me.) I wish to express my sincere thanks, as well, to the anonymous reviewers at Oxford University Press, whose insightful comments proved invaluable.

Pascal Bastien has been extraordinarily generous in sharing with me the fruits of his research, and although I have tried to include him diligently in the endnotes of this book, it would be impossible to cite adequately the conversations that we have had over the years that have contributed to my understanding of the subject. I truly appreciate his generosity and his collegiality.

Above all, I owe thanks to my family. My four children, Alexander, Talia, Lily, and Laney, were much more understanding and patient than they ought to have been when their father disappeared into his office for hours on end, trying to make sense of the past, when he should have been enjoying the present with them. As always, my greatest debt is to my wife and colleague, Page Herrlinger. Although at times I suspected her of rifling through my notes for ideas about which method of capital punishment might be most appropriate for someone who spent a decade writing a book, she nevertheless took up the slack when I needed her to, allowing me the precious commodity of time. I am truly grateful, and although I would never admit it to her in person, I am in awe of her generosity.

Introduction
Reading and Writing a History of Punishment

In the early days of January 1386, in the Norman town of Falaise, a horrible and revolting crime took place, a crime that would eventually become infamous in the annals of history. On that January day, more than six centuries ago, an intruder entered the home of Jonnet le Maçon. The motive for the intrusion was undoubtedly food, something that must have been in short supply so long after the harvests of the previous fall, and the intruder was hungry, ravenously hungry. Whether there was no food to be found in the house, or whether the food that the intruder did find was insufficient, we do not know. What we do know, however, is that at some point after entering the home, the intruder came upon a small child—a boy of approximately three months of age—lying in his crib. It was then that the heinous crime took place. With the parents apparently nowhere in sight, the intruder fell upon and began eating the infant, taking bites directly out of the little boy's face.

The child would die as a result of his wounds. The authorities quickly identified a suspect, and although we do not know exactly what happened next, it is probable that the suspect was placed into custody and that formal judicial proceedings were initiated. We do know that the intruder was found guilty of the crime, and was condemned to be dragged through the streets of the town—probably tied to a hurdle that was attached to a horse or donkey—and then hanged at the place of justice, the usual punishment for those who had been convicted of homicide. This sentence was duly carried out on 9 January 1386 by the official executioner of Falaise, who was paid 10 sols 10 deniers for his services.

What made this particular crime and this punishment so infamous? Was it perhaps the fact that cannibalism was involved? No. In fact, no cannibalism technically took place, as the intruder was a three-year-old sow. Was it then, perhaps, the very fact that judicial proceedings had been undertaken against a pig, or the fact that an animal had been condemned to die at the hands of the official executioner? As odd as it may sound to us today, neither the crime itself, the judicial proceedings, nor the punishment were all that unusual in pre-modern France. As for the crime, it would seem that infants were eaten by animals—usually pigs—with surprising frequency at this time. There are more than thirty documented cases of pigs who were accused of homicide, and this number only includes those cases whose records have survived; nor does it include the many horses, bulls, oxen, and dogs who were accused of killing people. In all of these cases, if guilt was established—by no means a foregone conclusion—then the convicted animal was subject to the very same punishment a human being would have suffered for the crime of murder: drawing and hanging.

In addition to being prosecuted for murder, animals in the pre-modern period were also tried for the crime of having sexual relations with people and, if they were found guilty, suffered the same punishments as human beings: burning at the stake, very often alongside their human partners in crime. All together, the number of documented cases involving the criminal trial of animals in France from the thirteenth through the seventeenth century numbers more than a hundred; this number may be a conservative estimate, however, as the documents of bestiality trials were often burned after the trial so that no records would remain of that "sin which cannot be named."

Why did the inhabitants of medieval and early modern France—as well as parts of what is today Germany, the Netherlands, Switzerland, and Italy—subject animals to criminal prosecution and punishment? The efforts that many historians, both professional and amateur, have undertaken to answer this question are, I think, every bit as interesting as the question itself. In the course of this book, I will add my own interpretation of animal trials and executions to the long line of those that have already been written. For the moment, however, for the purposes of this introduction, I would like to carefully reconstruct the story not of the crime and the punishment that took place in 1386, but rather the story of the story: how a not entirely unusual crime and punishment grew into the historical legend of the infamous Sow of Falaise. By reconstructing the making of this legend, I hope to show how modern conceptions of punishment have a tendency to color our reading of the penal past. In other words, by looking at what historians over time have tended to "see" that—truth be told—simply is not there, we can gain some very interesting insights into our own, modern assumptions about the essential purpose of punishment.

THE SOW OF FALAISE: THE MAKING OF AN HISTORICAL LEGEND

Although the Sow of Falaise may not be a household name, in the rarefied circles of penal historians of pre-modern Europe she is indisputably infamous. But why? There are, after all, other cases that, at least from a juridical standpoint, are decidedly more interesting. Take, for example, the case of another sow who in the year 1457 was convicted of having murdered five-year-old Jehan Martin, but whose six piglets, although stained with blood and found at the scene of the crime, could not be immediately condemned because, unlike their mother, they had not been caught in the act. The bloodstains were, of course, incriminating, but they were not conclusive, and the court decided to remand the piglets to the custody of their owner, who promised to return them to the court "if it is discovered that they did eat the said Jehan Martin."[1] There is also the case of the donkey who was caught *in flagrante delicto* with a man, but who was exonerated by the judges in view of the fact that she had apparently been an unwilling victim of a human aggressor.[2]

With the Sow of Falaise, however, there were no interesting questions of culpability, no semi-incriminating evidence, no possibility of exoneration. Instead, it was a cut-and-dried case of homicide. Yet, surprisingly, the case of the Sow of Falaise has been written about more than any other animal punishment in the history of France and, one might suspect, the world. Again: Why?

The key to understanding how this one case became so well known lies less in the facts of the crime itself than in the successive retelling of the facts by generations of historians, both amateur and professional. For, like a child's game of "telephone" or "Chinese Whispers," in which an original message is gradually altered by successive recipients, who either do not hear the original message correctly or who allow their imaginations to substitute a new version for the one delivered to them, the story of the Sow of Falaise underwent some profound and rather interesting changes in the course of its successive retelling over the centuries.

For nearly four hundred years after the crime occurred, the story of the Sow of Falaise seems to have disappeared into oblivion. Then, in 1764, Claude François Blondeau de Charnage had the idea of publishing a kind of inventory of official records gathered from local archives. Included in this random compilation of various bits and pieces of paper was a receipt of payment to the executioner of Falaise, which, although Charnage correctly lumped it together with other documents from 1386–87, he mistakenly labeled as an "Original receipt dated January 9, 1396 [sic]." Thinking that it was curious enough to interest his readers, Charnage transcribed the receipt of payment for 10 sols 10 deniers under the heading "Norman Simplicity":

> for his efforts and salary for having dragged and then hanged at the [place of] Justice in Falaise a sow of approximately three years of age who had eaten the face of the child of Jonnet le Maçon, who was in his crib & who was approximately three months old, in such a way that the said infant died from [the injuries], and [an additional] ten s[oux] tournois for a new glove[3] when the Hangman performed the said execution: this receipt is given to Regnaud Rigaut, Vicomte de Falaise; the Hangman declares that he is well satisfied with this sum and that he makes no further claims on the King our Sire and the said Vicomte.

From this receipt, Charnage deduced that the "sow underwent a trial, and that she was declared guilty in true juridical fashion."[4]

To the best of my knowledge, this receipt constitutes the full extent of the written evidence that has ever been found pertaining to the Sow of Falaise. And from this meager documentation an entire historical legend would be born.

There was a mild flurry of interest following Charnage's publication of the receipt. In the next year or two, the story made the rounds, along with the story of a homicidal bull who had been executed in Moisy in 1314, in the circles of those who liked to share interesting and arcane information.[5] Then, five years after Charnage had first published the receipt, the Abbé Béziers published a history of Caen and its surrounding region in which he saw fit to include the anecdote, taken directly from Charnage, of the trial and punishment of the Sow of Falaise, describing it as "a singular event which very well characterizes the coarseness of its age."

Béziers' version of the story was more or less faithful to Charnage's retelling, but with a few subtle changes. In the first place, he inexplicably altered the name of the father of the Sow's victim from Jonnet le Maçon to Journet le Maçon—a harmless enough alteration, but the first in what would prove to be an endless succession of name changes. Béziers also related the details of another case in which a homicidal bull had been put on trial and executed in Beauvais in 1499 because of, in the words of the court sentence, "the abhorrence of the crime." Béziers concluded, therefore, that the case of the Sow of Falaise was "ridiculous" but not unique.[6]

The next person to pick up the story of the Sow of Falaise was A. Brillon, who included it in his *Dictionnaire de Jurisprudence*, published in 1786. Under the heading "Animal," and citing Béziers as his source, Brillon related the events more or less as Béziers had described them, with one or two minor exceptions. Previous accounts of the story had left it unclear whether "Maçon," meaning mason, was part of the father's name or his occupation. Brillon opted definitively for the latter, and also slightly altered the father's name. Here is his account of the story:

> In 1396, the hangman of Falaise, after a formal judgment, preceded by a juridical inquiry, dragged "and then hanged, at the [place of] Justice in this town, a sow of approximately three years of age who had eaten the face of the infant of Journu, the mason, who was in his crib and approximately three months of age, in such a manner that the said infant died from [injuries]."[7]

Minor details have been changed, but the story remains more or less the same. If anything, as historians became more familiar with the existence of other animal trials in the period, the story of the Sow of Falaise was beginning to seem less unique and possibly less interesting. But an amateur historian and priest by the name of P. G. Langevin would change all that, and make sure that the Sow of Falaise would live in infamy.

Abbé Langevin's first retelling of the story appeared in a history of Falaise published in 1814. His account begins curiously enough, with an important correction followed by some strange alterations to the story: "According to…Blondeau [de Charnage]…in 1396 (*read* 1386), [the vicomte of Falaise] had the public executioner hang a sow who had eaten the arm of the infant of a man named Jonet, a mason, [as the child lay] in his crib." Here, Langevin is the first to include the correct date, having clearly taken the trouble to notice Charnage's mistake, which had been obvious within the context of the other documents he reproduced. But, strangely, the sow has now eaten the child's arm rather than his face, and the father, now definitively a mason, goes by the name of Jonet. But it is in the next few sentences that Langevin dramatically rewrote the story: "In thus punishing the sow, [the vicomte] deprived the negligent individual who owned her [of his sow], and…obliged him to attend the execution. The father of the child was also obliged to attend, as punishment for not having kept an eye on his child."[8]

Where do these new details come from? I am fairly certain that this new information concerning the pig owner's and the father's forced attendance at the execution was derived from Langevin's own impression of what *must* have taken place rather than from any other source. Langevin essentially took a story that, from a modern perspective, was incomprehensible, or as Béziers had put it, "ridiculous," and made it comprehensible by transforming it into a much more "rational" punishment of negligent people—the pig owner and the father.

Punishment may be about many things, but in the last instance, we citizens of the modern world have an almost visceral need to believe that it is *primarily* about one thing: deterrence. When all is said and done, we suspect that the *real* reason to punish is to prevent crime. Penal deterrence, we believe, works on two different levels. In the first place, it dissuades the actual offenders who commit crimes from committing other crimes in the future, either by teaching them that criminal actions have negative consequences, or by rendering them physically incapable of committing other crimes (through incarceration or the death penalty). On another, more general level, we believe in the basic principle of exemplary deterrence: the idea that the very fact of punishing one offender "sends a message" to all would-be miscreants that the commission of a crime has negative consequences.

The punishment of a pig for murder violates our modern understanding of the essential purpose of punishment because it punishes an animal, which we ordinarily do not believe to be capable of criminal intent, and because it does not lend itself very well to the principle of exemplary deterrence. Langevin's rewriting of the story of the Sow of Falaise allowed an incomprehensible anecdote from the past to fit neatly into the modern paradigm of penal deterrence. Yes, it was true; they had punished a pig. But the *real* purpose of the execution was to teach a lesson to the pig's owner and to the boy's father—and presumably to *other* pig owners and fathers—about negligence and about what can happen when pigs and little boys are left without proper supervision.

Langevin and his readers may have wondered, however, whether there was not a more straightforward way of punishing the pig owner and the father than through the prosecution and punishment of the pig. Why were the owner and father themselves not put on trial for negligence, rather than the pig? These thoughts must have occurred to Langevin himself, because twelve years later, in 1826, he published a "supplement" to his history of Falaise, in which he revealed some startling new details about the Sow of Falaise:

> This sow, who had eaten not only the arm but also the face of this child, suffered, before being hanged, the punishment of talion [i.e. an eye for an eye]. They cut off her snout, in the place of which they put the mask of a human face; [the sow] was dressed in a jacket, an *haut-de-chausses* [trunk hose worn by boys and men], breeches on the hind legs, and white gloves on the forelegs; and then she was hanged in accordance with the decreed sentence "because of the abhorrence of the crime."[9]

There is so much added to the story in these few sentences that it is difficult to know where to begin. Langevin's account begins with a half-correction to his earlier account. Now, the sow had eaten "not only" the arm but also the face of the child. But it is the startling addition of the pig's mutilation and anthropomorphosis that allows Langevin to "explain away," so to speak, the inconvenient fact that the authorities had punished the sow rather than the negligent human beings. Now, in some vague way, it made sense that they had punished the Sow: the execution was a kind of primitive judicial form of *retaliation*, the word itself being derived from the *lex talionis*, the injunction that all injuries would be repaid in kind, an eye for an eye, a tooth for a tooth. In this new version of the story, the severing of the snout essentially accomplished two things: it disfigured the pig just as the pig had disfigured the child; and the mask, along with the clothing appropriate for a little boy, transformed the female pig into a male child so that the crime could be re-enacted on the body of the criminal, tit for tat. The punishment was not, then, as it first appeared, the punishment of a pig. Instead, it was the anthropomorphosis of a sow so that the pig-turned-little-boy could suffer the very same punishments that she had inflicted on the child.

This new information obviously made the execution of the Sow of Falaise appear in an entirely different light. What was Langevin's source for this new information? This is unclear. The phrase "because of the abhorrence of the crime" is credited to Brillon, with the implication that he is the source for the additional details. But the story of the severed snout and the human mask, and the details about the human clothing, are nowhere to be found in Brillon, and neither is the phrase "because of the abhorrence of the crime," which can be found instead, as we have seen, in Béziers, however not in reference to the Sow of Falaise but rather to the Bull of Beauvais.

Langevin had one last historical bombshell to drop, which ensured that the legend of the Sow of Falaise would be a subject of fascination for generations to come:

> This singular event is painted in fresco on the western wall of the wing or the meridian intersection of the church of the Holy Trinity in Falaise. The aforementioned infant and his brother, sleeping side by side in a crib, are represented on this wall, near the staircase leading to the bell tower. And then, near the middle of this wall, are painted the gallows, [with] the sow dressed in human form, being hanged in the presence of the vicomte, on horseback, a feather in his hat, a fist at his side, watching over the whole affair.

A painting? An original fresco from the fourteenth century? This, then, was Langevin's evidence. The fresco, which so clearly represented all the new details of the story, would stand as proof to all who might have any doubts as to the veracity of the story. They would only need to enter the church of Falaise, gaze at the fresco for themselves, and their doubts would be dispelled by this work of art that served almost as a kind of window onto the penal past. It was almost too good to be true.

It was strange, of course, that no one had ever mentioned the fresco before, but there it was, for all to see. Or, perhaps not. As Langevin informed his readers, "Ever since the entire church was whitewashed around 1820 [i.e. six years earlier], one can no longer see this painting." But, Langevin consoled his readers, "When the white disappears, the painting will reappear, as this has already happened [in places?], although the frame for the banner which was recently put there has obscured a part of it."[10]

All of these new details precipitated renewed interest–even a fascination–with the case, which has continued unabated in some circles to the present day. The very same year in which Langevin's supplement was published (1826), another book undertook the task of assembling all the details related to the Sow of Falaise in one place. The authoritative *Statistique de l'arrondissement de Falaise*, compiled by several different local authorities on town history, provided a composite history of the case, based on all previous retellings, including both of Langevin's. Prefacing their definitive account with the remark that while "the anecdote contains little of interest in itself, it nevertheless familiarizes us very well with the coarseness of our ancestors at the time," the authors told the story as follows:

> In 1386, a sow devoured the son of a workman in the city, named Janet. This accident came to the attention of the judge, who condemned the animal to publically suffer the punishment of talion. The child had had his face and arm torn to pieces; the sow was mutilated in a like manner, and then hanged by the hangman. The execution took place on the public square, in the presence of all the townspeople. The vicomte-judge presided over all of this "on horseback, with a feather in his hat and fist at his side." To complete the horror, the father of the victim was required to attend this execution; they wanted to punish him, according to the historian of this event, for having failed to watch over his child. When the animal was brought to the place of execution, he had on human clothes, a jacket, *hauts-de-chausses* and gloves. Affixed to his head was a mask representing a human face.
>
> This event seemed so remarkable in its day, that the memory of it was conserved in the form of a fresco painting which could be seen, six years ago, in the church of the Holy Trinity.[11]

Here, after yet another alteration to the father's name, we have everything in one place: the claim that the father had been forced to attend "for having failed to watch over his child" (although the forced attendance of the negligent pig owner is missing from this version); the details of the sow's anthropomorphosis, her transformation into a little boy, and her mutilation in precisely the same manner in which she herself had mutilated her victim; and last, but certainly not least, the details of the fresco, which served as a kind of living proof of all that had transpired (at least until the date of the whitewashing, six years earlier). Future historians, most of whom would base their accounts on the *Statistique*'s definitive compilation, would not fail to see that the trial and punishment of the Sow of Falaise was at one and the same time both an exercise in deterrence intended to teach a lesson to negligent parents, and a kind of primitive exercise in retaliation in which the pig suffered exactly the same punishments that she herself had inflicted. Future historians would not fail to see this, because the interpretations had been planted there, in all the imaginary details supplied by Abbé Langevin.

Over the course of the nineteenth century, the legend of the Sow of Falaise, replete with all the details of the severed snout and the human mask and clothing, would be reproduced in a number of articles and books.[12] In 1872, not content to rely on a picture that had disappeared beneath whitewash, the author of *L'Homme et la Bête*, Arthur Mangin, commissioned a recreation of the fresco, which he used as the frontispiece to his book, in which the sow, dressed plainly in human clothing (although sans human mask) is about to be hanged by the executioner, the noose dangling above her head (Fig. 1). Gathered beneath the scaffold is a large and boisterous crowd that would seem to comprise the entire population of the town of Falaise: men, women, and children. Interestingly, the only figure who appears to be paying attention to the action on the scaffold is a little boy, hoisted on his father's shoulders, who seems to be applauding the execution almost as if it represents the revenge of all little boys against the miscreant sow.

Supplice d'une truie.

Fig. 1. The Execution of the Sow of Falaise. Frontispiece to Arthur Mangin, *L'Homme et la Bête* (Paris, 1872).

In the twentieth century, the *Statistique*'s version of events, along with Mangin's recreated picture, would make its way into a book that was to become (and still is to this day) the most widely read text on the subject of animal trials: E. P. Evans's *The Criminal Prosecution and Capital Punishment of Animals*, published in 1906. Evans, like so many before him, cites the version from the *Statistique*, opining that the punishment, in which the sow was "mangled and maimed in the head and forelegs" just as the animal itself had "torn the face and arms" of the child, was clearly "a strict application of the *lex talionis*, the primitive retributive principle of taking an eye for an eye and a tooth for a tooth." Citing both the *Statistique* and Langevin, Evans goes on to describe the location of the fresco that represented all of this in living color, but which was sadly whitewashed in 1820, without a true copy ever being made.[13]

Over the course of the twentieth century, the legend of the Sow of Falaise appeared in countless articles, magazines, and books, most of which have cited the numerous works that had told the story before them as if they were separate, corroborative pieces of evidence, rather than a long and increasingly distorted retelling of the same story derived from the same source, which, we should remember, is merely the executioner's receipt that does not reveal much more than the simple fact that a sow was dragged and hanged for killing a small boy. Somehow, though, the illusion has persisted that a veritable trove of evidence exists, which corroborates the imagined details of the case, although the only evidence that has ever existed—apart from the alleged fresco—was the original receipt with scant details.[14]

Evans's book was reprinted in 1987, with the cover sporting a detail of the recreated picture from 1872: the sow, appropriately colored pink in an otherwise black-and-white illustration, is grimacing in pain as the executioner pulls at her neck. This edition of the book, published in the form of an inexpensive paperback, fueled a surge of renewed interest in the Sow of Falaise. Among the most recent versions of the story are some that, in addition to the usual name changes, have claimed it was not only the sow's owner and the father of her victim who were forced to attend her execution, but that "a multitude of pigs" were also required to attend so that they too might learn a lesson from the spectacle.[15]

And so, at the end of this historians' game of "telephone," we have made our way from a relatively simple story of a sow who killed a little boy by eating his face and was drawn and hanged for her crime, to the complicated legend of the Sow of Falaise, who ate the face and arm of a mason's son and, for her crime, was dressed in little boy's clothing, had her snout severed and a human mask affixed in its place. She was then hanged before an audience that included not only the entire town of Falaise but also the father of her victim, her owner, and a "multitude of pigs," all of whom were forced to attend so that they might learn from her example. That is certainly quite a change from the original story.

A DISTANT MIRROR? READING HISTORICAL NARRATIVES OF THE SOW OF FALAISE

What can we learn from this comedy of errors and exaggerations? Quite a bit, I think. Certainly some of the alterations to the story are innocent enough, and do not dramatically alter the essential facts or our interpretation of it. The changes in the father's name, for example, do little to alter the essence of the story. Nevertheless, they do offer an interesting visual tableau that illustrates how the story mutated over time: from the original Jonnet le Maçon, successive authors changed the name to Journet le Maçon; Journu, the mason; Jonet, the mason; Janet; Ionnet le Maux; Jounet le Maux, who was a mason; and finally the attribution of the name Jean le Maux to the infant victim, whose father was a mason.

Other changes to the story are much more consequential, however, and much more important for our purposes. Most notably, the addition of new details by Abbé Langevin between 1814 and 1826 radically altered the story itself. What Langevin did was to plant something in the past—more familiar, more comprehensible, and, in the end, more reassuring. He essentially hid, among the artifacts of the past, what we might think of as a faux-antique, cracked, and smoky mirror in which we imagined that we were seeing something entirely new when, in fact, we were seeing a very fuzzy reflection of ourselves.

Historians, particularly present-day historians, are always on their guard against anachronisms, always careful not to allow their own modern-day assumptions to color their readings of the past. But there are clearly certain visceral assumptions that, despite our best efforts, we historians have great difficulty not bringing along with us on our journeys into the past. Langevin played upon those assumptions by supplying the details, which enabled us to rewrite the story in a way that made intuitive sense to us. Thanks to him, we could understand the execution of the Sow of Falaise to be the story of our own cultural ancestors, caught between a primitive, almost crude form of retaliation and an early, almost infantile and simplistic attempt at modern penal deterrence. The people of fourteenth-century Falaise were shown to be what we so often assume the inhabitants of the past to be: coarser, more simplistic versions of ourselves.

My intention here is not to cast supercilious aspersions on the methods and practices of other historians, and my use of the phrase "we historians" is not a rhetorical flourish because, as I think it only fair to confess, I too played my own small, ignoble part in this historian's game of "telephone." When I was at the beginning of this project, I published some of my initial reflections in an article in which, like so many others before me, I repeated the story of the Sow of Falaise, citing the work of previous historians, primarily Evans and Sorel. The story seemed such a neat fit for some of the arguments that I was just beginning to formulate, that I thought it expedient not to look this evidentiary gift horse too closely in the mouth. The only indication I gave to readers that I might, even then, have had some questions as to the provenance and authenticity of the information was my use of the phrase, "If accurate, these details would seem to indicate..." at the beginning of my interpretative paragraph.[16]

Let me say very clearly that what is in doubt here is not the fact that judicial proceedings were undertaken against animals or that animals suffered the death penalty at the hands of official executioners. Such cases were indisputably a feature of the judicial landscape in certain regions of France and neighboring countries from roughly the thirteenth to the seventeenth century.

There is, in other words, nothing particularly extraordinary about the Sow of Falaise within the context of her time. The only thing that sets this story apart from the other hundred or so documented cases of animal executions in France is what subsequent historians made of it and the way it was molded to fit our preconceptions about the essential nature of punishment and about the coarseness of past practices. To a great extent we owe these preconceptions to the penal reformers of the eighteenth century, who subscribed to the belief that the essential function of punishment was deterrence, and that any form of punishment that imperfectly accomplished that aim was either nonsensical or "barbaric."

FROM THE BARBARIANS' POINT OF VIEW: NARRATIVES OF PUNISHMENT AS HISTORICAL ANTHROPOLOGY

Perhaps more than anyone else, Michel Foucault challenged the basic assumptions of the Enlightenment reformers, and in his seminal book *Discipline and Punish* endeavored to recover the logic of pre-modern punishment from an Enlightenment discourse that had declared it to be beyond logic. Arguing that punishment in the early modern period did not "fall upon the body indiscriminately" and that it was instead "calculated according to detailed rules," Foucault took an approach to the past that was almost anthropological in nature.[17] He took care to avoid imposing modern preconceptions and value judgments onto the past, and as much as possible attempted to see past penal practices within the broadest context possible. Beneath their undeniably repressive exterior, he argued, the punishments of pre-modern France had various "positive" functions:

> We must first rid ourselves of the illusion that penality is above all (if not exclusively) a means of reducing crime... [W]e must show that punitive measures are not simply "negative" mechanisms that make it possible to repress, to prevent, to exclude, to eliminate; but that they are linked to a whole series of positive and useful effects which it is their task to support....[18]

One of these positive functions, he argued, was to allow a kind of "ceremonial" in which injured sovereignty—wounded by the affront of crime—was restored: "[The execution] is a ceremonial by which a momentarily injured sovereignty is reconstituted. It restores sovereignty by manifesting it at its most spectacular. The public execution... belongs to a whole series of great rituals in which power is eclipsed and restored...."[19]

Rather than being sheer repression, in other words, executions could be seen as functioning in a more constructive, positive sense, as a celebration of the invincibility of sovereign majesty. But they also functioned, he suggested, in a more basic, positive sense, by allowing the community as a whole to come to terms with the crime by ritually re-enacting it: "A public execution justified justice, in that it published the truth of the crime in the very body of the man to be executed.... There were even some cases of an almost theatrical reproduction of the crime in the execution of the guilty man—with the same instruments, the same gestures."[20]

As much as Foucault may have encouraged his readers to look at the past with a fresh eye, however, there is no doubt that some of the more powerful passages in *Discipline and Punish*—precisely the ones that stick in the reader's mind—tend to perpetuate the narrow characterization of executions as exemplary deterrence through terror. In seeming contrast to his warning to look beyond the obvious "repressive" effects of power for less obvious, more positive effects, the following passage, for example, leaves us with a characterization of pre-modern juridical power that is very difficult to spin as anything but repression: "by breaking the law, the offender has touched the very person of the prince; and it is the prince—or at least those to whom he has delegated his force [i.e. the executioner]—who seizes upon the body of the condemned man and displays it marked, beaten, broken. The ceremony of punishment, then, is an exercise of 'terror.'"[21] Or again: "The aim was to make an example, not only by making people aware that the slightest offence was likely to be punished, but by arousing feelings of terror by the spectacle of power letting its anger fall upon the guilty person."[22]

We should note, however, that Foucault stops short of saying that executions were perceived as spectacles of "terror" by spectators themselves and, a short time after the publication of *Discipline and Punish*, he gave a lecture in which he spoke of the importance of drawing a careful distinction between "conscious intention" and "real effects."[23] On another occasion, speaking specifically about the divergence between penal theory and practice, he argued that we need look no further than the modern penal system in order to see how intent could dramatically diverge from actual practices: "Obviously the effects only rarely coincide with the ends; thus the objective of the corrective prison, of the means of rehabilitating the individual, has not been attained; the effect has been rather the inverse, and the prison has been led rather to the behavior of delinquency."[24]

In the years since its initial publication, *Discipline and Punish* has exerted an enormous influence on a variety of different academic disciplines, and in particular Foucault's characterization of executions as displays of sovereign majesty, as exemplified by the execution of Robert-François Damiens in 1757 (for the attempted regicide of Louis XV), has become, as David Garland put it, "an archetypal image that has shaped much thinking about the subject ever since."[25] In much of this scholarship, passages emphasizing repression and terror have had a tendency to drown out countervailing suggestions in Foucault's work, and although he himself seemed somewhat reticent to equate intention with effect, certain assumptions about the spectators who attended these spectacles of "terror" have made their way into the literature on punishment. Just to cite one example, the sociologist David Armstrong has suggested that the crowds who watched executions "saw in the marking of one body by another an overt manifestation of the power of sovereignty over its subjects. Thus for the ordinary people power was glimpsed only with the concrete spectacle of the sovereign's hold over other bodies."[26]

As I hope to make clear in this book, however, spectators of executions in early modern France did *not* tend to see the penal spectacle as a manifestation of political sovereignty. Neither were they terrified. In fact, they *loved* attending executions. From the sixteenth to the middle of the eighteenth century, public executions in France were extraordinarily popular with spectators from all social classes, many of whom were so desperate to watch that they rented out windows overlooking the place of execution at exorbitant sums, or staked out prime viewing spots near the scaffold or on nearby rooftops, often days in advance. Even before this culture of spectatorship developed in the sixteenth century, those who attended executions were much more likely to understand them as meaningful rituals, which allowed the community at large to find redemption through the atonement of the individual condemned, rather than as any kind of display of sovereign majesty.

While it may be true that sovereign authority was uppermost in the minds of those who staged the graphic and protracted spectacles of the regicides François Ravaillac and Damiens, such a reading is much harder to impose on more ordinary executions of the day. Foucault's suggestion that "In every offence there was a *crimen majestatis* and...in the least criminal a potential regicide" has struck some historians of the period as overblown.[27] As Pascal Bastien has recently pointed out, in the day-to-day practice of punishment in eighteenth-century France "'policing' functions were privileged over the urban representation of royal justice, and...arbitration and negotiation...[were] strongly preferred to repression."[28] Every little crime did not, in fact, prompt the sovereign's mace to come crashing down.

But we might also ask: Where, in this vision of punishment as a great ceremonial of the restoration of sovereign power, does our Sow of Falaise fit in, not to mention all the other animal executions that took place over so many centuries? And what are we to make of the countless executions in effigy, which in certain regions and at certain times may well have constituted the near majority of executions? French law up to the Revolution insisted that if a person (and even, on occasion, an animal) had been convicted of a crime but could not be located, then their punishment would take place anyway, enacted on a representation of their body. These executions, which were innumerable, are exceedingly difficult to square with the idea of punishment as an "exercise in 'terror'" performed for the purpose of restoring sovereign authority.

In the end, I think it is fair to say that Foucault's conception of early modern punishment allowed for both positive and negative aspects, but with a rather pronounced emphasis on the latter. His work called into question the Enlightenment characterization of pre-modern punishment as an exercise in illogical barbarity, but in the end, he left largely unchallenged the prevailing assumption that punishment's primary purpose was exemplary deterrence. Although he took care to caution us not to mistake intentions for actual practices, his passages that so powerfully convey the logic of early modern executions imply a kind of unity of theory and practice, as if the "ceremony of punishment," the "exercise of 'terror,'" and the "ceremonial" of reconstituted sovereignty were perceived and understood in the same way by those who staged the penal spectacles and those who watched them.

Although Foucault's characterization of early modern punishment has proved enormously influential, we should not forget that *Discipline and Punish* was primarily concerned with the modern penal system and that, at least to a certain extent, pre-modern justice was less a serious object of study in itself than an elegant theoretical foil to the logic of modern punishment. If he saw modern punishment, epitomized by Jeremy Bentham's Panopticon, as endeavoring to prevent misbehavior in advance through constant, non-visible surveillance, then pre-modern punishment was its antithesis, punishing sporadically, after the fact, in a spectacular fashion, and with great expenditure of force. From Foucault's vantage point, the Enlightenment reforms that replaced public corporal and capital punishment with the modern prison system stemmed less from humanitarian sensibilities than from a desire to punish more effectively and with greater economy of effort.

In the years since the publication of *Discipline and Punish*, several historians of the early modern period have taken issue with Foucault's history of punishment, many of them arguing that Enlightenment reforms resulted much more from a shift in sensibilities than from any desire on the part of reformers to control society by placing it into a stranglehold of conformity. Pieter Spierenburg, for example, has taken inspiration from the historical sociologist Norbert Elias, and has argued that the Enlightenment reforms are part of a broader "civilizing process" through which the peoples of Europe gradually came to have greater self-control and a greater degree of empathy for one another. Spierenburg and, more recently, Lynn Hunt, have pointed to a dramatic shift in cultural sensibilities that took place in the eighteenth century when individuals suddenly found the spectacle of public executions intolerable. Although these historians largely reject Foucault's reading of Enlightenment reforms, they nevertheless seem to agree with his characterization of pre-modern executions as an exercise in terror whose primary function was to support sovereign authority and deter crime, an exercise that, in their view, became impracticable as sensibilities changed.[29]

Another group of historians have, over the past two decades or so, taken more of an anthropological approach to the penal practices of the past, not unlike the one employed by Foucault, but devoid of his arguably presentist agenda. Historians of France and Switzerland such as Esther Cohen, Michel Bée, Michel Porret, Robert Muchembled, Nicole Gonthier, Claude Gauvard, and Pascal Bastien, and historians of Germany such as Richard J. Evans and Richard van Dülmen, have, to varying degrees, approached the past in a manner not dissimilar to the way in which anthropologists approach the study of foreign cultures. Clifford Geertz described the task of the anthropologist as being neither some sort of magical, empathetic communion with a foreign culture nor a description of that culture in *our* terms, but rather an effort to, as he put it, "figure out what the devil *they* think they are up to."[30] In a similar fashion, these historians have been less interested in explaining how pre-modern practices evolved into modern ones than in explaining past practices on their own terms, as rituals that made sense to the people who participated in them.[31]

Several of these historians have highlighted the ways in which the ritual of public executions functioned as a ceremony of collective healing, allowing the community to overcome the atrocity of the crime itself. Michel Bée, in particular, has focused specifically on the markedly religious character of pre-modern executions, relating how those who attended often prayed, sang, and cried together with the "patient" on the scaffold, and presenting a picture of these executions that make them seem much more like real-life Passion Plays than the spectacles of "terror" described by Foucault.[32] In contrast to Bée's reading of executions as a kind of redemptive, communal experience in which the criminal, through the sacrifice of his or her own body, allows the community to heal, Esther Cohen has paid particular attention to the more exclusionary aspects of pre-modern executions. This approach is informed by the writings of the anthropologist Victor Turner, who explored how rites of passage often make use of a symbolic or actual casting-out as a prelude to eventual reincorporation. In early Christian Europe this sometimes took the form of pilgrimages as penance for sins, and in the case of secular crimes, it can be seen in various aspects of the penal ritual, ranging from public humiliation and shaming to banishment and death.[33]

Although the analysis of public executions presented in this book is very much informed by the interpretations of several of these more anthropologically minded historians, my ultimate aim is somewhat different. Rather than hoping to shed light exclusively on past penal practices and their meaning within the context of their time, I am also very much interested in learning how these punishments in the past have informed our understanding of the theory and practice of punishment in the present. How, in short, did we get from there to here? Punishment is no longer a ritual; in fact, it is largely invisible. At what point did this happen? And if punishment was, at some moment in the past, a form of collective healing that allowed the community to recover from the consequences of a crime that had already taken place, then why and how did punishment become so obsessively preoccupied with deterring crimes that had yet to take place?

In many ways, this book might be seen as attempting a kind of anthropologically-informed presentism, an approach that is equally informed by the approaches of Foucault, on the one hand, and Cohen, Bée et al., on the other—a history that seeks not only to understand the past on its own terms but which also attempts to trace the evolution of ideas and practices forward to the modern age. I wanted to understand not only the origins of contemporary penal practices but also of our present-day preoccupation with deterrence. If, as Foucault suggested, modern incarceration could be seen as actually fostering recidivism rather than deterring crime (and if innumerable contemporary studies question the link between capital punishment and deterrence), then why do we cling so tenaciously to the idea that these penal practices not only should but actually *do* deter crime? How, historically, did our penal theories, our conceptions of the fundamental purpose of punishment, come to differ from the actual effects of our penal practices?

To answer these questions, I realized I had to dispense with the notion that punishment was in any sense a monolithic concept, and recognize that it is an agglomeration of theories, practices, and perceptions, each of which had its own separate historical trajectory. As I endeavored to trace each of these back in time, I quickly discovered that their roots took me farther back, much farther back, than I had ever imagined I might be prepared to go. I am, by training, a historian of early modern France, but the history of spectacular capital punishment in France—by which I mean the era in which executions were performed in public, before an audience—stretched at least as far back as the eleventh century, and the various strands of theory and practice that comprised medieval punishment stretched back even farther in time.

The first chapters of this book discuss the evolution of the theory and practice of punishment in France from the fall of the Roman Empire through the Middle Ages, and although I have strayed far from my field of expertise, I have made every effort to familiarize myself with the relevant historiography, and have sought the advice of friends and colleagues who are experts in the field. While any historian who strays beyond the chronological boundaries of his or her period of expertise risks making mistakes, I was convinced that the potential advantages of a history of punishment *à la longue durée*, one that sought to explicate how precisely the theory and practice of punishment in the Middle Ages related to later theories and practices, outweighed these risks.

The sub-disciplines of medieval legal history and canon-law history can be particularly daunting to anyone who does not have decades of experience. As the scholar of canon law James Brundage wrote, "I should...alert readers that canonical waters, although alluring, can also be treacherous and warn historians that they must be prepared to steer carefully when they embark on investigations that may bring them into the vicinity of canonical shoals."[34] I took Brundage's warning to heart and did my absolute best to steer very carefully. To push his metaphor slightly further, I also did my best to steer clear of the Siren call of historiographical debates, which seem particularly prevalent in these waters, where I was entirely out of my element; I did, however, acknowledge these debates, when appropriate.

As I traced the various strands of penal thought and practice back in time, I came to realize that the divergence between intent and effects that Foucault and others have noted, the "disconnect" between theory and practice, was itself a historical phenomenon. I learned, in short, that the various conceptual strands comprising what we call punishment each had its own separate roots, its own separate evolution, its own historical trajectory. In other words, the theoretical intent of punishment envisaged by jurists, philosophers, and government officials; the actual penal practices that developed over time, the various rituals that were performed, the staging of the penal spectacle; and the ways in which people perceived executions, the ways they either participated or gawked, or refused to watch—all were very different things. The theories, the practices, and the perceptions of punishment developed independently, from discrete origins, and, over time, they have often functioned at cross purposes with one another.

Seen from this perspective, the three schools of historical interpretation of punishment that I outlined above might be seen not so much to disagree with one another as to concentrate on different aspects of penal history. If we consider that Foucault focused on the *theory* of punishment and the intentions of those who staged the penal spectacles, and on the intentions of Enlightenment reformers who sought to transform those spectacles; if we observe that historians like Spierenburg are charting a shift in the *perception* of punishment in the middle of the eighteenth century; and if we recognize that Cohen and Bée are exploring aspects of ritual penal *practice* in the pre-modern period; then all of their different interpretations do not so much contradict one another as they reveal different portions of a bigger picture.

Although this is a book that concentrates primarily on the history of punishment in France, the evolution of penal thought and practice that it describes may well describe that of European history more generally, and perhaps even that of Western society at large. Readers may wonder, therefore, why I focus more or less exclusively on the history of France. Perhaps the most compelling reason is that I wanted to finish this book in my lifetime, and as the project had already forced me back to the sixth century, and had taken an astoundingly long time to research and write, the prospect of broadening the scope of my analysis even further was not only daunting but terrifying. From a more defensibly intellectual point of view, however, it is my firm belief that the best way to trace a concept through time is to follow the strands within a given culture, in much the same way that a scientist would not trace a genetic mutation by skipping around from species to species. When it was a clear matter of cross-cultural fertilization of ideas and practices, I followed the trail outside of France: the intellectual movement surrounding the "discovery" of Justinian's compilation of Roman law known as the *Corpus Iuris Civilis* in eleventh- and twelfth-century Italy, for instance, or the rise of a cross-Channel discourse of sentimentality in seventeenth- and eighteenth-century Britain and France. The lion's share of the story, however, is a French story, even if, as I have suggested, it is not meant to be understood as unique to the history of France.

Because this book ranges over such a broad expanse of time, it seems appropriate to offer readers at least a rough roadmap to help them find sections that may be of particular interest to them. Although I would like to believe all of the sections of this book are essential to the story that it tells, I do recognize that it is a complicated story and that different readers may very well be seeking different things. I would therefore suggest that those who are primarily interested in legal history might direct the bulk of their attention to the first two chapters, which chart the evolution of criminal law in Europe from the fall of the Roman Empire in the fifth century through to the thirteenth century; they may also wish to read chapter 10, which discusses the death penalty in relation to the Revolutionary penal code of 1791. Readers who are more interested in the ritual and spectacle of executions and the ways in which people watched them may, on the contrary, find the first two chapters of the book rather slow going, and might prefer to begin with chapter 3. For those readers willing to make it through the entirety of the book, I would like to think that I can promise a thorough picture of the evolution of punishment over time: its theory, its practice, and the way contemporaries made sense of it.

Finally, a last word on the subject with which this introduction began: the Sow of Falaise. I recently came across a book published in 1880 on the history of Falaise that mentions the case of the infamous Sow, relating all the assorted details of the case, culled from the usual sources: the severed snout, the human mask and clothing, the father and the owner forced to attend, and the Vicomte de Falaise watching over the whole affair with a feather in his cap, etcetera, all of which had supposedly been represented in a fresco that had sadly been whitewashed back in 1820. Unlike so many others, however, who had been content to pass along the story without digging into any of the facts, the author of the book, J.-M. Hurel, claims to have actually undertaken a bit of investigative journalism, hoping to verify at least some parts of the story told by previous historians. Here, in his own words, is what Hurel claims to have found:

> Last year, the desire to verify this strange event, buried in the footnotes of abbé Langevin's *Recherches Historiques*, led me to examine the wall [of the church]. After having washed and scrubbed [the wall], after a very long time of passing the sponge over the wall again and again, we found, in part, what we were looking for.
>
> We saw, and one can still see today, the vicomte on his horse, with a severe expression, wearing a green outfit, a red plume waving [in his hat], with his arm extended toward a hanging object.
>
> Was it the condemned animal? Probably, but the clothing which Brillon [sic] gave him was not to be seen. The hanged [body] seems to have been covered with a shirt or a sack. We thought we could make out two long, hanging legs and arms which were made to go behind the back.
>
> These figurines, which are 25 to 30 centimeters in height, are located about 15 centimeters under the rope which comes out from the wall, and 1 meter 45 [centimeters] from the door which leads to the church bells.
>
> It is in this spot that one would find, if he were to continue in these investigations, the child of the mason and his brother, asleep in their crib.[35]

Is it possible that the fresco mentioned by Langevin exists after all? Do these details prove his story or do they, instead, show that many of the details in his story were fabrications? Or did Hurel make the whole thing up? We will probably never know.

Last year, however, in the naive belief that I could settle the question once and for all, I forced my friend and colleague Ian Burney to accompany me on an expedition to the town of Falaise. Carrying a copy of Hurel's account as if it were a treasure map, we entered the church and, searching under the bell tower, located the spot where, we were nearly certain, there had been a rope that used to protrude from the wall, just as Hurel had described. Sure enough, we both noticed an unmistakable splash of color that seemed to linger just beneath the surface, almost showing through in several spots. Could it be that the fresco did, in fact, exist after all? Perhaps. But, it turned out that we were in the wrong church. When we finally made our way to the correct church, a few streets away, again following the directions, we were disappointed to find that the area where the fresco was meant to be is currently a storeroom, closed to the public. So much for our attempt at historical archeology.

Maybe at some point in the future, a more talented and intrepid band of historians will inveigle their way into the church of the Holy Trinity in Falaise, will secure access to the forbidden storeroom, and receive permission to uncover the mural that has remained hidden beneath whitewash for nearly two centuries now. Perhaps this mural will be definitively dated to the fourteenth century, and will clearly reveal, in color, the image of a pig, dressed in little boy's clothes, wearing a human mask in the place of a severed snout, about to be executed, while down beneath the scaffold, reluctantly watching, are the chastened, negligent father and pig owner, accompanied by a multitude of pigs, duly taking notes, mindful of the lesson they are being taught. If this indeed happens, then I shall certainly be forced to eat my words. In the meantime, I will stick to the version of the story I have presented here.

PART I

THE ROOTS OF MODERN PUNISHMENT IN PRE-MODERN EUROPE

1

The Fall and Rise of Rome

Compensation, Atonement, and Deterrence in the Early Middle Ages

As I began to research the history of capital punishment in France, I was struck by the extent to which the writings of jurists and government officials, which invariably stressed the exemplary power of the death penalty as a deterrent, seemed at odds with various penal practices that appeared to have much more to do with involving audiences in time-honored rituals than with terrifying them. As a historian of early modern France, I knew that the country had historically been divided between two different legal "realms": a *pays de droit écrit* in the southern region, where Roman law had survived the fall of the empire and had remained the law of the land up to the Revolution, and a *pays de coutumes* in the north, where the Salian Franks, who had occupied the region in the fifth century, had replaced Roman law with their own customary laws of Germanic origin. I wondered whether the "disconnect" between penal theory and practice might not be at least partly a consequence of France's bifurcated legal heritage.

Reading more extensively on the origins of the *pays de droit écrit* and the *pays de coutumes*, however, I came to realize that things might not be as straightforward as I had at first imagined. The neat divisions between a Roman south and a customary, and presumably Germanic, north, turned out to be anything but neat. Penal practices did differ from region to region, but not along any kind of clear axis, and rather than being the results of purely Roman or Germanic influences, they seemed to be more of a hodgepodge of customs derived from a variety of different sources, not the least important of which were the penitential practices of Catholics.

I began to wonder why, like most historians of the early modern period, I tended to accept at face value the reality of a juridically divided France, and I have come to suspect that it is primarily because so many of the seventeenth- and eighteenth-century sources that we early modern historians read accept this division implicitly, as a simple matter of fact. Jurists, philosophers, historians, and even royal ordinances referred to the legal division of France almost as if it were an actual border, stretching from La Rochelle in the west almost to Geneva in the east. Although they rarely addressed how, precisely, this border came into existence, the assumption seems to have been that it occurred when the Roman province of Gaul fell to invading barbarian tribes in the fifth century, and somehow the former Roman subjects in the south were able to cling to Roman law much more successfully than those in the north.

Montesquieu was one of the few to attempt a more precise historical explanation of France's division into two juridical realms. In *L'Esprit des lois*, he argued that the inhabitants of the early Middle Ages had been more or less free to choose, as individuals, by which system of law they would be bound. Since northern France had been conquered by the Salian Franks, whereas southern regions had initially been conquered by the Visigoths, Montesquieu surmised that the inhabitants of the north must have had more of an incentive to "choose" the law of their conquerors than did those of the south:

> I say that Roman law fell into disuse among the Franks because of the great advantages there were in being a barbarian Frank or a man living under Salic law: everyone was driven to abandon Roman law in order to live under Salic law.... On the other hand, in the land of the Visigoths, Visigothic law gave no civil advantage to Visigoths over Romans, and the Romans had no need to stop living under their own law to live under another. They therefore retained their laws, and did not adopt those of the Visigoths.[1]

By the ninth century, Montesquieu argued, these individual choices of one legal system over another had coalesced, and had come to be associated with certain regions of France rather than with individuals. He cites, as proof, Charles the Bald's edict of Pistes (864), which makes a vague reference to "those regions which follow Roman law."[2]

Although Montesquieu's analysis would prove very influential, successive generations of scholars of medieval law and history would poke holes in his argument. Writing in the early nineteenth century, for example, the legal historian Friedrich Carl von Savigny not only challenged the notion that individuals had been free to choose which law code they followed, but also wondered how Montesquieu explained why former Roman subjects in southern France did not "choose" Salic law when they too were conquered by the Salian Franks less than a century after the conquest in the north.[3]

Although many questioned Montesquieu's explanation, most legal scholars through the mid-twentieth century nevertheless tended to view the history of French law in terms of national ideal-types, with the law of the *pays de droit écrit* discussed as if it were purely and simply Roman law, and the law of the *pays de coutumes* treated as if it were a pure expression of the Germanic peoples. As the noted nineteenth-century jurist Joseph Ortolan characterized the division:

> The law, having become associated with territories [rather than individuals] was Roman law in the South, whether because of the influence of numbers or authority, or because of the depth of the roots [of Roman influence] in the soil, and in the North, [it was] customary law... in which, from the earliest days of the monarchy, Germanic law predominated.[4]

Because the various systems of law had taken on an explicitly national character, European legal history of the late nineteenth and early twentieth centuries often seemed to be debating whether European civilization was more indebted to Roman or to Germanic influences. As the historian Katherine Fischer Drew observed, German scholars had a tendency to see "the origin of all free and democratic institutions as coming out of the forests of Germany."[5]

The legal historian Paul Viollet, writing at the end of the nineteenth century, was among the first to problematize the idea that France had been neatly divided between two ideal types of law, suggesting that the situation was far more complex and decidedly messier: "It would be very false and very dangerous to exaggerate the importance of this distinction between the *pays de droit écrit* and *pays coutumier*. The customs and statutes of the so-called pays de droit écrit are far from being the pure and simple reproduction of Roman law."[6] Nevertheless, characterizations of France's legal heritage as divided between a Roman south and a Germanic north persisted well into the twentieth century, and it has only been in recent decades that scholars of medieval history and law have begun seriously to question the terms of the debate.

The legal scholar Jean Gaudemet has gone so far as to suggest that Roman law was virtually unknown in France in any practical and meaningful sense after the fall of Rome, not only in the north but also in the supposedly Roman south. In Gaudemet's eyes, the *pays du droit écrit*, rather than being the province in which Roman law survived, is perhaps more accurately described as the province in which it may have decayed less completely than in the north. Conversely, recent scholarship has questioned just how German the so-called Germanic tribes who are supposed to have imposed their laws on northern France could possibly have been. As P. S. Barnwell has pointed out, "the 'barbarian' peoples who were settled in the west in the fifth century were not long-established political and ethnic groups, but relatively recent confederations, some still in the process of formation."[7] Far from coming out of the forests of Germany, with the purity of their customs intact, these tribes were often conglomerations of tribal groups that had lived either in or on the frontiers of the empire for generations, and had therefore been significantly influenced by Roman customs. As for the Germanic law codes that they supposedly brought with them, Barnwell suggests that these might well have been derived from Roman provincial law, and that they were not so much law codes as long-established extrajudicial customs in the Roman provinces designed to meet the needs of people who did not have regular access to courts of law and lawyers. Salic law, according to this view, is more a kind of cheat-sheet for arbitration than any coherent body of law, much less the expression of Germanic tribes.

Indeed, much recent scholarship has argued that, far from being governed in a traditional sense by one legal code or another, as the legal apparatus of the empire disappeared, much of European society, France included, resorted to informal, extrajudicial "peace-making" to settle disputes. In the absence of strong central governments intent on punishing wrongdoing, acts that we today might characterize as crimes were instead dealt with as instances of one party harming another; injured parties, or their surviving kin, could seek redress through compensation, which was not simply intended to "pay off" the victims but in and of itself was a way of righting wrongs. Justice was done, both in the eyes of the victim and of the community at large, when offenders were made to pay literally for their crimes.[8]

If, for all practical purposes, Roman law did not survive the fall of Rome in the *pays du droit écrit*, and if the Germanic legal codes in northern France may not be either Germanic or legal codes in the traditional sense, but rather a kind of list of what had previously been unwritten extrajudicial customs, then how can we explain the disconnect between French legal theory and practice? And how should we understand the relationship between France's past and its present?

As I endeavor to explain in this chapter, the influence of Roman law on France, and indeed on the rest of western Europe, had little to do with the survival of Roman law after the fall of Rome, and nearly everything to do with a renaissance in Roman legal studies that took place in Italy in the early to mid-twelfth century, and which spread outward into southern France, into England, and eventually to the rest of Europe. The division of France into southern and northern juridical realms may have more to do with the proliferation of law schools in southern regions of France (and the papal ban against teaching Roman law in Paris) in the thirteenth century than with any other single factor. If there was a division between the north and the south, then it is likely that it was much more recent than early modern authors seemed to think. As for the idea that northern regions of France were comparatively uninfluenced by Roman law, this would seem to be largely untrue, at least with respect to penal law. As I discuss both in this and the following chapter, the tide of Roman law that swept through western Europe in the twelfth and thirteenth centuries left nothing untouched. The customals of northern France were very much influenced by the renaissance in Roman legal studies, something that can be measured rather concretely by observing the ways in which a legal culture of compensation for damages (regardless of intent) was superseded by a decidedly Roman obsession with criminal intent, malice aforethought, and the prevention of crime through exemplary deterrence.

In this chapter, my aim is to give a broad overview of the legal, and more specifically, the penal culture of France from the fall of Rome through the renaissance of Roman legal studies in the twelfth and thirteenth centuries. Although the chapter ranges over a broad chronological span, its aim is fairly specific: to isolate, as much as possible, the various strands of thought and practice that would eventually comprise modern punishment. Although these separate strands would, in the modern era, be braided into the general concept of punishment, they were, in their origin and in their purpose, entirely separate from one another, and often functioned at cross purposes: the culture of compensation and "payback," which can be found in the legal texts of the "barbarian" tribes as well as in the earliest written customals of the twelfth and thirteenth centuries; the Catholic practices of public penance, of atonement and redemption; and the new interest in, perhaps even obsession with, criminal intent and deterrence sparked by the renaissance in Roman legal studies that began in the early twelfth century.

ROMAN LAW AFTER THE FALL OF ROME: DETERRENCE DECONTEXTUALIZED

In the year 507, the Salian Franks, having conquered most of the northern portion of Gaul, swept toward the south, defeating the Visigoths at the battle of Vouillé, and pushing them toward and eventually over the Pyrenees into Spain. In the year prior to his defeat at the battle of Vouillé, the Visigoth king Alaric II had somewhat optimistically commissioned a compilation of Roman laws that is commonly referred to as the *Breviarium Alaricum* (*Alaric's Breviary*). The precise timing of Alaric's decision to commission the *Breviary* only a year before the Franks invaded southern Gaul may well have been an attempt to curry favor with his Gallo-Roman subjects, in anticipation of that invasion, by magnanimously providing them with a concise book of their own laws (the ruling Visigoths were governed by their own laws, the so-called code of Euric). As Alaric himself declared in the "Commonitorium", which preceded the *Breviary* and explained its purpose, his intent was to "correct" whatever might be "obscure" or "ambiguous" in Roman laws so that the end result would be plain and clear.[9]

The text was prepared with the aid of jurists schooled in Roman law, and was based largely on the *Theodosian Code*, a compilation of laws issued by Roman emperors from 313 to 438, the year in which it was promulgated. But Alaric's *Breviary* was not a classic compilation of previous laws, replete with interpretations and commentaries; it was more of a pragmatic triage in which irrelevant laws were tossed unceremoniously by the wayside and laws that might be of use were retained. Gaudemet, who has written more on the *Breviary* than anyone else, wondered whether "juridical composition seemed too difficult" to those who compiled the *Breviary*, remarking that "they opted for the easiest but also the most rapid solution."[10]

Although Alaric himself would be killed in battle in the year following the compilation of the *Breviary*, and although the Visigoths would abandon Gaul, Alaric's abridged compendium of Roman laws was to survive for a very long time. After the Salian Franks defeated the Visigoths and incorporated southern Gaul into the Frankish kingdom, they retained the *Breviary* for the use of their Gallo-Roman subjects, and the *Breviary* proved so useful in its condensation of the nuts and bolts of Roman law that it eventually came to be used throughout the Frankish kingdom for other erstwhile Roman subjects. As the Salian Franks expanded their territory, the Visigothic compendium of Roman laws came with them, and even in those places where other compendia of Roman laws existed, such as in Burgundy, Alaric's *Breviary* seems to have gradually superseded them in importance.[11] Manuscripts of the code have been found across present-day France and Germany, far from southern Gaul where it originated.[12] In fact, it is probably safe to say that the *Breviary* was the most important and widely known text of Roman law in western Europe from the sixth until the end of the eleventh century, when the much more extensive compilation of Roman laws known as the *Corpus Iuris Civilis* supplanted it in importance. This latter text, although it was compiled by the Byzantine Emperor Justinian only two decades after Alaric's *Breviary*, would remained virtually unknown in the West until its "rediscovery" in Pisa at the end of the eleventh century, a subject to which we will return at the end of this chapter.

The bulk of penal laws in the *Breviary* was based on the ninth book of the *Theodosian Code*, which contained rather straightforward punishments for a variety of different crimes. The general tenor of these punishments, as they were contained in the original *Theodosian Code*, is one of exemplary deterrence. Those, for example, who indulged in the "shameful custom" of sodomy, and specifically of "acting the part of a woman's," were threatened with having to "expiate a crime of this kind in avenging flames in the sight of the people."[13] An individual found guilty of parricide was to be sewn into a leather sack with serpents and tossed alive into the sea (or a river if the sea was not close by), and be denied a proper burial, so that "while still alive he may begin to lose the enjoyment of all the elements, that the heavens may be taken away from him while he is living and the earth, when he is dead." (9-15-1) And those found guilty of kidnapping children, if freeborn would be killed by sword in a "gladiatorial show," and if a slave "shall be thrown to the wild beasts at the first public spectacle" (9-18-1).

Within the original *Theodosian Code*, these exemplary punishments had been expressed as part of a general framework of imperial sovereign authority in which a crime could be seen as an affront to the emperor's authority. This can be seen explicitly where the *Theodosian Code* refers to high-ranking members of society who engaged in wizardry as "almost violat[ing] Our imperial majesty itself," and stipulated that the offender should be "delivered to the torture horse, iron claws shall tear his sides, and he shall suffer punishment worthy of his crime." (9-16-6).

When those who compiled the *Breviary* conducted their pragmatic winnowing of Roman laws, they not surprisingly excised a number of laws that they deemed irrelevant to the new post-Roman reality, such as the punishment decreed by the *Theodosian Code* for individuals who damaged the levees of the Nile (9-32-1). But, interestingly, the drafters of the *Breviary* also omitted sections of the *Theodosian Code* that dealt explicitly with insults to imperial authority, an omission that was, as Gaudemet noted, somewhat "more surprising."[14] The section quoted above, for example, consigning wizards who "almost violate" Imperial majesty to the torture horse, was omitted from the *Breviary*, as was the Julian law on high treason, which mandated the torture, regardless of rank, of those who were found guilty or who falsely accused others of treasonous designs.[15] While there is evidence to suggest that the Visigothic kings were also protective of their imperial majesty (at least by the seventh century),[16] perhaps the references to royal majesty in the *Theodosian Code* seemed too specifically related to the majesty of an emperor and an empire that had ceased to exist in western Europe. Whatever the reason, the overall effect of this excision is very important. Exemplary deterrence was effectively ripped from its original context of imperial authority, a framework in which many crimes could be regarded as an assault on the emperor himself, and spectacular punishments, which were intended to teach a lesson about the consequences of flouting authority, were now made to stand on their own, as conceptual orphans.

Because of a dearth of evidence, historians know very little about the actual penal practices of the early Middle Ages and the extent to which any of the punishments that Alaric's *Breviary* borrowed from the *Theodosian Code* may actually have been performed. The laws of the Salian Franks, although they hardly ever imposed the death penalty, nevertheless include punishments for "anyone [who] presumes to take down a living man from a gallows [*furca*]," suggesting that capital punishment was being carried out, but whether these hangings were performed in accordance with punishments stipulated in the *Breviary*, or whether they were done according to some other system of punishments whose texts have not survived, we cannot be sure.[17] It is doubtful whether the Gallo-Roman subjects of the Salian Franks followed the letter of the law, which prescribed that they should throw kidnapping slaves to wild beasts in a gladiatorial show, but if Roman-style punishments continued for any length of time, the exemplary and spectacular nature of the sentence must have begun to seem strange in a realm and an era that were so different from the imperial context in which those punishments had originally been devised.

THE LAWS OF THE SALIAN FRANKS: PUNISHMENT AS PAYBACK

Most historians agree that the collection of laws known as the *Pactus legis Salicae* was promulgated by the Frankish king Clovis in the early sixth century, but beyond that there is little consensus about the origins of this text, or the extent to which it can be considered a true and complete legal code of the Salian Franks.[18] Whereas earlier generations of historians tended to view the Salic laws, along with the laws of the Ripurian Franks and the Burgundians, as "a nearly pure Germanic artifact in which Roman adulteration plays a weak role,"[19] historians have more recently come to question whether Salic laws may not owe as much if not more to provincial Roman procedures for adjudication and the resolution of disputes than to anything that might be described as Germanic.[20] However, regardless of whether Salic laws are aptly described as a legal code or whether they can truly be called Germanic, our specific aim here is to understand their internal logic and to compare and contrast that logic to other conceptions of punishment in the Middle Ages, so that we can understand how various strands of medieval penal thought would become part of later theories and practices.

To the modern reader, the laws of the Salian Franks look less like a book of laws than like a price list for every imaginable crime performed in every conceivable manner. The section entitled "Concerning the Theft of Pigs," for example, contains twenty articles that stipulate varying fines depending upon whether the pig was one year old or two years old, whether the swineherd was present or not, and whether the pig was a boar (gelded or non-gelded) or a sow (breeding or non-breeding). The same punctilious levying of fines is applied to different ways of stealing cattle (fourteen different situations); sheep, dogs, and birds (around five different ways each); and even to the theft of bees.[21] Punishments for direct offenses against people are equally precise and stipulate the just compensation for crimes that range from touching the hand (or arm, or finger) of a free woman, to theft, rape, and homicide. Interestingly, Salic law ascribes a different worth, or "wergeld"— literally the price of a human being in gold—to victims depending upon whether they were Frank or Roman, free or slave, old or young, male or female. (The life of a male Frank was worth 8,000 denarii, as was the life of free girls or women who had passed menopause; free women of childbearing age, however, were worth 24,000. By contrast, the life of Gallo-Romans was worth between 2,500 and 12,000 denarii, depending upon their status.)[22]

The legal historian Jean Carbasse has suggested that penal laws like those of the Salian Franks, in which punishments are expressed almost entirely in terms of monetary fines, exist at a midpoint between primitive societies, which allow direct vengeance by injured parties, and more advanced societies in which the state takes over control of all aspects of punishment.[23] Harold Berman sees a similar kind of progression from the law of talion (an eye for an eye) to one of monetary substitution for the injury (money for an eye), which, he argues, "gave dignity to a settlement short of violence, while not altering the basic raison d'être of the remedy, which was the redemption of the honor of the household and the kin."[24] For both Carbasse and Berman, a fundamental purpose of Salic penal laws was to prevent a cycle of retributive violence—not to deter crime, as we might understand this concept, but rather to prevent the blood feuds that were so often the consequence of harmful acts.

But if we put aside, for a moment, the overall aim of Salic penal laws, and focus instead on their mechanics, their internal logic, we begin to realize the enormous care that was put into determining *precisely* how much damage a given act had inflicted so that the offender could make a complete restitution and the victim could be fully compensated for his or her loss. Even if, for example, a stolen pig was returned to the owner, the offender was still required to compensate the victim for loss of use. While this care in determining damages is consistent with a system that sought to prevent feuding, there was an added element to some penalties in Salic law—which speaks to something beyond this narrow purpose. Even after the pig was returned, and even after the victim was compensated for loss of use, the offender was still required to pay an additional monetary fine, which presumably represented a kind of compensation for the very fact of the crime itself.

Taking note of the fact that Salic law, like Visigothic law, forbade the private settlement of disputes, Maurizio Lupoi has suggested that the public nature of justice was an essential aspect of the law, "since it had exemplary value: it demonstrated that the law had been applied, and it publicized the fact of reconciliation, and thus strengthened the social fabric."[25] We would be wrong, however, to make too much of the exemplary nature of punishments in Salic law, as its primary intent is so clearly one of restitution. In contrast to Roman law, Salic law is almost entirely unconcerned with the degree of intentionality or malice aforethought, and is infinitely more interested in the worth of the victim. The concept of involuntary manslaughter, for example, would have made little sense within this context: either someone had been killed or they hadn't. In this respect, the logic that governed Salic law is much closer to the one that governs modern insurance companies than it is to modern penal systems. The person or family who suffered a loss had to be compensated regardless of the intent of the person who caused the damage, and the argument that one had not intended to cause injury would have made as little sense as the argument of an individual in modern society who endeavors to explain to an insurance company that he or she had not intended to cause an accident. Compensation had very little to do with intent, and everything to do with the extent of the damage and the worth of the victim.

If we put aside the modern distinction between crimes and civil damages, we can appreciate the ways in which what we now see as two entirely separate categories of harm might have informed each other in the early Middle Ages. The idea that the offender should literally "pay" for his crime lies at the root of later medieval penal practices, which would similarly seek a carefully calculated equivalence between the crime and the corresponding corporal punishment. We will have ample occasion to explore these penal rituals in their context, but for the moment I would simply like to establish this principle, which we might call penal *payback*, and which we can witness in many of the law codes of western Europe in the early Middle Ages. (One might even argue that the concept of penal payback lingers to this day in the belief and the expression that criminals should "pay" for their crime, or in modern trials for manslaughter when damages are exacted or prison sentences levied even when there was no malicious intent and when the exemplary nature of the punishment is unclear.)

Enveloped within the principle of payback and yet at the same time a distinct concept unto itself is the aim of undoing or taking back the crime. The act of making restitution does not merely compensate the victim of the crime, it also endeavors to make things as they were before the crime took place. The restitution of a pig or the monetary compensation that enables the purchase of a replacement makes things "as they were." Not all damages can be made right through monetary compensation, of course, and the insistence on the public nature of the punishment served no doubt to help restore the honor of the victim; this was especially true when the victim's reputation had been directly attacked through slanderous comments (ranging from calling someone a pederast to a liar or a rabbit).[26] We will be able to trace the continuation of this intent to undo the original crime in later medieval penal sentences that involve a repetition of the original crime on the body of the offender, serving as a kind of ritual transference of wounds from the victim to the offender, and we can also detect its equivalent in modern times in the judicial practice of not only levying damages on those who commit slander but also in demanding a public retraction of the original comments.[27]

Although the concept of penal restitution was primarily monetary in Salic law, there were situations in which a different kind of restitution was stipulated. If the offender was a freeman and the crime was of a very serious nature, then Salic law stipulated that he should pay "with his life," a phrase that historians have variously interpreted either as a straightforward death sentence or as a sentence of enslavement, the proceeds of which would be given to the victim as compensation for the crime.[28] If the offender was already a slave, and was unable to compensate monetarily, then Salic law provided for compensation in flesh. A slave, for example, who was found guilty of stealing something worth 2 denarii, would, in addition to returning the stolen object (or its monetary value) and to compensating the owner for loss of use, also be required to compensate for the crime itself by receiving 120 lashes. The compensatory nature of this corporal punishment is made clear by the fact that the slave could "spare his back" by paying 120 denarii, or 1 denarius in lieu of each lash.[29] More serious crimes demanded more serious forms of monetary or corporal compensation: the owner of a slave who had stolen an object worth 40 denarii would be liable for the return of the object or its value, and the slave himself "shall be castrated or pay two hundred forty denarii."[30] Finally, there were rare situations in which no monetary punishment or its corporal equivalent would be sufficient to compensate for the crime, and death was deemed the appropriate punishment. In many of these cases, however, the penalty of death would seem to be the non-Frank's or the slave's equivalent to the Frank's monetary fine. If, for example, a slave was found guilty of a serious theft "for which a freeman would be liable to pay eighteen hundred denarii and the slave confessed during torture, he shall be subjected to capital punishment."[31]

Although capital punishments are exceedingly rare in the original laws of the Salian Franks, they were slightly more common in amendments known as capitularies, which were added over the course of the sixth century. But here too, they tended to be applied for very serious crimes and only to those who were not free Franks. Only at the very end of the sixth century do we find cases in which the death penalty was applied to free Franks, and these appear to be limited to an individual who "marries his father's wife" and those who commit homicide with no rational justification whatsoever. With respect to the latter, the capitulary of King Childebert decreed that "We order that whoever by rashly daring deed kills another man without cause shall lose his life. He may not redeem himself with a price nor make composition [i.e. compensation]... because it is just that he who is known to kill deserves to die."[32]

Apart from these very few exceptions, the various forms of exemplary corporal and capital punishments, which were common in the *Theodosian Code* and would eventually become standard practice in later medieval Europe, are not to be found in Salic law. As noted, the primary intent of punishment in Salic law was restitution, almost always by monetary fine, and even on those occasions when "payment" was demanded in flesh or with the offender's life, restitution and compensation rather than deterrence remained the clear objective.

Among the legal codes of other "barbarian" tribes, one finds a similar concern with the principle of compensation and restitution. The laws of the Burgundians, of the Ripurian Franks, who lived east of the Rhine, and of the Lombards, who had settled in what is today northern and central Italy, contain similarly punctilious determinations of monetary fines and wergelds, and their use of the death penalty would seem to have been very rare.[33] Apart from a few minor exceptions, therefore, the so-called barbarian tribes who ruled the territories of western Europe after the fall of the Roman Empire were far less prone to inflicting corporal or capital punishment than the Romans themselves had been. While it is possible that they may have permitted their subject Roman populations to continue to practice exemplary justice, at least for a time, it would appear that the early Middle Ages were decidedly less bloody in terms of penal practice than the periods either before or after.

CHRISTIAN PENANCE AND ATONEMENT

If corporal and capital punishment and indeed the whole agenda of exemplary penal deterrence seem to have more or less disappeared for several centuries after the fall of Rome, they began to make their reappearance around the turn of the ninth century. Charlemagne's capitulary of the year 802 is often considered to be the founding legislation of the Holy Roman Empire. For our purposes, it might also be seen as the harbinger of modern punishment, because it combines, in one piece of legislation, several different discrete strands of penal theory: compensation, deterrence, and a decidedly Christian emphasis on penance and atonement. Although these three elements of penal law would, over time, meld together into an amalgam, in Charlemagne's capitulary, deterrence, compensation, and atonement are layered on top of one another in such a way that they are still easily identifiable as discrete concepts. The following warning to those who would commit murder so perfectly exemplifies this incomplete fusion of different penal aims that it merits quoting at length:

> With every kind of protestation we command that men leave off and shun murders, through which many of the Christian people perish. If God forbids hatred and enmity to his followers, much more does he forbid murders. For how can any one hope to be pleasing to God who has slain His son who is nearest to Him? Or how can any one believe that Christ will be gracious to him who has slain his brother. It is a great and inevitable risk to arouse the hatred of men besides incurring that of God the Father and of Christ the ruler of Heaven.... [B]y what rashness can any one hope to evade His wrath? Therefore we have taken care to avoid, by every possible regulation, that the people committed to us to be ruled over perish by this evil. For he who has not feared that God will be angry with him, will by no means find us gentle and gracious; we wish rather to punish with the greatest severity him who dares to commit the crime of murder.
>
> Lest, then, crime increase, and in order that very great discord may not arise among men, wherever under the devil's suasion, a murder has occurred, the guilty one shall straightway hasten to make his amends, and shall, with all celerity, compound worthily with the relatives of the dead man for the evil done. And this we firmly decree under fur bane, that the relatives of the dead man shall by no means dare to carry further their enmity on account or the evil inflicted, or refuse to make peace with him who seeks it; but, pledging their faith, they shall make a lasting peace, and the guilty man shall make no delay in paying the wergeld.
>
> When, moreover, through the influence of sin, this shall have happened, that any one shall have slain his brothers or his relative, he shall straightway submit himself to the penance imposed, according as his bishop decides, and without any circumvention. But by the help of God he shall strive to work out his atonement; and he shall pay the fine for the slain man according to the law, and shall fully be reconciled to his relatives.[34]

In the above passage, there is a focus on compensation, which is expressly undertaken so that "very great discord may not arise among men." But alongside the principle of just compensation and the prevention of a blood feud we can also see an emphasis on deterring crime, which is more typical of Roman jurisprudence. Indeed, perhaps the strongest message in the above passage is the threat to would-be murderers that their actions will reap consequences, not only in the hereafter, but in the here and now, and "with the greatest severity." The intent here is clearly to deter or prevent future criminal acts.

Finally, we have the newest ingredient in the mix: penance and atonement. Penance, in and of itself, was of course not new at all. For several centuries, bishops had been prescribing public penance for a variety of sins. But Charlemagne's capitulary is evidence of what might be described as a kind of cross-fertilization between two completely different penal species, in which each gave attributes to the other. Not only would secular law begin to borrow from Christian concepts of penance and atonement and public forms of expiation, but Christian concepts of penance would be forever changed by contemporary secular conceptions of punishments, as sins began to be compensated by monetary payments.

Penance, as it had been practiced in the late Roman Empire and the early years of the Frankish kingdom, was a very different thing from the penance that developed later in the Middle Ages. It was a once-in-a-lifetime act of expiation, undertaken solely under the auspices of a bishop, with profound and irreversible consequences for the penitent. Although the actual detailing of the sins committed was conducted privately between the penitent and the bishop, the act of penance itself was necessarily public. Generally speaking, penitents would appear before the congregation at the beginning of the Lenten season, with shaven head and in sackcloth and with some sort of hood or head covering in goat's hair.[35] The penitents would then throw themselves to the ground, rolling under the feet of the faithful, who in turn were encouraged to weep in sympathy with them. Here is a fifth-century account of the practice of penance in Rome itself:

> [The penitents] stand with downcast eyes and with the seeming [i.e. countenance] of mourners. When the Divine Liturgy is concluded...with wailing and lamentation they cast themselves prostrate on the ground. Also the whole multitude of the Church with loud crying are suffused in tears. After this the bishop first arises and raises the prostate ones, and having prayed in such sort as is fitting on behalf of the sinners who are doing penance, he dismisses them.[36]

The interesting thing here is the public interchange between sinners, on the one hand, who admitted their guilt and expressed their contrition, and the community, on the other, who were, according to the religious historian Cyrille Vogel, "explicitly invited to pray, to cry, and to moan for and with the penitents."[37] In the words of Caesarius, bishop of Arles in the first part of the sixth century, penance was necessarily public so that the sinner, by his example, could help deter others from committing sin: "as often as we see any of our brethren or sisters seeking penance in public, we can and ought to kindle in ourselves, God inspiring us, a great compunction of Divine fear." And the sinner, in turn, might derive strength from the support and tears of the community: "considering the multitude of his sins [the sinner] sees that he is not alone sufficient to deal with such grave evils, and desires to seek the aid of all the people."[38]

After this act of public contrition, penitents were then ritually expelled from the Church into the outside world, where they were required to perform their specified penance, which usually involved a specific combination of fasts and abstentions from alcohol, meat, and sexual relations, self-inflicted corporal punishments, and pilgrimages. After the penance was completed—weeks, months, or sometimes years later—the penitent would again be received into the Church in a ceremony of reconciliation. After being readmitted into the community, he or she could again take communion, but readmitted penitents could never again function as normal members of society; they were forbidden to marry, or if they were already married, they were forbidden to cohabit with their spouses; and they were denied all possibility of important public positions or clerical office. In essence, public penance absolved an individual of sin, and although they had made their peace with God and the Church, they would forever be marked with a kind of infamy in their daily life.[39]

This was the classical conception of penance, at any rate, and the extent to which it was carried out in actual practice is difficult to tell. But the fact that the price of penance seemed too high to contemporaries is revealed by the sudden appearance of radical innovations in the practice of penance in the early Middle Ages, which had the effect of making penance, to put it bluntly, cheaper and easier. Beginning around the middle of the sixth century, an entirely different form of penance came into existence in the monasteries of Ireland, England, and Scotland, and in many respects it was almost the opposite of the classical form of public penance. It could be performed privately; it could be decided by a local priest without the need for consultation with a bishop; and it could be performed more than once. In fact, parishioners were encouraged to perform a penance each time they sinned. But what makes this new form of private penance so interesting for our purposes is that monetary payments could now be used as compensation for sinful acts.

Already familiar with a penal system in which most crimes could be paid for by some sort of compensation, whether monetary or corporeal, the inhabitants of western Europe embraced this new system of penance enthusiastically. By the year 589, bishops in Visigothic Spain were already complaining that "people, in certain regions of Spain, have been performing penance for their mistakes, not in conformity with canonical prescriptions, but in an indignant manner, which is to say that each time that they have sinned they demand priestly absolution."[40] By the middle of the seventh century, certain bishops in the Frankish kingdom were actively encouraging sinners to undergo "expiatory penance each time that they are confessed [of their sins]."[41]

Throughout western Europe, books known as penitentials began to proliferate, which were essentially the religious equivalent of contemporary secular law codes: price lists for an innumerable variety of sins. According to Vogel, penitentials imposed a "precise *taxation* of faults," which ranged from corporal mortifications and obligatory recitations of psalms to fasts and pilgrimages. But they also included monetary fines payable to a church or monastery, which Vogel suggests were clearly "in imitation of the legal compensation of Germanic law (wergeld)."[42] In the ninth century, there was something of a backlash against the new form of penance, when some bishops began to call for public penance for those convicted of a public crime,[43] while others complained that "Almost everywhere the classical form of penance has gone out of use" and called upon the emperor to do something about it.[44] Bishops at a council in Paris went so far as to suggest that "each bishop track down these little books [i.e. penitentials], filled with errors, in his diocese and have them burned so that in the future ignorant priests will no longer use them to deceive people."[45]

In the end, there was a compromise. Public and notorious sins would be punished publically, according to the old practice, and private or hidden sins could be atoned for secretly, through private confession to a priest and the secret performance of penance. Interestingly, the distinction between public and private seems to have had less to do with the crime itself than with whether people knew about it. Even a so-called "capital sin," such as incest, if it had been committed in secret, could be atoned for, paid for, in secret.[46] This dual penitential system would last until the Fourth Lateran Council in 1215, when yearly, private confession was mandated. Although many have seen this as the de facto end of public penance, Mary Mansfield has shown that, at least in certain parts of France, public penance lived on through the medieval period.[47] As we will see in later chapters, this long tradition of public penance would resonate within medieval rituals of public execution.

Religious penance, therefore, came to resemble the secular punishments of Salic law, gradually shifting from a public spectacle of atonement to non-spectacular, often secret, compensation. The extent to which a logic of compensation had made its way into conceptions of religious penance can be seen very clearly in the writings of Anselm of Canterbury, who spoke of sin as an offence against the honor of God and which incurred a "debt" demanding compensation. Just as Salic law required not simply the restitution of the stolen object (or the wergeld of a victim) but also additional compensation for loss of use and injury to the victim's honor, so too did Anselm insist that "it is not sufficient merely to repay [to God] what has been taken away: rather, he ought to pay back more than he took, in proportion to the insult which he has inflicted.... Therefore, everyone who sins is under an obligation to repay God the honour which he has violently taken from him, and this is the satisfaction which every sinner is obliged to give to God."[48]

If religious penance can be seen as taking on attributes of secular compensation, then the reverse was true as well, as secular punishments began to incorporate elements of public spectacles of penance. Charlemagne's predecessors Carloman and Pippin had insisted on public penance for certain crimes such as impersonating a priest and various sexual offences,[49] but it was Charlemagne who would expand the practice of public penance to a wide variety of secular crimes and who would combine it with a renewed stress on deterrence and an old commitment to compensation.

If we return to Charlemagne's capitulary of 802, we can see just how much religious and secular punishments had become two sides of the same coin. Those who committed the crime of murder were required both to pay a wergeld and to make their amends to the Church because their act had wounded both the victim's family and God. The sin of adultery, according to the Capitulary of 802, was not simply a sin, but a crime against the entire Christian community, which must be punished so that "others may have fear of doing the same: so that uncleanness may be altogether removed from the Christian people, and that the guilty man may fully atone by such penance as shall be imposed on him by his bishop."[50]

This interchangeability of sin and crime seemed to call for a more proactive approach to wrongdoing. In contrast to earlier Salic law, which took effect only when the injured party leveled an accusation, Charlemagne made use of *missi dominici*, or royal emissaries, whom he ordered to "diligently investigate all cases where any man claims that injustice has been done to him by any one."[51] Behind these first beginnings of an inquisitorial sensibility was a clear sense that the spiritual well-being of the community was at stake, and that no one "dare to conceal thieves, robbers, or murderers, adulterers, magicians and wizards or witches, or any godless men, but will rather give them up that they may be bettered and chastised by the law: so that, God permitting, all these evils may be removed from the Christian people."[52] If the old system permitted aggrieved family members to seek restitution by legal means, now for the sake of Christian purity the entire community could seek restitution through the medium of the state. But rather than focusing exclusively on compensation after the fact, the community now believed itself to have a vested interest in preventing future crimes. Charlemagne's successor, Louis the Pious, went so far as to speak of using punishment in order to "terrify" by example.[53]

At the time of Charlemagne's death (814), his empire comprised vast portions of western and central Europe, and the inhabitants of these lands were therefore subject to the same combination of penal compensation, Christian penance, and exemplary deterrence. Upon his death, Charlemagne's empire was divided among his offspring, and although the successor states were all theoretically still bound by the same laws, in practice the next several centuries saw an implosion of political, legal, and administrative order. The relative uniformity of law splintered into thousands of little fiefdoms and cities, each with its own separate set of laws and customs, and the promise of a more or less common penal order of Europe evaporated.[54]

Or did it? Looking at the big picture, one might almost say that a remarkably similar hybrid of compensation, penance, and exemplary deterrence had spread throughout the former western Roman Empire. Of course there were differences, but every region of western Europe including the British Isles experienced a remarkably similar evolution in the conception of punishment. Catholic rituals of public penance, and a concern with the Christian community as a whole, had been layered on top of various practices of secular compensation (Salic, Burgundian, Saxon, etcetera), which had primarily been concerned with the righting of individual wrongs, all of which in turn had been layered on top of a foundation of Roman law, with its interest in criminal intent and exemplary deterrence. This layering process had served to roughly homogenize penal practice and theory throughout western and central Europe, and even after the Carolingian Empire had fallen, there were invasions and counter-invasions—most notably by the Normans—which served to mix the pot even more, so to speak, spreading a rudimentary, common penal culture where differences might otherwise have developed.

We begin to get a sense, therefore, of a kind of pan-European phenomenon in which a hybrid of different penal systems and practices spread through the continent, homogenized by successive invasions and by other cultural motors such as trade and texts. Although there was certainly no unified legal system such as had existed under the Roman Empire, or even during the reign of Charlemagne, within the thousands of different fiefdoms and independent cities that dotted the landscape of medieval Europe there was nevertheless a surprising commonality, and a shared conception of the fundamentals of justice. As Esther Cohen has remarked, similarities existed not only within specific regions but throughout Europe as a whole, where "the vocabulary of justice showed a remarkable consistency."[55]

But there was to be one last homogenizing force that completes the story of the evolutionary roots of punishment in Europe and whose effects are still being felt in the present day. This was the renaissance in Roman legal studies associated with the discovery—or rediscovery—toward the end of the eleventh century of the *Corpus Iuris Civilis*, the compilation of Roman legal texts that had been put together by the Byzantine Emperor Justinian half a millennium before. In the fields of both secular and canon law, the study of the *Corpus Iuris Civilis* was instrumental in effecting a profound theoretical revolution in which the degree of malicious intent would replace the extent of actual harm as the standard for determining culpability, and exemplary deterrence would become the overriding theoretical aim of punishment.

THE RENAISSANCE OF ROMAN LEGAL STUDIES IN MEDIEVAL EUROPE

Shortly after the fall of the Roman Empire in the West, the Byzantine emperor Justinian ordered the most ambitious compilation of secular law in history. Known variously as the *Justinian Code*, or the *Corpus Iuris Civilis*, it comprised several parts of the known body of Roman law: the *Code*, the *Institutes*, the *Novels*, and, undoubtedly the most important part for our purposes, the *Digest*. Justinian's compilation would be known very briefly in western Europe when the Byzantines attempted a momentarily successful reconquest of Italy in the first half of the sixth century. But even then, it seems to have been barely read. As Gaudemet put it: "Too learned and too complicated, the *Digest* had scarcely any audience. The *Code* knew slightly more success...but remained unknown in Gaul, and Italy itself ignored it soon enough."[56] When the Byzantines lost most of Italy again around 568, Justinian's compilation seems to have departed with the Byzantine armies, and it remained lost to the western world for several centuries.

Then, at some moment between the years 1050 and 1075, a long-forgotten copy of Justinian's vast legal undertaking was "discovered" in Italy. The story has traditionally been told that the sudden discovery of the *Corpus Iuris Civilis* was the spark that ignited an intellectual revolution. A scholar by the name of Irnerius was the first to devote himself to the serious study of Justinian's compilation, and by the early twelfth century he had gathered around him a group of four students eager to join him in his work. Known collectively as the "four doctors," Irnerius's students were said to have carried on the master's work, each of them, in turn, gathering around him a similar coterie of eager students. With this exponential growth of scholars dedicated to studying the *Corpus Iuris Civilis* from one generation to the next, the study of Roman law was reborn.

The impact of the rediscovery of the *Justinian Code* was unquestionably enormous, but it begs the question of why Europeans of the High Middle Ages would regard a text that had been compiled some six or seven centuries earlier, and which contained principles that had been articulated well before that in a profoundly different context, as the ultimate authority in jurisprudence. Was this a simple question of Europeans emerging from the "dark ages" and recovering a lost, more rational way of thinking from their distant past?

In recent years, historians have come to question various aspects of the traditional story. Some have focused their attention on the mysterious Irnerius, about whom little is known, suggesting that the role of this one individual has been greatly exaggerated, and that the renaissance in Roman legal studies is more properly understood as the work of a whole generation of legal scholars.[57] Historians have also challenged the notion that Roman law had been suddenly "rediscovered" at the end of the eleventh century. As we have already seen, scholars in the former province of Gaul, as well as in other areas of western and central Europe, were familiar with the *Theodosian Code*, or at least those parts of it that had been included in Alaric's *Breviary*. In Italy, familiarity with Roman law was even more extensive, and scholars there had been familiar with, or at least knew about, some of the texts that were contained in the *Corpus Iuris Civilis* throughout the early Middle Ages.[58]

The one part of Justinian's compilation that was comparatively unknown in western Europe, however, was the *Digest*, the most theoretical and most complex part of the *Corpus Iuris Civilis*. While historians of an earlier generation, like Hermann Kantorowicz and Stephan Kuttner, tended to imply that the discovery of the *Digest* sparked an intellectual revolution,[59] Charles Radding has argued that the *Digest* would have been meaningless had it not been for a "revival of juridical culture in Italy in the eleventh century…that created an audience capable of understanding what the book had to teach."[60] Other historians have focused more explicitly on the circumstances surrounding the accidental "discovery" of Justinian's compilation, with the implication that the timing of its appearance was no accident. Harold Berman has argued that the papacy under Gregory VII was in the process of a radical reorganization and was beginning to take on the characteristics of a sovereign state with great ambitions to assert authority over the people and property of the Roman Catholic Church across Europe. What the *Corpus Iuris Civilis* provided, Berman suggests, was something of an administrative blueprint for a papacy preparing to make itself the preeminent sovereign political power in Europe; it was no mere legal code, but contained within its pages an exploration of the very principles of justice and the theoretical foundations of the law. Echoing Hobbes's statement that "the Papacy is no other than the *ghost* of the deceased *Roman empire,* sitting crowned on the grave thereof," Berman sees papal reformers as availing themselves of the principles of a dead empire in order to build the foundation for a new one, a foundation that monarchs across the European continent would soon emulate.[61]

Whether the renaissance in Roman legal studies was precipitated by Irnerius or by an entire generation of scholars, whether it was sparked by the discovery of Justinian's compilation, or whether that discovery was itself the consequence of a broader intellectual revolution, what is essential for our purposes here is the simple fact that this revolution in thought took place. From the second half of the twelfth century onward, scholars who would come to be known as "the glossators", after the numerous "glosses" that they wrote on Justinian's compilation, set about analyzing and cross-referencing the various cases and arguments contained in the *Corpus Iuris Civilis*, attempting to resolve apparent contradictions on the basis of underlying principles. By the turn of the thirteenth century, Bologna had become a Mecca for jurisprudence, and thousands of students from all over Europe were gathering there to learn from the glossators, forming "nations" of students from as many as thirteen different countries at what would eventually become the University of Bologna. These students added their own textual interpretations and insights to the growing corpus of glosses, and when they returned to their home countries they brought back with them a deep knowledge, and often a copy, of Justinian's texts. In the year 1240, some 96,000 glosses on Justinian's compilation were compiled into a companion text known as the *Glossa ordinaria*.[62]

The ripple effects from this revolution in jurisprudence were felt outside Italy as early as around 1130, when scholars who had studied in Bologna founded a law school in the Rhone valley, in southeastern France. By the turn of the thirteenth century, scholars from Bologna and their pupils had founded law schools in Montpellier, Toulouse, and Orleans. In 1219, Pope Honorius III issued a papal bull forbidding the study of secular law in Paris, fearing that its study threatened to eclipse religious learning in that city.[63] Law schools were also established in Catalonia and in England, where the Bologna-schooled scholar Vacarius taught law and compiled the so-called "poor-man's" version of Justinian's compilation, because it was shorter and cheaper, a text that was used in law classes at Oxford. By the second half of the thirteenth century, the law school founded by Bolognese scholars in Montpellier, benefitting from the ban on the study of secular law in Paris, became the new center of Roman legal studies in Europe, supplanting even Bologna in importance.[64] As scholars from Bologna spread the legal gospel of Justinian to the rest of Europe, they achieved a Roman cultural conquest of the very same territories that Roman armies had occupied a millennium before. The overall effect was one of a new, or renewed, homogenization. As Peter Stein observed, "in every European country a university-trained lawyer was necessarily a Roman lawyer. Such lawyers came to share a common legal culture, based on the same texts, expounded in the same language, Latin."[65]

The role of scholars of canon law in the spread of Roman legal principles is a fundamental part of this story. One can see the growing influence of Roman legal studies on canonists by looking at successive recensions, or versions, of the twelfth-century canon lawyer Gratian's *Decretum*, the earliest of which makes only a limited use of Roman legal concepts, but later versions of which are replete with extensive quotations from the *Corpus Iuris Civilis*.[66] As James Brundage writes, canon law and a revived Roman law developed "a symbiotic relationship" by the early thirteenth century, with scholars from both fields freely borrowing terms and concepts from the other. Canonists accepted Roman law as a kind of supplement to canon law, and over time there developed a conception of a *ius commune*, or general law, which embodied the principles of a combined romano-canonical law.[67]

Scholars of canon law have tended to highlight the role of twelfth- and thirteenth-century canonists in spreading the theory and practice of Roman law, not only within canon law but within secular law as well. As one twentieth-century scholar of canon law wrote, "It is thanks to them [the canonists] that a number of principles of roman law passed into the penal law of modern societies."[68] Scholars of Roman law, by contrast, while often acknowledging the importance of canonists, nevertheless tend to see their role as being somewhat less crucial to developments: "Roman law and canon law worked upon each other, with Roman law the dominant partner, to form eventually the *ius commune*, virtually a common learned law for Western Europe."[69] But let us leave aside, for the moment, the question of whether canonists and canon law influenced the Roman legal renaissance or vice versa,[70] and return to the subject of the *Corpus Iuris Civilis* itself, with the aim of understanding the logic of punishment that is inherent to it, and to the *Digest* in particular.

In stark contrast to Salic law and the other "barbarian" legal codes of the early Middle Ages, the overriding concern of the *Digest* is not so much to stipulate penalties but to establish the rationale according to which penalties ought ideally to be determined. Central to this task was a deep interest in the questions of intentionality and liability: To what extent had someone *intended* to cause harm? And to what extent, even in the absence of any kind of malicious intent, ought someone to have *foreseen* that harm might occur, making that individual liable for damages? Distinctions were made between criminal cases involving malicious intent, in which punishment was called for, and civil cases involving liability, in which damages were due. But the *Digest* is not Manichean in its outlook, acknowledging an entire spectrum of intent and liability, which called for harsher or milder punishments, greater or lesser damages. That these concepts should seem so rational to us, in the twenty-first century, is eloquent testimony to the long-lasting and revolutionary impact of the *Corpus Iuris Civilis* on European conceptions of justice from the eleventh century to the present day.

If we look briefly at the text of the *Digest* itself, we can see just how carefully the questions of liability and intent were studied. The *Digest*'s treatment of liability is easiest to see in those cases in which malicious intent is entirely absent. A section entitled "If a Four-Footed Animal is Alleged to have Committed Pauperies" discusses a variety of contrasting cases in which animals caused damage, and the extent to which their owners were liable for it. Here, intentionality is dismissed at the outset because "an animal is incapable of committing a legal wrong because it is devoid of reason."[71] But liability was another question, and tended to be a function of the preventability or foreseeability of the harm:

> Take the case of a dog which, while being taken out on a lead by someone, breaks loose on account of its wildness and does some harm to someone else: If it could have been better restrained by someone else or if it should never have been taken to that particular place … the person who had the dog on the lead will be liable.[72]

Similarly, in the section entitled "Those who Pour or Throw Things out of Buildings," liability would seem to exist in proportion to preventability:

> [I]t is in the public interest that everyone should move about and gather together without fear or danger. It should be a matter of little interest whether the place [where the harm occurs] is public or private ground, so long as the public pass there, because the edict is concerned with protecting passersby rather than regulating public streets, and those places where people habitually pass by should at all times enjoy equal safety. (9, 3, 1, 1–2)

If, in other words, it was conceivable that someone might happen by, then the person throwing things out of buildings ought to have foreseen that harm might have resulted from his actions, regardless of whether those actions were committed on public or private property.

When it was a question of criminal punishment rather than civil damages, the intent of the offender was of paramount concern. Although intent would, at first glance, seem to be an entirely different question from foreseeability, they are very much related. For, if one *intends* to perpetrate a crime, then the consequences of that crime can be seen in advance; if, on the contrary, a crime is committed without prior intent, then the consequences are not foreseeable. Criminal liability, which like its civil counterpart is directly related to the foreseeability of damage, is determined by the degree of prior intent, and the severity of punishment is therefore determined according to the absence or presence of prior intent. If, for example, one committed homicide in the heat of an argument, then punishment would be less severe than if one had planned the homicide in advance because the consequences were less foreseeable, and therefore less preventable:

> The deified Hadrian wrote in a rescript that he who kills a man, if he committed this act without the intention of causing death, could be acquitted; and he who did not kill a man but wounded him with the intention of killing ought to be found guilty of homicide. On this account, it should be laid down that if someone draws his sword or strikes with a weapon, he undoubtedly did so with the intention of causing death; but if he struck someone with a key or a saucepan in the course of a brawl, although he strikes [the blow] with iron, yet it was not with the intention of killing. From this it is deduced that he who has killed a man in a brawl by accident rather than design should suffer a lighter penalty. (48, 8, 1, 3)

The principle here is that someone who intended to commit homicide but did not manage to do it ought to be punished more severely than someone who did not intend to commit homicide but somehow ended up doing it.

The crucial thing about the *Digest* is, once again, the extent to which it is a *forward-looking* text. As a means of preventing future harm, in the public interest, it analyzes all past or hypothetical acts of harm, whether civil or criminal, to determine the extent to which they may have been preventable and similar harm might be prevented in the future. Salic law had been forward-looking only in the extent to which it can be said to have aimed to prevent the outbreak of disturbances and blood feuds, but its primary intent was retroactive: how could damage be compensated, restitution made, so that the harm itself could be undone. The principles contained in the *Digest* represent, therefore, the inverse of the priorities of Salic law. If damages were to be paid for injury, it was not simply to make reparations, but so that the threat of paying damages would ideally make an individual think twice before he or she took that aggressive dog on a walk or threw that chamber pot out the window. The more serious the crime, the more serious—but also the more *spectacular*—the punishment, because the fundamental purpose of punishment was to dissuade those with malicious intent from committing damaging acts. Severe bodily punishments that were necessarily public and spectacular were mandated so that, as Valentinian III had put it in 382, "the punishment of one might inspire fear in the greater number."[73] While such punishments might not effectively dissuade the man with the key or saucepan from killing someone in the heat of a brawl, the fear of severe punishments would, in theory, deter someone with prior intent who had the time to reflect on the consequences of his or her actions. It was for this reason that, in contrast to Salic law, intent trumped actual damages when determining appropriate punishments. As Emperor Hadrian wrote, "In crimes it is the intention, not the issue, to which regard is paid." (48, 8, 14)

Underneath the massive compilation of cases, both actual and hypothetical, contained in *Corpus Iuris Civilis* lay an entire logical foundation of penal principles that weighed culpability on the basis of malicious intent, and assessed appropriate punishments largely on the basis of their potential to deter crimes from being committed in the future. And it is here that we can begin to see why the principles contained in the *Corpus Iuris Civilis* would have been attractive to the leadership of the Church at the time.

One need not necessarily embrace the full-blown arguments of Berman and others who link the Church's interest in the *Corpus Iuris Civilis* to its sovereign ambitions in order to accept that the reforming popes may have had practical motives for paying attention to Justinian's compilation, and to its theory of crime and punishment in particular. A particularly compelling argument has been put forward by legal historian Richard Fraher, who suggests that the papacy was especially attracted to the idea of using the sweeping powers of inquisition afforded by Roman legal procedure in order to uncover and eradicate vice within the clergy. For Fraher, the roots of a modern, proactive, deterrent approach to crime may very well date back to Gregory VII's campaign in the late eleventh century to stamp out clerical concubinage and simony, the act of buying ecclesiastical offices.[74]

Fraher's argument sheds light on the extent to which the very definition of a criminal act was shifting around this time. Whereas Salic law, like other "barbarian" legal codes, had focused almost exclusively on individual misdeeds and the harm they did to specific individuals, the Church's attack on clerical vice viewed both sin and injury as a collective concept, affecting the Church as a whole. The religious historian Gerd Tellenbach paraphrases the motivation behind Gregory VII's anti-simony campaign as follows:

> When a simoniac usurps the rights of Christ, when against His will a church is married to an evil man, through whom the Savior scorns to become mystically present, then the connection between Christ and the church ceases. The church is no longer His Bride, but becomes a harlot....[75]

When certain crimes were perceived as having an effect upon the community as a whole, the damage that was caused was more abstract than the specific injuries addressed by Salic law. This conception of a more collective injury was inadequately repaired by monetary compensation, but called instead for punishments that were iconographic and spectacular, more qualitative than quantitative, punishments that would allow not only for individual atonement but for the redemption of the community as a whole. Furthermore, the more abstract understanding of "crime" as a general phenomenon meant that the public punishment of one crime could serve as a non-specific lesson to deter the commission of other crimes. The ideal punishment was, therefore, one that allowed the individual criminal to expiate the particular crime committed, which allowed the community to heal from the injury inflicted on it, and which sent a message to others who were contemplating committing a crime, any crime, in the future.

Canon law had traditionally stressed the "medicinal" role of punishment, the idea that a primary purpose of punishing was to correct or reform the individual offender.[76] While the idea of punishment as a corrective would continue to be emphasized, at least rhetorically, in canon as well as secular law throughout the Middle Ages, and indeed in the modern period as well, from the eleventh century onward a new stress on crime prevention, on deterrence, came to monopolize thinking about punishment. As Brundage writes, the reforming popes took "an energetic and vigorous approach to penal law. Bishops and other prelates, the reformers believed, should seek out offenders against orthodox belief and behavior. Once detected, offenders ought to be put on public trial for their misdeeds and, when convicted, their punishment should likewise be public and ferocious enough to make other potential offenders think twice before imitating the miscreants."[77]

In stark contrast to Anselm's conception of punishment as the repayment of a debt owed to God, discussed above, the rhetoric of the reforming popes often betrayed a decidedly Roman sensibility. Innocent III not only argued that the failure to punish created "an audacity of impunity, through which those who were bad become worse," but he was instrumental in recasting heresy as a form of divine *lèse majesté*.[78] At the same time, Innocent's insistence that his campaign to stamp out crime was in the "public interest" was something that, as both Fraher and Ken Pennington have noted, was clearly borrowed from the *Corpus Iuris Civilis*.[79]

The rise in Roman legal studies, which began in Italy and spread out across the European continent, would bring about a revolution in both the theory and practice of punishment, as punishment itself became nearly synonymous with deterrence, and as public spectacles of pain and death were increasingly regarded as the most efficient means of deterring crime. In the words of the French philosopher and theologian Durandus de St. Pourçain, writing in the fourteenth century, "Some are not born to obey reverently, but out of terror, not to shun evil out of shame, but on account of penalties."[80]

This revolution in penal thought affected both canon and secular law, and there is no question that canon lawyers helped to serve as a conduit for Roman legal theory and practice, not only through the criminal prosecution of wrongdoing clerics who fell under their jurisdiction, but also through the prosecution of lay individuals who were accused of sins such as heresy and sexual offenses that were deemed to fall under the province of Church authority. Nevertheless, members of the clergy were expressly banned by the Fourth Lateran Council of 1215 from participating in the practice of capital punishment in any capacity whatsoever: "No cleric may pronounce a sentence of death, or execute such a sentence, or be present at its execution.... Nor may any cleric write or dictate letters destined for the execution of such a sentence. Wherefore, in the chanceries of the princes let this matter be committed to laymen and not to clerics."[81] While the Church vigorously pursued capital cases such as heresy and sodomy, no sooner was guilt established than the condemned was "abandoned" to secular authorities in order for justice to be done: "We excommunicate and anathematize every heresy that raises against the holy, orthodox and Catholic faith.... Those condemned, being handed over to the secular rulers of their bailiffs, let them be abandoned, to be punished with due justice, clerics being first degraded from their orders."[82] If canon and secular law both played a role in the revolution of penal theory that began around the turn of the eleventh century, the Church purposely distanced itself from the spectacular punishments that were the logical result of that revolution.

Rather than seeing France's complex legal history as one characterized by a geographical split between Roman law in the south and customary law in the north, we would do better to understand it as the product of a gradual layering of separate penal traditions on top of one another. In this sense, France's history is not very different from that of the rest of western Europe. On the decayed foundations of Roman law was layered a theory and practice of penal compensation, payback, and the righting of wrongs; on top of this were layered Catholic practices of atonement, expiation, public apology and forgiveness, expulsion, reincorporation, and redemption; and on top of these was yet another layer of Roman law, and a preoccupation with deterring crime in the public interest, with malicious intent, and with exemplary deterrence.

Although there is always the temptation to find coherence in any system, the conception of punishment in European society did not evolve in a straightforward, linear fashion. Each successive conception of punishment did not replace the preceding one, so much as it pushed it beneath the surface, sometimes completely obscuring it, sometimes allowing it to rise back up. Although at first these various penal influences combined together in such a way that each of the constituent ingredients, layered on top of one another, was still readily identifiable, over time they began to lose their distinct characteristics and congealed into a nearly indistinguishable mass, a kind of half-baked cultural lasagna of penal theories and customs, which existed through the Middle Ages, into the early modern period, and which arguably still exists today.

2

Criminal Intent and Spectacular Punishment
The Infiltration of Roman Legal Theory and Practice into French Customary Law

In the wake of the "rediscovery" of the *Justinian Code* in Italy in the latter half of the eleventh century, law schools mushroomed across the European continent. Beginning in Italy, and spreading outward to France and Britain in the thirteenth century, Roman legal studies became the intellectual fashion of the day, with the number of legal scholars rising exponentially. In France, law schools were founded in Montpellier, Orléans, Toulouse, and Paris, and by the second half of the thirteenth century, Montpellier had replaced Bologna as the primary center of Roman legal studies in Europe.

As these law schools were being founded, and as the influence and authority of Roman law was spreading, there was, somewhat surprisingly, a sudden impetus to compile and to commit to writing regional customary laws and practices, which had traditionally been passed down from one generation to the next in oral form. The earliest compilations of customary laws were written outside of Capetian France, in the region surrounding Avignon as early as 1154, and somewhat later in Norman-controlled areas of Britain and in French Normandy. Glanvill's *On the Laws and Customs of England* was probably the first truly comprehensive compilation of customary laws, appearing around 1190, and was followed about a decade afterwards by the Norman *Très Ancien Coutumier*, which had much in common with Glanvill's text. After the French conquest of Normandy in 1204, the *Coutumier* was absorbed into France proper, and eventually acquired a semi-official status under the French monarchy. In the second half of the thirteenth century, codifications of customary laws were compiled in many other regions of France. Among the more prominent of these customals were: the *Conseil de Pierre de Fontaines* (*c*.1253), which made a first attempt to put the customs of the Vermandois region into writing; the *Grand Coutumier de Normandie* (*c*.1255), which updated the customary laws of French Normandy; the *Livre de Jostice et de Plet* (*c*.1260–70) and the *Etablissements de Saint Louis* (1272–73), which detailed the customary laws of the Orléans region; and Philippe de Beaumanoir's *Coutumes du comté de Clermont en Beauvaisis* (*c*.1283).[1]

Although most of the thirteenth-century customals appeared in northern France, the so-called *pays de coutumes*, several customals appeared in southern areas as well, where written Roman law has traditionally been thought to have held sway. The first written *coutumes* of Agen, Bordeaux, Provence, and Toulouse, for example, all date from the thirteenth century.² Over the course of the fourteenth and fifteenth centuries, several other important customals appeared, including Jacques d'Ableiges's *Grand Coutumier de France* (*c*.1380); Jean Boutillier's *Somme rural* (*c*.1385); the *Coutumes et stilles observez et gardez ès pays d'Anjou et du Maine* (1411); and the *Coutume de Vermandois* (1448). Finally, in 1454, Charles VII ordered that the customary laws of *all* the regions of France be put into written form, a process that continued up to the French Revolution, when all laws and customs were superseded by the new legal code.

The codification of customary laws throughout France (and indeed throughout Europe as a whole) was undertaken with the purpose of preserving these local customs and protecting them from outside influences, the most important of which was Roman law, with its innumerable glosses, and its abundant prestige. As Philippe de Beaumanoir wrote at the beginning of his *Coutumes de Beauvaisis*, "It seemed to me, and to others as well, that it would be good and profitable to write down and register all customs that are now in use so that they may be maintained without change from now on. Because memories are fleeting and the lives of people are short, that which is not written is soon forgotten."³

Although codification was perceived as a bulwark to change, the act of putting customary practice into written legal form paradoxically altered its very nature. One of the essential characteristics of customary laws was their adaptable nature; although their authority lay in their traditional use, customary laws were nevertheless subtly altered and updated as they passed from one generation to the next. As Esther Cohen put it, written customary laws were something of a "contradiction in terms."⁴ The act of writing them down fixed them in time, transforming living and fluid customs and rituals into objectified practice. In written form, enumerated and arranged, customary laws inevitably invited comparison to Roman laws, and many authors of customals could not resist the temptation to imbue customary laws with a kind of theoretical coherence they did not naturally possess, in the hope that they would not seem inferior by comparison. In the end, therefore, despite the best efforts of those who endeavored to compile these laws faithfully so as to preserve them from Roman influence, the very act of arranging them in written form inherently Romanized them.⁵

Earlier generations of historians tended to regard French customals as descended from "Germanic" law, and if they were willing to acknowledge a modicum of Roman influence on specific customals, they nevertheless subscribed to the idea that customary law was distinct from Roman law, the traditional division of France into a *pays de droit écrit* and a *pays de coutumes* being a reflection of that distinction. In this chapter, however, I am interested in tracing the incursion of Roman principles into customary penal laws, and the extent to which that incursion may have blurred or even erased many of the distinctions between the two bodies of law.

As we have seen, Salic law, like other "barbarian" legal codes from which customary laws are often thought to have been derived, was more or less unconcerned with the intent of the perpetrator, rarely making any distinction between premeditated acts, acts undertaken spontaneously, and complete accidents.⁶ If someone had been injured, it mattered little what the intentions of the person who had caused the injury may have been, as the primary concern was the compensation of the victim, regardless of intent. By the same token, if no injury had been sustained, then no crime had been committed, and no compensation was due.

In marked contrast to this conception of crime and punishment, Roman law considered the intent of those who perpetrated crimes to be of paramount importance. Because Roman law was primarily concerned with the prevention of crimes in the future in the name of the public interest, rather than with compensating particular victims or their families after the fact, Roman jurists drew important distinctions between degrees of intentionality, which would have a direct bearing on the severity of the penalty. Premeditated murder demanded the severest and most spectacular of penalties because it was believed that such penalties were indispensable to deterring future murderers. Murders that were committed without premeditation, however, merited less severe penalties; committed in the heat of the moment, these crimes were seen as being less preventable, as the perpetrator had little or no time to weigh the consequences of his or her actions. Accidental homicides, which were by definition unpreventable, called for the lightest of penalties and sometimes no penalty at all.

The concepts of intent and malice aforethought can, therefore, be used as cultural "genetic" markers that allow us to trace the genealogy of modern law as it developed through the medieval and early modern periods. Even the most cursory glance at customary laws that were compiled from roughly the thirteenth century onward reveals a pronounced interest in the intentions of the offender. This was true not only in the simple sense of a differentiation between intentional crime and accidental injury, but in a more subtle and complex differentiation between degrees of culpability, along the lines of what one finds in Roman jurisprudence.

Scholars of religion and canon law have tended to see this incursion of intentionality into customary law as the result of the influence of contemporary theologians and canonists, for whom intentionality had become a preoccupation, rather than as a direct result of Roman legal studies. Indeed, there is perhaps no one in the twelfth century who devoted more time and attention to the subject of intentionality than the theologian Peter Abelard, who in his writings drew a careful distinction between intentions and deeds. For Abelard, good deeds could be either good or evil in intent, and evil deeds could similarly arise from either good or evil intentions, but good intentions were inherently good, and evil ones, inherently evil. In his eyes, "God alone...considers not so much what is done as in what mind it may be done, [and] truly considers the guilt in our intention...."[7] Although Abelard's argument was meant to be applicable to sin rather than secular crimes, twelfth-century canonists endeavored to extend the principle of intentionality beyond sin to include canon-law crimes, arguing that these too should be defined by malicious intent rather than by deeds alone.[8]

Scholars of canon law have long argued that this twelfth-century redefinition of sin and canon-law crimes as a function of intent was largely responsible for the eventual incursion of the principle of intentionality into secular law. This argument has been made since at least the 1930s, when Stephan Kuttner, a scholar of criminal law who eventually became one of the foremost scholars of medieval canon law, expressed this view in his seminal book *Kanonistische Schuldlehre*.[9] Around the same time, the legal scholar Francis Bowes Sayre put forward a very similar argument in his important article "Mens Rea," in which he expressed the conviction that canon law's conception of sin had exerted a profound influence on the conception of criminal intent, or *mens rea*—literally guilty mind—in English common law.[10]

While neither Kuttner nor Sayre disputed the idea that the canonists themselves derived their views on intentionality from Roman law, they and the vast majority of scholars of canon law who came after them have insisted that the jurists who studied and practiced canon law were the primary conduit for the spread of these (originally Roman) concepts into Western jurisprudence. Although this is certainly a plausible argument, it is also plausible that secular jurists, like the canonists themselves, derived their views on intentionality directly from Roman law. The legal scholar Guyora Binder has recently argued that "we cannot simply assume canon law's influence on criminal law,"[11] and Jean Gaudemet has suggested that the question of who influenced whom is largely unknowable:

> It is not always easy, and sometimes not even possible, to establish in any concrete way, which of the two influences [canon or Roman] was decisive, for the very simple reason that medieval Canon law... drew abundantly from Roman law. In this situation, juridical reasoning, the institution, the procedure which manifests itself as "canonesque," might it not be in reality Roman?... Canon law is so impregnated with Roman [law] that it is not always possible to resolve the problem of the "fount of influence."[12]

For our purposes here, what truly matters is the very fact that intentionality inserted itself into European conceptions of crime and punishment from the twelfth century onward. It may very well be that theologians and canonists were the first to articulate the relevance of intentionality to penal law and that their contributions were instrumental; it may also be that secular jurists simply arrived at similar conclusions slightly later, through their own encounters with the principles of Roman law contained in the *Corpus Iuris Civilis*. Or, it may be that the preoccupation with intentionality in both canon and secular law was a testament to the close relationship and interconnections between the two juridical realms. Regardless of its provenance, the essential point is that intentionality entered the European juridical consciousness in the twelfth century, and quickly came to monopolize conceptions of both crime and punishment. Culpability became a function of prior malicious intent, and punishment came to be virtually synonymous with deterrence. The following pages trace the incursion of intentionality into customary law, and the consequent rise of spectacular punishments that were intended to deter malicious intent.

INTENTIONALITY AND CUSTOMARY LAW

Sometimes the intrusion of Roman law into French customals is not terribly difficult to see. Pierre de Fontaines' *Conseil*, for example, which was written around 1253, and which purported to be a book "about the usages and the customs of the

Vermandois,"[13] is a rather thinly disguised regurgitation of Roman law. As Paul Viollet remarked, Fontaines did little more than "continuously translate the *Digest* and the *Code*, and acquainted us with precious few customary practices."[14]

While Fontaines' text is something of an extreme example, many other customary authors found it equally difficult to resist the temptation to cite Roman law in works that were ostensibly devoted to customary practices. The author of the *Livre de Jostice et de Plet*, for example, a customal compiled around 1260–70, had the habit of intersplicing Roman and customary laws without any attempt to reconcile the different principles that underlay them, as if the mere citation of Roman laws lent a certain air of respectability to his text. The chapter on punishments begins with six articles that essentially list general principles taken directly from the *Digest*.[15] This is followed, without any transition whatsoever, by a list of crimes, in no discernible order, from gambling and sodomy to theft and murder. The crimes and their respective punishments are presented as a price list, in a manner that recalls the articles of Salic law, which similarly sought to define the precise compensation for every imaginable crime: "If someone cracks open someone's head and he recovers his health, he [who dealt the blow] owes sixty sous to the grand justice."[16]

A more subtle case of borrowing from Roman law is presented by Beaumanoir's *Coutumes de Beauvaisis*, which was compiled roughly two decades after the *Livre de Jostice et de Plet*. Beaumanoir makes no direct references to Roman law and, at first glance, the detailed listing of injuries and crimes is similar to the list of injuries in Salic law. Beaumanoir, for example, drew careful distinctions between assaults that resulted in the flow of blood, depending on whether blood flowed "through the nose" (in which case the fine for assault was not increased) or "through punctured skin" (in which case the penalty was greater).[17] On the surface, then, Beaumanoir's customal seems like a text that preserves preexisting penal customs, relatively unadulterated by the new wave of Roman legal studies. As we have already seen, this was Beaumanoir's stated intention—"to write down and register all customs that are now in use"—and his text is often cited as a classic customal of the period.

One can, nevertheless, discern a decidedly Roman preoccupation with the intent of the criminal in Beaumanoir's customal. With respect to murders, he draws a distinction between premeditated murders, which he labeled "*traisons*," or treachery, and simple *homicides*, which he defined as murders that occurred during the heat of an argument [*en chaude mellee*].[18] Moreover, he takes pains to exclude from punishment people who commit murder by reason of insanity because, as he writes, "they do not know what they are doing."[19] There is perhaps no better place to see how Beaumanoir's conception of crime differs from earlier Salic law than in his discussion of the appropriate punishment for someone caught stealing game from a private reserve. Whereas Salic law would have paid attention only to the value of the animal taken, Beaumanoir was concerned with the extent to which the crime was premeditated: "[T]hey should be [hanged] if they are apprehended at night, because it would be apparent that they had gone there with the intent to steal [*par courage d'embler*]. But if they go there by day, in the way that a certain carefree attitude can lead people to do stupid things, they should be let off with a monetary fine."[20] It would be going too far to suggest that Beaumanoir's customal was simply Roman law dressed in customary garb, as he does not go so far as to criminalize mere intent in the absence of an actual crime.[21] But in its subtle absorption of the theoretical foundations of Roman law, Beaumanoir's customal is in many respects emblematic of the process by which Roman law inserted itself into European conceptions of crime and punishment.

Given Beaumanoir's attention to malicious intent, it is not surprising to find that he embraced Roman law's preoccupation with penal deterrence. In fact, he even occasionally suggested that existing custom fell short in this regard, and advocated altering customal penalties so that they might better deter wrongdoing:

> It's an annoying thing when our custom allows a petty commoner to injure a great man [*homme vaillant*] and only pay a fine of five sous; for this reason, I am of the opinion that a long prison sentence should be handed down to him so that, for fear of going to prison, good-for-nothing people [*musart*] will correct themselves [and refrain] from undertaking foolish acts.[22]

Over the next century and a half, the idea that deterrence was a primary, if not *the* primary, aim of punishment gradually found its way into the customals of France. When, in 1411, the *Coutumes de l'Anjou* outlined why wrongdoers should be punished, it listed four basic reasons: "1) for their misdeeds; 2) to give fear and example to others so that they will not do evil; 3) to remove said evildoers from the community of the good so that they do not make them worse; 4) to prevent the evils that they might still do if they escape."[23] Of these four reasons, only the first pertains, albeit somewhat vaguely, to the crime that was actually committed; the remaining three involve the prevention of future crimes that might be committed, either by the criminal himself or by others.

So much, in fact, did deterrence become the preoccupation of medieval jurisprudence that some jurists went so far as to suggest that the law justified the prevention and punishment of a crime before it had technically occurred. As Alexander Murray has suggested, Roman law had been somewhat ambivalent on this point, reluctant to punish *nuda cogitatio*, or bare thought, except in the rarest of cases, such as when someone "even tries to rape" a consecrated virgin.[24] From this clause in the Codex, medieval jurists writing after the mid-thirteenth century extrapolated the right to punish mere intent in the case of "atrocious" crimes, a category that would eventually include certain kinds of homicide and heresy. The French jurist Pierre de Belleperche, writing at the end of the thirteenth century, went one step further, justifying the punishment of intent not simply in atrocious crimes but in situations where the intent to commit a crime was patently obvious. For Belleperche, the strict limits of Roman jurisprudence, which mandated punishment only in the most heinous of attempted crimes, was a bit formalistic if not downright silly: "A thief gets a key to your room in order to steal, but you catch him before he has taken anything. Does he not remain a thief? The *Digest* says no and refuses to punish him as a thief." For Belleperche, however, where there was blatant intent to commit a crime, punishment was called for, whether the crime was atrocious or ordinary: "[T]he distinction between graver and lesser offences is *not* one I find applicable here. Just ask yourself what you think is permissible to a householder who actually finds a thief trying to steal, and catches him in the attempt, even if nothing has been stolen? Do you think the householder would not hand him over to the executioner? He most certainly should and rightly so."[25] For Belleperche, the target of punishment was criminal intent rather than crime.

LÈSE-MAJESTÉ AND TREASON IN CUSTOMARY LAW

Although the preoccupation with criminal intent can be viewed as a clear marker of Roman influence on customary law, certain influences are so blatant that one hardly needs a marker. Perhaps the clearest example is the Roman conception of *crimen laesae majestatis* and its eventual incorporation into customary law as *lèse-majesté*, a term that acknowledged the Roman antecedents of the concept. We have already seen how, shortly after the rediscovery of the *Corpus Iuris Civilis*, Pope Gregory VII had made use of Roman legal principles to pursue his war on moral crimes such as simony, a crime that he intended to ferret out and eradicate in the "public interest."[26] A little over a century later, his successor Innocent III similarly availed himself of the Roman principle of *crimen laesae majestatis*, adapting it to his campaign against heresy.

In the Roman context, *crimen laesae majestatis*, a crime of wounded majesty, had referred originally to an assault upon the majesty, the sovereignty of the Roman people. During the imperial period, however, the crime of wounded majesty was reinterpreted as a direct assault upon or betrayal of the emperor or, by extension, his ministers. Innocent essentially argued that if disloyalty or attacks upon the emperor could be construed as a crime against majesty, then it stood to reason that the spiritual crime of heresy or aberrant faith could similarly be construed as a crime against Divine Majesty. This juristic move was something of a conceptual stretch in two respects. First, Innocent's decretal took a law that had been applicable to observable acts of disloyalty and applied that law to interior belief, thereby blurring the boundaries between spiritual and physical crimes.[27] Second, Innocent resurrected a concept that had been intimately bound up with Roman conceptions of sovereign authority, a concept that had not been in practical use for nearly a thousand years, and deposited it, so to speak, into the European political context of the turn of the thirteenth century.[28]

Like Innocent, the secular monarchs of Europe resurrected the long-moribund concept of *crimen laesae majestatis*, availing themselves of the traditional, political version of the concept as a means of defending their newly theorized sovereignty. As early as the 1180s, *lèse majesté* made its appearance in English legal texts, and by 1199 Innocent himself was encouraging the applicability of the concept of lèse-majesté to crimes against the king of France.[29] One does not, however, find the crime of lèse-majesté mentioned in the earliest French customals, a fact that is not particularly surprising, given that they were ostensibly devoted to the laws and practices of specific regions rather than the realm as a whole. Royal jurists, however, had begun to explore the concept by the late fourteenth century, and the term "lèse-majesté" made an appearance in legislation in the year 1372.[30]

Shortly after its appearance in royal legislation, the crime of lèse-majesté appeared in Jean Boutillier's *Somme rural* (c.1385), topping a list of nineteen capital crimes. Boutillier, whose compilation comprised the customary laws of the Somme region, defined the crime of lèse-majesté as "laboring or scheming in any way whatsoever against the noble majesty of the King our Sire," and he straightforwardly acknowledged the Roman origin of the concept, obligingly referring his readers to the appropriate passage in the *Digest*: the Julian Laws on Treason (Book 48, 4).[31]

Immediately following the crime of lèse-majesté in Boutillier's list of capital crimes is the crime of *trahison* (a term that is usually translated into English as *treason*, but which, at least for the moment, I will keep in its original French so as not to color it with its modern connotations). At first glance, *trahison* would seem to be a lesser form of lèse-majesté, committed not against one's king but rather against one's lord: "The second [capital crime] is *trahison* which is done by someone against his Lord, or against another person. If it is against one's lord, in whatever manner it is undertaken, it is a capital crime." For Boutillier, the crime of *trahison* was "such a detestable and very-horrible thing" that someone "who had so much as only thought of such a sin or crime" was subject to capital punishment; in other words, intent alone without the act was sufficient to merit death.[32] So "very-horrible" was the crime that it deserved an equally horrible punishment:

> [they] must suffer the penalty of traitors such as being *tonnelé* [disemboweled?], quartered and flayed, and everything that belongs to them assigned to the seigneur, but also their children if they have any must be forced into exile & left to die a deserved death there, and the reason for this is that, so horrible and detestable is the crime of *trahison* that it by nature infects the seed [*la semence*] of the offender & for this reason the roots, the trunk, and the seed must all be destroyed, so that no more of their kind can be made....[33]

As a source for his writings on the punishment of traitors, Boutillier once again cites the Julian laws contained in the *Digest*. But it would seem that the *Theodisian Code* was even more of an inspiration here, for we find in Book IX of the latter work almost all of Boutillier's thoughts on the suitable punishment for traitors, as if they were imported lock, stock, and barrel without much in the way of reflection.[34]

Boutillier appears, therefore, to have "lifted" the Roman concept of lèse-majesté and applied it to attacks against the sovereign authority of the French king as well as to attacks on one's lord. But he went further than Roman jurists by suggesting that the concept could be applied not only to physical attacks against the king but also to attacks on his representation, a category that included the crime of counterfeiting. Although Roman law had been rather ambiguous as to whether counterfeiting could be considered a *crimen laesae majestatis*, only considering it to be so in the late imperial period, Boutillier, along with many of his fellow customary authors, clearly considered counterfeiting as equal to an attack on the person of the king, and made it a capital offense, usually punishable by being boiled alive.[35]

Boutillier and his contemporaries might therefore be seen as seizing upon the law of late imperial Rome, when sovereign authority had been fully invested in the person of the emperor and when any crime against either him or his representation was considered a crime deserving of the most severe punishment. In this sense, then, there hardly seems anything at all that is "customary" about Boutillier's conception of *trahison*. Yet, if we take a second look at his reasoning, we see that something else seems to be at work here, and that Boutillier and his fellow customary authors did not so much import the Roman concept of lèse-majeste and impose it anachronistically onto the fourteenth century as endeavor to merge it with pre-existing traditional, customary concepts of disloyalty and betrayal signified by the term *trahison*.

As we saw above, Boutillier used the word *trahison* to speak not only of crimes against the king but also of crimes against one's seigneur. But he also included in the definition of *trahison*—and one almost misses it upon a first reading—a rather vague allusion to crimes "against another person." Boutillier never explicitly lays out what he means by *trahison* against someone who was not one's king or one's lord, but simply refers to those who have "betrayed [*trahy*] and plotted against [*espié*]" another individual as deserving the death penalty.[36] If Boutillier is himself somewhat elusive on the definition of what precisely constituted the "very-horrible" crime of *trahison*, other customals provide crucial clues. The English customal *Britton*, written in French around 1280, includes a section "De Tresouns" ("On Treasons") in which the author differentiates between high treason (*graund tresoun*) and ordinary treason. The former includes direct attacks on the king as well as on one's lord, and includes within this category various forms of counterfeiting. But it is the definition of ordinary treason that is particularly interesting, and would seem to be analogous to Boutillier's concept of *trahison* as betrayal: "Treason [*tresun*] consists of any mischief, which a man knowingly does, or procures to be done, to one to whom he pretends to be a friend."[37] Around the same time, the author of the *Livre de Jostice et de Plet* (c.1260–1270) defines the concept as follows: "To commit a crime at night is traïson; to break a truce is *traïson*; to strike when one does not see the blow coming; to strike, without challenging [first], and so close that one cannot fend off the blow."[38] Finally, Beaumanoir gives the following definition: "Traïsons are when someone does not show any signs of hatred and [nevertheless] one hates mortally, so much so that, because of hatred, one kills or has killed, or one beats or has beaten to the point of great harm the person whom he hates treacherously [*par traïson*]."[39]

Trahison, no matter how one spells it, was understood in the late thirteenth century as a concept that is probably best expressed in English by the words "treachery," "betrayal," and "disloyalty." But *trahison* was more than that; it was *duplicitous* disloyalty. It was declaring peace and then attacking; it was striking from behind, murdering at night. *Trahison* in many respects presents us with a mirror image of the contemporary understanding of virtuous behavior. The opposite of *trahison* would be honesty, forthrightness, trustworthiness, and loyalty. For these customary authors writing at the turn of the fourteenth century, *trahison* was not simply a crime of one individual against another. Precisely because it was characterized by duplicity, an act of *trahison* committed by someone who hated and yet who did not "show any signs of hatred" had the effect of sowing doubt and suspicion in a society where trust and faith in others were indispensable. *Trahison*, in short, threatened to dissolve the essential bonds uniting one individual to another.

Although these bonds of trust might be between a man and his friend, many of the bonds in medieval society were, of course, hierarchical in nature: between a man and his lord, between a lord and his suzerain (and it was indeed only men, for women and children were bound respectively to their husbands and fathers rather than to other men). But even these hierarchical relationships were characterized by a mutual relationship. A man promised his lord loyalty, and in return a lord promised his man protection; these were essentially debts that could be called due when necessary. Perhaps the clearest expression of the mutuality of this binding contract can be found in Jean d'Ibelin's *Assizes of Jerusalem* (*c*.1265), which, while acknowledging that "a man owes his lord reverence in all matters," nevertheless maintains that both a man and his lord "must steadfastly and sincerely keep faith with the other."[40] Nearly the same sentiments were expressed by Beaumanoir two decades later in his customal: "We say, and it is true according to our custom, that just as much as a man owes faith and loyalty to his lord by virtue of his homage, every bit as much do lords owe it to their man."[41] So personal were these bonds, however, that although one was bound to one's lord, one was not bound to *his* lord. Or, as the thirteenth-century jurist John de Blanot put it, "the man of my man is not my man."[42]

If we understand the nature of the bond that tied each man to his lord, we can begin to understand how the local seigneur came gradually to insert himself into the judicial equation. In contrast to Salic law, for example, which had sought to adjudicate between two individuals, later customary law often takes into account the fact that a crime not only had an impact on its direct victim but also on the lord who had sworn to protect his man.[43] Damage therefore had to be paid not only to repair the actual injury caused, but also to make reparations for the breach of peace and to compensate the lord who was sworn to protect his man's interests. Over time, the local seigneur gradually displaced the direct victim as the identified injured party, and as a consequence of this, compensation increasingly found its way into the purses of the seigneurs.

In many ways, the twelfth and thirteenth centuries mark a midpoint in this gradual redefinition of criminal injury, and sentences handed down in the period often directed that fines be shared by the victim and his lord. For example, in 1240 the town charter of Bergues, in Flanders, stipulated that anyone who attacked someone and created an open wound would be liable to pay 3 livres to the victim and 6 to the count.[44] The *Coutumes* of Caumont, a town in southwestern France, stipulated around 1289 that an adulterous couple caught in the act would be forced to run naked and tied together through the streets of town, but could be spared this punishment if the condemned paid 65 *sous* to the seigneur and an unspecified fine to the woman's relatives.[45]

Not only does the sentence of the adulterers of Caumont seem to stand at the midpoint between private compensation and fines due to local authorities, it also stands on another important threshold. According to Jean Carbasse, there was a clear trend over time in the punishment of adultery from shaming rituals, such as being forced to run naked, toward simple monetary fines.[46] This is part of a broader trend in which certain crimes that were considered less serious in terms of their public threat were beginning to be punished by civil fines and, on the contrary, those crimes that were regarded as a true threat to public order—particularly crimes involving premeditation and clear malice aforethought—were increasingly seen as mandating exemplary, public, corporal punishment rather than compensation.

Through the thirteenth and, in some areas, into the fourteenth century, penal sentences often wavered between monetary and corporal punishments for the same crimes, even for crimes as serious as homicide. In areas under its direct control, the royal government endeavored to stamp out this practice of paying for serious crimes with money, as it so clearly violated the principle of exemplary deterrence. In 1267, for example, Louis IX abolished the "bad custom" that had allowed citizens of Tournai to avoid corporal punishment for the crime of homicide by paying a fine. Finally, in 1357, the dauphin Charles abolished the practice of compensation throughout the entire realm, arguing that this traditional practice had effectively allowed the crime to "remain, without being duly punished, against reason and good Justice."[47] Charles clearly shared Innocent's view that the failure to punish crimes created "an audacity of impunity."[48] For Charles, as for his successors, the only real punishments for those who had the audacity to threaten public order would be punishments that were both corporal and spectacular.

Despite this royal ordinance and the general trend toward mandatory corporal and capital punishments for serious, premeditated criminal offenses, the practice of compensation nevertheless lingered for quite some time, whether as court-ordered fines or as private transactions between the offender and the victim's family. Compensation seemed particularly appropriate in cases where premeditation was absent (homicides that took place in the heat of the moment, for example). Even in those areas where compensation had effectively been abolished, the practice of banishment, replete with confiscation of assets, served as a more palatable alternative for localities that could not quite reconcile themselves to the new penal severity.[49] In fact, I would venture to suggest that the widespread practice of punishing by effigy those offenders who had fled before they could be punished may very well have originated as a tacitly accepted means of obeying the letter of the law, while skirting it in spirit.[50] Nevertheless, the overall trend was, as we will see, toward increasingly corporal and increasingly spectacular punishments.

HIGH JUSTICE, LOW JUSTICE, AND THE SPECTACULARIZATION OF PUNISHMENT

The variety and inconsistency of penal practice in medieval France would seem to make any generalization extraordinarily difficult. Each region had its own peculiarities, and even within the same regions, punishments could differ significantly from one town to another. Customary law almost seemed to revel in exceptionality, and the modern reader who searches for patterns and endeavors to discern what logic might have underlain the various punishments can feel frustrated at nearly every turn. Even within a given text of the customary laws of one particular region, any general rule invariably has an exception and the inevitable exception to the exception.[51]

Given the variation of customs within given regions, it is perhaps not surprising that corporal and capital punishments were susceptible to great variation across regional divides. Most customary laws called for male murderers to be hanged, whereas in the south-west, custom apparently demanded that they be buried alive with their victims.[52] Counterfeiters suffered mutilation in some regions, were hanged in others, and were boiled alive as well as hanged in still others. If we take into account a lack of consistency in the actual application of these customary laws, we realize the difficulties involved in painting any kind of general picture of punishment in medieval France.[53]

Nevertheless, it is possible to identify certain trends over time, across all regions of France, and indeed across much of continental Europe. One of the most important of these trends was a dramatic increase in the severity and the spectacularity of punishments from the twelfth through the sixteenth century. As customary law took intentionality increasingly into account and as the prevention of crime became a priority, spectacular corporal and capital punishments seemed to offer the ideal means of deterring crime. Corporal punishments were seen to deter individual criminals from reoffending, whether by the simple act of teaching a lesson or by mutilations that made recidivism less likely: the severing of a blasphemer's tongue, for instance, or the dismemberment of a thief. Capital punishment, of course, made recidivism impossible, and was also seen as sending a powerful message to those in the community who might be contemplating the commission of a crime.

One can see the beginnings of this process of spectacularization in the *Très Ancien Coutumier*, compiled around 1200, which differentiated between an ordinary form of the death penalty, usually hanging, for crimes such as theft, and a more spectacular form of capital punishment for more egregious crimes. A man who killed either his father or his mother on purpose was not simply hanged, but was to be drawn and hanged (*traîné et pendu*) and, because hanging was considered to be an inappropriate punishment for women, a woman found guilty of killing either parent was to be burned alive. Furthermore, a man who killed his lord—even if it was an accident—was also to be drawn and hanged.[54]

From a modern vantage point, it may well seem that the distinction between being merely hanged, and being first drawn and then hanged, is not terribly meaningful; the difference was, however, profound to contemporaries. Hanging, to put it bluntly, did not take very long and usually took place on the outskirts of town. The process of drawing someone, which involved their being tied to a hurdle and dragged through the center of town, usually by a horse or donkey, before being brought outside of town to be hanged, allowed for a kind of spectacle that preceded and led up to (both in a chronological and spatial sense) the punishment of death. Simple hanging might be seen as not all that different from the way in which Salic law had occasionally mandated that an individual criminal "pay with his life." But drawing and hanging was more than simple corporal compensation; it reflected a burgeoning desire to spectacularize the punishment of particularly egregious crimes for the purpose of exemplary deterrence.

In Beaumanoir's customal, which appeared some eighty years later, the list of crimes that were punishable by the aggravated, spectacular punishment of drawing as well as hanging was expanded beyond parricides to include *all* murders as well as rape, which crimes also entailed the forfeiture of the offender's assets to the lord.[55] While the right to draw and hang an offender was reserved for lords who possessed the privilege of "high" justice, the simple hanging of thieves was not a matter of high justice, and could be performed by those who merely possessed the right of "low" justice. Beaumanoir and his contemporaries apparently still regarded the death sentence for thieves as a kind of tit for tat payment for the crime, or as Beaumanoir had put it: "the thief loses his life for his theft."[56] The fact that hanging thieves remained a function of low justice enables us to note a very important point: apart from the difference in the confiscation of the offender's assets, the fundamental, essential difference between the execution of high and low justice was not the presence or absence of a sentence of death; rather, it was the degree of spectacle.

For Beaumanoir and his contemporaries, the question of whether a case could be adjudicated by a lord with low justice or whether it passed to one with high justice was of paramount importance, as it had an impact both on the disposition of the offender's assets and on the spectacularity of the punishment. This distinction was so important that in the event of someone being gravely wounded, it was customary for the offending party to be held in a prison belonging to the lord with high justice until the fate of the victim could be known for certain:

> If the wounded person recovers, the individual who has high justice must return the prisoner to the individual who has low [justice], so that [the latter] can claim his fine according to the misdeed; and if the wounded person dies from the injury done to him, the vengeance for this misdeed belongs to the individual who holds high justice.[57]

While the distinction between low and high justice had important financial ramifications, and could determine whether or not one's estate was forfeit, no less important was the element of spectacle associated with the respective categories of justice. The extent to which contemporaries considered the presence or absence of spectacle to be crucial can be seen in the case of a man who was about to be hanged for theft in early fourteenth–century Noisy, near Paris. When he confessed on the gallows to a previously unknown homicide, he was brought back to town, *drawn*, and then once again brought to the gallows for hanging.[58]

The spectacularization of punishment is a process that can be observed not only in the growing number of crimes subject to drawing and hanging but also in the expanding range of punishments, both capital and non-capital, that incorporated elements of spectacle. We have already noted how the *Très Ancien Coutumier* had mandated burning at the stake for women guilty of parricide because it was inappropriate to hang women. In Beaumanoir's customal, the penalty of burning was extended to an entirely different group of offenders, not in lieu of hanging, but as a purposeful penalty that was deemed particularly suited to the crime: "He who errs against the faith through misbelief, from which he does not wish return to see the truth, or he who commits sodomy, must be burned [*ars*] and forfeit all his assets."[59] Also included in Beaumanoir's customal is a penalty that would be commonly employed throughout France for the crime of counterfeiting: "The counterfeiter must be boiled and then hanged and they forfeit all their assets...."[60] As a direct assault on sovereign authority, the crime of counterfeiting called for a punishment that was even more horrible, more spectacular, than other aggravated, spectacular punishments.

Although one is always on shaky ground when attempting to read punishments as the staging of some sort of literal message, it is not unreasonable to suggest that *some* of these spectacular punishments hint at and perhaps even endeavor to re-present an image of the original crime. Drawing, as an actual dragging through the dirt, might be seen as a way of doing to the honor of the offender what he, through his crime, had done to the honor of the victim and, by extension, to the lord. The punishment of burning, the usual punishment for heretics and sodomites throughout the medieval and early modern periods, can be seen as a representation of their unnatural passions. The word that Beaumanoir used to refer to burning at the stake, "*ars*," and the phrase used throughout the medieval and early modern periods for such sentences, "*ars et brulé*," is derived from the Latin verb *ardere*, a word that the *Dictionarium Latinogallicum* of 1552 translates as "to burn" not only in a literal sense but also in the figurative sense of "to burn with love."[61] We can also observe the contemporary equation of unnatural passion and burning in the imagery used by a fifteenth-century Franciscan friar—admittedly in Italy and not France—who urged the people of Florence to spit whenever sodomy was mentioned: "Spit hard! Maybe the water of your spit will extinguish their fire."[62] The fact that unnatural sexual partners (whether of the same sex, or of different species) were often sentenced to be consumed by the same flame is, I think, also relevant in this respect, as it consumed them together as they themselves were consumed in the act of unnatural passions. Finally, the punishment of boiling alive those who had been found guilty of counterfeiting, an act that usually involved the melting down of metals and the changing of their form into an unnatural image, can be seen as a reenactment of the original crime by melting, so to speak, and thereby altering, the body of the counterfeiter. One can certainly push these affinities too far, and I would not claim that all punishments can be read in this way. But, at least in certain instances, we would be wrong to ignore what would seem to be an attempt to recall or re-present the original crime within the punishment itself.

If we examine the *Livre de Jostice et de Plet* (*c*.1260–70), a rough contemporary of Beaumanoir's text, we can see that many of the same spectacular penalties had made their way into this customal as well. If, like Beaumanoir, this text stipulated that heretics and sodomites be burned alive, it nevertheless suggested a somewhat more forgiving, three-strikes-and-you're-out policy for sodomites: "Those who are sodomites must lose their testicles. And if they do it a second time they must lose a limb or other part of the body [*membre*]. And if they do it a third time, they must be burned." The same punishment was mandated for women as well, making obvious allowances for anatomical differences: "A woman who does it must lose a limb or other part of the body [*membre*] the first two times, and the third time must be burned. And all of their goods are [forfeit] to the king."[63] However, in contrast to the customals of Beaumanoir and others that mandated boiling for counterfeiters, the *Livre de Jostice et de Plet* called only for simple hanging. Conversely, this same text mandated spectacular punishments for certain crimes that other customals passed over in silence. Anyone who disturbed the king's peace, for example, or any serf who tried to kill his lord, was subject to being burned at the stake, and anyone who fled before the enemies of the king or his ministers was to be either burned or hanged on the *fourches*.[64]

This reference to the *fourches*, circa 1260–70, or *fourches patibulaires* as they were often called, is one of the earliest references to this apparatus that I have seen, and its appearance in a text of customary law at this particular moment in time is rather telling.[65] The word *fourches* is derived from the Latin word *furca*, or fork, and refers to the forked trees from which people were hanged in classical times. The *fourches* that spread throughout France from the middle of the thirteenth century onward were comprised of stone pillars with wooden beams in between them, and they were built to accommodate several bodies at the same time (Fig. 2). They were, in short, a concrete manifestation of the growing spectacularization of capital punishment. Situated on a hilltop so as to maximize their visibility, the *fourches* were used as a place of execution as well as to display the corpses afterwards. On occasion, bodies executed elsewhere by other means were transported to the *fourches* for exhibition.

The *fourches* were not, however, the first apparatus in the Middle Ages that was explicitly intended to spectacularize punishment. That honor would have to go to the pillory as well as the *échelle*, or ladder, both of which seem to have first appeared in what is today northeastern France around the middle of the twelfth century, before quickly spreading to other areas. The pillory was a device that held an individual, with his hands, neck, and, sometimes feet, immobile, so that others could look at him. (The *échelle*, an ordinary wooden ladder, performed the same function of holding the offender in place without the need for a special device). Perhaps the best way to think of the pillory, as it was originally used, is as a rudimentary precursor to the *fourches*; the pillory represents the first attempt to spectacularize penal practice in a way that does not quite manage to weave visibility into the punishment itself (as the *fourches* would later do). The pillory, in short, was a kind of crude "add-on" to punishments that already existed. Its purpose was to transfix offenders in time and space, holding them motionless before the gaze of onlookers, before a comparatively less spectacular form of punishment was carried out.

The earliest mention of a pillory that I have come across is from the 1168 charter of the town of Saint-Omer, in Flanders (present-day Pas-de-Calais), where those who had failed to pay their fines for a variety of offenses were sentenced to the "pellori" before being banished from town. This particular sentence, which

Fig. 2. Fourches patibulaires. Eugène Viollet-le-Duc, *Dictionnaire raisonné de l'architecture française du XIe au XVIe siècle* (Paris, 1868), 5:561.

condemned the offender to "stand, transfixed, all day Saturday from morning till night," allowed for an extended period of visibility that preceded the inherently non-visible punishment of banishment.[66] Mention of a pillory also appears in the town charter of nearby Abbeville in 1184, as a punishment levied by municipal magistrates on convicted thieves prior to their being handed over to the officers of the viscount for further punishment.[67] On occasion, the pillory was added to a punishment that was already spectacular, particularly when it involved a question of moral offenses. In 1389, for example, judges argued whether to sentence the madam of a brothel to the pillory or to burning, and eventually decided to do both.[68]

The pillory, then, at least initially, was less a punishment in itself than a kind of addendum to other punishments, meant to compensate either for the rapidity of a punishment such as hanging or the invisibility of a punishment such as prison or banishment. To a certain extent, the appearance of the *fourches*, roughly a century after the pillory, as well as the spread of several other forms of spectacular capital punishments, obviated the need for the pillory as a supplement. But rather than disappearing, the pillory became a punishment in its own right, as we can see in the royal ordinance of 1347, which declared that all first-time blasphemers should be displayed on the pillory where "one can throw in their eyes one or several [bits of] filth, without stones or other things that might injure them." Even here, however, where it was a punishment unto itself, the pillory seems to serve as a kind of first installment to future punishments, which could be deferred as long as the individual did not reoffend. The ordinance of 1347 goes on to stipulate that an individual who committed blasphemy for a second time would be "condemned [again] to the pillory and will have the upper lip split with a hot iron; in the case of another recidivism, they will have the lower lip split with a hot iron; and the fourth time, they will have both lips cut off, and the fifth time, the tongue."[69]

Punishments involving the mutilation or the severing of lips, tongues, ears, and other parts of the body can be found in many of the earliest legal texts, but rather than being intended for display, these earlier forms of punishment fell squarely within the realm of corporal compensation. The charter of Tournai in 1187, for example, legislated mutilation according to the ancient law of talion—a limb for a limb—but with a twist that recalls earlier Salic law: monetary compensation could be made in lieu of a limb, provided that one had made peace with one's victim.[70]

While mutilation as corporal compensation continued into the thirteenth century, it was increasingly used for social transgressions and, as we saw in the case of sodomites who progressively lost parts of their bodies each time they reoffended, as a kind of warning or down payment on future punishments. The *Etablissement de Saint Louis*, for example, listed a series of lesser thefts for which the punishment was, at least in the first instance, mutilation rather than the death penalty:

> Whoever steals anything from a church, whoever makes counterfeit money, whoever steals the plowshare from the field, whoever steals other things, such as clothes, coins, and other small things, he must lose an ear at the first offence, a foot from the second offence, and on the third offense he is subject to hanging; because, one does not go from large limbs to small ones, but from small ones to large.[71]

Here, as with the pillory, mutilation functions as a kind of warning or promise of future punishments in the case of recidivism, but perhaps because mutilation was, in and of itself, beginning to seem insufficiently spectacular, it was sometimes combined with the pillory. In 1460, for example, in the town of Amiens, a woman who had been convicted of theft was sentenced "to be led to the pillory on a scaffold, and there to have her ear cut off"; although the woman herself was then banished forever, her ear remained behind, attached to the pillory by the executioner.[72]

Around the same time that mutilations were moving from the realm of corporal compensation into that of spectacular deterrence, customals and charters began to mention the punishment of public whipping. According to the *Livre de Jostice et de*

Plet, those who ran houses of prostitution "must be whipped and thrown out of town, and their assets are [forfeited] to the king,"[73] and Jacques Chiffoleau has estimated that in the early fourteenth century, public whippings were taking place roughly every three days in the papal city of Avignon.[74] As in the case of the pillory, public whippings often served to spectacularize a punishment that would otherwise have been more or less invisible; also like the pillory, public whippings were used for first-time offenders as a kind of warning. In 1335, for example, in Paris, a nine-year-old boy who confessed to theft was "in view of his young age... beaten and corrected with a switch in lieu of punishment."[75] No doubt because they were used in similar ways, as ancillary punishments and as warnings, the fifteenth-century customal of Anjou and Maine described whipping and the pillory as being roughly equivalent.[76]

Over the course of the twelfth and thirteenth centuries, therefore, new devices such as the pillory and the *fourches* added elements of spectacle to punishments that had traditionally been either invisible or compensatory. At roughly the same time, punishments that were in and of themselves spectacular—drawing, burning, boiling, etcetera—were beginning to be used for crimes that involved clear malice aforethought. This trend continued in the fourteenth and fifteenth centuries, which witnessed an ever-expanding assortment of graphic, visible, capital punishments intended both to punish individual criminals and to deter future ones. Women, who had traditionally been burned at the stake rather than hanged, began to be buried alive as early as the mid-fourteenth century, and beheading had become a punishment in northeastern France by the early 1340s, eventually becoming the exclusive method of executing members of the nobility who had committed a capital crime.[77]

The trend toward increasingly spectacular punishments only intensified over time, as greater crimes needed to be differentiated from lesser ones that were themselves being punished by ever more spectacular methods. In Boutillier's *Somme rural*, compiled around 1385, we observe one of the earliest references in a juridical text to the punishment of the wheel, which called for the offender to be strapped to the spokes of a large wheel, where he (it was applied exclusively to men) would have his bones and his limbs broken by an iron bar, after which he would be turned skyward until death ensued, which could take anywhere from a few minutes to many hours (Fig. 3).[78] It was around the same time, in *Somme rural* as well as in other customals, that quartering and flaying were being presented as the appropriate punishment for the crime of lèse-majesté.[79]

Within this environment of ever more painful, protracted, and spectacular punishments, the old dividing lines between high and low justice must have seemed increasingly outdated and untenable. At the time when Beaumanoir had written the *Coutumes des Beauvaisis*, only those few exceptional cases that had merited both the confiscation of the offender's estate and the aggravated punishment of drawing and hanging had belonged to high justice, whereas most other penalties, including simple hanging, had been relegated to the jurisdiction of low justice. But with the rise of the *fourches* and the advent of so many different spectacular punishments over the course of the fourteenth century, there was clearly a need to clarify and, to a certain extent, to reconfigure the old juridical divisions.

Fig. 3. The Wheel, from *Les Grandes Misères de la Guerre* by Jacques Callot (Paris, 1633). University of Michigan Museum of Art.

Compiled around the end of the fourteenth century, *Le Grand Coutumier de France*, presumed to have been written by Jacques d'Ableiges, attempted to clarify the distinctions between high and low justice once and for all. Recognizing the futility of establishing a clear division between spectacular and unspectacular punishments in an age when so many punishments were spectacular, the *Grand Coutumier* posited the existence of "middle justice," a category allowing for limited amounts of spectacle but without the right to seize the assets of the offender, a privilege that remained the exclusive right of high justice. The *Grand Coutumier* reserved for high justice those egregious cases in which malice aforethought was most clear, and therefore where spectacular deterrence could have the greatest opportunity to prevent crime. To middle justice, the *Grand Coutumier* relegated those crimes that had been committed without malice aforethought—crimes, in other words, that might still merit the death penalty but seemed less suited to the exemplarity of spectacular deterrence:

> Some say that in the regions of customary law only three cases are reputed to be [matters of] high justice, namely: arson, rape, and murder. And they draw a distinction between murder and homicide [*occision*]. Because one calls it murder when the event comes about consciously, with forethought, or with malice [*scientement, et apensément, ou par aguet*] and it is therefore a matter of high justice. But one calls it homicide [*occision*] when the event has not come about in a deliberate or planned manner, but is done in the heat of the moment, and is therefore a matter of middle justice, which means simple hanging [*pendre seulement*]. But the three other preceding cases [i.e. arson, rape, and murder] involve drawing and hanging.[80]

In addition to the crimes enumerated above that fell into the category of high justice, the *Grand Coutumier* remarked that "some people" would add sodomy and heresy. "He who has high justice," therefore, had "the power to draw and to burn." But he also had the right to erect a "*fourches* of three pillars, or more if he wishes."[81]

D'Ableiges goes on to speak of the mistaken assumption on the part of many people that the possession of a *fourche* of fewer than three pillars implied that their owner did not possess high justice, and he stressed the fact that while those with high justice had the right to construct a *fourche* with three or more pillars, they were under no obligation to do so.

If all this seems confusing to the modern reader, it would appear that it seemed equally confusing at the time, and the text goes on for quite some time, endeavoring to differentiate between *fourches* with wooden beams on the outside or the inside, and with or without footings, as indications of high or middle justice. In all of these distinctions, one cannot help seeing a kind of desperation to distinguish between things that were becoming increasingly indistinguishable. If the degree of spectacle had originally been the basis for a distinction between high and low justice, such distinctions were clearly becoming more difficult in an age when nearly all punishments were, at least to some extent, spectacular. The *Grand Coutumier* does, however, seem to be on more solid ground when it declares categorically that "the pillory and the ladder are the sign of high justice and only those with high justice can have them, and there is no real difference between these two things, and whoever has a ladder can have a pillory."[82] Here, perhaps more than in any other distinction, we can see that the fundamental distinguishing feature of high justice lay not in its severity or even its claim to the entire estate of the offender, but rather in the spectacularity of the punishments that those with high justice were entitled to execute. The pillory and the ladder, devices that were purely spectacular in the sense that they caused no physical pain but were exclusively intended for display, were, as D'Ableiges put it, the quintessential "sign of high justice."[83]

THE HOMOGENIZATION OF JUSTICE

Although the distinction between high and low justice was originally a function of the degree of spectacle, over time, those with the privilege of high justice came increasingly to arrogate punishments that had traditionally fallen to those meting out low justice. Consequently, whereas earlier customals had focused on distinguishing between high and low justice, by the turn of the sixteenth century many customals were concerned with distinguishing between various categories and sub-categories of high justice. In the customal of Maine (1535), for example, above the category of simple high *justicier* there were now superior jurisdictions, such as the right of *chastellenie*, and at the top rung of judicial privilege in Maine were the count viscount of Beaumont and the barons under his suzerainty, with each successive rung having the right to bigger, more elaborate *fourches*.[84]

It was also around the turn of the sixteenth century that an increasing number of cases were declared to be *cas royaux*, the exclusive province of royal justice. In Arras, for example, in 1499, the officers of royal justice were granted jurisdiction not only over cases of lèse-majesté, where the direct involvement of the king's justice seemed reasonable enough, but also over cases involving illicit assembly and the repeal of orders of banishment.[85] As more and more cases fell within the jurisdiction of royal justice or to those few people who had the highest jurisdictions, the inevitable effect was one of a general homogenization of sentences and penal practices, and this was perhaps even more true in the south of France, where competing jurisdictions of high justice were rare compared with other parts of the country.[86] This process helped to facilitate a general movement toward what some had been calling "common law," a notion that had been articulated, however vaguely, since the thirteenth century, which held that customary laws, despite their apparent differences, obeyed certain general principles. Where customary laws were in general agreement, common law could be said to exist; where they disagreed, there was no common law, but only the customs of a particular region.[87] By the mid-sixteenth century, Charles du Moulin was expressing the hope that a uniform customary code for all of France could be drafted, based upon the customs of the Paris region.[88]

If the gradual homogenization of French penal practices can be seen both as the natural by-product of a consolidation of jurisdictions as well as a reflection of a belief shared by many jurists in the underlying existence of common law, it was also the result of a conscious plan on the part of successive royal administrations to bring about the gradual centralization of justice throughout the realm. Royal ordinances such as those of Blois in 1498, of Villers-Cotterêts in 1539, and the Criminal Ordinance of 1670, all served to establish the inquisitorial model of justice as the law of the land, and helped to streamline and unify legal procedures throughout France.[89] At the same time, the principle of judicial discretion, one derived largely from Roman law, encouraged local judges to tailor their rulings to particular circumstances rather than being bound by the letter of the law, allowing them, at the urging of royal officials, to bend customary law to the royal will.[90] When, at the direction of the royal government, regional customals were edited in the sixteenth century, many of the specific punishments contained in earlier versions of customals and charters were purposely left out, and several texts explicitly left the penalty to the judge's discretion. The new customal for the city of Touraine, for example, crossed out six of eight articles detailing specific punishments and replaced them with the following sentence: "The penalties for the crimes mentioned in these articles will be remitted to the discretion of the judges so that they may judge according to their conscience on the basis of the ordinances of the king and written justice [*raison écrite*]."[91]

From the twelfth to the sixteenth century, a preoccupation with criminal intent and malice aforethought, derived from Roman law, came to infiltrate the logic of customary law, and led to a rise in spectacular, theoretically exemplary punishments calculated to dissuade those with criminal intent from carrying out their crimes. The increasing severity and spectacularity of punishments, combined with an administration of justice that reserved the execution of the most spectacular forms of punishment for those with the highest judicial privileges, resulted in a greater homogeneity of penal practice, a process aided by a movement among jurists to identify the common foundation of French law, as well as by royal administrative efforts to streamline judicial procedures. By the sixteenth century, the theory and the practice of punishment in France had reached a point where they can be said to have had a relatively stable and more or less national character. One of the consequences of the spectacularity and homogeneity of punishments, as we will see in the following chapter, was the development of a bureaucracy of executioners, who were charged with the task of staging these increasingly elaborate spectacles.

PART II

EXECUTIONERS AND THE RITUAL OF EXECUTION

3

Extraordinary Beings
The Life and Work of Executioners

The appearance of professional executioners in the early thirteenth century occurred, perhaps not surprisingly, at the same time as the rise of spectacular punishments. As the staging of executions became more complex and more specifically geared to audiences, professional executioners appeared across northern and central Europe to oversee the production of these penal spectacles. These individuals, who gradually developed into a separate caste of people, related not only by profession but often by blood as well, saw their fortunes rise and fall with the fate of the spectacular punishments that they helped to make possible.

Remarkably little attention has been paid to executioners in scholarly works devoted to the subject of capital punishment.[1] Foucault's euphemistic reference to executioners in *Discipline and Punish* as "those to whom [the Prince] has delegated his force,"[2] is emblematic of a general glossing over of the executioner's role: the executioner almost seems like a bit player, a henchman who is simply following orders, an individual whose role might almost be performed by someone else. But the executioner was very far from a cog in the wheel of ancien régime justice. He was, rather, the central player on the penal stage, the one who coaxed meaning from the flesh of the condemned, and who transformed the body of the patient—the term is derived from the Latin verb *patior*, to suffer—into the visual representation of justice. By focusing on the person of the executioner, and by forcing this figure, who has been allowed to lurk in the shadows of historical narrative, to take the center stage of our analysis, I hope to shed new light on the complex rituals that these individuals oversaw and arrive at a perspective that more nearly approaches the way in which executions were understood and experienced by the historical actors themselves.[3]

A RACE OF OUTCASTS

More than we may realize, our contemporary conception of the executioner as a mere agent of the law, who transparently carries out the sentence of the court, is itself a relatively modern notion purposefully invented and handed down to us by Enlightenment reformers who were trying to put in place a new, and more "rational" penal system. This vision of the executioner as a modern, bureaucratic court officer was constructed in reaction to the prevailing and long-standing conception of him as an extraordinary being, someone whose touch was so profane that he could not come into contact with other people or objects without profoundly altering them.

The status of the executioner is best understood not as the status of an individual, but rather of an entire outcast race of people who inhabited many of the countries of northern and central Europe. In some respects not unlike the Jews of Europe, executioners and their families performed essential yet problematic tasks, the practice of which was forbidden to others. Also like the Jews, many aspects of the executioner's daily existence and, in particular, the extent to which he was allowed to come into contact with ordinary people, were carefully circumscribed; his place of residence was restricted to a specific area of town set aside for him, usually on the outskirts, and he would wear a special patch or other mark signifying his difference. In other respects, however, executioners possessed certain privileges that, oddly enough, they shared with European royalty: they held their offices in largely hereditary dynasties that spanned the borders of several European countries; they had the exclusive right to seize specified goods from sellers in the public marketplace; and they were reputed to have the ability to cure certain diseases with their touch.[4]

This peculiar combination of opprobrium and privilege was precisely what the eighteenth-century reformers endeavored to do away with when they attempted to remake executioners into agents of rational modern justice. But public opinion was not so easily swayed. Half a millennium of otherness could not be erased overnight and, despite the best efforts of penal reformers and revolutionary legislators who insisted on referring to the executioner as the "agent of the law," people continued to view executioners and their families almost as a separate species of humanity. As the essayist Louis-Sébastien Mercier wrote in the 1780s, the apparent ordinariness of the executioner's appearance belied an essential, unalterable, and fundamental difference:

> Nothing distinguishes this man from other citizens, even while he is exercising his terrible functions.... His hair is curled, powdered, braided; below, [he wears] white silks and court shoes with which to climb the fatal scaffold, which seems revolting to me, for he ought to wear, in these terrible moments, the mark of the law of death.... The exterior of this man ought to proclaim who he is.[5]

Mercier's assessment would be repeated in the early nineteenth century by Joseph de Maistre in the following well-known passage from his *Soirées de Saint-Petersbourg*:

> This head, this heart, are they made like ours? do they not have something odd or foreign to our nature?... On the exterior he is made just as we are; he is born, like us; but he is an extraordinary being.... No sooner do the authorities designate the place that he will live, no sooner has he taken possession, than other dwellings recede so as to be out of sight of his. It is in the midst of this solitude and this empty space that encircles him... [that he] lives with his female and his little ones.... Is he a man? Yes: God receives him in his temples and allows him to pray. He is not a criminal. And yet no tongue will consent to say, for example, that he is virtuous, that he is an honest man, that he is worthy of esteem etc. No moral elegy is appropriate to him, as all presuppose relations with other men, and he has none.[6]

Although we might expect that the otherness of the executioner was solely a function of his work, his outcast status was largely inherited rather than earned. As a general rule, executioners were born executioners, the descendants of a long line of executioners, who for generations had existed as a caste of untouchables. They did not, in fact, have to execute anyone in order to be despised and reviled: the children, the wives, the brothers, sisters, and cousins of executioners were all tainted. Many of the women who became the wives of executioners—*les bourelles*, as they were known—were themselves born into executioner families; the fact that they had always been excluded from society made it nearly inevitable that they would marry someone in the profession, as few other people would consider them to be suitable spouses. One rarely chose to become part of this race of outcasts, unless one had absolutely no other prospects.

Where did this profane race of people come from? The concept of an official executioner—someone who executed justice for a living rather than doing it once or occasionally—dates from the early thirteenth century; prior to this time, if some sort of corporal punishment was called for, it was usually carried out by the victim, the victim's family, by the judges themselves, or by criminals who agreed to perform the execution of justice in return for a reduced sentence.[7] Over the course of the thirteenth and fourteenth centuries, however, many cities and towns, particularly in the northern and central parts of Europe, began investing the task of executing justice in individuals whose occupation it would henceforth be to carry out all the sentences handed down by local authorities. Normandy seems to have been among the earliest regions to have instituted the office of executioner, with Nicolas Jouhanne (a.k.a. "*la justice*") having taken the position in the *vicomté* of Caux by 1202, and most of the major towns of Normandy following suit over the next hundred years.[8] The trend seems to have gradually spread outside of Normandy to other areas of northern and central France, with Paris having an official executioner by 1275, Saint Omer, near the Dutch border, in 1363, Blois in 1376, Rouen in 1400, Amiens in 1401, and Dijon toward the east by 1403.[9] The same trend seems to have occurred outside of France as well, although apparently not quite as early as in Normandy. The city of Augsburg had an official executioner by 1276 and the papal city of Avignon had one by the first half of the fourteenth century.[10]

In certain locations, the institution of the office of executioner seems to have given rise almost immediately to an hereditary dynasty. Nicolas "la justice" Jouhanne, who took office in 1202, was to be the first in a very long line of Jouhannes or Jouennes (as they would later spell their name) who would continue to serve as official executioners in various towns and cities across northern France well into the nineteenth century.[11] In other places, dynasties, or even lengthy terms in office for that matter, took much longer to be established. Beginning in the last quarter of the sixteenth century, however, a general trend toward stable tenures in office and dynastic succession had become common in northern France, and this would eventually spread to other areas as well.

The town of Arras is fairly typical of this gradual trend over time toward established, hereditary dynasties. Between 1400 and 1600, Arras had roughly forty-five executioners, or an average tenure in office of less than five years. Several of these individuals appear to have been of relatively unsavory character and were either forced out of office or ended up on the scaffold themselves.[12] Toward the end of this period there is evidence that local authorities were beginning to select their executioners with more care, because in 1577 the new candidate for the position in Arras presented references attesting to his good character, including one from his parish priest. (Such testaments of good character and "catholicity" would become increasingly common by the seventeenth century.)[13] Despite the testaments to his good character, however, the individual appointed to the office that year lasted no longer than the others, and the next fifty years or so would see the same rapid rate of turnover. In 1631, however, a father and son team took the job and they were to last in office for an unprecedented thirty-eight years. From this point onward, the typical tenure in office was much longer than it had ever been before in Arras, and three separate father-son successions would take Arras into the nineteenth century.[14]

A similar trend can be seen in the office of executioner in Paris, although the tenure there even before the establishment of hereditary dynasties was significantly longer than in Arras. From 1460 until 1594, the typical length in office in Paris was roughly twenty years.[15] In 1594, however, Jehan Guillaume became executioner of Paris, initiating a family dynasty of executioners that, with one brief exception, would occupy the office of executioner of Paris for nearly a century (and more than two hundred future executioners across France would be able to trace their roots to this original patriarch of the Guillaume family).[16] In 1687, when the reign of Guillaume executioners came to an end in Paris, they were succeeded by an even more long-lived and celebrated dynasty of Parisian executioners, the Sanson family. Charles Sanson, who took the position in 1688, was the first of many Sansons who would hold the office into the middle of the nineteenth century, the most infamous being Charles Henri Sanson who executed Louis XVI by guillotine in 1793.

The family dynasties in Arras and Paris were by no means unique. The Desmorest dynasty was itself an offshoot of the Guillaume dynasty in Paris, and was founded when the daughter of Jehan Guillaume married Pierre Desmorest, who was her father's aide. She gave birth to Louis Desmorest, who assumed the position of executioner in Laon in 1664. He would be followed by nearly fifty Desmorests who would hold the office of executioner in various towns across the north of France into the nineteenth century, including Laon itself, Etampes, and Châlons. The Ferey family dynasty began when François Ferey became executioner of Coutances in 1717, the first of some twenty Fereys who would hold the office in important cities such as Rouen and Orléans into the nineteenth century.[17]

Hereditary dynasties of executioners became so well established in France that the right of succession would eventually be written into the letters of provision establishing the executioner in office.[18] In fact, it was not uncommon for sons or other close relatives to accede to the office even if they had not yet achieved the age of majority. Louis Desmorest, the founding member of the Desmorest dynasty and grandson of Jehan Guillaume of Paris, was named the official executioner of Laon at the age of ten, with a regent performing his functions until he had reached the age of twenty. Perhaps the most extreme example of this practice was the case of Jean Baptiste François Carlier, a descendant of both the Guillaume and the Ferey families, who upon the death of his father in 1741 was named the official executioner of Pontoise—even though he was barely one year old.[19]

Outside of France, hereditary dynasties became the norm as well.[20] In fact, some dynasties spanned across national boundaries. The Dalembourg family, for example, occupied the post of executioner in various parts of France, Germany, The Netherlands, Switzerland, and Austria, and the Dalembourgs were related to the Spirkels and the Backs, both of whom practiced across widespread areas of German-speaking Europe.[21] This common culture with respect to executioners seems to have been restricted to northern Europe, however, and northern France would seem to have had more in common with parts of Germany and Switzerland than with southern France where, up until the eighteenth century, towns were more apt to forego official executioners and instead made use of convicted criminals to perform executions.[22] The same is true of the French colony of Quebec, whose first official executioner accepted the position to avoid being punished for the crime of sodomy, and whose second executioner was part of a convicted pair who agreed to execute his erstwhile partner in crime in return for exoneration.[23] By the early eighteenth century, however, the official position of executioner had spread to many areas of southern France as well.

How are we to explain the rise of this closely interrelated caste of people, who gradually came to occupy most of the official posts of executioner in the cities and towns of northern France, the Netherlands, and German-speaking northern and central Europe? Perhaps the endogamy of executioners was the result of the opprobrium attached to their profession, with few people willing to practice the profession or marry someone who did, unless they were already part of the extended family of executioners. Perhaps the endogamy of executioners was itself the cause of the opprobrium, as practitioners of this very problematic profession came to be quite literally a separate tribe or race of people. Most likely the endogamy and the revulsion attached to the profession were mutually reinforcing. As executioners became more reviled, they increasingly married their own kind, in turn making them seem even stranger.

As executioners coalesced into a people separate from all others, they found themselves the object of increasingly restrictive prohibitions and obligatory marks of difference that would ensure their continued ostracism. But the development of an expertise, almost a "craft," practiced largely by a group of interrelated families, put executioners in the position of being able to negotiate an impressive variety of rights and privileges that had the potential, particularly in larger towns, to make them very wealthy. From a modern vantage point that tends to see wealth as a great equalizer, the privileges and wealth of the executioner seem difficult to reconcile with the fact that they were universally reviled and ostracized. From a pre-modern vantage point, however, there seems to have been nothing odd about this combination. Indeed, executioners shared attributes with a variety of other groups and castes with whom one might not expect them to have much in common. Like feudal lords, executioners possessed enormously lucrative and exclusive rights and privileges; in common with actors and prostitutes, they practiced a problematic profession that made them social and civil outcasts;[24] and in common with Jews and lepers, they wore visible signs and marks of their essential difference and untouchability. Although each of these groups incorporated various elements of otherness, executioners would seem to be unique in their differing from mainstream society in virtually *all* respects: economically, professionally, socially, and, ultimately, genetically.

A PEOPLE APART: DUTIES, PRIVILEGES, AND RESTRICTIONS

Although executioners did, of course, execute people, the day-to-day performance of their office called upon them to do many other things, a fact that is alluded to in their official title: *maitre des hautes et basses oeuvres*—the master of high and low works. The execution of high works referred to cases of "high justice," which, by the early modern period included almost all forms of capital punishment, as well as non-capital sentences involving a certain degree of spectacularity, such as the pillory, whipping, or mutilation.[25] Just as judicial jurisdictions were divided between those who had the right to deal with cases of high and low (and sometimes middle) justice, so the work of the executioner was divided into the different categories of high and low works, although normally the same individual performed both, particularly in smaller towns.

The low works of the executioner included a variety of day-to-day tasks related to hygiene or policing, which he had the exclusive privilege of performing. In many areas, executioners were accorded a monopoly on the right to maintain public sewers and latrines—a dubious privilege one might think, but a fairly lucrative one.[26] On the boundaries between hygiene and policing, executioners were also often charged with the task of managing stray dogs.[27] Similarly, but with greater potential benefit for the executioner, he was charged with enforcing local regulations regarding livestock. In Dijon, for example, where a town ordinance from 1452 declared that "it has for a very long time been a custom that no inhabitant of the city can have or nourish pigs or sows, whether big or small," it was the executioner's job to kill any of these animals that he found in the city, and he had the right to cut off the pig's head and neck up to its forelegs and take it for his own profit, leaving the remainder of the animal for the offending owner.[28] In most towns, executioners were granted exclusive domain over the carcasses of all animals found dead in the streets, the skins of which brought them considerable additional revenue.[29]

In addition to the seizure of wayward, illicit, or dead animals, several of the executioner's other "low" duties were important sources of income. In sixteenth-century Dijon, the executioner was charged with preventing lepers who were not from Dijon from seeking alms within the city (except, apparently, on certain holidays when this restriction was lifted and foreign lepers could descend on the city at will). If the executioner found a foreign leper within the city limits, he was accorded the right, if he saw fit, to seize the leper's pouch and small cask—leper appurtenances, it would seem—and to seize possession of the leper's alms along with 12 deniers tournois in fines. In other areas, not only in France but in Germany as well, executioners were charged with overseeing all lepers, whether foreign or domestic, and were entitled to exact a kind of tribute from them. Along similar lines, executioners in many areas were put in charge of prostitutes, from whom, as in the case of lepers, they exacted tribute. In sixteenth-century Troyes, for example, the executioner was entitled to collect a one-time fee of 5 sous from prostitutes as well as 1 liard, several times throughout the year, from lepers.[30]

Related, one suspects, to the logic of overseeing prostitutes, executioners in parts of France and Germany were put in charge of morally problematic activities such as gambling. In some towns, like Strasbourg and Arras, executioners were granted the privilege of running gaming houses themselves up until the early sixteenth century, when this right was rescinded.[31] In Dijon, by contrast, the executioner was charged with the task of ferreting out other people's clandestine gambling dens, with the right to seize for himself the monies being wagered. As part of their policing of a locality's general moral and physical well-being, some executioners were entrusted with the duty of enforcing ordinances against public urination and defecation as well as blasphemy. The executioner of Dijon was apparently particularly adept at nabbing *in flagrante delicto* those who relieved themselves in public, from whom he was entitled to exact a fine. Similarly, if he happened to overhear a blasphemous utterance, the executioner of Dijon could report the offender to authorities and, provided there was another witness, could pocket the resulting fine.[32]

Although all of these various *basses oeuvres* no doubt added up to considerable sums for many executioners, the bulk of their income in most areas of France derived from a privilege called *havage*, the exclusive right to seize a specified quantity of goods from sellers in the public marketplace. Depending upon the specific rights of the executioner in a particular locality and upon the size of the marketplace, the rights of havage could produce revenues that ranged from a comfortable living to a very sizeable income.

The origin of the rights of havage is fairly obscure, but it would seem that it had originally been a feudal right, and there is evidence of its existence as early as 1080.[33] The etymology of the term '*havage*' is equally obscure. According to some, the word derives from the low-Breton word *havaich* or *hauvach*, which signifies "a handful." According to others, it comes from the old French verb *haver*, meaning "to take or grab hold of." Still others have suggested that the word is derived from the verb *avoir*, "to have."[34] Whatever its etymology, at some point in time the extremely lucrative right of havage was ceded to executioners as their primary form of remuneration. This appears to have happened as early as 1302 in Chartres, where the right of havage was originally imposed upon merchants who were not from the town, almost as a kind of protectionist tariff.[35] Town regulations from Dijon in 1452 also make it clear that the havage was, at least in its origin, intended to be imposed on foreign merchants only. Each town had its own remarkably precise list of items that executioners were entitled to seize in the local marketplace, and the list for Dijon is fairly typical. A short excerpt should convey the general idea:

> Firstly, from each foreign maker of patisseries or baker that he finds on any day of the week, selling cakes or bread in the said city or suburbs [of Dijon], [the executioner may take] one little cake or one little bread up to the estimation of the value of the third of a *petit blanc* [i.e. approximately 1 denier].
>
> Item from each large basket of eggs which is being carried by horse or around the neck, four eggs.
>
> Item from little bags or baskets which contain a gross of eggs or more, [at least] one egg. And if there are as many as one hundred, two eggs.
>
> Item from each cartload of garlic and onions, two bunches [*glennes*].
>
> Item from a loaded horse or from those who carry them around the neck, from each horse or large bagful of said garlic and onions, one bunch.
>
> Item from garlic and onions that are not in bunches, from each large bagful one two-handed handful or *hané* [a cup equivalent to the same] and from little bags, a one-handed handful which the vendor will dole out.[36]

We can probably stop there, although the list continues with the same punctiliousness through innumerable items: ceramic pots, pears, apples, kindling, turnips, prunes, herring, etcetera. At the end of the list, however, is the important stipulation that "All of these things are to be levied and taken by the said executioner from foreign and traveling merchants [*marchans estrangers et forains*] and not from others."[37]

We can begin to see something, now, of the logic of the executioner's sphere of activity, at least in its origin. He was charged with the task of patrolling the margins of society, a kind of metaphysical as well as literal border guard. It was his job to keep illicit or stray animals at bay; to clear away dead animals and sewage; to keep foreign lepers from entering the city, and to keep tabs on local ones as well as on prostitutes; and to manage the comings and goings of merchants from out of town. With respect to the citizens of the town, he was a kind of policeman, enforcing ordinances of moral and physical hygiene. With respect to outcasts and foreigners, his function was not unlike that of a *seigneur*, exacting tribute and enforcing order.

While the executioner had authority over those who stood outside of society, he was not allowed to come into contact with non-blasphemous, non-soiling, upstanding citizens of the town or, for that matter, with their property. Touching a leper, a prostitute, or a dead animal was one thing, but touching ordinary people, their animals, or their food, was a different matter. Although foreign merchants might be technically within the executioner's domain, the rules governing how the executioner was to take hold of merchants' produce were carefully circumscribed. The stipulation, in the above excerpt from the description of the Dijon executioner's rights of havage, that the vendor would himself dole out the necessary amount of garlic and onions from a bag is clearly a measure to protect the remaining food from contamination by the executioner's hands (and probably had as much to do with protecting the livelihood of the merchants as with protecting the citizens of the town from eating food touched by the executioner). This fear of the executioner's touch is made explicit in the instructions as to how the executioner was to proceed if a merchant should refuse to accord him his just due:

> It is not customary nor reasonable for the said executioner to touch with his hand any of the items mentioned above relating to food, which should not, as has been said, be rigorously refused to him; in the event [that these items are refused] he may not yet, upon first refusal, put his hand upon them, but must only pretend to do so. And if he should be refused a second time, he may take his just due as gently as he possibly can without making a scene.[38]

As an extra precautionary measure to protect produce and people from the executioner's touch, it apparently became customary for executioners to carry a special spoon that they were required to use in the exercise of their right of havage. According to the *Encyclopédie* as well as several other eighteenth-century sources, the executioner of Paris used a tin-plated spoon "because of the infamy of his profession," whereas in other parts of France the spoon was said to be a long-handled wooden one.[39]

Although it is unclear precisely when spoons were introduced as a means of mediating the executioner's touch as he circulated in the marketplace, we do know that by the mid-fifteenth century, executioners were eliciting from townspeople many of the same feelings of revulsion and horror as the lepers and other outcasts whom they were charged with overseeing.[40] Over the course of the early modern period, towns took proactive measures to separate executioners, both visually and physically, from the general populace. It was understood that as they performed their duties, both high and low, and as they exercised their rights of havage, they would necessarily come into close proximity with ordinary townspeople, but every effort was made to set them apart and prevent unnecessary contact.

Visually, executioners in most localities, both in France as well as Germany, were required to wear the mark of their office at all times. In fifteenth-century Arras, the executioner wore a special cloak in the city colors, on the front of which was embroidered an image of the gallows, and on the back, a ladder. In Amiens, the costume of the executioner was half green and half yellow, although the stipulated colors seem to have changed every few years.[41] In Dijon, the executioner was required to carry with him a "special little white stick or painted [in white] of a foot and a half in length which he must carry as the sign of his office;" he also wore a special insignia in orange velour, embroidered in his clothing, which depicted a gallows with a rope hanging down and a ladder.[42]

On one level, these special robes, staffs, and insignia were similar to the ceremonial robes that were worn by many office holders in the municipalities and guilds of medieval Europe, some of which still exist today. But there was something more going on here than the mere sartorial expression of the dignity of office, and there is no clearer evidence of this than the innumerable squabbles that broke out between executioners, intent on not wearing the visible marks of their office, and municipal authorities, equally intent on forcing them to do so. In 1452, as quoted above, the ordinances of Dijon stated simply that the executioner "must carry as a sign of his office" the prescribed little white stick. A century later, in 1551, the ordinance was amended slightly to read that the executioner "must *always* carry [the white stick] as the sign of his office *no matter where he goes*, and where he shall be found without said little stick, the gentlemen magistrates may order a fine of three *livres* five *solz*."[43] Eight years later, after a new executioner had taken office, it would seem that the authorities were still having difficulties. The executioner was apparently carrying his stick alright, but he was refusing to wear the mandated robes and special orange velour insignia depicting the gallows. Instead, he had substituted an outfit of his own design, which the authorities branded an "indecent outfit." They therefore reiterated the sartorial requirements of his office, and threatened him with expulsion if he refused. For good measure, they also elongated his "little" stick to a medium-sized stick of two and a half feet in length.

The following year, however, in apparent response to the executioner's increasingly clever attempts to obey the letter but not the spirit of the law, authorities insisted that the executioner should wear the insignia of office where people could actually *see* it: on his sleeve or on his shoulder. And then, in 1569, they gave up the game of second-guessing the executioner, and from this point onward town officials saw to the manufacture of the robe of office themselves. But no one had stipulated that the executioner could not cover the insignia with a coat, and so in 1607 there was a new ordinance mandating that the insignia of office be worn both on the coat and on the robe of office. The remainder of the seventeenth century would see further fine-tuning, second-guessing, and increased penalties for disobedience.[44]

We can see, therefore, that the executioner's robes and insignia reflected the contradictory nature of an office that was both a hereditary privilege and the exclusive lot of a race of pariahs. In the latter sense, the marks of his office were not unlike the visible signs of otherness that lepers, Jews, and prostitutes were required to wear both in France and in Germany.[45] But these visible marks were also related to general sumptuary laws that were enacted to ensure that individuals did not dress above their station in life (so they would not be mistakenly accorded a respect that was not their due). As Kathy Stuart has written with respect to the imposition of marks of difference for the executioner in sixteenth-century Frankfurt, the problem seems to have arisen because honorable people were "mistakenly showing him respect;" the obligation to wear red, white, and green stripes on his clothing would ensure that he would never again be mistaken for an honorable person.[46]

In France, as opposed to Germany, one cannot help getting the impression that it was less a question of honor and dishonor than the executioner's fundamental, essential otherness. To confuse someone of low socioeconomic standing with someone of a higher standing might have been awkward for all concerned, but to confuse an executioner with an ordinary person, whether high or low, would have been nothing short of awful. In fact, it formed the basis of an oft-told early modern horror story/urban legend that usually involved unsuspecting individuals dining or sharing a glass with the executioner without realizing the true identity of their new companion, or a young man who falls in love with a young woman without realizing that she is the executioner's daughter.[47] Throughout the early modern period, and indeed through the Revolution as well, one of the most effective means of impugning someone's moral character was to insinuate that they had been seen dining with the executioner.⁴⁸

One last thing that the executioner shared with other outcasts was their enforced physical separation from the community. Particularly as the office became established and hereditary, townspeople took pains to ensure that the now permanent presence of the executioner was as far removed from them as possible. This revulsion for the executioner seems to have become even more keenly felt over time, and the turn of the eighteenth century saw the inhabitants of several towns and cities endeavoring to move executioners and their families to houses even farther out of town and out of sight.⁴⁹ In the southern town of Roussillon, for example, the executioner was housed on an "isolated piece of land such as befits a man of this ilk."⁵⁰ Although, as Christians, they were permitted to attend church, receive communion, and be buried on consecrated ground, executioners and their families were nevertheless cordoned off and isolated in special pews and in special sections of cemeteries for fear that their presence, whether alive or dead, would contaminate others.⁵¹ As late as 1781, the executioner's presence was still considered so intolerable that a near riot erupted in Rouen when the executioner and his family attempted to attend a theatrical performance.⁵²

Given the feelings of revulsion that the presence of the executioner provoked when he came into close proximity with others, we can understand how his presence in the marketplace, no matter how regular, expected, and sanctioned by local ordinances, was nevertheless extraordinarily problematic. It is not difficult to imagine the shudder that went through the crowd at the approach of this figure, dressed in his required ceremonial robes, bearing perhaps the insignia of the gallows, accompanied by his wife, and by his aides (often drawn from the ranks of younger siblings or cousins). And all these people—individuals whom one usually caught sight of only when they were rooting around in sewers, skinning dead animals, harassing lepers and prostitutes, and, of course, rending the flesh of live human beings on the scaffold—would fan out across the marketplace and begin to demand their allotted egg, their measure of butter, and their herring, etcetera. Spoon or no spoon, they made everyone cringe.

The exacting of havage, even though it was initially directed only at foreign and traveling merchants, necessarily entailed the executioner's presence among the local citizenry in the marketplace, the very heart of the city. The distinction between who was local and who was foreign was not always entirely clear, and although townspeople might have suffered the executioner's presence in their midst, the slightest indication that he was taking more than his just due sent them running to the town council demanding that he be put in his place. In fifteenth-century Châlons-sur-Marne, local inhabitants complained that the executioner was "taking and demanding many things around the city that he should not take," and town officials took it upon themselves to admonish him "not to levy anything that is not contained in the enumerations [of his rights of havage]...."⁵³ Sometimes these disputes could be rather petty: In 1552, the executioner of Dijon was forced by local officials to return an egg that he had taken unjustly.⁵⁴

An interesting case, with somewhat more at stake than a lone egg, was a dispute that erupted in Troyes in 1536. Because royal and municipal authorities of the *échevinage* of Troyes possessed overlapping jurisdictions over various cases of high justice, Troyes had the dubious distinction of possessing not one but two executioners.[55] Although townspeople were themselves largely exempt from havage—apart from the interesting obligation to hand over a pastry and some fruit to the executioner on Saturdays during Lent and on New Year's Day[56]—they nevertheless were very much disturbed by the idea of two executioners, along with their families and their various aides, walking around the marketplace and touching things. In the following statement by local authorities, one can sense the distaste, if not the outrage, at the sight of all these rapacious outcasts descending on local produce like a plague of locusts:

> Presently, as there are not so many executions to perform in the said city [of Troyes], to the point that one lone [executioner] would have free time on his hands, nevertheless there are two principal executioners.... [Along with their aides] they number eight or nine who want to profit as much as possible from the office, and they place themselves at the gates of said city and the public markets, and there is not wood, kindling, eggs, cheese, butter and other produce and provision that are brought into this city that is not taxed by them; and furthermore, often times their companions and aides assist them in the markets and streets of Troyes and because they do not have any written receipts, there is no butter, cheese, fruit or anything else that is not tainted by their hands...[57]

Although the townspeople of Troyes were themselves exempt from havage (apart from the occasional pastry, etcetera), citizens of the town were not happy about the burden placed on the local economy by the executioner's—or in this case the two executioners'—havage. Local authorities reprimanded the executioners for "imposing an incredible servitude upon the said city and an exaction and pillage upon the people [which was] very damaging and harmful to the public welfare and which should not be tolerated."[58] Equally as important, however, and as the above paragraph implies, was the fact that townspeople simply could not stand the fact that these outcasts were "taint[ing] by their hands" all of the goods and produce on sale.

Because the executioner's presence in the marketplace was so consistently problematic, several towns experimented with ways of at least partially circumventing the havage or limiting the amount of physical contact between executioners and merchants during its collection. In St. Omer, for example, in 1448, authorities decided to substitute a weekly salary of 10 sous for the executioner's right to seize a percentage of eggs brought into the town by outside merchants, because the process had proved "very unpleasant for people [coming to St. Omer] from outside...."[59] In the following century, city officials in Dijon attempted to put a stop to the practice, which was common in many towns, whereby executioners would mark those merchants who had paid their due with a piece of chalk so that these merchants could be more easily differentiated from those who had not yet paid up. The executioner's touch, even mediated by a piece of chalk, was simply too unpleasant to allow on any kind of routine basis.[60]

Discomfort with the executioner's right of havage was, therefore, present very early on, even when havage was still primarily directed at foreign and traveling merchants. From the sixteenth to the eighteenth century, however, the havage rights of executioners gradually became more extensive, with many of the old distinctions between local and foreign merchants disappearing, and many townspeople no longer exempt from giving the executioner a share of their produce. In early eighteenth-century Poitiers, for example, the only items exempted were those grown by local townspeople in their gardens and for their own personal consumption.[61] This extension of havage rights to virtually all goods sold by all people in the marketplace was made even more lucrative in some localities by the right of executioners to exact a double levy on days when an execution was performed, almost as a kind of price of admission to the penal spectacle; and in major towns such as Paris and Rouen, executioners were entitled to seize goods from marketplaces in surrounding localities as well.[62] These increases in the rights of havage ultimately had two important and interrelated consequences: executioners in this period became increasingly wealthy, and their presence in the marketplace became increasingly intolerable.

As early as 1620, when Jehan Guillaume, the patriarch of the Guillaume dynasty of executioners, died in Paris, he had amassed enough wealth to be accorded an elaborate funeral presided over by thirty priests, and if we look at the extensive rights of havage enjoyed by those who succeeded him in office over the next century, we can begin to get a sense of the basis for that wealth. For example, here is just a partial list of the rights granted in 1688 to the executioner Charles Sanson over goods sold in the markets of Paris:

> …[T]he said Sanson…[shall have] and hold and henceforth exercise, enjoy, and use the rights of havage in the fairgrounds and marketplaces of our said city provost and viscounty of Paris…[amounting to] the right to levy from each merchant bringing in eggs on his back or in his arms, one egg, from each saddlebag two eggs, from each cart a half *quarteron* [equaling an eighth of a pound], and from each basket of apples, pears, grapes and other produce coming either by ground or by water in boats carrying a horse-load's worth, one *sous*, from each horse a like sum, and from each cart two *sous*, from those who bring whether by ground or by water green peas, medlars, hempseed, mustard seed, poulavin, millet, walnuts, cuttlefish, chestnuts, hazelnuts and green walnuts, a whole spoonful such as he has always taken; from each traveling merchant who brings whether on his back or in his arms butter, cheeses, poultry and freshwater fish six *deniers*, from each horse one *sous*, from each cart or wagon two *sous*…

The list meanders on, through oranges, lemons, oysters, charcoal, and various beverages, and ends up providing an exhaustive look at what was available for sale in early modern Parisian markets. In fact, one could get a very interesting and accurate sense of the regional variety of produce and goods sold in marketplaces throughout the country by making one's way through the various provisions of havage throughout the realm.[63]

In addition to proceeds from the havage, executioners in many localities were entitled to receive monetary payments in a kind of penal piece system. These payments varied widely from town to town, and in an attempt to lessen some of the local variations, regional *parlements* in the early eighteenth century endeavored to set standard fees within each region. In a series of twenty-seven articles, the parlement of Bordeaux laid out a price list for various forms of punishment: 30 livres for beheading, 20 for burning at the stake and scattering the ashes to the wind, and 6 for cutting off someone's hand. Differences between regions persisted, however, and a beheading that would have cost local authorities 30 livres in Bordeaux or in Flanders, cost 100 livres in Paris. Burning at the stake and scattering the ashes cost 90 livres, however, no matter whether it was performed in Paris or Flanders, but was a comparative bargain at only 20 livres in Bordeaux.[64] Executioners were also often compensated for travel expenses to neighboring towns and for meals along the way.

When one adds up all of their various sources of revenue—payments per execution, income from the various *basses oeuvres* and other minor privileges, and the extensive proceeds from the right of havage—one begins to see just how wealthy executioners were, particularly in the larger urban areas. According to the historian Pierre Lefranc, when the executioner of Poitiers remarried in 1745, the list of possessions that he provided to the local notary was impressive:

> Four pages of fine, tight handwriting were necessary to complete the account, because the household of the executioner of Poitiers seemed like that of a well-to-do bourgeois: walnut furniture, a bed '*à la duchesse*,' a copper cauldron in the kitchen, an abundance of linens, dozens of tablecloths and shirts, 16 women's hats, a large supply of linen yarn, 9 marks of silverware, 1,000 livres in cash; in the wine cellar 8 full barrels of new red wine, and 13 empty ones, etc.[65]

In addition to their material possessions, executioners shared one other thing with the upper stratum of society: literacy. All could sign their names, and a good many of them were capable of writing competent and, on occasion, even eloquent letters.[66]

Although wealth was one of the consequences of the executioner's extensive havage in the early modern period, so too was increased animosity. If townspeople had bristled at the exaction of havage in earlier times, when they themselves had been largely exempt, they became overtly hostile as the executioner's spoon increasingly came to be pointed in their direction. In many localities, executioners repeatedly sought help from local authorities in enforcing their rights of havage, complaining both of harassment and refusals to accord them their due. Some towns responded to these troubles by posting notices reminding people of the executioner's rights and by threatening to levy fines on those who taunted him or flouted the havage. In 1741, the king's attorney reminded the citizens of Falaise that it was "in violation of public order that the executioners be insulted either in the streets or in the marketplaces when they come to this town [to perform] the execution of criminal sentences or to collect the rights which are accorded to them by ordinances and regulations." Those who refused to accord the executioner his rights of havage, or who allowed their children to taunt or harass him and his aides in the performance of his duties or the collection of his rights, would be subject to a fine of 20 livres.[67]

Other towns attempted to circumvent the problem by replacing the havage with an annual salary. In 1615, local authorities in Dijon expressed the hope that they would be preventing "popular agitation" when they succeeded in convincing the executioner to forego his rights of havage in exchange for an annual salary of 90 livres a year. The problem, however, was that havage was becoming intolerable at precisely the moment when it was becoming extraordinarily lucrative, and it would not be very long before 90 livres would seem a paltry sum in exchange for the bounty of havage. Nearly fifty years after the executioner of Dijon had ceded his rights of havage, his successor bought back those same rights, not only foregoing his salary of 90 livres but paying the town 300 livres a year to enjoy the privilege. By 1711, however, it was the executioner's turn to propose the idea of replacing the havage with a salary, and thereby put an end to the "difficulties with unpleasant consequences" to which he and his aides were "continually" being subjected. Now, however, the executioner's salary would be 700 livres a year, representing nearly an eightfold increase in revenues over the course of a century.[68] The town of Chalon-sur-Saône followed suit in 1718, and shortly afterwards, even the executioner of Paris was persuaded to abandon his extraordinarily lucrative rights in favor of a fixed annual salary.[69]

In those areas where the practice of havage survived into the middle of the eighteenth century, disputes between executioners and locals often turned ugly. In 1744, when the executioner of Poitiers, accompanied by his aide and his daughter, attempted to claim his right to levy a tax on a cartload of wood entering the town, they were blatantly refused. A crowd of a dozen or so people began to gather. A brawl ensued, and although the executioner was able to escape, his aide and his daughter were not so fortunate, and were roughed up by the crowd. The daughter's cape and head covering were trampled underfoot, and someone went so far as to call her a *bougresse* (female bugger).[70]

THE END OF AN ERA: THE ABOLITION OF HAVAGE

In April of 1775, partly in response to a series of bad harvests but also as part of comptroller general Anne–Robert–Jacques Turgot's broad vision for the deregulation of the grain trade, the royal government announced an end to all levies and duties imposed on grains in Dijon and several of the other larger towns of Burgundy. Very quickly, towns from across France begged the government for a similar decree, and on 3 June 1775 the government declared the abolition of all duties imposed on grain throughout the entire realm. Although the right of havage had not been the primary target of the decree, it is clear that this privilege and the disturbances provoked by executioners trying to exercise it, was nevertheless very much on the minds of the king and his ministers: "His Majesty, in suspending the exaction of rights [on grains] belonging to cities, believes it even less permissible to allow to subsist those [rights] which are levied by the Executioners of High Justice, whose collection can excite more troubles and encounter greater opposition in the markets [than the levies imposed by cities]."[71]

Theoretically, executioners still retained the right of havage over non-grain items, but because grains constituted such a large part of their income, their privileges had effectively been wiped out in the stroke of a pen; it would not be long before the havage disappeared entirely.[72] Consequently, royal officials and local authorities found themselves scrambling to determine some other equitable method for compensating executioners. The latter, or at least those among them who had not already negotiated an annual salary prior to 1775, effectively found themselves at the mercy of bureaucrats. A retrospective study undertaken in the early years of the Revolution would determine that in many areas of the country the annual income of executioners dropped precipitously after 1775, with some making a third and sometimes even a quarter of what they had made before that date.[73]

The year 1775 would mark, therefore, the beginning of lean times for executioners, and a researcher in the archives can easily get the impression that from this moment on, they spent infinitely more time crafting letters begging officials for money than they did executing people. Jean-François Joly de Fleury, administrator general of finances, and essentially a successor of Turgot, found himself handling many of these requests. As he would remark in January 1783, "Among the executioners of Champagne, there is not one who does not fervently desire the reestablishment of the rights of havage or who does not ask for an increase [in salary] proportionate to what they enjoyed before the suppression [of those rights]."[74] But by 1783, the restoration of the havage seemed unimaginable:

> I do not think I have to stress the disadvantages that would result from a restoration of these rights.... The mere sight of the executioner sends people from the countryside fleeing and along with them all the produce that they bring for sale. If some among them are more reasonable [and do not flee] they can barely stand the executioner's... designating those who have paid by marking them with a cross on their stomachs in yellow chalk. There is not one of them who would not be ready to perform any sacrifice [so as not] to be reduced to such a debased position [*servitude*].[75]

In the years before the Revolution, the traditional executioner who trawled the marketplaces of France in his obligatory, colorful robes of office, marking with chalk those who gave him his due, and threatening to touch the produce of those who did not, was on the verge of extinction. Executioners, who for generations had been among the more visible inhabitants of the towns of France as they performed their functions, high and low, became increasingly invisible, their appearance more and more confined to the spectacle of execution alone. A new kind of executioner was seemingly called for by an emerging penal system: not some extraordinary being who caused a kerfuffle every time he made an appearance among ordinary folk, but someone utterly unremarkable, someone who would be content to stay out of the limelight, and who would gratefully accept whatever the authorities chose to pay him. As the *intendant* of Picardie reported at the moment of the abolition of the havage in June of 1775, "The minister [Turgot] has remarked to me that it would perhaps be desirable if this class of men [could be] chosen from among criminals to whom one granted life [in return for becoming an executioner], [and] could not lay claim to anything more than the bare necessities."[76]

An important blow to the executioner's status as a privileged individual came on the night of 4 August 1789, when the National Assembly voted to abolish all feudal privileges. Once the Assembly's decisions were enacted into law, in March of 1790, executioners were no longer able to seize any goods in the marketplace, nor were they able to continue exercising their traditional monopoly on the curing of animal skins and sewer cleaning, which had constituted a sizeable portion of their income. Because executioners were often prevented by contemporary prejudices from exercising any occupation other than that of executioner, many became entirely dependent on penal functions as a sole means of support. In some locations, where executions had been relatively rare and where executioners had derived the majority of their income from their privileges, the consequences of the Assembly's reforms proved devastating. And when, as a consequence of the Revolutionary penal code of 1791, many traditional forms of spectacular justice were replaced with incarceration, executioners, who for centuries had derived an income from the communities in which they lived, now effectively became wards of the state, entirely dependent on administrators for support.

As they had done after the 1775 decision abolishing the right of havage, executioners besieged the minister of justice with letters in the wake of 1791, pleading for financial assistance. As Pierre Joseph Outredebanque, the executioner of Arras, complained to the Minister of Justice Duport, "[the petitioner] has seen himself reduced to [sterile speculation] by the wisdom of the decrees of the gentlemen of the National Assembly." And he begged the minister "to take the supplicant under the wings of your benevolent protection and accord him a sufficient annual and permanent pension...."[77] Michel Benoist, the executioner of Brives in the Limousin, barraged the minister of justice with several letters between 1791 and 1792, lamenting the "sad situation to which he has been reduced for a long time." In a letter from October of 1791 he begged the minister to "allow yourself to be softened by [the supplicant's] tears in an advanced age.... Only you can return his life to him." Three months later, he declared himself to be "without bread, without money, and without any source of support." And, writing yet again, several months later, he described himself as "groaning under the weight of misery."[78] Similarly, François Chesdeville, executioner of Dijon, wrote a letter to the administrators of his department in February of 1791 in which he offered to spare them a full "exposition of the extent of his repugnance [for his profession] and of his suffering," if they would give him a raise as a pension for his elderly mother, who was bedridden.[79] In October of that year, Pierre André Louis Desmorest, executioner of Estampes, complained to Minister Duport that local officials had decided to reduce a salary already agreed upon, despite the fact that he was fifty years old, that his age as well as contemporary prejudices precluded his finding another occupation, that he had significant expenses and debts, and that he had the obligation "to nourish and care for an infirm, eighty-two-year-old mother."[80]

Even the uncle of the executioner of Paris, Nicolas Charles Gabriel Sanson, wrote to Duport concerning his "unfortunate position." Seventy-two years old, "infirm and at the edge of his grave," with a son as destitute as he was, he had no choice but to "throw himself at your feet to beg of you, as well as of the Minister of the Interior, to accord the petitioner the support necessary for his subsistence and his infirmities, [in the form] of a retirement pension in whatever amount you choose." Although he eventually found refuge at the home of his famous nephew in Paris, he nevertheless wrote, in a letter to the Committee on Legislation, that he was "reduced to the most abject misery and necessity, without clothes and with no means of attaining them."[81] Things would only get worse for executioners when the invention and deployment of the guillotine in 1792 would deprive them of their starring role on the penal stage, and the machine's efficiency would more or less render their expertise obsolete.[82]

For nearly half a millennium, from the thirteenth to the end of the eighteenth century, the act of putting someone into the hands of the executioner for punishment could not have been farther from the simple and transparent act of carrying out the king's justice. To be placed into the hands of the executioner was to be given over to someone brimming with infamy, someone whose very being exuded otherness, someone who was situated at the extreme opposite pole from everything that was clean, upstanding, and good, and who dealt with everything that was cast off from society: everything unclean, unwanted, and dead. To be passed into those hands that delved in sewage and trafficked in offal, hands that corralled lepers and whores, was to pass into another realm.

4

The Execution of Justice
The Ritual of Punishment in Medieval and Early Modern France

By the fourteenth century, all of the building blocks were in place that would comprise the early modern penal ritual. Spectacular elements had been added to older punishments of corporal compensation, such as simple hanging and mutilation, so as to update them and bring them into line with the legal thinking of the day, which placed a premium on exemplary deterrence. Dragging the condemned through town prior to execution, exhibiting the condemned in the town square prior to mutilation, had initially served as a means of spectacularizing death penalties that had previously been primarily compensatory rather than visual and exemplary. Eventually, spectacular elements were woven directly into the death penalties themselves. Burnings and beheadings became elaborately staged moral lessons. The *fourches patibulaires*, built on the highest hills on the outskirts of towns and capable of exhibiting numerous corpses at the same time, came to serve as formidable stages on which the simple act of hanging, which had always carried within it the germ of exemplarity, could be transformed into grand penal spectacles. So powerfully important was the visible lesson of exemplary justice perceived to be, that the bodies and parts of bodies of those executed by means other than hanging were often brought to the *fourches* for display after death. Overseeing all of this, from beginning to end, and acting as a kind of master of ceremonies, at least in the northern two-thirds of France (as well as in Dutch and German-speaking areas to the east), was the executioner, institutionalized in the official position of *maître des hautes oeuvres*.

Although most, if not all, forms of punishment had taken on spectacular elements by the fourteenth century, they existed more as a kind of fragmentary collection of penal strategies, loosely connected by the theoretical imperative of exemplary deterrence, than as any kind of coherent ritual. At the end of the fourteenth century, however, a royal ordinance was passed that, probably more than any other single factor, helped to standardize ritual practice. In February of 1396, abrogating all customary laws that decreed otherwise, Charles VI declared:

> That henceforth, all people who are condemned to death for their misdeeds will...be provided and administered the sacrament of confession...even in cases in which [the condemned] are so overcome with sadness or emotion, that they do not know that they want [confession] or ask for it.[1]

The universal requirement that local officials provide a priest to administer confession to condemned criminals as they prepared to make their way to the place of execution essentially provided public executions throughout the realm with an identical opening act. Set in motion was a process that eventually culminated in the development of a fairly standard ritual of execution, with similar stages and a similar rhythm, which would last, more or less unchanged, until the promulgation of the Revolutionary penal code of 1791.

We might tend to think of punishments such as the pillory, public whipping, banishment, and branding as entirely distinct from punishments resulting in the death of the condemned. Of course, if we consider only the end result, they are profoundly different. Considered within the context of the entire penal ritual that came into existence at the turn of the fifteenth century, however, all of these different punishments might be seen as representing varying levels of completion of the very same journey that every condemned criminal was required to take. This journey was essentially a penal pilgrimage, the successive stages of which condemned criminals were obligated to complete depending upon the seriousness of their crimes.

The first leg of the journey, on which all those who had been convicted of a serious crime necessarily embarked, involved the public appearance of the condemned and his or her acknowledgment of wrongdoing. Shame was inherent in the act of public display, but it was made even more pronounced by the touch of the executioner's infamous hand. Remorse was the ideal outcome of this public shaming, and it is fair to say that, at least until the early sixteenth century, it was the usual outcome. The pillory, although it had initially served as a means of spectacularizing other non-spectacular punishments, eventually became a penal device unto itself, epitomizing, more than any other device or practice, the combined elements of display and shame that were the essential function of this first stage.

For some, the punishment ended at the conclusion of this first leg of the penal pilgrimage, and the offender could return home to his or her family, chastened but unmarked. For others, who had committed more serious crimes, the second stage of the journey would be required. This involved the ritual casting out of the condemned: the identification of the offender as separate from the community and no longer welcome within it, which sometimes entailed the mutilation or branding of the condemned as a visible mark of their difference. If the banishment was temporary, the offender would be allowed to return after a specified period of time to resume his or her place within the community; if, however, the banishment was permanent, the offender was warned never to return, usually under penalty of death. Permanent banishment was, by the logic of the day, considered a capital punishment, in that it demanded the "civil death" of the offender and the confiscation of his or her assets. With the emergence of the modern state, these simple expulsions would prove more complicated, as neighboring states came to resist the idea of receiving each other's unwanted citizens, and different forms of exclusion, such as confinement in the king's galleys (and, much later, exile to overseas colonies), would eventually replace banishment.

The last and final stage of the penal pilgrimage was death, a stage that in many ways allowed for the most variability in terms of ritual. Depending upon the nature of the sentence, death could be over in an instant, or at the conclusion of a protracted spectacle that stretched over many hours; it could be performed in town, or on the outskirts; and it could be performed on a live body, on a dead body, or on the effigy of a body. Despite these differences, all punishments that resulted in death, or even the representation of death, contained within them all three stages of the penal ritual. They began, like every other punishment, with exhibition and shame; they proceeded to the ritual separation of the offender from the community and the performance of casting out; and they ended with the death of the condemned. Not unlike the punishment of banishment, which could be either temporary or permanent, punishments resulting in death allowed for two post-mortem possibilities: reincorporation into the community or permanent exclusion. Many who suffered the death penalty, by undergoing the ultimate penance in reparation for their crimes, were allowed a Christian burial on consecrated ground, particularly after the ordinance of 1396 that mandated last confessions. Others were permanently excluded either through a sentence stipulating that the criminal's body be burned and the ashes thrown "to the winds" or one that ordered the criminal's corpse to be left on the gibbet to rot.

If the authorities themselves, through the use of exemplary and spectacular punishments, seemed intent on "sending a message," it is not at all clear that this message was being received and understood by the crowds who flocked to public executions, often in great numbers. The very willingness of so many people to gather around the scaffold and take an active part in the penal ritual, often praying, crying, and singing with the condemned, serves as eloquent testimony to a fundamental "disconnect" between contemporary theory and practice. The inhabitants of medieval and early modern France did not attend public executions so that they could be the object of the government's didactic lesson; rather, they attended for many of the same reasons that people had taken part in earlier rituals of public penance: to witness an act of atonement and to take part in an act of collective healing. So profoundly important was the penal ritual to the community that it would take place even in the absence of a live, human, criminal body. The surprisingly common punishment of effigies of escaped criminals, the standard practice of punishing the cadavers of dead criminals, and the not uncommon execution of animals that had committed crimes, all point to a ritual logic very much at odds with the prevailing, contemporary theory of exemplary deterrence.

THE FIRST STAGE: DISPLAY AND SHAME

As we have seen, the touch of the executioner was a powerful and carefully regulated thing. Because they were extraordinary beings, outcast from the rest of society, executioners were forbidden to come into contact with the accused until the trial had been concluded and guilt had been established. For an executioner to have touched the body of the accused prior to a guilty verdict would have been to impart a mark of infamy prematurely. The absence of the executioner did not, however, necessarily translate into an absence of pain prior to conviction, since judicial torture for the purpose of ascertaining guilt had been common practice since the advent of inquisitorial procedures. Rather than being performed by the executioner, however, the task of administering the *question préparatoire*—questioning accompanied by pain—fell to the official *questionnaire*, who was often a relative of the executioner but whose touch did not carry the same taint. An eighteenth-century treatise on criminal procedure stressed that questioning was "not inflicted as a penalty, but merely in order to force the accused to tell the truth. This is why the *question* [*préparatoire*] in and of itself carries no mark of infamy...."[2]

Even after an individual had been declared guilty, it was not at all inevitable that the executioner would play a part in carrying out the sentence, as the seriousness of the offense had to be of a certain magnitude for the executioner's presence to be warranted. There existed several sentencing options that stopped short of infamy, which were intended as a kind of gentle reproof or warning, including: simple monetary fines, the confiscation of property, and the forced payment of alms.[3]

More severe than simple fines, but still not of a severity that demanded the presence of the executioner, were those punishments administered privately, within the confines of the court. Minors, for example, were sometimes sentenced to a whipping at the hands of the jailer as a foretaste of what they might receive in public from the executioner should they not mend their ways. Also included in this category was the *amende honorable sèche*, which called for the convicted party to beg the forgiveness of offended parties within the confines of the court.[4] Again, neither of these punishments were performed publicly, and although they may have entailed a certain degree of shame, their aim was not exemplary deterrence, but rather a deterrence of any future wrongdoing that might be committed by the individual punished.

Of an entirely different nature were those punishments that were carried out in public, all of which demanded the presence and the touch of the executioner, and all of which involved the display and humiliation of the guilty party. Although there were certain alterations to the ritual of public punishment over time, the basic elements of the essential ritual remained more or less the same throughout much of the medieval and early modern periods. The convicted criminal's induction into spectacular justice began, interestingly enough, with a private reading of the sentence behind the prison walls. The *greffier-criminel*, or court clerk, along with several other officers of the court, would enter the prison, take the prisoner from his or her cell, and, after placing the prisoner in a kneeling position, would read the entire judgment aloud.[5] The following is a typical description of this first, private reading, as reported by an eighteenth-century *greffier*:

> In the year one thousand seven hundred thirty five, the fifth day of October, at the hour of noon, we, the attorneys and greffier-criminel of the court, assisted by Mssrs. Francois Iannet and Claude Nicolas Mignot, bailiffs [*huissiers*] of the court, descended into the prison of the conciergerie of the palace for the reading of the judgment [*arrêt*] rendered this day against the accused Pierre Bernard... [to whom], being on his knees, we read the said judgment which condemns him to be beaten and whipped, naked

[ie. from the waist up], with a birch rod, and with a rope around his neck, by the executioner of high justice at the main crossroads and customary places of this city, and in particular across from the main door of the enclosure of the Temple and on [that] spot branded with a hot iron in the form of the three letters GAL on the right shoulder; this done, [he will be] led and delivered to the *galères* [i.e the convict ships] of the king in order to be detained there and to serve said lord king as a slave.[6]

After the reading of the sentence, the convicted prisoner would normally be asked whether he or she had "anything to declare." As there would be many further opportunities to name one's accomplices, the normal reply to this question was that the prisoner had "nothing to declare." In cases of capital crimes, if there was a strong suspicion that the condemned had not acted alone, but had not yet named accomplices, the court could order the convicted criminal to undergo the *question préalable*, or evidentiary torture, for the purposes of forcing the naming of names.[7] Otherwise, after the reading of the sentence, those who had been condemned to death would be provided with a confessor; those sentenced to any other penalty would immediately confront the first, true moment of the penal ritual: the executioner's touch.

Many of the documents, even those that detail the ritual of punishment in which the condemned was not sentenced to death, present the moment of the executioner's first touch as a rude surprise. In the case of Pierre Bernard, above, who was sentenced to the galleys rather than to death, and was therefore not provided with a confessor, the transition from the reading of his sentence to the executioner's entry on the scene is remarkably abrupt. Even from a textual vantage point within the *procès verbal*, or official account, of the execution, the transition is jarring: "... and the assets of said Bernard... [shall be] confiscated by the crown... not including the prior confiscation of five hundred *livres* in fines payable to the seigneur of the justice of the Temple said Bernard was at that instant seized by the executioner of high justice and led outside the door of the said prison...." If this moment of "seizure" seems abrupt in narration, we can only imagine how much of a shock it must have been to the condemned. As the *procès-verbaux* of many executions testify, prisoners often found themselves surprised, confused, or despairing at the moment of being seized by the executioner. Here is one such account from 1763: "When the judgment was read to him, confirming the sentence that he had not expected, having thought of the murder [he had committed] as a trifling thing, he was very surprised to see himself seized by the executioner. He began to cry, and threw himself on the collar of his confessor, saying to him... 'I really need you.'"[8]

In and of itself, almost regardless of the sentence imposed, the executioner's touch would have been profoundly disturbing. An inhabitant of medieval and early modern France, particularly in larger towns and cities, saw executioners only in carefully circumscribed situations, such as when they came to collect their just due from vendors in the marketplace, or when they trafficked in the carcasses of dead animals or the sale of the clothes of execution victims, or, of course, when they were performing executions. But executioners were expressly forbidden to touch ordinary, law-abiding citizens. To feel, therefore, the touch of the executioner, of this being who epitomized untouchability, was to realize, suddenly, that one was no longer an ordinary citizen, safe from the profanity of his touch, and that one had, in effect, entered his realm and become his subject.

For some, the sojourn in the executioner's realm would last only a few hours, but it was an experience that would nonetheless leave them profoundly marked, either symbolically or literally. For others, it was the beginning of a journey into liminality, the start of a long or even permanent exile, with the forced abandonment of their entire lives, their loved ones, and their possessions. For still others, it would mean that they became the executioner's *patient*—literally, he who suffers. For this last group, once they had been seized by the executioner, it was the portent of certain death. While there was always the hope of a last-minute *grace*, a pardon that would bring the condemned back from the abyss and once again into the world of the living, their fate was nearly certain, and it was the task of their appointed confessor to help them reconcile themselves to the fact that their final hours were at hand.

From the moment of the executioner's first touch, everything unfolded precisely according to the sentence handed down by the court. The first phase of the sentence, no matter what the crime or the punishment, was invariably one in which the condemned was displayed to the public. Immediately, there would be a public reading of the sentence outside the prison door "in the presence of the people," and then, particularly if the punishment was capital in nature (either banishment or death), the condemned would usually be loaded into a special cart waiting outside the prison. Variously called a *charrette* or a *tombereau*, this was an open cart so that the condemned would be plainly visible to onlookers; one eighteenth-century account describes this vehicle as "the cart which is used to pick up the muck [*boue*] of the city."[9] As Pierre Bernard's *procès-verbal* contains a fairly detailed description of his public display and shaming, we might as well continue to follow his journey, after the executioner had seized him and taken him out the door of the prison:

> [Bernard], having been attached to the base of the cart, we, the *greffier-criminel* of the above named court read the judgment of condemnation rendered against him in the presence of the people; the cry of the executioner performed in the accustomed manner, the said Bernard was beaten and whipped by the said executioner of high justice for the first time.

After this first public beating in front of the prison, Bernard was then transported, as the judgment had stipulated, to "the main crossroads and customary places of this city," and each time the ritual was repeated in precisely the same order: the sentence was read, the executioner uttered his "cry,"[10] Bernard was beaten and whipped, and then the entire group moved on to the next spot. This happened four times, and then:

> Finally, we led the said Bernard to the main door of the Temple where we read the said judgment of condemnation rendered against the said Bernard in the presence of the people; the cry of the executioner made in the accustomed manner, the said Bernard was beaten and whipped, naked, with birches, for the last time, and then branded with a hot iron in the form of the three letters GAL and then we detached him from the said cart and entrusted a certain Chenedy... [with the task] of conducting the said

Bernard to the tour St. Bernard in order to be attached to the chain [of galley slaves headed for the southern ports].

The punishment of Bernard functioned like a travelling show, moving through the city of Paris, repeating the scripted performance without variation. The final beating and the branding of Bernard marked the conclusion of the first stage of punishment, involving shaming and display, and the beginning of the second phase, in which the condemned was cast out of the community and into his new life as a galley slave.

In contrast to punishments like whipping, which tended to move about the city, giving repeat performances, the punishment of the pillory essentially functioned in an inverse manner: it remained rooted in one spot, and onlookers passed through. Despite this difference, the two punishments served an identical purpose: to display and to humiliate the offender, and to allow "the people," before whom the judgment was read, to *see justice done* in a very literal sense. The pillory represents the purest form of the first phase of punishment because it was so clearly a device that shamed through the act of displaying. Prior to the fourteenth century, as we have seen, the pillory was used either as a spectacular addendum to less visible punishments or as a kind of promise or precursor of future punishments for first-time offenders.[11] Over time, however, although the pillory continued to be used as an accessory to banishment and other punishments, it also became a punishment in itself. By the turn of the sixteenth century, many larger cities possessed massive pillory towers in the center of town, which served to heighten—in both a literal and figurative sense—the spectacular potential of the pillory (Fig. 4). In Dijon, for example, the pillory tower was a brick and stone structure with eighteen interior wooden steps, and was covered with a roof of gilded lead. Visible at the top was a pillar, to which the hands and feet of the offender were attached with chains.[12]

Like those who were condemned to public whippings, individuals sentenced to the pillory also suffered the touch of the executioner, who shepherded the convicted criminal from the prison to the place of the pillory (which functioned as a kind of "business address" for the executioner, who, as we have seen, was not allowed to live within the walls of most cities and towns). As they were led to the pillory, many convicted criminals were obligated to wear some sort of sign that detailed the specific crime they had committed. Placards reading such things as "Crook," "Would-be Psychic and Sorcerer," "Debauched Libertine [Who Plays] with Little Girls," or "Aggravated Disturber of the Public Peace" were worn around the neck or posted nearby. Sometimes, as an added indignity, the offender was required to wear a paper bonnet. As the criminal was being chained to the pillory, a public reading of the sentence would be given, and then the criminal was simply required to stay there for a specified number of hours, while people looked on. Sometimes, the sentence stipulated that exhibition in the pillory was to be repeated over a period of days, with the sentence read aloud each time.[13]

Public whipping, the pillory, as well as other forms of public humiliation such as the forced naked march of adulterers, or the obligation to ride an ass backwards through town, entailed a form of public display combined with humiliation.[14]

Fig. 4. Gruet au pilori des Halles. Facsimile of the original illustration, in Paul Lacroix, *XVIIIe siècle, Institutions, usages et costumes* (Paris, 1875), 305.

Related to these punishments, but more complex in its origins and its purpose, was the punishment of the *amende honorable*. The public form of the amende honorable, like its private, or *sèche*, counterpart, prevailed upon individuals to beg forgiveness, not of the injured party but rather of God, the king, and justice. Literally the "fine of honor," the amende honorable was required of those who committed crimes that were understood to be an attack on divine, royal, or public honor, a category including such varied acts as sacrilege, sedition, and poisoning, as well as crimes of fraud such as counterfeiting.[15] The condemned was required to walk barefoot, or "with only a shirt" or in some other manner either literally or figuratively signifying nakedness, with a candle of specified weight in hand, and was usually brought to the entryway of a prominent church or to the scene of the crime. There, the condemned would get down on his or her knees and publicly beg forgiveness, often wearing a rope around the neck (Fig. 5). Here is the standard form for those sentenced to perform the amende honorable, which was repeated with only minor variations from the fifteenth to the eighteenth century:

> ... [the said individual] duly charged and convicted of [fill in the crime], as reparation for which we have ordered him to perform the amende honorable, naked, [save only for] a shirt, with a rope around the neck, holding in his hands a candle of burning wax weighing two pounds, [at the appointed place] gathering an audience, and there, being bare-headed and on his knees, shall say and declare in a raised and intelligible voice, that with malice and against good judgment, he did [fill in the criminal act], of which act he now repents, and begs pardon of God, of the King, and of Justice...[16]

The similarities between the amende honorable and the practice of public penance, discussed in the first chapter, are striking. Although the public penance of earlier times had been eclipsed by private penance, and by the introduction of mandatory, yearly private confession for sins, public penance endured in a multitude of forms throughout the Middle Ages.[17] The bare head or feet and the sparse clothes of the condemned who performed the amende honorable would have been instantly recognizable to contemporaries as the sign of penitence, as would the candle that he or she carried. Jean-Marie Moeglin has traced many of the similarities between

Fig. 164. — Amende honorable de Desrues, à Notre-Dame.

Fig. 5. Antoine François Derues faisant amende-honorable devant Notre Dame, 1777. Bibliothèque Nationale de France.

these two forms of public contrition and, as Moeglin shows, several thirteenth-century acts of mandated public penance shared very specific attributes with the later juridical form of the amende honorable, namely: the requirement to perform the ritual in bare feet, either shirtless or in a loose-fitting shirt; and the carrying of *verges*, or sticks, in the hand. The fact that penitents were sometimes publicly beaten with the sticks they carried might also suggest that public penance was a cultural precursor not only of the amende honorable but of public whipping as well.[18]

The performance of the amende honorable was, at one and the same time, a way for the convicted criminal to show remorse as well as to pay his or her debt to society through the act of public penance. If we recall the discussion of Anselm's concept of sin as incurring a debt to God, we can see how the amende honorable developed as an "amende"—literally a fine.[19] In an age when one's obedience to and honor of God were being increasingly likened to the respect that one owed the king, the public performance of the amende honorable was meant to pay one's debt to both.

Of course the amende honorable differed in one key respect from other forms of public display and humiliation. Unlike punishments such as public whipping and the pillory, which merely required the passive participation of the condemned, who simply had to stand there and be displayed or beaten, the amende honorable required the condemned criminal's active participation. In the vast majority of cases, this does not appear to have been a problem, and the condemned almost always dutifully played the role of the penitent sinner. Occasionally, however, convicted criminals simply refused to play along. Although the law provided for aggravated penalties in the case of those who refused to perform an amende honorable prior to a period of banishment, there was obviously little that could be done to force cooperation in the case of individuals who had been condemned to death and therefore had little to lose. Such cases were, however, surprisingly uncommon.[20]

Sometimes, the amende honorable constituted the entirety of the sentence, and therefore amounted to what the eighteenth-century jurist Daniel Jousse termed a penalty that was "purely defamatory [*infamante*]."[21] In this case, it performed a function similar to the earlier, abbreviated form of public penance in which sinners were required to appear in church on Ash Wednesday, barefoot and remorseful, whereupon they were publicly expelled, only to be welcomed back into the fold on Maundy Thursday.[22] The act of public humiliation and the display of remorse essentially compensated for the sin or crime, and allowed for the offender's reconciliation with and reincorporation into the community. More often, however, the amende honorable served as a kind of threshold to social expulsion, a gateway to the next stage of punishment in which the convicted criminal was ritually, and sometimes quite literally, cast out from the social body.

THE SECOND STAGE: EXPULSION AND LIMINALITY

On those occasions when the amende honorable served as a preface to other punishments, such as banishment, a sentence in the galleys, or death, it is best understood as an induction into otherness. The historian Esther Cohen, more than anyone else, has explored the ways in which punishment in the Middle Ages can be seen, at least in part, as rituals of enforced marginality. Invoking cultural anthropologist Victor Turner's conception of liminality, Cohen writes that "Whether temporary or permanent, the liminal status imposed upon offenders was a means of demarcating the boundaries between the normative community and those who had offended against it.... The purpose was twofold: the liminalization of an offender not only lessened his danger to normative society; it also drew by contrast the boundaries of the established community."[23] To this, I would only add that the sight of the convicted criminal in the clutches of the executioner—the very personification of otherness in pre-modern France—served as a graphic visual representation of the condemned's new status, and may very well have served as a reminder, to those who witnessed it, of the common etymological roots between the condemned and the damned (*condamné* and *damné*).

Cohen also suggests that certain aspects of the medieval ritual of punishment owe a cultural debt to the earlier Salic practice of *chrenecruda*, whereby someone who had committed homicide but was unable to pay the wergeld was required to debase themselves and separate themselves from the community symbolically. Indeed, the similarities are too close to be ignored. Salic law stipulated that if someone was truly unable to compensate monetarily for the crime of homicide, the guilty party should throw dirt onto his relatives, and then, "in a loose-fitting shirt, and barefoot, with a stick in his hand he must jump over the fence [of his house]."[24] Here, many centuries before the amende honorable, we have the same bare feet and the wearing of "only a shirt," and it seems reasonable to assume that the stick carried in the *chrenecruda* was a precursor of the sticks, or *verges*, that appear in later instances of public penance and of the two-pound candle carried by those who performed the amende honorable.

Like the earlier penitents who were either whipped in public or who self-flagellated prior to their expulsion, those condemned to banishment were often sentenced either to a public whipping, as we saw in the case of Bernard above, or to a stint in the pillory. A cortege would then usually accompany the individual to the outskirts of town, where he or she would either be cast out or, in the early modern period, handed over to the chain of galley slaves to be taken away. According to Nicole Gonthier, the procession of the banished, which sometimes called for the condemned to be either partially or completely naked, could last an entire day from the first reading of the sentence, through the whipping or display on the pillory, to the arrival of the cortege on the outskirts of town.[25]

As odd as it may sound, permanent banishment or the galleys represented more of a definitive exclusion from society than did most punishments involving death. Especially after the imposition of mandatory confession, many of those who were condemned to death, but who were allowed a proper burial on consecrated ground, ultimately found a reincorporation of sorts into the community after death. Permanent banishment, however, meant exclusion without the possibility of reconciliation. For this reason, many sentences involving banishment were accompanied by various forms of mutilation or branding, an act that visually differentiated the condemned from others in the community.

As we have seen, the practice of mutilating the bodies of condemned criminals can be found in the earliest texts of customary law, but had traditionally been used primarily as a means of corporal compensation: either in retaliation for mutilating someone else or as a kind of "price" for returning from banishment. Over the course of the medieval period, however, mutilations came to be used more and more as a punishment for those who had committed transgressions such as sodomy or blasphemy, as well as for those who had committed theft. The act of severing the limb and sexual organs of sodomites, mutilating the lips and severing the tongue of blasphemers, and removing the ears, eyes, hands, or feet of those convicted of theft served several different functions at once. In part, they were still a form of corporal compensation, a way for criminals to pay for their crimes with the offending part of the body. In part, these punishments were also a form of crime control and deterrence in the sense that to deprive a sodomite of sexual organs, a blasphemer of a tongue, and a thief of hands, eyes, or feet, was to prevent—or at least significantly lessen—the possibility of recidivism. But all of these acts of mutilation also permanently and visibly marked offenders as different, setting them apart from the community at large.[26]

Mutilation was much more frequently used before 1600 than after, and was eventually replaced by branding in the case of thieves and others who were sentenced to banishment or the galleys. The gradual disappearance of mutilation and the rise of branding reflects the extent to which the principle of corporal compensation was slowly giving way to theories of deterrence. Branding essentially retained the marking aspects of mutilation while dispensing with what was beginning to seem like the crude idea of "paying" for a crime with a part of one's body. Originally, the brand of the *fleur de lis* had been used, but the royal declaration of 4 March 1724 replaced the fleur de lis with a brand of "V" for those who committed theft, and "GAL" for those sentenced to the galleys. These markings were meant to facilitate the identification of repeat offenders, so that those who had previously been convicted for theft would be recognizable by their "V" and could therefore be sentenced to the galleys (and receive an additional brand of "GAL") for a second offense; female offenders, who were not eligible for the galleys, were marked by a double "V" for repeat offenses, and sent to a *maison de force*, or prison workhouse.[27] Although the marking of thieves had the practical effect of making them identifiable and subject to greater penalties for repeat offenses, it also served to set them apart from others. In contrast to earlier forms of punishment, one did not simply pay for one's crime once; one kept paying, for the rest of one's life, by bearing the stigma of the offense.

Although mutilation was performed far less frequently after 1600 or so, it continued to be used in cases of crimes that were seen as particularly egregious. Parricides as well as those who were convicted of direct attacks on the sovereign were subject to the severing of the offending hand prior to the penalty of death. But here, rather than being a matter of marking the criminal's body, or even of corporal compensation, the act of severing the hand would seem to be a way of marking the crime itself as particularly odious, and of distinguishing the penalty of the parricide from penalties inflicted on those who were guilty of less egregious crimes.

THE THIRD STAGE: DEATH AS REINTEGRATION OR AS THE ULTIMATE EXILE

Unlike the journey of the expelled, the journey of those condemned to death combined elements of ostracism and expulsion with those of compassion and forgiveness, and, at least in the afterlife, a promise of reintegration. Executions resulting in death are marked, therefore, by what Cohen has aptly described as a "tension between ejection and reconciliation [which] permeated the entire procedure." Although she has tended to focus on the ways in which the reconciliatory aspects of executions made them "secular rituals of communal meaning," Cohen notes that the decision in 1396 to mandate religious confession in all death-penalty cases "introduced a strong religious element into what had hitherto been a secular ceremony."[28] Indeed, most accounts of public executions in the medieval and early modern periods reveal that they had an unmistakably religious character. Particularly before the seventeenth century, those who journeyed toward their deaths were often seen not simply as criminals getting their just desserts, but as performers in a kind of real-life Passion play in which the meaning of life and death, crime and reparation, sin and redemption, were all intertwined.[29] Even after the seventeenth century, when the practice of attending executions as a form of entertainment would become widespread, particularly penitent or sorrowful patients were still able to elicit deep spiritual feelings from those in attendance.

The ritual for those condemned to death began, as in the case of all punishments, with a private reading of the sentence behind closed doors. Then, virtually at the moment of seizure by the executioner, the condemned was provided with a confessor—in Paris, this was usually a doctor at the Sorbonne—who served as a reminder that condemnation in this world did not necessarily preclude salvation in the next. The confessor would normally lead the condemned into the prison chapel for prayers, and for the Benediction of the Blessed Sacrament, after which they would proceed, together with the executioner, outside the door of the prison, where a public reading of the sentence would take place. Then the condemned, accompanied by the executioner and the confessor, would begin the journey toward the place of execution.

Particularly in smaller towns, a bell would often toll to mark the beginning of the procession to the place of execution, and onlookers would gather to watch. The procession sometimes took place on foot, or on a horse or mule. In Paris, however, particularly in the seventeenth and eighteenth century, the condemned was usually seated in an open cart, or tumbrel. On this journey, accompanied by both confessor and executioner, the condemned might find the opportunity to reconcile him or herself to the fate that lay in store and find solace in the words of the confessor. As one witness reported in 1736, "I saw [the condemned] pass by.... He seemed... to be very remorseful...and seemed to be listening to the confessor and was devoutly kissing the crucifix...."[30]

If the amende honorable was to be performed, the procession would stop at a church—in Paris, usually the main entry to Notre Dame cathedral—where the condemned would kneel, holding a two-pound tapered candle, with a cord around the neck, and beg forgiveness of God, King, and Justice. He or she would then once again board the cart to the place of execution, which, until well into the sixteenth century, was often located outside of town, rather than in the marketplace or some other main square where later executions would take place. In fourteenth- and fifteenth-century Paris, although beheadings were conducted in the city center, usually at the place of the pillory, most other forms of execution took place either outside the gate of Saint-Honoré, or at the fourches at Monfaucon and Montigny, to the north of the city, with the route toward the place of execution usually going along the rue Saint-Denis. Each town seems to have had its own assortment of routes out of the city toward the place of execution, which sometimes varied depending on the nature of the crime and punishment.[31]

In Paris, as the procession wended its way through town, it would often make several stops, either at the scene of the crime or to perform public readings of the judgment in various parts of the city. After 1500 or so, it was customary for the procession to stop in front of the convent of Filles-Dieu where the condemned criminal would receive a glass of wine and a piece of bread as a last meal from the nuns of the convent, as well as a crucifix to carry on the final leg of the journey to the scaffold. Here is an account of the procession of Jacques de Beaune, seigneur de Semblançay, found guilty of defrauding the king, as he made his way toward the gibbet of Montfaucon:

> ...[H]e left the Bastille and was put on a mule, wearing a bonnet on his head, without being tied....[A]ccompanying him, were the lieutenant-criminel along with...all the archers, cross-bowmen, and hackbutiers of Paris, the men of the watch on horseback and on foot, the sergeants of the Châtelet and many townspeople, in great number. His public cry [i.e. reading] was done in three places: namely the porte Bauldetz [near today's rue Saint-Antoine], in front of the Châtelet, and at the gibbet. He was accorded his wine and his bread in front of the church of Filles-Dieu by the [nuns of] the convent, as they have the custom of doing for poor criminals. He was given a wooden, red crucifix to carry in his hand, and his bonnet was taken off and he was made bareheaded, and was led to the gibbet bareheaded.[32]

Contemporaries would not have had difficulty drawing the parallels between the journey of the condemned toward the place of execution and Christ's passage along the Via Dolorosa. The meal of wine and bread, if not exactly a Eucharistic offering, nevertheless recalled to all who witnessed it the body and blood of Christ, as did, no doubt, the proffered Cross which the condemned carried on his way to the gallows.[33]

While the customary practice of the Filles-Dieu appears to have died out in the early modern period, confessors continued to take great care to impart a religious character to executions through the Revolutionary period, often taking last-minute confessions and consoling the patient to the very end. The following account, from

1737, of the final hours of a man who had been sentenced to be burned at the stake for stealing and desecrating objects from a church, gives some indication of the efforts to which priests often went to impart the appropriate religious character to executions:

> Pascal was in the hands of his Confessor from the reading of his sentence to the moment of execution. [His Confessor] gave him full confession, made him feel the true horror of his crime, and brought him to ask very humble pardon of God, and to put his confidence in divine mercy. He appeared to be in this frame of mind when, about a half hour before he was to leave the prison [for the execution] he asked to eat a chicken. It was no use reminding him that it was a fast day; he responded that he had eaten [chicken] on Friday, and that he would eat it on Saturday. He was made to understand that it was too late, and that none would be found in the city. Finally, by means of reminding him of his past crimes, his present situation, and the moment that would decide his happy or unhappy eternity, he was [made to] be satisfied with a glass of wine and a piece of bread.... Along the entire way [to the execution] Pascal seemed [greatly] affected. His lips were constantly glued to the crucifix, and whenever the movement of the cart took it away [from his lips] he immediately sought out again this adorable object of his salvation. Arriving in front of the Place de Saint-Etienne...Pascal once again made confession...[and] begged his Confessor not to abandon him.... At the stake [where he was to be burned], Pascal confessed to a sin that he had forgotten and recommended himself to the prayers of those in attendance; he [and his accomplice] were both burned alive, crying for [God's] mercy [*criant misericorde*], and all the people were singing the *Salve Regina* in order to obtain from God the grace to have a good death.[34]

A similar account of the "conversion" of an irreverent criminal into a truly devout and penitent Catholic can be found in another pamphlet from the very same year. In this case, a young woman who had been found guilty of murder seems almost Christ-like in her final hours, even quoting Jesus's words at the hour of his execution (John 17:1):

> At half past noon, they came to call her. She rose immediately and said: "Let us go. My God, be praised. The hour is come," remembering these words of Jesus Christ which we had read to her.... She had a Crucifix forever in her hands, and did not let go of it until she arrived at the scaffold.... Word of her penitence brought a multitude of people to the [Place de Grève where]... people assembled to pray. She arrived there with modesty and an air of piety which was plainly visible on her face and which edified those who were present.... This spectacle, which was watched by the light of many torches, seemed more like the sacrifice of a Penitent than the punishment of a Criminal. The moment having arrived, the Executioners had her descend from the Cart and brought her to the foot of the ladder.... The Doctor [of the Sorbonne] who accompanied her intoned the *Salve Regina*. She sang the entire thing along with the people in a strong and melodious voice.[35]

More than any other historian, Michel Bée has drawn attention to the ways in which spectators at executions behaved as if they were at a religious ceremony, praying with the patient and even alternating verses of prayers and hymns. Inspired by the writings of Marcel Mauss, Georges Bataille, and Roger Caillois, Bée has characterized public executions in ancien régime France as a "spectacle of sacrifice" that allowed both the criminal to atone for his wrongdoing and the community to heal from it:

> [T]he criminal, who has violated the prohibition of murder, has by his act entered into the world of the sacred; he has endowed himself with an energy that renders his presence harmful and contagious; he introduces disorder into society and in the relations between [society] with the divine; the only reconciliation possible between the murderer and the society rests therefore in the sacrifice which frees him from his stain....[36]

As an example of the ways in which nominally secular executions could function as religious rituals, Bée cites the following account of an execution that took place in 1760:

> [The patient]... helped with the singing of the Salve Regina, which being finished he kissed the Cross: having turned toward the people, he exhorted them to pray to God for his soul.... Having received the blows of the iron bar on the wheel, he started singing the Veni Creator. After he had finished the first verse, the public sang the second, the patient took up the third and so on until the end. He then asked the hangman to beg the people to say the Miserere in Latin for him while he recited it in French. M. Méritte, the priest, took up the "Parce Domine, parce populo tuo ne in aeternum irascaris nobis." The public repeated it; then M. Méritte sang the Miserere. After the final verse, the public again repeated Parce populo tuo. Then the priest and the patient followed with the second verse in a strong and energetic voice. Around the middle of the Miserere the voice of the patient became weak.[37]

Although, as we will see, such pronounced religious feeling and compassion for the condemned was less common in the eighteenth century than in earlier times, it nevertheless seems clear that, even accounting for the moralistic and didactic intentions of those who reported the beautiful deaths of repentant criminals, executions had the potential to be profoundly moving, even spiritual, events.

As Pascal Bastien has recently pointed out, Bée's uniform characterization of executions as rituals of sacrifice is not particularly useful in explaining the vast majority of executions of judicial sentences that did not result in death, as well as those executions in which crowds were unsympathetic toward the condemned.[38] I would add to this that the tendency among the French public from the sixteenth century onward to view executions increasingly as a form of entertainment suggests that Bée's characterization must be applied selectively.[39] Moreover, when sentences stipulated that the remains of a criminal be burned and the ashes scattered to the winds, the authorities were clearly trying to prevent the kind of reintegration that Bée describes; likewise, when the corpse of the condemned was ordered to be left to rot and displayed to the public, the explicit intent to "terrorize" would-be malefactors took precedence over any kind of reintegration.[40]

Nevertheless, with Bastien's caveats in mind, and with the recognition that the authorities' intent in staging executions may have had little to do with how people actually perceived them, it seems fair to say that many pre-modern executions resulting in death were indeed experienced by witnesses as a moving and spiritual ceremony in which the community found great meaning and redemption, and the patient secured (post-mortem) reintegration. As we have already seen in the examples above, it was customary, as the execution neared its end, for all those present to sing the *Salve Regina*, a prayer that asks the Virgin Mary "to turn your merciful gaze toward us" with the hope of reconciliation after "this exile." Sometimes, of course, the singing of the *Salve Regina* was more or less rote form. At other times, as in the cases cited above, it could be the climax of a profoundly moving ritual, with the patient and all those in attendance singing, praying, and dissolving into tears.[41]

In certain parts of France, the religious aspects of executions were perhaps more pronounced than in others. In common with parts of Italy and Spain, southern areas of France were home to confraternities of lay penitents who took upon themselves the task of accompanying those condemned to death on their journey to the scaffold. Clad from head to foot in the color of their confraternity, replete with a tall, pointy hat (Fig. 6), these penitents—who were ordinary members of secular society but who belonged to these semi-secret brotherhoods as a form both of sociability and public service—helped to imbue the execution of death sentences with an aura of pronounced religiosity.

Among those confraternities with a specific mandate to officiate at the execution of death sentences was the order of *pénitents noirs*, or black penitents. Modeled on the confraternity of St. John the beheaded, originally founded by Florentines in Rome in the fifteenth century, the *penitents noirs*, who were sometimes known as the *confrérie de la Misericorde*, were established in Lyon, Avignon, and many other

Fig. 6. Les pénitents de Limoges (retrospective exhibition at the Palace of Industry, *Histoire du costume*), *Le Monde illustré* (10 October 1874), no. 913.

French, as well as Belgian, towns. Another group of lay penitents who officiated at executions was the confraternity of the *Sanch* in Perpignan, a group founded in the fifteenth century when Perpignan belonged to Spain, but which continued to flourish after the town was annexed to France in 1659, and which, in fact, still exists today. Another group, the *pénitents pourpres*, or purple penitents, was founded in Limoges in the seventeenth century.[42] The role that confraternities of penitents played in executions can be seen in the following article from the constitution of the purple penitents, drafted in 1662:

> Art. 6. In so much as one of the principle aims in establishing the pious company of charity is the assistance and consolation of the miserable patients condemned to the ultimate punishment, it is in these sad moments that the light of zeal and charity of the confraternal members must shine forth. As soon as the Rector is warned of an execution, he will assemble all the members of the confraternity in the church of St. Aurelien where the regalia will be brought for the convenience of said confraternal members, after which they will leave the said church, marching two by two in a procession in order to make their way to the prison, and once arriving there they will march in a procession before the patient, accompanied by two ecclesiastical brothers who will exhort [the patient] to die well; these [brothers] will be covered in a black cloth. On the way, they will sing the prayers for the dying, until the execution has been done, after which will be sung the Psalm De profundis, during which time the members of the confraternity will untie the body [of the patient] and will put it in a shroud in sight of everyone and said body will be carried in a coffin by four of the brothers... and the body will be carried to the church of St. Cessadre or St. Aurelien... in order to be buried in the designated place on the following day, the brothers singing, along the way, the Miserere, the De profundis, and other psalms destined for the souls of purgatory.[43]

So deeply meaningful and extraordinarily important were penal rituals to members of the community, that on those rare occasions when the ritual was interrupted, the crowd immediately responded with frustration and anger, almost as if a spell had been broken, and they suddenly realized that what, moments before, had seemed sacred, now appeared disturbingly profane. Executioners, in common with dramatic actors of the time, were the object of considerable scorn and contempt "offstage" in the course of their ordinary lives, but they could nevertheless command great respect and complete attention in the midst of their performances on their respective stages. Just as audiences could sometimes turn against dramatic actors when plays did not go well or when actors flubbed their lines, so too did the crowds who attended penal spectacles in the medieval and early modern periods routinely vent their rage on executioners when the ritual faltered. There are countless instances in which crowds assaulted, chased, and sometimes even killed executioners when executions were botched, almost as if those present had suddenly been surprised to see the executioner revealed before them not as the master of an important ritual but as the detested pariah they had always known him to be.[44]

It is within this context of the extraordinary significance that the penal ritual held for the community that we should approach the subject of executions of non-human and inanimate bodies. If we understand how the ritual of execution was absolutely indispensable to the community as a means of overcoming the fact of the crime and healing from the wound inflicted by it, then we can see how the ritual absolutely *had* to take place even in the absence of a live, human body. If the person who committed the crime could not be found, or had run away, then the penal ritual would take place all the same, performed on an effigy of the condemned. If the convicted criminal died before he or she could be punished, or if the crime was suicide, then the punishment would be enacted on the cadaver. And if the convicted criminal was an animal, then the logic of the day demanded that the ritual be performed on the body of the animal.

BEYOND DETERRENCE: THE EXECUTION OF INANIMATE AND NON-HUMAN BODIES

Although the origin of the use of effigies in public executions in France is unclear, and a scholarly study focusing on the subject has, to my knowledge, yet to be written, it appears that effigies were in use at least as early as the first half of the fourteenth century and continued to be a common feature of French criminal justice through the eighteenth century.[45] Contrary to the way we understand the word today, effigies that were used for the purposes of criminal justice, particularly in the early modern period, usually took the form of paintings of the condemned, which were commissioned by the authorities from local artists.[46] Here is how the *Encyclopédie* described the use of effigies in the eighteenth century:

> In Paris, paintings that serve as effigies are simply a rough drawing made by pen, which represents a man being hanged or on the wheel, depending on the sentence; but in the provinces where executions are more rare, effigies are ordinarily painted and colored so that they resemble the accused as much as possible; he is represented in his regular clothing and with everything that can capture [his likeness] so that it will have a greater impression on the people.[47]

Most commonly, effigies appear to have been not simply a representation of the condemned, but a representation of the condemned *being* executed. In this sense, then, they were less a simulacra of the condemned than of the execution itself. On occasion, however, instead of representing the execution within the painting, it was the painting itself that was, so to speak, executed. In Caen in 1706, for example, the painting of a woman who had been condemned in absentia for murder was requisitioned from her abandoned belongings, was displayed on the place of justice for a day, and then burned by the executioner:

> They burned the effigy of Marie-Anne Le Blanc.... It was put on display all day long on a gibbet at the pillory. It was her portrait that they found at her house, in the course of the search and inventory of her belongings. It was a very good painting of a woman of distinction and pleasure and the portrait was a very strong likeness. The entire town went there [to see it] out of curiosity.[48]

Often, even when the execution was itself represented in the painting, the authorities "hung" the painting on a gibbet, not only for purposes of display but also as a means of "executing" the painting.⁴⁹ According to Michel Porret, executions by effigy in eighteenth-century Geneva involved a procession of a painting of the condemned from the prison to the gallows, exactly as would have taken place if the condemned had been present. Moreover, if the sentence called for the convicted criminal to be whipped, then the painting was carried through the city and whipped.⁵⁰

More visually effective, no doubt, than burning or manhandling paintings was to use life-sized effigies in the form of mannequins. Although these appear to have been significantly less common, there are several cases of particularly prominent individuals whose execution called for three-dimensional representations, particularly before 1600. In 1562, for example, local authorities went to great expense to construct and elaborately clothe the mannequins, replete with facial likenesses, of several wealthy bourgeois Protestants condemned for heresy.⁵¹ In 1539, when an auditor at the Châtelet by the name of Jean Frolo was found guilty of murder and condemned to perform the amende honorable, to have his hand cut off before the house of his victim, and to be hanged, the entire sentence was apparently performed using an elaborately constructed dummy, as documented by the following receipt:

> For having made a figure of said Frolo, four *livres* eight *sous parisis*; for a candle weighing two pounds in wax, twelve *sous parisis*, for a ruffled shirt to put on the said figure, eight *sous parisis*; for a pair of black breeches to put on said figure, twenty *sous parisis*, for the rental of a robe of black cloth, as much again for the semi-worsted cuffs (stuffed with wool) and with a surrounding border [in the style of] a barrister, with a pourpoint of black velour, *twelve sous parisis*.⁵²

Perhaps to avoid such odd sights as an effigy performing the amende honorable, the royal Criminal Ordinances of 1670 attempted to standardize the use of effigies, decreeing that henceforth they were to be used only for individuals who had been sentenced to "natural death" (meaning *actual* rather than civil death) and not for condemnations involving the galleys, the amende honorable, perpetual banishment, branding or whipping; these latter sentences were to be "only written on a board [*tableau*] without any effigy; and both the effigies and the boards shall be put up in the public square. And all other condemnations in absentia will only be signified [in writing] and a copy delivered to the domicile or residence of the condemned...."⁵³ The basic intention of the Ordinance was therefore to restrict *visual* representations of executions to sentences involving natural death, and to mandate written representations of all other sentences.

As strange as all this may seem from a modern perspective, perhaps the most surprising aspect of executions in effigy is how extraordinarily common they were. Julius Ruff has estimated that one-third of all cases involving the death penalty in eighteenth-century Libourne and Bazas, in southwestern France, were tried in the absence of an actual defendant;⁵⁴ Benoît Garnot has suggested similar numbers for eighteenth-century Burgundy, finding that 40 percent of all death-penalty cases that came before the parlement were adjudicated *en contumace*, meaning in absentia, or literally, in willful "rebellion" or contempt of court;⁵⁵ and Michel Porret has found that an astonishing 85 percent of capital sentences in Geneva in the period from 1755 to 1790 were executed in effigy.[56] It appears that the number of cases executed in effigy sometimes seemed ridiculously high even to contemporaries. In 1665, for example, during the mass trials of the Auvergne nobility that took place in the town of Clermont, 347 people were sentenced to death, of whom apparently 324 were executed in effigy.[57] As Esprit Fléchier wryly noted in his *Mémoires sur les grands jours*, this extraordinary number of executions in effigy gave rise to its own sort of spectacle:

> In one day nearly thirty [criminals] were [executed] in effigy at the same time. It was quite a sight to see so many paintings on display at the place of executions, and in each one of them an executioner [was portrayed] cutting off a head. These non-bloody executions, and these genteel [*honnêtes*] representations, which were only slightly infamous, constituted an even more agreeable spectacle in the sense that there was justice without any blood spilled. The paintings remained there for a day, and all the people came out of curiosity to see this bunch of criminals in portraiture, who were dying incessantly and who were not dying at all, who were ready to receive the [final] blow without fear, and who will not cease being evil in reality, even as they appear unhappy in representation [*en figure*].[58]

Related, in certain respects, to the punishment of effigies was the practice of punishing the cadavers of criminals who had died before they could be executed. For the most part, this category was comprised of individuals who had committed suicide and who were, like most individuals convicted of premeditated murder, sentenced to be drawn and hanged.[59] In many places, suicides were punished on a different *fourche* or gallows from ordinary criminals, and it is unclear whether this was done to further stigmatize the body of the suicide or out of respect for the bodies of ordinary criminals who, unlike the suicide, still had the possibility of a Christian burial.[60] In addition to the punishment of suicides, the execution of cadavers was also performed on convicted criminals who had died before they could be brought to justice. In one such execution that was doubly removed from that of a living body, a corpse that proved too rotten to execute was executed in effigy in the form of "wood carved into the semblance of a man."[61]

There are, no doubt, ways in which the execution of effigies and cadavers can be seen as setting an example to others. The very fact that those guilty of capital offenses would have their assets seized by the Crown without the possibility of leaving anything to their heirs was, undoubtedly, something that had the potential to deter individuals from committing crimes or killing themselves, and executions of effigies and cadavers can therefore be seen, at least in part, as a form of advertising the essential fact and the inescapability of punishment. As we saw in the article from the *Encyclopédie*, there was clearly a widely held conviction that the purpose of executions in effigy was to make some sort of "impression on the people."

But there are also many aspects of the punishment of both effigies and cadavers that point to a purpose beyond deterrence. The spectators who came to see the painting of Marie Le Blanc be burned "alive," and those who flocked to the spectacle of hundreds of beheaded nobles in portraiture, are described by the sources as coming "out of curiosity." If the intent was to set an example for them, one wonders whether the intent and the effect were not, at least to a certain extent, at odds with each other.

The execution of effigies and cadavers affords us a unique window onto a fundamental disconnect between an execution ritual, which had evolved very gradually over time, and the rise of the theory of exemplary deterrence, which had developed independently of that ritual but that contemporary jurists often insisted on reading into penal practice no matter the obstacles. The execution of effigies and cadavers, in other words, offers us an even starker contrast between the logic of the ritual itself, on the one hand, and the theoretical intent retroactively superimposed upon that ritual, on the other, than can be seen in the ordinary execution of live bodies. The rhetoric of jurists aside, bodies—even dead and imaginary ones—needed to be punished from the perspective of those who actually participated in the ritual, not to teach a lesson, to send a message, or to make an impression, but rather so that the fact of the crime itself could be overcome. I do not mean to suggest that onlookers felt the same sense of spiritual investment with respect to executions of effigies and cadavers that they felt with the execution of living people, or that they sang and prayed with a portrait, a mannequin, or a cadaver. Rather, I want to suggest that these executions provided a means—the only available means—for the community to put the crime behind them and move on. In this sense, they are not unlike the ritual of a funeral, which marks the fact of a death, and allows the community a certain sense of what we would today call "closure."

A reading of executions as closure and overcoming rather than as deterrence also helps to explain a certain category of executions that otherwise presents something of a conundrum: the spectacular punishment of crimes that were so horrible as to be classified as *offensa cujus nominatio crimen est* (an offense whose very utterance is a crime), a category that included both bestiality and homosexuality under the general rubric of sodomy. For these crimes, it was sometimes the case that the minutes of the trial would be burned, so that no trace of the unnatural act would remain.[62] Given this attitude, we might expect a kind of unspectacular version of punishment, for fear that the punishment of these unspeakable crimes might call attention to the crime itself. But we would be wrong. The sentence, for example, in 1470 of a man and a mare who had been found guilty of having sexual relations somewhat paradoxically called for an elaborately staged burning of both offenders for the purposes of effacing their memory:

> [H]aving seen the deposition and confession of said Simon, messeigneurs condemn him to be consumed by flame and burned [*ars et brulé*] by the sergeant of high justice [i.e. the executioner] near the place of justice of said city, until death and that he should be burned and consumed by flame into dust, and also order that said mare be consumed by flame and burned next to said Simon and said place of justice, and consumed into dust so that never shall there be memory of said Simon nor of said mare.

In attendance at the execution of Simon and the mare were some five to six thousand spectators, who watched as the great bell in the church belfry tolled to mark the occasion.[63]

So here we have a crime that was, by contemporary standards, so horrible and unnatural that one dared not mention it, and yet the punishment of the crime was so public, so spectacular, that this unmentionable crime could not help being—for lack of a better word—advertised by its punishment. Clearly, in the punishment of bestiality, as for the punishment of sodomy in general, the need to overcome the atrocity of the act took precedence over the need not to publicize something that people dared not mention. In fact, the necessity of overcoming the crime itself through a spectacle of closure was so important that it could take place even in the absence of one of the principal actors—even if, in other words, an effigy had to be used in the place of one half of the illicit couple. In 1606, in the town of Chartres, a dog and a man were tried and convicted of sodomy. But whereas the dog participated physically in the execution, the man was tried in absentia and an effigy of him was burned together with his canine co-conspirator:

> For reparation and punishment of the crime we condemn the said Guyard to be hanged and strangled on the gallows which will be erected for this purpose at the corral of the horses' market in said city of Chartres....And prior to said execution of death, the said dog will be felled by the executioner of high justice in said place, and the dead bodies, both of said Guyard and of said dog burned and reduced to ashes if the said Guyard can be taken and apprehended in his person, and if not with respect to said Guyard, the sentence will be executed in effigy by a portrait which will be attached to said gallows, and we will declare each and all of his possessions acquired and confiscated...[64]

We can now see that, within the context of the medieval and early modern ritual of punishment, the only thing that was extraordinary about the Sow of Falaise, the story with which this book began, was what later historians made of it. As with the punishment of effigies and cadavers, the punishment of animals made perfect sense at the time. If a crime had been committed, then the law required that a punishment be performed. Ideally, no doubt, the punishment would be performed on a live human body. Failing that, a dead body, the representation of a body, or an animal body would do.

The punishment of animals was a fact of pre-modern justice, just as the crimes committed by animals were a fact of pre-modern life. E. P. Evans's *The Criminal Prosecution and Capital Punishment of Animals* documents nearly one hundred cases of animals executed in France between the thirteenth and the seventeenth centuries for the crimes of homicide and sexual relations with people.[65] But Evans's history, which remains the most complete account of animal executions in Europe despite its having been published more than a century ago, is surely incomplete; not only does it omit animal executions cited in other sources but it does not include those trials and executions of animals whose records were burned, and of which no trace remains.

In a sense, it misses the point to count the number of animal executions, just as it would be pointless to count the number of bodies executed in effigy or after death. Suffice to say that in many regions of France—not to mention parts of present-day Belgium, Switzerland, and Germany—whenever a crime was committed by an animal, the animal was punished. The same standards were applied to crimes involving animals as to human crimes: official investigations were undertaken to ascertain the facts of the case, and to identify the party or parties responsible; once suspects were identified, guilt was by no means a foregone conclusion. In a case of homicide involving a sow and her piglets, for example, several of the piglets were exonerated as it could not be definitively proved that they had participated in the crime.[66] Animals who had committed crimes but had fled the jurisdiction before they could be apprehended were punished in effigy, no different from any other criminal who had fled the scene.[67] To read deterrence into the punishment of an animal in effigy would be, it seems to me, not only difficult but far-fetched.

Animals were punished in pre-modern Europe not because anyone thought that animals "intended" to commit the crime, but because the origin of the ritual of punishment went back to a time before intent had been made a fundamental part of penal practice. As we have seen, Salic law had been infinitely more interested in compensating for damages than in punishing intent. While this compensation had usually been in the form of monetary fines, on occasion the offender had been required to "pay with his life," especially if the offender was a slave without material assets. As French law gradually moved away from compensation toward the public, corporal punishment of criminal intent, strange hybrids appeared that seemed to incorporate elements of both legal paradigms. To cite an example, the *Très Ancien Coutumier*, compiled around 1200, had decreed the death penalty for a serf who killed his lord accidentally.[68] In this case the disparity of the offender and the victim created what we might call an "atrocity" that needed redressing, setting right, regardless of what criminal theories of intent were beginning to say. Atrocious crimes without intent demanded public punishment not as an example, but as a kind of public ritual of overcoming, and it is in an analogous sense that I think we must understand the punishment of animals: as the righting, the overcoming, of an atrocity.[69]

The public execution of animals, therefore, could only have originated *after* theories of compensation had been largely abandoned (and Salic law did not, incidentally, punish animals, but instead fined their owners who made compensation on their behalf) and *before* a Roman theory of criminal intent and malice aforethought had come to monopolize legal thinking. If a crime had been committed, it had to be punished, and punishment took the form of the established penal ritual, regardless of whether the criminal was human or animal, dead or alive, present or represented.

RECONCILING THE IRRECONCILABLE: SIXTEENTH-CENTURY JURISTS ON CUSTOMARY PRACTICE AND DETERRENCE THEORY

Although animal punishments were performed through the seventeenth century (and even, occasionally, as late as the eighteenth), jurists were keenly aware of the problem that these executions posed for contemporary legal theories of culpability as well as penal theories of exemplary deterrence. Even as early as 1285, Philippe de Beaumanoir, who compiled a list of the customs in the Beauvaisis region but who, as we have seen, had been influenced by the renaissance in Roman legal studies, declared that the common practice of punishing animals made little sense, at least from the vantage point of criminal intent:

> Some individuals who have [the right of] justice in their land bring animals to justice when they kill someone—such as when a sow kills a child, he draws and hangs her, or another beast. But this is senseless [*mes c'est nient a fere*] because dumb beasts have no understanding of what is good and what is evil, and for this reason it is justice lost because justice must be done to avenge a misdeed and so that he who has done the misdeed knows and understands that for this misdeed he has incurred this penalty; but such understanding does not exist among dumb beasts, and therefore he who, according to justice, puts a dumb beast to death for a misdeed has involved himself in the matter for no purpose [*se melle il de nient*].[70]

These words by Beaumanoir represent one of the few explicit references to animal punishments among French customals. On the surface, it seems strange that customals shied away from discussing the common custom of punishing animals when the ostensible purpose of these texts was to offer a compilation of traditional customs; after all, almost every other imaginable offense and its corresponding punishment found a place in the customals. It would seem, however, that the increasing tendency to define criminal offenses as an act involving malicious intent, and the corresponding tendency to see punishment as a means of deterring malice by example, combined to make the very existence of animal punishments a logical affront to contemporary juridical sensibilities.

Only in the fifteenth and early sixteenth century, when it became common to publish court decisions and arrêts, do we find animal punishments mentioned, but only as a point of fact, and usually without much in the way of commentary.[71] In the last half of the sixteenth century, however, an intellectual revolution took place that would prompt a critical reassessment of the relevance of classical Roman law to a French nation separated geographically, culturally, and chronologically from ancient Rome, and this intellectual movement would prompt a renewed interest in native French customary penal practices. It was within this context that animal trials were finally discussed explicitly in juridical texts, more or less for the first time since Beaumanoir.

In the sixteenth century, several scholars took aim at Europe's long infatuation with the *Corpus Iuris Civilis*, seeing it not as a fount of universal legal knowledge, as previous generations of jurists had seen it, but as a historical document that was the product of a specific time and place. Among the earliest of these scholars was Guillaume Budé who, around the turn of the sixteenth century, embarked upon a textual analysis of Roman laws, and concluded that those who had originally compiled the *Corpus Iuris Civilis* had irreparably distorted Roman legal texts, and that every successive gloss was simply compounding nonsense.[72] Several decades later, François Hotman pushed many of Budé's findings to a logical conclusion, not only joining him in his critique of Justinian's compilation of Roman law, but taking aim at generations of jurists who had so slavishly followed what they thought was Roman law. Moreover, Hotman declared that the example of ancient Rome had "no value" for sixteenth-century France for the simple reason that "these two commonwealths are not in any way alike."[73] Instead, Hotman and others like him insisted on the relevance of traditional French customary laws. In the words of the sixteenth-century jurist François Baudouin, "Base it is...to know nothing of the law in which we dwell. But baser still by far to seem like strangers in our country and our home."[74]

It is at this moment in time, within the context of a celebration of French customs at the expense of "foreign" influence, that we find in Jean Duret's *Traicté des peines et amendes*, first published in 1573, not only one of the first explicit references to animal executions since Beaumanoir's but also, in contrast to the earlier jurist, an attempt to defend their rationale:

> If animals do not simply wound but kill or eat [people], such as experience has shown us [in the case of] small children eaten by pigs, they forfeit their life [*la mort y eschet*] and they are condemned to be hanged and strangled as if they were possessed of reason, in order to erase the memory of the enormity of the deed.[75]

Even in this short passage, we can glimpse both a sensitivity to a ritual that seeks to overcome the horror of the crime rather than simply deter, as well as a tacit acknowledgment, with the phrase "as if they were possessed of reason," that a core principle of the contemporary understanding of crime was *reasoned* intent.

A contemporary of Hotman, Jean Bodin was beginning to formulate an approach to the historical study of law that would find a compromise between earlier scholars' uncritical acceptance of the authority of Roman law, on the one hand, and the more recent championing of customary law, on the other. While he, too, criticized the *Corpus Iuris Civilis*, writing that those responsible for its compilation had "muddied the sources of law to such an extent that one can barely extract anything that is not soiled with mud and excrement,"[76] Bodin nevertheless advocated the synthesis of French customary law with the "best" laws from other times and places, including Roman law.

Informing Bodin's intellectual position was a preconception that underlying all the apparent differences and even contradictions among the laws of the many peoples of the earth was a hidden universal law that gave coherence to the apparent disunity. His belief in these universal legal principles gave rise to a desire on Bodin's part to synthesize the particular and the abstract, the practice and the theory of law, regardless of their apparent contradictions. The best jurisprudence, he argued, demanded a willingness to reconcile the customs and practices of the age with the eternal laws of all ages. This did not mean changing existing laws and customs so that they would conform to eternal laws; rather, it meant finding the kernel of "reason" that these existing customs held within them.

It was ideas such as these that prompted a generation of legal scholars to endeavor to find the kernel of reason within the executions of animals (along with dead bodies and effigies), and to undertake the unenviable (and impossible) task of reconciling these punishments with the principles of exemplary deterrence. While Bodin himself never weighed in on this particular subject, Pierre Ayrault did. He was Bodin's contemporary and, like him, both a native of the town of Angers and a practicing jurist as well as a scholar of law. In a 1576 text, which reads almost as if

Bodin could have written it, Ayrault sought to synthesize contemporary French legal customs and practices with the "best" practices of classical jurisprudence, among which was the principle of exemplary deterrence: "Justice in all its forms of execution tends more toward example than toward punishment.... *Exempla sunt omnium tormenta paucorum* [The torments of the few are the examples of the many], says Saint Cyprian: & for this reason the Latins called even he who was punished and executed *Exemplum*."[77]

But it would not be until several years later that Ayrault decided to tackle the thorny issue of the punishment of inanimate and inhuman bodies head on, in an essay entitled "Des procès faits aux cadavres, à la mémoire, aux bestes brutes, choses inanimées et aux contumax" [1591] ("Trials against cadavers, the memory (of dead people), brute animals, inanimate things and (defendants) in absentia"). As Ayrault readily admitted at the very beginning of the essay, the punishment of dead bodies seemed, at least on the surface, to be patently silly and pointless:

> Let us see, first of all, before entering into formalities, if it is not entirely ridiculous and idiotic [*inepte*], even cruel, even barbarous, to do battle against shadows, which is to say to cite and call to justice that which cannot in truth appear nor defend itself, and where there is neither crime, nor correction, nor gain to be had.[78]

Indeed, from the perspective of Roman jurisprudence, there were many aspects of contemporary penal practice that, Ayrault admitted, seemed silly:

> What gain or what example could there be in dragging armorial bearings on the ground, in throwing ashes to the wind & (something even more barbarous) in seizing hold of or decapitating a dead body. Even a bear does not assault the dead...said Aesop.
>
> What good are these trials, then, without the accused, these judgments, without examples. If the Romans, so as not to fall into such absurdities and mockeries, made it through a long stretch of time without thinking it a good idea even to try people in absentia (but having, in the end, accepted the idea, never condemned them to death), would there be any apparent purpose [*apparance*] in practicing [trials and executions] against the dead? And, even more so, [to prosecute and execute] animals, who have— neither dead or alive—any will or intention to do evil? Do we want to be like Xerxes who gave blows of the whip to the sea & who wrote letters to the Athos mountain as if it could give him a response?[79]

Ayrault did not, however, advocate the abolition of these "absurdities," but rather, like Bodin, sought to find the kernel of reason and universal legal principles (read: exemplary deterrence) that lay within these ostensibly "ridiculous and idiotic" penal practices. In the following passage, the modern reader almost feels sorry for Ayrault as he valiantly struggles to force the square peg of deterrence theory into the round hole of animal executions:

> The principal aim of justice is example.... If we see a pig hanged and strangled for having eaten a child (a punishment which is familiar to us), it is to induce fathers & mothers, nursemaids, servants not to leave their children all alone, or to lock up their animals well so that they cannot injure or harm [the children]. If we see an ox stoned to death & its flesh thrown to dogs for homicide, & if we see a hive of honeybees

burned for the same reason, it is in order to make us abhor homicide, since it is punished in brute animals.[80]

In a similar fashion, despite the fact that he himself had questioned whether the execution of cadavers was not "barbarous," Ayrault nevertheless endeavored to reconcile the practice with the theory of exemplary deterrence:

> In all accusations or punishments one seeks primarily [to set] an example: an example, I say, for the survivors & those who have not committed a crime, not for those who are beyond remedy. Following this line of reasoning (*which is general and universal*) that which has been done to the dead was done for [the benefit of] the living.... [An] execution performed on those who have neither feeling nor [possibility] of improvement has an effect upon [*redonde*] those who still have them.[81]

That said, Ayrault cannot quite help admitting that, if it were up to him, "I would rather bury [the body] without ceremony…".[82]

Although the rise of spectacular punishment was largely inspired by Roman legal theories of exemplary deterrence, public executions gradually coalesced into a ritual that was more indebted to the practice of public penance in the early Middle Ages (and to a lesser extent to earlier practices of corporal compensation) than to anything in ancient Rome. Far from being "terrified" by the example of what they saw, audiences willingly participated in public executions as a means of overcoming the fact of the crime itself and healing from the wound inflicted by the offense. Public executions were, at least until the dawn of the early modern period, experienced as a spiritually moving ritual, with witnesses frequently praying, singing, and crying along with the condemned. Even in the case of executions of justice in which the offender was merely humiliated or banished rather than killed, the ritual had more to do with the marginalization of the criminal and the reaffirmation of social norms than with exemplary deterrence. The importance of the ritual itself, quite apart from any deterrent message, can be seen in the absolute necessity of public execution even in the absence of a live, human body.

When jurists like Bodin and Ayrault, writing at the dawn of the early modern age, went to great lengths to read deterrence into rituals that were so clearly about something very different, they exemplified a trend that has only increased over time: a willful desire to see exemplary deterrence as a universal principle of both the theory and practice of justice, even in the face of all evidence to the contrary. As we will see in the following chapters, when the ritual of execution began to attract a new kind of spectator—people who were eager to watch executions more as a form of entertainment than out of a desire to participate in a communal ritual—jurists would continue to cling to the idea that the primary purpose of punishment was to set an example and strike fear in the hearts of spectators.

PART III

SPECTATORS AND SPECTACLE

5

From Ritual to Spectacle
The Rise of the Penal Voyeur in Early Modern France

Although the seventeenth and eighteenth centuries undoubtedly mark the high point of a public fascination with watching executions, there is no question that there was a good deal of interest in executions long before the eighteenth century. Specific figures with respect to attendance are hard to come by, and when the sources do mention a number, common sense would seem to dictate that it be taken with a grain of salt. One chronicler, for example, ventured to guess that some two hundred thousand people turned out to watch the execution of the Comte de Saint Pol for treason in 1475—an unlikely figure given that it would seem to exceed most estimates of the entire population of Paris at the time.[1]

What does seem clear, however, is that executions consistently drew crowds throughout much of the late medieval and early modern periods. Beneath what would appear to be a relatively constant viewership and a more or less unchanging penal practice, however, profound transformations were taking shape in the way people watched executions. Prior to the middle of the sixteenth century, those who attended executions—I will resist calling them "spectators"—did so largely out of a sincere desire to participate in a ceremony that held profound personal meaning for them, and not because they wanted to gawk from a distance at the suffering of others. These were less "spectacles" in the way that we understand the word today than they were rituals in which those who attended saw themselves as full participants rather than onlookers. When, as was usually the case, the condemned participated fully in the ritual of repentance, seeking forgiveness from divine and earthly authorities, witnesses usually bridged the physical distance between themselves and the patient through prayer, tears, and empathy. The public transformation of the condemned criminal into a repentant sinner enabled the entire community to undergo a kind of healing that many experienced as profoundly beautiful and uplifting. On those occasions when the crime was particularly egregious or when the condemned refused to play the role of repentant sinner, however, crowds still managed to participate in the ritual of execution by venting their rage on the condemned, transgressing the physical distance between them by hurled objects, shouted insults, and even direct blows.[2]

Beginning around the second decade of the sixteenth century, certain novelties emerged in the viewing habits of some of the individuals who attended executions. While many people continued to participate in the ritual of execution in the traditional manner, others began to experience executions in profoundly new ways: as a form of spectacle in which one could watch the suffering of another out of simple curiosity and without actually taking part or sharing in the traditional communal ritual of healing and redemption. These new spectators began snapping up prime viewing spots from which to watch noteworthy executions unfold, often bidding up the price of windows overlooking the scaffold to exorbitant sums.

There was a certain amount of variation among these new penal voyeurs: some watched with an almost clinical detachment, while others seemed to revel in the dramatic tragedy of the scene unfolding before them. But whether they watched coldly or with the delightful frisson that came with watching a real-life tragedy being played out before their eyes, they expressed, by modern standards, remarkably little sympathy for the actual person being executed. This chapter explores the new voyeuristic ways of watching during that window of time when one could appreciate the spectacle of execution with no compunction whatsoever, a window that would be slammed shut in the eighteenth century, when marked changes in the culture of sentiment would spell the end of this unselfconscious fascination with the sufferings of others.

WATCHING EXECUTIONS BEFORE THE SIXTEENTH CENTURY

In contrast to the abundance of first-hand accounts of executions in later periods, descriptions of executions prior to the mid-sixteenth century are relatively scarce. The historian Claude Gauvard has counted approximately one hundred such accounts for the entire period from the beginning of the fourteenth through the fifteenth century, roughly one quarter of which are to be found in the same text, *Journal d'un bourgeois de Paris*, which covers the period from 1405 to 1449.[3] Gauvard has suggested that there are so few accounts of these early executions because they happened so frequently and in so many places that they were hardly worthy of notice; executions were, in other words, simply part of the fabric of life in the late Middle Ages, and one took notice of them only when something strange happened, something that would make them stand apart from the normal and the banal.

I think Gauvard is right to suggest that those executions discussed in detail are the ones that somehow defied normal expectations. Indeed, many accounts of executions are to be found in chronicles that list various unexpected, surprising, and odd phenomena such as earthquakes, bolts of lightning, and monstrosities. Within this context, it must have made sense to include unusual or odd executions. When, for example, Pierre des Essarts, superintendent of finances under Charles VI, was executed in 1413, the fact of his execution might have merited a brief mention in a chronicle because of his importance, but it was his strange behavior that prompted the author of *Journal d'un bourgeois de Paris* to narrate what actually transpired on the scaffold: "[The condemned] never stopped laughing..., so that most people took him for a madman, and all those who saw him wept so piteously that you will never hear of more tears [shed] for the death of a man, and he, all alone, kept laughing...."[4] The odd behavior of the condemned made the execution stand out, made it memorable, and therefore fit to be included in a text that chronicled the notable and the unusual. Just as these chronicles would have passed over ordinary weather in silence but had quite a bit to say about extraordinary weather events, so too did they forsake run-of-the-mill executions for those that defied expectations—those, for example, in which the condemned criminal was spared at the last minute by a broken rope or by a woman who offered to marry him (an act which, by custom, demanded that the condemned be released).[5]

Gauvard is, therefore, right to point out that pre-sixteenth-century sources focus on unusual executions. But her suggestion that ordinary executions are not mentioned because they are banal is, I suspect, not right. The difference between executions that escaped narration and those that are chronicled lies less in the difference between the banal and the unusual than in the difference between ritual and spectacle. What I would like to suggest is that those executions that proceeded as planned were important rituals which, at least up through the turn of the sixteenth century, seemed ill-suited to narration. Even if elements of spectacle had increasingly been incorporated into punishment after the thirteenth century for the express purpose of making them serve the interests of exemplary deterrence, those who attended executions seem to have been oblivious to these intentions, and instead experienced executions as a variation on traditional public penance. Executions, in short, were rituals in which one took part and that most likely elicited strong emotions, but one would have been no more likely to describe them than to narrate the moment of Eucharistic transubstantiation during a church service, an event that, although it occurred routinely, can hardly be described as banal. Interruptions or unusual behavior in the course of executions, like the laughing des Essarts, had the effect of transforming an execution from ordinary ritual into an extraordinary event, something akin, perhaps, to dropping the consecrated Host in the middle of Communion. Like any other unusual event, it demanded chronicling, but the ritual that it interrupted was by no means banal.

If we look at some of the accounts of executions prior to the mid-sixteenth century that do exist, we can see that very few of them actually contain any information at all about what transpired on the scaffold, betraying a clear reluctance to narrate the moment of execution itself. Writers often provided detailed descriptions of what happened *before* the execution, frequently spelling out exactly what the court sentence or *arrêt* stipulated in terms of the precise punishments that were about to take place. But at the moment of execution, in account after account, we encounter something of a narrative black hole in which we are told simply that the sentence was performed. Almost nothing is mentioned concerning the size of the crowds, the behavior of the condemned, or the reaction of those who attended; little or nothing is said about any last words that might have been spoken or about the actions of the executioner. No sooner, however, do we pass the moment in the text when the sentence has been executed than the narrative resumes, providing details of what happened to the corpse of the condemned after the execution.

Accounts of executions, in short, narrated *around* the moment of execution. In the following description, for example, of the 1409 execution of Jean Montaigu, grand master of the king's household, although the author goes to great lengths to describe the outfit worn by the condemned as he made his way to the scaffold, and provides details about Montaigu's body immediately after the execution, the execution itself gets decidedly short shrift:

> The seventeenth day of said month of October [1409], [Montaigu]...was put in a cart, dressed in his livery, a greatcoat of white and red, with a like hood, one stocking red and the other white, gilded spurs, his hands tied in front of him, a wooden cross between his hands, sitting high in the cart, two trumpets preceding him, and in this state was led to [Les] Halles. There his head was cut off, after which the body was brought to the gibbet of Paris, and hanged from the highest, in shirtsleeves, with stockings and gilded spurs...[6]

In contrast to the extended description of the outfit worn by Montaigu, both living and dead, the simple description "his head was cut off" is remarkably terse. There is no description of the crowd's reaction, no description of Montaigu's mood, no account of any words he may have spoken on the scaffold, and no report of the executioner's actions or demeanor.[7]

More than a century later, in a different anonymous chronicle with the same title, *Journal d'un bourgeois de Paris*, accounts of executions tend to follow more or less the same pattern. Many of the accounts are simply summations of the court sentence, ending with the simple phrase letting us know that justice was done: "*ce qui fut fait*—which [sentence] was carried out." Here is a typical example:

> In the said year [1524], Saturday the twentieth of August, master Jacques Fleury, who was a student in Paris, was hanged and strangled, having been a murderer, rapist of girls and women, and a thief. [He] was taken at d'Estrepigny, near Gisors in Normandy...and was condemned to be hanged and strangled on the Place Maubert in Paris, on the gallows, and then taken down and his body cut in four quarters and put at the four gates of the University of Paris and his head put on the gallows; which [sentence] was carried out the same day [*ce qui fut faict*].[8]

We might assume that this particular author was acquainted with the court sentence but simply did not have sufficient details to provide much information about what transpired on the scaffold, other than the fact that the execution was carried out. But the pattern is nearly ubiquitous in texts of the period, and does not appear to change with respect to the absence or presence of the author at executions. Standing out as exceptions to this general rule are narratives of executions that were unexpectedly interrupted. Here is an example from the sixteenth-century *Journal d'un bourgeois de Paris*, which tellingly had no difficulty giving details about an execution that, in the end, did not take place:

> In the said year fifteen hundred and twenty-three, Tuesday the seventeenth of February, the criminal sentence was pronounced against monsieur de Saint Vallier, in the court of Parlement;...he was condemned to be decapitated on the place de Grève in Paris, on a scaffold, and all his goods confiscated by the King.... This same day, after [the sentence] had been pronounced, he was led after dinner on horseback, bare-headed and his hands tied, being in a woolen robe with fox fur trim, to

the place de Grève, and had behind him an archer of the city, on the same horse, who held him from behind because he was weak as a result of not eating or drinking since the pronouncement of his sentence due to unhappiness. A doctor in theology named monsieur Merlin had been given to him for confession ... as he was led to the scaffold which had been prepared on the said place de Grève; there were ... [many officials] ... and a great number of people along the streets and at the [place de] Grève.

Arriving at the [place de] Grève, he was delivered into the hands of two executioners, one named Rotillon, the other named Macé, who took him and put him in a doublet, and in this state he was put on the scaffold, being still bare-headed with his hands tied, and this being done, they put him on his knees, to beg pardon of God and of justice, and [he] was ready to receive death and he was surely expecting it; and after there was a space of time of about an hour, he was given a stool to lean against the scaffold, still bare-headed, where he prayed to God, awaiting the hour of his death; after which, came by horseback one of the servants of the chancellor, who was then in Paris, who began to shout in a loud voice, saying "Holla, holla; Stop, stop. Here is the [letter of] remission from the King." ... He immediately thanked God and kissed the scaffold twice, making a sign of the cross many times. This done, [he] was brought back on horseback to the Conciergerie, more happy than when he had left...."[9]

Here, in contrast to most other accounts, the author provides a wealth of information about what took place on the scaffold in the course of an execution that never came to pass. Interrupted ritual became a kind of spectacle, something one could watch with a sense of curiosity, something one could narrate.

Apart from executions that, for one reason or another, were not actually carried out, detailed accounts of executions that did in fact take place are exceedingly rare, but they do exist. A text that has come to be known as the *Chronique scandaleuse*, attributed to Jean de Troyes, includes an account of the execution in 1475 of Louis de Luxembourg, Comte de Saint Pol, for the crime of lèse-majesté, in which full details are given about what took place as the execution was performed. The account begins with the usual attention to details concerning the journey to the scaffold, and the performance of the amende honorable, but then, at the moment when we might expect to be told simply that the sentence had been executed, the author gives us an unusually detailed, blow-by-blow account of the execution:

> He went down on his knees before the little scaffold, and turned his face, and his two knees forming an arrow, toward Notre Dame, in order to give his speech, which he did for a rather long time, with sorrowful tears and great contrition, always with the cross before his eyes, which was held for him by master Jehan Sordun, which cross he kissed often and with great reverence, and very pitifully crying.
>
> And after said speech was finished, and he had raised himself to his feet, Petit Jehan, son of Henry Cousin, then master executioner of high justice, came to him, bringing a medium-sized rope with which he tied the hands of said Saint Pol, which he suffered rather benignly. And after, said Petit Jehan led him up the said little scaffold, upon which he stopped, and turned his face toward [many officers of] ... the King, our sire, who were there in great number, begging forgiveness of the king to them, and asking them to recommend his soul.... And also turned toward the people ... begging them

also to pray for his soul; and then he got down on his knees... where he was diligently blindfolded by said Petit Jean, [and he was] still speaking to God and to his confessors, and frequently kissing the cross. And forthwith, said Petit Jehan seized his sword which his father had loaned to him, with which he made the head fly off from the shoulders so quickly and so mortally that [Saint Pol's] body fell to the ground at the same time as the head, which head was immediately taken by the hair by said Petit Jehan, and washed in a bucket of water that was nearby, and then put on the supports of said little scaffold, and shown to the onlookers [*regardants*] of said execution, who numbered very well two hundred thousand people or more.[10]

This account of Saint Pol's execution, so unusual in its explicit detail, is the exception that proves the rule. Perhaps the author saw fit to narrate the details because of the extraordinary number of people attending, or perhaps due to Saint Pol's prominence. Whatever the reason, the importance of this account lies less in what it tells us about this particular execution than in its revealing what is missing from so many of the other accounts: all the details that are hidden beneath the blanket phrase *ce qui fut fait*, those ubiquitous, euphemistic four words, which function as a narrative ellipsis.

SPECTACULAR NOVELTIES

Beginning in the 1520s, something changed. Up until this time, there had always been a question as to whether condemned criminals would, so to speak, go with the script, admitting their crimes and begging forgiveness of God, the king, and justice. Repentance, although very strongly encouraged, could not exactly be forced, particularly for criminals who had already been sentenced to death and had nothing to lose by refusing to play along. Although most condemned criminals do indeed seem to have chosen repentance, there were rare occasions when individuals adamantly refused to repent, thereby depriving the community of its ritual of atonement and redemption.[11] In the 1520s, however, a new kind of condemned criminal came on the scene. Lutherans who had been condemned as heretics began showing up at the scaffold, and rather than being pitifully repentant or obstinately unrepentant they tended to be perplexingly joyful—an attitude for which no one seemed quite prepared.

News traveled quickly of the early executions of Lutherans outside of France, and of their odd behavior at executions. The author of the early sixteenth-century *Journal d'un bourgeois de Paris*, normally someone who avoided details about executions, could not help repeating the news that when three Lutherans were executed by the authorities in Antwerp in 1523, "two of them were burned in a fire, and as they were being put into it, they joyfully sang *Te Deum laudamus*, but the third repented."[12] Almost from this moment forward, people became fixated on the behavior of condemned Protestants at the moment of execution. The essential question on everyone's mind was whether these heretics would, at the last moment, repent (and therefore fit the traditional model of the condemned criminal as repentant sinner), or whether, on the contrary, they would remain steadfast in their heretical convictions and proceed unrepentant and even joyful to the scaffold, thereby defying convention.

In 1525, when Lutherans began to be condemned and executed in France itself, chroniclers, like everyone else, found themselves drawn to the moment of execution, inevitably commenting on whether the condemned had, in the last instant, repented or not. Such comments mark the beginning of a systematic incursion into what had previously been a space that lay beyond the realm of narrative representation. Perhaps it was the oddity of the Lutheran's joyful march to death that first attracted the attention of chroniclers. Or perhaps it was the fact that their refusal to participate in a ceremony of communal redemption effectively short-circuited the ceremony, thereby making the event something that could be narrated as spectacle rather than experienced as ritual. What is clear, however, is that from the 1520s onward, the executions of condemned Protestants were no longer something that could merely be summarized by the traditional, terse assurance that justice had been done.

Predictably enough, authors who were hostile to Lutherans tended to report events rather differently from those who were sympathetic. Those who supported the repression of Lutherans tended to dwell on their executions only if they ended in sincere repentance and a return to the Catholic fold. In 1525, for example, the *Journal d'un bourgeois de Paris* offers the following account of a Lutheran who repented at the stake:

> A young man of about twenty-eight, with a degree in law... was led by the executioner in a tumbrel before the church of Notre Dame de Paris and before the church of Saint Geneviève, by order of the court, where he performed the amende honorable, begging forgiveness of God, of the Virgin Mary and of Saint Geneviève—this, because he had held the doctrine of Luther and said blasphemous things about [*mesdit*] God, Our Lady, and the Saints of Paradise. From there, he was led to the place Maubert where he had his tongue pierced, and was then strangled and burned, dying nonetheless very repentant and recognizing having well deserved death.[13]

When, however, the heretic proved unrepentant, the anonymous bourgeois de Paris reverted to the default mode in which very little was mentioned about the execution. In 1526, for example, when a Lutheran could not be made to perform the amende honorable because "he was saying he had done no wrong," we are told simply the fact that he was burned at the Place de Grève, and that despite the best efforts of his confessor, he "died in this error."[14]

Another interesting example of a contemporary author's account of an unrepentant Lutheran is the case of Louis Berquin in 1529. Berquin had translated Luther and Erasmus into French and was initially sentenced by the Parlement to perform an amende honorable, to participate in the public burning of his writings, and to be confined with only bread and water for the rest of his days. Berquin made the mistake of appealing his case or, more probably, he sought to provoke the authorities. In any event, he lost his appeal, and was subsequently sentenced to death. In the following description, the author provides numerous details about Berquin's performance of the amende honorable and his exhibition at the pillory;

once Berquin's appeal prompts the authorities to change his sentence to burning at the stake, however, the free-flowing narrative abruptly stops, and the execution of his death sentence is reported in the traditional, terse form:

> Friday the 16th day of April [1529] after Easter, Louis Berquin, squire, seigneur of said place, who because of his heresy was condemned to perform an amende honorable before the church of Notre Dame de Paris, a torch in his hand, and there to beg forgiveness of God and of the Virgin Mary for the books that he produced and which he wanted to use against our faith, and from there [was condemned to be] led to the place de Grève, and put upon a scaffold so that said Berquin could be shown, so that all could see him, and before him a great fire made in order to burn all said books in his presence, so that there would never be any knowledge or memory of them; and then led into a tumbrel to take a turn in the pillory and there to have his tongue pierced and a fleur de lys [branded] on his forehead, and then sent to the prisons of monsieur de Paris to live out the rest of his life. And to see the said execution [of the amende honorable, book burning, and pillory] as Berquin was leaving the Palais [where he was being held] were more than twenty thousand people. And he, having been thus condemned, appealed to the court of Rome and to the Grand Council, and for that reason by order of the court of Parlement, the following day... was condemned to be put in a tumbrel and led to [the place de] Grève and to be burned, which was done [*ce qui fut faict*] on the year and day stated.[15]

As for those sympathetic to the Lutherans, whenever the condemned went to the execution unrepentant and steadfast in their unwavering devotion to the "true religion," authors tended to dwell on the execution, providing ample details about the condemned's demeanor and the mood of the crowd, etcetera. Here, for example, is an account in a later Protestant text of Berquin's execution:

> Berquin, upon leaving the prison, gave no indication of a faint or troubled heart when the executioner read aloud the court order in a horrible voice, nor when he was led to the ordained place for the final punishment where, upon arrival, he spoke to the people; but there were few who could hear him, so great was the noise and tumult of those who had been posted there by the Sorbonnists in order to make noise, so that the voice of this sainted Martyr of the Lord was not heard on the threshold of his death. His Sorbonnic enemies & Monks not sated by the cruel punishment of this noble personage, stirred up little children to scream in the streets that Berquin was a heretic: so great was the rage of these supporters of Satan...[16]

This passage comes from Jean Crespin's *Histoire des martyrs persecutéz et mis à mort pour la vérité de l'Evangile*, first published in 1554 in Geneva, where Crespin had sought refuge. As the title suggests, the entire point of Crespin's work was to focus on the moment of execution of Protestant martyrs, and to draw the connection between contemporary executions and the executions of the first Christian martyrs in Roman times.[17]

Similarly skewed accounts were given of the execution of Alexandre Canu in 1534, who was burned at the stake for heresy. One author reported that Canu was able to give "a little harangue" before his death, which, although it started well enough, ended up being "not worth very much," and so the authorities cut it short and proceeded to the execution, whereupon the condemned kept screaming "Jesus" even while he was in the fire.[18] According to Crespin, however, Canu preached to the crowds the entire journey from the prison to the place of execution on the Place Maubert, and many said "that he was wrongly being put to death." In contrast to the "little harangue" that was abruptly cut off in the above account, Crespin's version of events has Canu delivering a sermon that was "excellent and marvelously effective, and which lasted a rather long time." In fact, Crespin claimed to offer the extended oration word-for-word in his text (some twenty years after the fact).[19]

Beginning in the 1520s, therefore, the traditional reserve associated with the narration of the ritual of execution began to disappear. By alternately reading Catholic texts of repentant heretics and Protestants accounts of steadfast martyrs, we can begin to get a fairly detailed description of most executions for heresy in the early sixteenth century. Given the ways in which these executions became a kind of moral battleground between Catholicism and Protestantism, people began to attend them for reasons other than the time-honored practice of communal redemption. People came, in short, to see what would happen: would the condemned repent or not? As the historian David Nicholls writes, crowds were "drawn to the burning of heretics by curiosity; they were novelties, and people wished to see how this new kind of criminal faced death."[20] As one contemporary put it, spectators in Agen had come to watch an execution in 1539 "as something novel [*comme chose nouvelle*]."[21] Spectators must have also been curious about what the condemned might say, as executions afforded one of the few opportunities to hear new religious ideas without fear of putting oneself in danger. The condemned, after all, had little to lose and could say whatever he or she wished, provided of course that the authorities allowed them to be heard.

The key point is that spectators increasingly came to watch the execution of Lutherans to see, in a new kind of detached way, what might happen, rather than to participate, themselves, in a pre-scripted, traditional ceremony. According to Nicholls, however, this phase was of limited duration, and by the 1550s Lutherans and other Protestants had come to be seen less as a novel, heretical minority and more as a real religious and political enemy. By the late 1550s, unrepentant Protestants were provoking the traditional rage and vengeance that crowds normally meted out on those whom they deemed unworthy of forgiveness, signaling, at least for some, a return to a more participatory, less voyeuristic, execution ritual, albeit with negative rather than positive emotions.[22] But something had changed in the contemporary mindset. The semi-sacred moment of death, sacrifice, and redemption whose script was known in advance had, at least briefly, been transformed into a spectacle whose outcome was not entirely certain. From the 1550s onward, it would seem that this mutation in viewing habits, this curiosity surrounding the final moments of the condemned on the scaffold, began to spread to other, more mundane, non-religious executions. A combined fascination with crime, criminals, and their punishment took hold of the French imagination, and from this point onward the simple repetition of the court sentence and the phrase "*ce qui fut fait*" would no longer suffice.

A NEW SPECTACULARITY: ANATOMY THEATERS, EXECUTIONS, AND THE DIARY OF FELIX PLATTER

In 1552, a young Swiss student by the name of Felix Platter journeyed from his home in Basel to the town of Montpellier, in the southern French region of Languedoc, to begin his studies at the prestigious medical school there. He would live in Montpellier for the next seven years, pursuing his study of medicine and joining in the general life of the town. During those years, Platter recorded his reflections on a variety of topics: everything from his life as a medical student, his relationship with his host family, his attendance at masked balls, and the comings and goings of various people in the city. Although he apparently took assiduous notes as the events were happening, the journal itself appears to be the product of some light, retrospective editing that Platter undertook half a century later (around 1612), after a successful career as a prominent physician back in Basel. Because the intervening years may very well have influenced how Platter recalled events or how he edited his original notes, his diary, although it contains fascinating information about various aspects of life in mid-sixteenth-century Europe, cannot be relied upon as a definitive, chronologically accurate source for the period it describes.[23]

Included in Platter's diary are the details of some fifteen public executions that he witnessed during his stay in Montpellier. Some of them were of Protestants who had been convicted of heresy, and like many others at the time, Platter could not help being drawn to the moment of execution: would the condemned repent or stay true to the faith? But, as a Protestant himself, Platter was understandably disturbed by these executions, and felt a great deal of sympathy for the victims. On one particularly rainy day, the executioner was having a great deal of difficulty getting a fire started underneath a Protestant that he was burning at the stake, and decided to go into the pharmacy owned by Platter's landlord in search of turpentine to get the fire going; after he had left, with turpentine in hand, Platter scolded the pharmacy employees for helping the executioner, but they promptly put him in his place: "They advised me to keep my mouth shut, because the same thing could happen to me, since I was a heretic."[24]

Platter's interest in these executions of Protestants is understandable enough; however, most of the executions that Platter discusses in his diary were for ordinary crimes, unrelated to religion. The simple fact that he recorded his reflections on these executions, sometimes in great detail, marks Platter's text as something new and unusual. While it would not have been out of the ordinary for him to record a few details about heretics or the execution of particularly prominent people, it is in fact extraordinary that he should have seen fit to write down his detailed reflections on the execution of common criminals, who had been convicted of such crimes as counterfeiting, theft, and murder.

So why would Platter record details about these sorts of executions whereas others had, up until this point, seemed unwilling or uninterested in doing so? We should not discount the possibility that his interest was fabricated retrospectively, and that he might have recalled happening upon these executions in 1552, but found them more meaningful and more interesting in retrospect than he did at the time. But it is also possible that, as a foreigner recently arrived in Montpellier, he took note of these executions at the time because of the fact that penal practices in Montpellier differed from those in his native city of Basel. Indeed, he writes that the very first moment when he had laid eyes on the city of Montpellier, in 1552, he was greeted by the, to him, strange sight of the corpses of execution victims, which had been strewn across olive trees on the outskirts of the city: "Pieces of human flesh hung from the olive trees; this sight gave me a very strange feeling."[25]

No doubt Platter took note of this sight at the time because the practice of displaying the corpses of execution victims was unfamiliar to him. Similarly, two years later, his description of a beheading and quartering suggests that at least part of his interest lay in the peculiarities of local customs compared with those in Basel: "They cut off the head upon the scaffold, and then cut off his four limbs, following the custom of the region."[26] That same year, he seemed similarly curious about an execution on a St. Andrew's cross, comparing it to executions by wheel back home:

> Behind the town trumpeters, sounding their trumpets, marched the criminal, accompanied by monks. He was a handsome young man, accomplice in a murder. He was led to a scaffold erected in front of the city hall; there two pieces of hollowed wood had been prepared in the shape of a St. Andrew's cross, upon which they were going to break his extremities. The condemned stood, recounting everything he had done in the form of a rhyme. It was very well delivered and in finishing he added [to the crowd]: "Pray to Holy Mary so that she may beg her son to take me to Paradise." The executioner undressed him, attached his arms and legs to the cross, just as in our country we tie those who are about to be broken on the wheel. After this, he took a heavy iron bar, called a *massa*, with a bit of an edge on one side, and beat his arms and legs. This resembles our punishment of the wheel, and is called there *massarrer*.[27]

Platter's detailed accounts of ordinary executions stand in marked contrast to previous accounts. While his interest in executions can be ascribed, at least to a certain extent, to the natural curiosity of a young man in a foreign country recounting things that are new and different from those back home, the detailed nature of his accounts suggests an interest that went far beyond the simple notation of differences between French and Swiss methods of execution. He had, to put it bluntly, developed a taste for executions in and of themselves. In fact he seems interested in dead bodies in general, and gives accounts of various escapades undertaken with his fellow medical students in search of cadavers to dissect. He clearly enjoyed these late-night, secret forays into graveyards, and recounts these expeditions with nostalgic glee. In the following passage, Platter confesses, with almost Frankensteinian enthusiasm, his thirst for scientific knowledge, and especially for the study of anatomy:

> I have always felt the desire to know everything about all that concerns medicine, even those aspects that many others neglect.... This desire to gain knowledge was such that, even outside of class and ordinary studies, I carefully watched the preparation of medicines in our pharmacy, something that would prove very useful to me later. I collected plants as well, which I attached to pieces of paper. But my main object of study was anatomy. Not only did I never miss attending the dissection of people or animals that

took place at the College, but I also took part in all the autopsies that were secretly practiced on cadavers, and even came to the point of holding the scalpel myself, despite the repulsion that I initially felt.[28]

His interest in anatomy was certainly not inappropriate for a medical student of the time, and Montpellier was, in fact, at the forefront of the relatively new study of human anatomy, and would become home to one of the earliest anatomy theaters in Europe.[29] But what is particularly interesting for our purposes is that, as Platter relates in the following passage from his journal, the dissection of a human cadaver attracted spectators not only from within the medical community but from the community at large:

> Beginning on 14 November [1552], in the old amphitheater, a dissection was being performed on the body of a boy who had died of an abscess in the chest (*pleuritide*). They found within the interior of the chest...only a bluish stain with neither swelling or abscess. The lung was attached in this region by ligaments that they were obliged to cut in order to remove it. Doctor Guichard presided over the anatomy session, and a barber operated. Aside from the students, there were also in attendance many persons of the nobility and of the bourgeoisie, even including some ladies, despite the fact that the autopsy was being performed on a man. There were even some monks in attendance.[30]

So, here we have a whole segment of Montpellier society interested in human anatomy: members of the nobility, the bourgeoisie, ladies, monks, and of course medical students, all gathering around the dissection of a corpse. It does not seem too much of a conceptual leap to imagine that the same crowd at the same time might have felt a similar curiosity about public executions, which also allowed spectators to look at the corpse of a stranger in a similarly theatrical setting. In fact, Platter reports in his journal that less than three years later he watched an execution in what would appear to be the same company of prominent local citizens. In July of 1555, he writes that he had dinner with a well-regarded local doctor, after which the doctor "took me to a house where there were many ladies as well as gentlemen, and from which I watched the execution."[31]

If we could completely trust the chronological accuracy of Platter's account, this would be perhaps the first written account of a new way of watching that had more in common with the way spectators observed public dissections than with the traditional manner of attending executions. Here we have, as in the case of the autopsy cited above, medical professionals as well as members of the community of a certain social standing, both "ladies as well as gentlemen," watching an execution. We are very far, here, from the concept of participatory communal redemption. After all, Platter and the others watched the execution from *inside* the house, presumably precluding any possibility of interaction with or participation in the ritual. Did this new way of watching executions as a spectacle spread from the anatomy theater to the scaffold? Or, conversely, was public interest in anatomy theaters perhaps related to the sudden interest in executions that had occurred in the wake of executions of Lutherans a few decades earlier? Or were anatomy theaters and executions both caught up in a rising tide of spectacularity? Although all of these possibilities are plausible, I suspect that this new, detached way of watching executions could not have come about were it not for the initial spectacularity of Protestant executions—those twenty-odd years in which people attended executions in order simply to see what might happen.

Platter himself had been drawn to both religious and ordinary criminal executions, albeit for very different reasons and experiencing rather different emotions at each. Whereas he had been moved by and felt sympathy for the Protestants who had been executed for heresy, he seemed to feel no particular emotions as he watched the executions of ordinary criminals. In the following entry from his diary, in which he describes the execution of a murderer in December of 1558, Platter's tone is almost clinical, not unlike the one he used to describe the dissection of the corpse quoted above:

> The guilty party, after having made a full confession, was condemned to be *massaré*.... After the reading of the judgment, the executioner had him get into a cart and he was placed on the knees of [the executioner's] wife. [The executioner] then began to torture him with red-hot pincers until they reached the house of the canon [whom he had murdered]. There [the executioner] cut off both his hands upon a chopping block that had been placed for this purpose on the cart. The [executioner's] wife blindfolded him, and as her husband cut off a hand, she would place the stump, from which a spurt of blood was escaping, into a kind of cone, which she solidly tied up to stop the hemorrhaging. He was then led to the Cour de Bayle, where he was decapitated, and cut up into four pieces, which were then hung from olive trees outside the city walls.[32]

If Platter's diaries could be trusted as unedited sources from the 1550s, then they would represent a pronounced departure from preexisting accounts (and indeed from most contemporary ones as well) not only because he wrote accounts of ordinary executions, but more particularly because of his tendency to describe these executions with a kind of objective, detached, clinical thoroughness. He was able to watch criminal executions in a way that indicates he saw himself to be absolutely *outside* the process. The spectacle might have been taking place in front of him, but he was able to observe it with a sense of critical distance; this was not a spectacle that he saw as intended for him, and not one from which he—or any of his companions in curiosity—derived any particular meaning or message.

I have no doubt that Platter describes a way of watching executions that was new. My only question is whether this way of watching first appeared, as his edited journals suggest, in the 1550s, or whether it appeared slightly later and was somehow mixed in with Platter's diary entries from the time. Although the exact date of its first appearance may be uncertain, there is no question that a new, more detached, less participatory way of watching did indeed come into existence in the second half of the sixteenth century (Fig. 7). This new way of watching most likely evolved from the initial, novel curiosity that first greeted the execution of heretics in the 1520s, but it was encouraged by an intentionally and increasingly spectacular form of punishment that practically begged for spectators. Although people would flock in ever greater numbers to these elaborately staged spectacles over the course of the early modern period, the way that they watched and the meaning

132   *Spectators and Spectacle*

Anne du Bourg Conseiller du Parlement de Paris bruslé a S.Iean en Greue le 21.Decembre 1559.

Anne du Bourg ayant esté mené sur vne charrette en la place
Sainct Iean en Greue à Paris de Ville, on luy a relevé le pourpoinct nuf
qu'à la chemise, est guindé en vne potence, là où il est estranglé,
& puis son corps jetté au feu.

Fig. 7. Execution of Anne du Bourg, 1559, reproduced in Alfred Franklin, ed., *Les Grandes Scènes historiques du XVIe siècle, reproduction fac-similé du recueil de J. Tortorel et J. Perrissin* (Paris, 1886). Note the presence of spectators in all of the windows

they derived from public executions would prove to be very different from what jurists and government officials intended.

MARKERS OF A SHIFT IN VIEWING HABITS: L'ESTOILE'S JOURNALS AND THE RISE OF CANARDS

The *Mémoires-Journaux* of Pierre de l'Estoile, which span the years 1574 to 1611, include detailed descriptions of virtually anything that L'Estoile considered to be noteworthy at the time, from affairs of state to the sighting of an armless man who could write.[33] Scattered among his journal entries are accounts of a significant number of executions, and because L'Estoile wrote for nearly forty years, we can gain an interesting perspective on how one individual's interest in executions evolved over the course of several decades at a crucial moment in the mutation of viewing habits.

The earliest executions mentioned in L'Estoile's journals are of Protestants who were condemned in 1574. These executions, unlike most of those that took place two decades earlier, are ostensibly for political crimes rather than for religious heresy, because by this point in time the Protestants represented a multifaceted threat to the Catholic monarchy, rather than a purely religious challenge. In the following account, of the execution of the Comte de Mongommeri, who had been convicted of lèse-majesté for leading Protestant forces against the king, we can see that it is not simply Mongommeri's political prominence that attracted L'Estoile's interest, but also the ever-present question of whether a Protestant would, in his final moments, repent and return to the Catholic faith:

> Saturday, the 26th of June, le comte de Mongommeri... was taken from the Conciergerie du Palais, put in a tumbrel, hands tied behind his back, with a priest and the executioner, and from there was led to the place de Grève.... [As he was] being led to the execution, he said in a loud voice that he was dying for his religion, and that he had never committed treason nor any other crime against his prince.... He did not want to confess to our Monsignor Vigor, archbishop of Narbonne... nor take or kiss the cross which we have the custom of presenting to all those who are led to the ultimate punishment; nor [did he want to] hear or look at the priest who had been put in the tumbrel next to him.... Having arrived at the scaffold, he begged the people to pray to God for him, recited aloud the Symbole, in the confession of which he protested to die. Then, having said his prayer to God in the mode of those of the [Protestant] Religion, [he] had his head cut off, which on the following Monday, the 8th of June, was put on a stake at the place de Grève and, that night, was taken down on the orders of the Queen Mother, who had attended the execution, and who was finally avenged... of the death of her husband the former king Henri...[34]

L'Estoile's interest in Montgommeri's execution seems to have been both a function of the usual interest in the final moments of Protestants on the scaffold as well as the traditional interest in the execution of people of great prominence (similar to what we saw with the execution of Saint Pol). Executions such as this one had, in short, more than one reason to attract the curious—a fact attested to by Huguenot rebel François de Bricqueville, sieur de Colombières, who, when he had refused to turn himself in along with Montgommeri in 1574, stated: "No, no... I do not have such a poltroon heart that I would surrender in order to be led to Paris and serve as a pastime and spectacle on the Place de Grève for those idiotic people...."[35]

One more thing in L'Estoile's account of Mongommeri's execution is worthy of our attention: the Queen Mother personally attended the execution. Although the attendance of royalty at executions would soon become unthinkable,[36] it would seem that, at least briefly, the royals were swept up in the vogue of attending executions. In 1582, L'Estoile reports that the king and queen watched the execution of Nicolas Salcède from a window "in a room of the Hôtel de Ville, expressly outfitted and done up for them."[37] Although it is possible that they watched this execution out of an interest in this particular case rather than out of a general interest in executions, a contemporary observer suggested that, at least for the king, the reason was the latter: "King Henry III took pleasure in watching people being hanged or put on the wheel. He always tried to see executions from some window or other."[38]

Many of the executions that L'Estoile mentions, and especially those on which he tends to dwell, involve Protestants. Unlike the execution of Montgommeri, however, many of these Protestants were convicted not of great acts of treason, but rather of ordinary criminal acts. In L'Estoile's account of a 1579 execution of a captain who had killed his wife and her lover, we can see that although the condemned remained true to his Protestant faith, he did not exactly go to his death singing hymns:

> When the court order was read to him, he said aloud that all his judges were cuckolds, and that if you looked hard at the list you wouldn't find one that wasn't, and that they were making him die because he couldn't stand to be a cuckold like them. Having arrived at the place of punishment, he did not want to be blindfolded, took the sword from the hangman, and, testing it on his finger to see if it cut well, said to the hangman, "My friend, dispatch me quickly; it all comes down to you, as your sword is a good one." And he died in this fashion, a real determined captain, having said his prayer to God aloud, in the mode of those of the [Huguenot] Religion.[39]

L'Estoile's interest in executions gradually spread from Protestants to ordinary criminals, with Protestant criminals serving as a kind of natural stepping stone. Because people had been reporting on executions of Protestants for nearly half a century by this point, L'Estoile's focus on the Protestant religion of condemned criminals allowed him a kind of alibi to recount the details of ordinary criminal executions, something that had not quite yet become commonplace.

By the 1590s, however, L'Estoile was writing accounts of criminal executions in which those put to death were Catholics, although even in these instances he tended to dwell on the subject of repentance, still perhaps seeking a kind of justification for his interest in criminal executions. In 1598, for example, L'Estoile writes of two sisters who had killed their father with the help of their lovers, who happened to be priests. Referring to the execution of one of the sisters, who was sentenced to be hanged and then burned, L'Estoile wrote that she exhibited "the most rare and steadfast resolution, contrition, and repentance of her sin, for a young girl of her age, that one had ever seen."[40]

By this point, L'Estoile had no need for the condemned to be Protestant in order to dwell on the punishment. All he really needed was a good crime to justify his interest. Although many of his earlier accounts of executions leave it unclear whether he was deriving his information from published court orders, hearsay, or personal experience, in 1600 he leaves no doubt that he was personally present, at least for the public reading, but presumably for the scene that followed as well:

> Monday, the 24th of [April], the provost-marshal of Sens was hanged at the Place de Grève. The reading aloud [of his court sentence], which I heard, carried [the words]: "For theft, murder, the rape of women and girls and other execrable crimes and excesses in great number perpetrated by him." He was also charged with having stolen from the brother of the First President, which he denied so assuredly and with such impudence that, traveling in the cart [on the way to the Grève], he cursed the Premier President, wishing aloud that he go to the Devil, adding the ugly contribution unworthy of a Christian who is going to his death: "Fuck him!" [a phrase] he repeated several times.[41]

L'Estoile's writings, therefore, serve as a kind of marker of shifting attitudes toward executions. From an interest in the execution of prominent Protestants, to an interest in Protestants who had committed crimes, by the turn of the seventeenth century L'Estoile had arrived at a more or less pure interest in the execution of people who had committed interesting crimes.

Perhaps the most concrete sign that crime and punishment were becoming the object of a novel, spectacular kind of interest was the birth of a new medium that catered to this interest. Broadsides known as *canards*, usually printed on one sheet of cheap paper with one rough-cut (and often recycled) illustration, began to focus on crimes and criminals at exactly this point in time. Canards, in some form or another, had come into existence within a generation of the invention of movable type, and from the late fifteenth century through the sixteenth had circulated sensationalized accounts of various natural disasters and miraculous phenomena. Only in 1574, however, did they begin to focus on crimes and criminals. Over the following sixty years, more than a hundred canards would be published that divulged all the "horrible" details of "scandalous" crimes to a literate and semi-literate public that proved increasingly eager to read them.[42]

For the most part, canards focused on criminals and crime rather than on executions per se. But because criminal trials in ancien régime France were secret proceedings, and because the only part of the criminal process that was visible to the public was the execution of the sentence, canards increasingly came to relate the details of executions as a kind of "last act" in the drama of a criminal's life. Conveniently, the moment of execution and, ideally, of repentance allowed canards to give all the details of sordid crimes and yet wrap everything up in a kind of cautionary morality tale.

The earliest canards focusing on crime are clearly more reticent than later ones when discussing the details of both crimes and executions. Interestingly, many of these early canards focus on crimes beyond the borders of France, in places like Naples, Switzerland, and Germany: close enough so that the obligatory assurances that the stories are absolutely true can have some credence, but far enough for readers to be titillated without being frightened. Quickly, however, their focus switched to France, and in the mid-1580s, the first canards appeared in which gallows speeches figure prominently. The first extant example of this is a canard published in 1583 that in its very title promises to tell the "bloody, cruel, and amazing story" of a woman who was driven to "inhumanely massacre her two little children and then her husband" but who delivered a "public speech on the duties of married husbands toward their wives and children." The canard is not at all unsympathetic toward the murderer, who is portrayed as having been driven to commit these horrible crimes by her husband's incessant boozing and gambling; the text claims to reproduce her entire gallows speech, in which she begs men everywhere to foreswear gambling, but when it comes to the actual moment of execution, there are only the words: "the executioner did his job."[43]

Twenty years later, in 1603, we are given a much more extensive account of the final moments of the condemned in a canard that tells the story of a brother and sister who were executed in Paris for the crimes of incest and adultery. Instead of a didactic gallows speech, however, there is a touching description of the penitence of the condemned siblings and of the crowd's pity for their fate:

The lady, addressing her brother, said, "Let us die, my brother. We have deserved it. And let us pray to God that he shows us mercy." And thus, with contrition in their hearts and confession on their lips, they were made participants in the sacrament of penance; and afterwards were conveyed in the tumbrel from there to the theater [of execution], where those who were present offered their prayers and most of their tears at [the sight] of such a piteous spectacle in which their tender youth and beauty moved even the hardest of hearts to pity.

The execution of the brother followed immediately after that of the sister:

The gentleman, kneeling down on the disgusting wet floor [of the scaffold], steaming with the blood of his sister...begged his confessor to go and console his poor father, which after having been promised to him, without being blindfolded, praying to God, he bid fall upon his neck the swift blade that he received with great steadfastness.

Lest readers got too carried away by the dramatic tragedy of it all, the canards gently brought them back to reality, assuring them that justice had been done and that "the atrocity of such enormous crimes made everyone admire the wisdom of the gentlemen of Parlement, and above all the constancy and integrity of our good king who, having been supplicated and begged many times to pardon them or commute their sentence to prison, stayed firm..."[44]

The parallel trajectories of canards and the writings of L'Estoile, both of which gradually came around to focusing on the mood and behavior of criminals on the scaffold at the moment of their death, is not at all surprising, given that L'Estoile was an avid consumer of canards. Indeed, several of the crimes and executions mentioned in his journals were also the subject of canards, and it is entirely possible that some of his information on criminals and executions may have been gleaned from canards rather than from direct experience.[45]

The period from the 1550s until the first decade of the seventeenth century, therefore, witnessed the birth of two related but somewhat different ways of watching executions. On the one hand, a new, almost clinically detached way of watching them came into existence, which we saw in the diaries of Thomas Platter, and which enabled viewers to observe executions without participating in the traditional ceremony of repentance and healing. On the other hand, the French public was beginning to show an insatiable appetite for sensationalistic and dramatic accounts of crimes, criminals, and executions, a craving that could be satisfied either by attending executions or, increasingly, by consuming broadsides and other kinds of texts devoted to the subject.

EXECUTIONS AS TRAGIC SPECTACLE: ROSSET'S *HISTOIRES TRAGIQUES*

In 1614, François de Rosset published *Les Histoires tragiques de nostre temps*, a runaway bestseller that contained titillating short stories whose subjects were "horrible" crimes such as murder, incest, parricide, rape, sodomy, and sorcery. Rosset's stories, with minor exceptions, were based on real incidents that had recently taken place in France, although the details were dramatized and romanticized for the benefit of his readers. His formula for romanticized true-crime stories proved so successful that Rosset would update his collection several times over the next few years, adding new tragically horrible stories as they occurred. The book was eventually translated into several different languages, and after Rosset's death others took on the task of updating the book, the last version of which was published in 1758—not coincidentally the year after Damiens' execution, and a time when it would suddenly no longer be entirely unproblematic to find entertainment value in executions.[46]

Many of Rosset's stories are based on contemporary canards, which in turn are based on actual crimes that had recently taken place. But Rosset had a tendency to add a veneer of fictional exoticism to these real-life events. Sometimes, particularly in cases involving important political figures with powerful friends still alive, the events are set in "Persia." Other stories take place in France, but the names of the characters were altered, and although these kinds of name changes were a convention of the times, Rosset's substitution of exotic names like Doralice and Lizaran for the more prosaic Marguerite and Julien, for example, added a layer of mystique to his stories.

Rosset's stories straddle the border between truth and fiction. Although most are based on real-life cases, to say that Rosset took poetic license would be an understatement. It seems all too clear, for example, that the moralizing sermons put in the mouths of condemned criminals as they mounted the scaffold were less a transcription of actual words than the author's attempt to provide a kind of moral veneer to what is, pretty clearly, a dirty book by contemporary standards. People read these accounts of rape, murder, and incest in order to be titillated, and the remorseful *mea culpa* put into the mouths of criminals immediately preceding their execution gave the reader a kind of alibi in the form of a morality tale. Rosset undoubtedly took many liberties with his stories, his ultimate aim being to please his readers rather than provide an accurate account of what had actually transpired. Nevertheless, his stories strove for an aura of verisimilitude that was sure to give his readers the special thrill that could only be derived from horror stories rooted in the realm of the plausible. Additionally, the fact that many of Rosset's stories had taken place only a few years—and sometimes only a few months—before his rendering of them in print must have made them all the more exciting to his readers.[47]

On the surface, all of Rosset's "tragic stories" are very similar: someone commits a horrible crime—I would say an unspeakable crime, but Rosset had a talent for speaking about such things as male rape and incest without explicitly going into all the details—and as a price for having committed that crime, the person usually dies a horrible death, often at the hands of the executioner. Beyond these surface similarities, however, there are some interesting differences. The dynamics of the executions tend to fall along a spectrum that ranges from unrepentant criminals, whose execution is attended by spectators very satisfied to see a miscreant get his or her just desserts, to deeply repentant—and often beautiful—criminals who are executed before tearful crowds (and, at least on one occasion, a tearful executioner).

Perhaps the best example of an unrepentant criminal in the *Histoires tragiques* is the case of the "execrable doctor Vanini," a defrocked monk who was put to death by the parlement of Toulouse in 1619 for the crime of human and divine lèse-majesté as a result of his blasphemous writings. According to Rosset's account of the execution, when Vanini was asked, as was the custom, to beg forgiveness of God, he replied that "he did not know what God was, and that consequently he would never beg forgiveness from an imaginary entity." When officials pressed him further, he replied, "Alright! I ask pardon of God, if there is one." (176) When Vanini was led up to the scaffold, Rosset writes that he "glanced from one side to the other, and having seen certain men that he knew among the great crowd of people that attended the end of this execrable [individual], he [threw out] these words to them: "You see, he said in a loud voice, a miserable Jew is the reason I am here." Rather than leaving it to his readers to put two and two together, Rosset duly informs them:

> He was speaking of Our Lord Jesus Christ, the king of kings and lord of lords, from whom this rabid dog was trying to strip divine majesty, to the great [scandal] of an infinity of people who were shouting that this blasphemer be exterminated; [the crowd] used other terms that I would not know how to write without horror and without offending the ears of those who are taking the trouble of reading this story. (177)

In this particular case, Rosset does not dwell on the execution, but merely tells us that the executioner removed Vanini's tongue before throwing his body on the fire and then scattering his ashes to the wind. In this execution at least, no one shed a tear.[48]

In the middle of the spectrum, between vengeful and tearful spectators, there is the story of "Dragontine," who was beheaded for bewitching the queen of "Persia." The story is a thinly veiled account of the real-life Leonora Galigai, lady-in-waiting to Marie de' Medici and executed in Paris for sorcery in 1617. Unlike Vanini, Dragontine is clearly repentant, and the signs of her repentance manage to soften at least some of those who witness the execution: "When everyone caught sight of this pitiful, disheveled woman, dark and shriveled, who held a silver cross in her hand and who was in between two priests, the just anger [of the crowd] melted just as the snows melt when touched by the sun." (68–9) Whereas Vanini was utterly unrepentant, Dragontine willingly played by convention, giving a speech of repentance before the enormous crowd:

> When she arrived at the place of execution, those who led her scarcely had enough room to make their way to the scaffold. The entire square was filled, and the windows and the rooftops were all filled with an infinity of people. One had never seen such a large crowd. Having mounted the stage of infamy [*infâme théâtre*], she glanced from one side to the other and then offered these words. "You see, gentlemen, the fickle nature of worldly things. You see, I say, an example which has perhaps no other example in the world. I accept death as a willing sufferer [*en patience*] because it is justly given to me."

Her contrition apparently went a long way toward winning the crowd over, and when the executioner beheaded her, Rosset writes that "the people, who had seen such noble resolve...were kind of moved with compassion." But this compassion was apparently not universal: "[S]ome of the more zealously patriotic [spectators] threw themselves upon the severed head and had a long game of pelote, even while the rest of her body was thrown on the fire that had been lit." (70–1)

Finally, at the far end of the spectrum, were the cases of individuals who, despite the fact that they had committed horrible crimes, were nevertheless so saintly in their repentance, not to mention so physically beautiful, that the crowd could not help being reduced to tears. Perhaps the best example of this is Rosset's version of a story that we have already come across: the brother and sister executed in Paris in 1603 for the crimes of incest and adultery. Here is Rosset's account of the execution, which describes spectators rushing to the scene, and shedding sweet tears, as if they were watching an extraordinarily moving tragic performance:

> The execution took place in the place de Grève. Never had one seen so many people flock to such a spectacle. The square was so filled that one practically suffocated. The windows and rooftops were all filled. The first who appeared on this stage of infamy [*infâme théâtre*] was Doralice [who showed] such courage and resolution that everyone admired her steadfastness. All those in attendance could not prevent their eyes from shedding tears for this beauty. So [beautiful] was she that one finds very few on earth who are comparable. One might have said, as she ascended the scaffold, that she was going to perform in a pretend tragedy and not a real one: never once did she change color. After having glanced from one side to the other, she raised her eyes to heaven and then, her hands joined together, she prayed [aloud for God's mercy]. (218–19)

The scene was so moving, Rosset tells us, that even the executioner "could not himself help from crying along with all the spectators." (220)

After the sister's execution, it was her brother's turn, and Rosset tells us that "All the people were still crying warm tears when they led her brother to the stage." Again, Rosset calls attention to the physical beauty of the condemned, telling us that the brother, Lizaran, was "the living portrait of his sister...and consequently endowed with great beauty." As his sister had done, the brother gave a speech filled with contrition and lamentation in response to which "all the people felt a great sadness." He had just finished the prayer *In manus tuas*, commending his spirit into the hands of God, when the executioner struck his fatal blow. (220–1) Rosset, after spending pages on the pity and the tragedy of it all, ends the story, very much like the canard upon which it was no doubt based, by reminding readers, in a few brief lines, that justice had been done: "Their execrable love hastened the end of their young lives. [Their punishment is] a memorable example which must make those who commit incest and adultery tremble with fear. God leaves nothing unpunished. His vengeance always finds the guilty if they persist in their evil ways." (221)

Similar in many respects to the story of the execution of the brother and sister is another of Rosset's tragic stories: the tale of Lystorac, based on the real-life execution of Thomas de Guémadeuc in 1617. Here again we have an individual of great physical and personal attractiveness: "His beauty and his courtliness together with his valor, his knowledge and his eloquence won over the soul of all who spent time with him. It was impossible to see him without loving him, nor to speak with him without being thrilled by the sweetness of his words." (368) Unfortunately, this beautiful, wonderful young man found himself in a position of power, and ended up doing some very nasty things. In the end, however, when he found himself on the scaffold, he recognized the justness of the verdict, and seemed truly repentant about his misdeeds. Rosset describes how the sight of this beautiful and contrite young man elicited a torrent of tears from those who watched:

> When the arrêt was read to him, he thanked the judges and said that he had merited an even more severe punishment. Being therefore resolved to death, and showing the most ample courage that one can imagine—instead of needing consolation, he seemed himself to be consoling those who endeavored to console him—but who can adequately describe the steadfastness that he showed when he mounted the scaffold…? His color never changed, and one might have said, seeing his assured countenance, that he was performing a character in a theatrical tragedy [*une feinte tragédie*].... Having finished a prayer [of lamentation and contrition], he put his own doublet down, without wanting to allow the executioner to touch him. One of his valets de chambre cut his hair, after which he got down on his knees, still pleading for God's mercy and asking the crowd to add their prayers to his. All the windows and the rooftops of the houses were occupied, and everyone, seeing such a beautiful gentleman, and touched by such contrition, cried bitterly and begged the heavenly powers [*la bonté céleste*] to treat his soul more gently than his body [was being treated on earth]. Finally, the executioner wanted to cover [Lystorac's] eyes, but his great courage did not permit this, nor did the memory of so many crimes that he had committed. "Oh executioner, he said, let your blow fall freely! If I had the courage before to shed innocent blood, God will give me the grace now to have the same [courage] to see his just hand thunder down upon my head and to see the end of this miserable life…." Having said this, [he] offer[ed] aloud [his prayer] *In manus tuas*, and the executioner separated his head from his body. This was the tragic end of Lystorac to whom heaven was not miserly in [giving] its greatest gifts. (383–4)

It is difficult to miss Rosset's efforts to situate these executions within the realm of the theatrical, as he very nearly beats us over the head with it. Even if he did not tell us that his more sympathetic characters seemed as if they were acting in "une feinte tragédie," we would undoubtedly be tipped off by behaviors that can only be described as theatrical: the obligatory glances back and forth, taking in the full extent of the packed house before the tragic hero or heroine launches into the monologue that is hypothetically meant for God's ear, but is actually a theatrical aside for the benefit of the audience. There is also the crush of spectators gathered around the "stage of infamy," a kind of penal parterre so immense that the overflowing crowd finds seating on the rooftops. And, last but not least, in almost every one of Rosset's execution scenes, there are the well-to-do spectators who have paid for the privilege of renting windows overlooking the square, the penal corollary of the theatrical loges.

What is going on here? We have semi-fictionalized accounts of real events in which the characters behave, Rosset tells us, almost like fictional characters in a play. If we could break this all down into separate parts, we might see that Rosset is striving for two separate things: the realism and exciting immediacy that comes when we know a story has some basis in fact, but also the relative freedom of emotion that we allow ourselves to feel for fictional characters, for people who do not actually exist. Rosset knew that it was far easier for readers to forget themselves, to weep hot tears and be overcome with pity for such beautiful characters as Doralice, Lizaran, and Lystorac in a far-off neverland, than for the real people upon whom those characters were based, whose respective crimes of incest, adultery, rape, and murder might not be quite so easy to put aside in real life.

We might assume that Rosset's tragic realism and his clear intention to elicit pity and tears from his readers is evidence of a rising *sensibilité* in the French public and of a new concern for the victims of execution. But we would be wrong. In the first place, such an assumption presupposes that those who attended executions prior to the seventeenth century felt nothing for the patient on the scaffold; as we have seen, however, those who gathered around the scaffold traditionally felt a deep sense of compassion for patients, often singing and praying with them until their final moments. In the second place, we would be mistaken in seeing in Rosset's tragic stories a deep and heartfelt concern for the actual victims of executions; in fact, I would argue, Rosset's stories and their popularity point to precisely the opposite trend.

In many respects, we might think of Rosset's readers as analogous to the new penal voyeurs, who were gathering in windows overlooking the scaffold at precisely the time that he was writing his tragic stories. Rosset's tragic realism made readers feel as if they were "almost there" at the scene of the execution, but with the relative freedom to experience their emotions as if they weren't, to forget themselves and sob with delight in private. In a way, the new penal voyeurs experienced a similar sense of being "almost there"; from behind their windows, at a considerable distance from the scaffold, they could gaze out at the real-life drama unfolding beneath them, and they could take it all in—the suffering of the patient, the compassion of the crowd—as if they were all characters in a magnificent spectacle, to which they themselves were not participants but spectators. They were beginning, in other words, to process the execution scenes played out before them almost as if they were watching one of Pierre Corneille's tragic heroes or heroines deliver a monologue prior to execution, peeking in on the most intimate moments of another person's life and death.[49] Outside the traditional framework of participation and compassion, they were free to feel a sense of tragic delight, or free to feel nothing at all. For them, the crowd gathered around the scaffold had become a kind of Greek chorus, reacting to the suffering of the condemned and expressing the compassion that they, seated up above in the windows, no longer felt.

The sixteenth century witnessed the birth of an entirely new kind of spectator who, rather than participating in the traditional ritual of penance and communal redemption, instead purchased seats overlooking the scaffold in order to watch events unfold from a distance. Some of these spectators, like Thomas Platter, cultivated an air of clinical detachment, and although they were interested in the details of executions, they had little or no emotional investment in them. Others, like the readers of Rosset's *Histoires tragiques*, seemed to revel in the tragic pity of the spectacle, and eagerly sought out details about the emotions of the patient and the reactions of the crowd. Not only were they entirely oblivious to the fact that the spectacle of execution was supposed to be a terrifying moral lesson, they had come to take a voyeuristic pleasure in watching. The various actors on the scaffold, even the crowd shouting or crying down below, were all part of the show. If someone, somewhere thought that these spectacles were staged for the purposes of deterring crime by example, it seems very clear that none of these spectators, watching from a distance, thought that *they* were the target audience.

For the time being, this new way of watching appears to have been largely restricted to relatively wealthy *amateurs* of executions, and most individuals probably continued to attend executions in the traditional manner, gathering around the scaffold and either weeping and praying with the condemned and rejoicing in his or her redemption and salvation, or heaping abuse upon and demanding vengeance against those individuals unworthy of redemption. The coming century and half, however, would see ever more celebrated and sensational criminal cases attracting more and more public attention and interest, with newspapers and broadsheets not only catering to the taste of these new consumers but helping to whip it up into a frenzied obsession with crime, criminals, and executions. Not unlike Norbert Elias's famous example of the fork, which appeared as an aristocratic affectation and gradually made its way down the social ladder to become an ingrained cultural habit of society at large, a voyeuristic fascination with executions would spread across the social classes by the eighteenth century.

This growing public fascination with and curiosity about executions were on a collision course with contemporary penal theory, which regarded exemplary deterrence as the very *raison d'être* of punishment. While the new penal voyeurism was still restricted to the relatively privileged members of society, few seemed to take notice of the discrepancy between the intent of the punishment and the way in which it was being perceived by these spectators. But as this new way of watching made its way down the social ladder, alarm bells were sounded. While it is doubtful that the praying, weeping crowds had *ever* been "terrified" by executions, this new way of watching seemed even further removed from the ideal of exemplary deterrence.

At the same time, another cultural crisis was looming on the horizon. Over the course of the seventeenth and eighteenth centuries, a revolution in sensibilities would sweep over both sides of the Channel, and human beings would be re-imagined as naturally benevolent and compassionate. The eager anticipation of *amateurs* who watched executions as if they were a dramatic performance, or perhaps even worse, the callous indifference of those in the windows who watched and felt nothing, would be difficult to square with the new view of human nature as instinctively compassionate.

The following chapters trace the growing conflicts between spectators desperate to watch people die on the scaffold, a penal theory predicated on their not being able to watch without being terrified, and a culture of sensibility that insisted they could not watch without horror.

6

Executions, Spectator Emotions, and the Naturalization of Sympathy

Whereas earlier generations had expressed a feeling of compassion—literally suffering *along with* the patient who suffered on the scaffold—a new breed of spectator had emerged over the course of the sixteenth century who developed an entirely different relationship to the spectacle of suffering. In contrast to those who had viewed themselves as participants in a ritual of communal redemption, these new spectators, physically and emotionally detached from the action on the scaffold, came to think of the sufferer more as an object of contemplation from whom one could have a certain critical distance, and consequently, a range of reactions. As we saw in the previous chapter, some spectators like Felix Platter seemed to take this objectification of the patient quite literally, evincing a flat, emotionless, almost clinical, interest in the details of executions; others exploited the new distance from the patient to take a kind of creative license, reveling in the tragic pity of those who suffered before them almost as if the sufferer were a character in a play or story.

Although these different ways of watching executions tended to coexist over the course of the seventeenth and eighteenth centuries, one can nevertheless discern broad trends and changes over time. The phenomenon of reveling in tragic pity seems to have been a largely seventeenth-century phenomenon, slowly waning toward the end of that century; the more emotionally detached form of spectatorship, however, in which the spectacle of execution could be appreciated as an object of curiosity without necessarily engendering any emotional response, seems to have become more prevalent over time, appearing first among the privileged classes and gradually making its way down the social ladder, so that by the early eighteenth century, it was fairly widespread.

Simultaneous with these changes in spectator viewing habits, a revolution in sensibilities was taking place—also occurring first among the privileged classes, and slowly making its way down the social ladder—a revolution that reimagined human beings to be instinctively sympathetic and benevolent. As the very *nature* of humanity came to be defined as having "humane" sensibilities, the practice of finding pleasure in the sufferings of others came to be seen as *unnatural* and inhuman. This chapter traces these two largely incompatible and yet nearly simultaneous trends in watching and making sense of executions from the turn of the sixteenth century to the middle of the eighteenth century: the growing tendency to watch executions as a form of spectacular entertainment, and the rise of a new sensibility that would claim it was impossible for human beings to witness the suffering of others without suffering themselves.

A RISING SPECTACULARITY

Although, as we have seen, the execution of notable individuals had tended to attract large crowds even before the early modern period, spectators in the seventeenth and eighteenth centuries flocked to executions of the notable and the famous with ever more excitement and eagerness, snapping up windows overlooking these executions as if they were prized seats in the loge at the latest theatrical sensation. In 1632, for example, when Louis de Marillac, Maréchal de France, was executed on the place de Grève, the *Gazette de Paris* reported that one hundred thousand people attended the execution and marveled at the fact that "each window was rented for eight *pistoles*."[1] The following year, thirty thousand people crowded into the provincial town of Troyes to watch the execution of the Chevalier de Jars, filling the main square and all the windows looking over it.[2]

Through the seventeenth and much of the eighteenth centuries, many of France's most illustrious and privileged inhabitants developed the hobby of watching executions as a form of entertainment, a hobby that was not restricted to the rare execution of privileged people but extended to all different kinds of executions, down to the most mundane. Although the king and queen no longer attended executions in the seventeenth century, as they had in the sixteenth, they may have been among the few who did not. Even Cardinal Richelieu apparently developed a fascination with executions and, according to Tallemant de Réaux, would "send for father Bernard who was exceedingly devout, and would make him recount the story of all the prisoners and hanging victims whose punishment he had attended [as a confessor]. He [Bernard] would say that the Cardinal used to receive him as a priest, but that the Chancellor [received him] as a henchman of the hangman."[3]

By the middle of the seventeenth century, however, the aristocratic penchant for watching executions was of such long standing that it became fashionable to affect an air of insouciance when speaking of them. In a letter written in 1659, Paul Scarron seemed barely able to muster enough enthusiasm to speak of the subject:

> I will tell you...for an utter lack of any other news, that they are hanging and breaking on the wheel here every day of the week, and even the hangman himself is getting tired of it, and that Madame ***, who, according to Monsieur de ***, likes nothing more than to watch [people] die in public, is beginning to have her fill of it, and that if it weren't for [the highwayman] Saint-Ange whom she wants to see broken on the wheel at whatever price, she would not have stepped foot in the Grève for a long time.[4]

Scarron's tone of affected *ennui* was not uncommon in the mid to late seventeenth century, and we can see the same, almost studied, indifference in the correspondence of Madame de Sévigné. In her case, however, one can almost always sense a barely repressed excitement lurking just beneath the surface. In a letter written in

1671, for example, as she relates to her daughter the various tidbits about executions gleaned from friends, almost as if they were scandalous passages from racy novels, we can sense a mixture of scintillation and enthusiasm underneath a veneer of flip dismissiveness:

> So, you saw a poor, old man that they were going to execute on the wheel. He behaved better than a certain comte de Frangipani, who was executed two months ago in Vienna along with several others who had plotted against the emperor. This Frangipani found himself so incapable of tolerating death in public that he had to be dragged to the punishment. He fought off the executioner; four people were needed to hold him. In the end, they succeeded in finishing the job, but not without hacking him to pieces [*charcuter*]. [But] that's exactly what I would do. Mme de Villars sent me this account that had been sent to her from Germany.[5]

Sévigné is clearly *trying* to be cavalier, affecting a tone that people had come to expect when speaking about such things. She seems, in other words, almost self-consciously insensitive when referring to executions. After relating the gruesome account of Frangipani's execution to her daughter, she segues nonchalantly into her next topic: a cure for toenail fungus.

Despite her efforts at insouciance, one can nevertheless occasionally sense very different emotions lying just beneath the surface in Sévigné's letters. Writing to her daughter in 1675 about the recent troubles in Brittany, during which countless people had been executed as a result of a tax rebellion, one can discern a feeling of compassion for those who suffered:

> You write very amusingly about our troubles; we are not as [subjected to being] broken on the wheel as we were: one in eight days, just to uphold justice. It is true that hanging seems a refreshing [change of pace] to me now. I have a completely different sense of justice since I have been in this region. Your men in the galleys seem [by comparison as if they were] a company of honest folk who have retired from the world in order to lead a quiet life. We have certainly sent them to you by the hundreds; those who stayed behind are more unfortunate than they.[6]

Tocqueville, and a few modern scholars who have echoed his views, saw in these comments by Sévigné an insensitivity to the sufferings of individuals who were not of her class:

> One would be wrong in thinking that madame de Sévigné...was an egotistical and barbarous creature: she loved her children with a passion, and showed herself to be very sensitive to the sufferings of her friends; and one notices even, in reading her, that she treated her servants and vassals with kindness and indulgence. But madame de Sévigné did not clearly conceive what suffering meant to anyone who was not a member of the nobility. In our day, the harshest man, writing to the most insensitive person, would never dare indulge in a cold-blooded manner in this kind of cruel badinage, and even if his personal morals permitted him to do it, the general morals of the nation would forbid him from doing so.[7]

In fact, as we have seen in her comments about the Comte de Frangipani, quoted above, Sévigné's insouciant and cavalier attitude extended to all execution victims, regardless of their social standing. But Tocqueville is nevertheless right to point out that she did not seem to care about execution victims in the same way that she cared for members of her family or her household. This would, however, be a reflection not of class prejudice but rather of her personal acquaintance with the sufferer, something that was, at the time, considered to be almost a prerequisite to the ability to sympathize, a subject to which I will return shortly.

Despite Sévigné's efforts at insouciance, we can occasionally glimpse moments in her letters when she cannot help expressing sympathy for the victims of certain executions, before seemingly catching herself. Referring, once again, to the executions in Brittany, and suggesting that the true perpetrators of the uprising had already fled the scene, she wrote: "The rebels of Rennes left a long time ago, and therefore the good will suffer [for the crimes] of the bad. But it is all well and good as long as the four thousand soldiers who are in Rennes...don't get in the way of me strolling in my woods, which are of a marvelous height and beauty."[8] If one is not predisposed to seeing callousness and class prejudice in her comments, then in another passage cited by Tocqueville as evidence of her insensitivity, I think one can read genuine feeling and concern that is quickly swept under the carpet:

> Do you want to know the latest from Rennes?... They've made a tax of one hundred thousand écus on townspeople, and if they don't come up with it in twenty-four hours it will be doubled and payable to soldiers. They turned an entire large street [of people] out of their homes and banished them, and forbade anyone from taking them in, under penalty of death, so that one saw all of these unfortunates, old people, pregnant women, wandering about in tears at the gates of this city, not knowing where to go, without any food or anything to sleep upon. Yesterday, they executed on the wheel the fiddler who started the dance by pillaging the stamp tax; he was cut into pieces after death, and the four quarters [of his body] were exposed in the four corners of the city.... He said upon dying that it had been the stamp tax farmers who had given him twenty-five écus to start the sedition, and no one could get anything else out of him. They took sixty townspeople, and will start hanging them tomorrow. This province is a fine example for others....[9]

Where Tocqueville sees heartlessness, I think we can see a struggle between compassion, insouciance, and sarcasm. Sévigné knew that contemporary conventions demanded she view executions as a form of amusing spectacle, but she could not help feeling something for these particular victims of justice.

Over the next few years, although Sévigné's accounts of executions betray the occasional trace of sympathy, as a general rule she seems to enjoy and even revel in the excitement of the penal spectacle. In 1676, only a year after the repression of the rebellion in Brittany, she became utterly obsessed with the trial and punishment of the Marquise de Brinvilliers, who had been accused of secretly poisoning a significant portion of her extended family (and of having plans to poison most of the rest of it). Brinvilliers had been having an adulterous affair, and her attempts at poisoning her relatives were in apparent retaliation for her family's efforts to put an end to that affair. She was also widely reputed (although the accusation was never proved) to have tested her poisons on unsuspecting paupers to whom she administered trial doses disguised as charitable offerings.[10]

The combination of poisoning, adultery, and the Marquise de Brinvilliers' social standing made her case so scandalously exciting that, in the summer of 1676, Parisian society could talk of little else. On a visit to Paris at the beginning of May, Madame de Sévigné wrote to her daughter that "The only thing one talks about here [in Paris] are the words, the actions and the movements of La Brinvilliers."[11] Upon leaving Paris and setting off toward her daughter's house, Sévigné wrote "Alas, What good will I be, heading back to you? I pity you for not having me in Paris any longer so that I can send you the latest on la Brinvilliers."[12] A month and a half later, she was headed back toward Paris, eager to find out the latest: "This affair occupies all of Paris, at the expense of matters relating to the [Franco-Dutch] war. When I arrive there [in Paris], my dearest, rest assured that I will leave you in the dark about nothing relating to such an extraordinary matter."[13]

In mid-July, when La Brinvilliers was found guilty of her crimes and sentenced to death, Sévigné made sure to be in Paris. As she related the details of the execution to her daughter, we can see the same tone of insouciance tinged with a modicum of sympathy that we saw in her accounts of previous executions. In fact, she begins her account of Brinvilliers' execution by playing on the fact that Parisians had been living and breathing La Brinvilliers for so many months, and now that she was dead, they still were: "Well it's done. La Brinvilliers is in the air. After the execution, her poor little body was thrown onto a great big fire, and her ashes to the wind, so that we are all breathing her in...." Sévigné goes on to describe the mood of the spectators as they watched Brinvilliers make her way toward the scaffold, and although she declares that all Paris was "moved" by the sight and that she herself "shivered" at seeing Brinvilliers go by, her tone seems devoid of any emotion or feeling. In fact, if she expresses any sadness at all, it is directed at the fact that her vantage point afforded her an inferior view, as apparently she was not among the lucky ones who had managed to procure one of the windows overlooking the square itself:

> At six o'clock she was led, naked but for a shirt and with the cord around her neck, to Notre-Dame in order to perform the amende honorable. And then she was put back into the tumbrel, where I saw her, thrown backwards on the straw, wearing a head covering and her shirt, a doctor [of the Sorbonne] next to her, and the hangman on the other side. In truth, it made me shiver. Those who saw the execution say that she mounted the scaffold with a good deal of courage. As for me, I was on the bridge of Notre-Dame... never were there so many people, nor Paris so moved or so attentive. And ask me what we saw, because as far as I am concerned I saw only a head-covering. But in the end, the day was devoted to this tragedy. I'll know more tomorrow, and will get back to you.[14]

Sévigné's matter-of-fact description of Brinvilliers' journey towards the Place de Grève stands in contrast to the mood of "Paris" that she describes as "so moved and so attentive." She sees herself, in other words, as qualitatively different from the crowds. For her, this was merely the final chapter of a titillating and scandalous case. For many around her, however, it was apparently a much more meaningful ceremony, a penitential journey toward redemption. As

Sévigné reported to her daughter in her next letter, on the day after Brinvilliers' execution, "they were looking for her bones because the people said that she was a saint."[15]

Although Sévigné reported that the crowd was "moved" by the execution, Edme Pirot, Brinvilliers' confessor who accompanied her in the tumbrel, had a somewhat different reading of the crowd, writing of a "continual murmur...in the streets along our route, continuing all the time up until the scaffold....[W]hile some were begging God for mercy on her behalf & were pitying her misfortune, a greater number insulted her and heaped curses upon her."[16] To Pirot, in short, the crowd was divided between those who felt compassion for Brinvilliers and those who felt she was unworthy of it.

Pirot's account of Brinvillier's execution is a rather curious text in that it recounts in labored detail virtually every second of Brinvilliers' journey toward the scaffold. (In fact, it takes considerably more time to make one's way through the several hundred pages of Pirot's text than it did for Brinvilliers to make her way from the prison to the scaffold.) Pirot's account, in itself, bears testimony to the multifaceted ways in which people were processing executions at the time. On the one hand, the text is a heartfelt description of Brinvilliers' spiritual journey toward redemption. On the other hand, it is the written representation of a spiritual process that no one had ever thought to put down on paper in quite the same way before.[17] Although it was never published in Pirot's lifetime, the text was clearly intended for readers—most probably those who would take up the task of being confessors in the future, but very possibly others with a more amateur interest in the Brinvilliers case. In fact, there are glimpses of a tragic realism that recall Rosset's *Histoires tragiques:*

> [The hangman] ripped the upper part of her shirt...in order to uncover her shoulders;....he blindfolded her, and found in her no resistance at all. She was like a lamb who is led to slaughter. She opened her mouth no more to complain to the hangman, who did with her whatever he wanted, than does the animal whom one shears and seizes in order to make it a victim of sacrifice.[18]

While it would be unduly cynical not to see genuine feeling in Pirot's account of the execution, I suspect it would be very naïve not to take note of a tragic writing style that betrays the fact that elements of the tragic-spectacular had made its way into the inner sanctum of the ritual of execution.[19] Although Pirot may have declared that he took "little pleasure in being looked at and observed by the thousand people who were in the windows on all sides" of the Place de Grève, one cannot shake the suspicion that his manuscript was written, at least in part, with these same spectators in mind.[20]

A little more than three years after La Brinvilliers' trial and execution, French society found itself once again transfixed by a case that involved not only poisoning but various other crimes including abortion and witchcraft. Catherine Monvoisin, better known as La Voisin, who was something of a fortune-teller and provider of strange potions to the rich and famous, became the object of enormous curiosity in the autumn and winter of 1679 when she was accused and tried for her various crimes. In February of 1680, when she was executed on the Place de Grève, Madame de Sévigné made sure to be on hand for the event, along with the rest of Parisian high society:

> At five o'clock, they bound her and, with a torch in hand, she appeared in the tumbrel, dressed in white—it's a kind of outfit to be burned in. She was all red [in the face] and you could see that she was pushing away the confessor and the crucifix with force. By the hôtel de Sully, we saw her pass—Mme de Chaulnes and Mme de Sully, the countess [and I], along with many others. At Notre Dame, she did not want to perform the amende honorable and, at the [place de] Grève, she did her best to avoid getting out of the tumbrel. She was pulled out by force. She was put on the pyre, seated and bound with irons. She was covered in straw. She swore a lot, and pushed the straw away five or six times, but in the end, the fire grew and one couldn't see her any more, and her ashes are now in the air. And that's the death of Mme Voisin, famous for her crimes and her impiety.[21]

While it seems clear that executions had become a form of entertainment for the privileged classes, from a modern perspective one cannot help wondering whether anyone found this development strange or problematic. For the time being, it would appear that they did not. If one did not know the context, one might almost think that the names of La Voisin and La Brinvilliers, so often bandied about in the correspondence of the well-to-do, referred to celebrated tragedians rather than the victims of executions. It must not have seemed all that unusual, therefore, when Thomas Corneille, brother of Pierre, co-authored *La Devineresse*, a play based on the life of La Voisin, which enjoyed unparalleled success when it was performed over the months before and after her execution. By this point in time, the wealthier classes had come to expect executions to be diverting, and one suspects it would have seemed strange, perhaps even *démodé*, for someone among the privileged classes to experience these events as a solemn affair rather than as an entertaining spectacle.

It was within this context of unreflecting, emotionally detached spectacularity that Jean de La Bruyère in 1688 made what was, quite possibly, the very first criticism of the practice of watching executions as a form of entertainment:

> They run to see the unfortunates; they line up in haste or they place themselves in windows in order to observe the demeanor and the countenance of a man who is condemned and who knows that he will die: vain, malicious, and inhuman curiosity. If men were wise, the public square would be devoid of people, and it would be established that it could only be ignominious to watch such spectacles.[22]

This passage, from *Les Caractères*, was but one among many such candid reflections on contemporary French society that La Bruyère offered in his book, and no doubt opinions such as these made him several enemies, not the least of whom was Thomas Corneille, the playright of *La Devinesse*, who would later oppose La Bruyère's election to the Académie Française.

With hindsight, we can see that La Bruyère's indictment of those who gawked at execution victims was the harbinger of new sensibilities that would not become common until several decades later. At the time, however, his statement was like a lone raindrop falling on a large pond without a ripple in sight. Spectators continued to flock to executions, untroubled by any moral compunctions whatsoever, and La Bruyère's words would seem to have had little or no effect on his contemporaries, at least for the moment.[23]

Why, all of a sudden, in 1688 did someone think to declare it "inhuman" to watch the spectacle of execution when people had been watching executions for several hundred years, and rushing to "place themselves in windows" for at least a century? Lynn Hunt, drawing upon Tocqueville's reflections on sympathy and class, has recently suggested that the advent of epistolary novels, in which characters of different social backgrounds expressed their innermost feelings, made it possible for readers to "empathize" across class lines in a way that they had never been able to do before.[24] But, as we have seen, the lack of "empathy," rather than characterizing all spectators prior to the eighteenth century, resulted from a novel way of watching, which first appeared in the sixteenth century. Moreover, as I have endeavored to show, a culture of voyeuristic insouciance drew little distinction in terms of empathy on the basis of class, and many of the most celebrated executions, from an entertainment standpoint, involved the execution of individuals of high social standing. Finally, La Bruyère's criticism predates the advent of the type of epistolary novel that Hunt is referring to by a good half century. So, if not from reading epistolary novels, where did La Bruyère's sensitivity come from?

I would like to suggest that what changed people's attitudes to executions was not the literary developments of the mid-eighteenth century, but rather a broader and more complicated shift in sensibilities that had been occurring since at least the middle of the seventeenth century—and in isolated cases, even earlier. In fact, one might see this cultural revolution in sensibilities as making possible the epistolary novel, rather than vice versa.

SENTIMENTAL JOURNEY: FROM STOIC INSENSITIVITY TO *SENSIBILITÉ*

In the 1580s, a century and a half before Samuel Richardson's *Pamela* and *Clarissa* or Jean-Jacques Rousseau's *Julie*, and well before the flowering of *sensibilité* in the seventeenth century, Michel de Montaigne gave voice to his then peculiar, if not extraordinary, discomfort at watching the spectacle of other people suffering. Referring to his inability to "watch the executions of justice, no matter how reasonable they may be, with a steady eye," Montaigne declared that "I experience great, tender compassion with the sufferings of others, and would easily cry for company's sake if, on any occasion at all, I can bring myself to cry. There is nothing that calls forth tears in me more than [other people's] tears, whether or not they are real, or feigned or painted."[25]

Clarifying that it was the sight of *suffering*, specifically, that bothered him, rather than the death penalty in general, Montaigne offered what may very well be the earliest suggestion for penal reform from a sentimental vantage point:

As far as justice is concerned, it seems to me that everything that is in excess of simple death is pure cruelty.... I would suggest that these examples of rigor by means of which one hopes to keep the people in their place [*en office*] would be exercised on the [dead] body of criminals: because seeing them deprived of a tomb, seeing them boiled and quartered, would have almost as great an impact on the common people than the penalties that are [currently] inflicted on the living.[26]

In many respects, Montaigne's critique of the spectacularization of pain anticipates the penal reformers of the eighteenth century. Unlike these later reformers, however, Montaigne did not argue from a universal perspective. For the most part he attributes his sensitivity not to some higher moral vantage point, but to his own, peculiar inability *not* to feel the sufferings of others. Montaigne saw himself as exceptional in crying "at any occasion at all," at not being able to bear seeing someone else suffer—not only human beings but animals as well: "I have never known even how to watch, without displeasure, the pursuit and killing of a defenseless, innocent animal who has never harmed anyone." Here again, his sensitivity is expressed as a peculiarity, almost a kind of affliction, and he describes himself as being "weak to the point of not being able to watch a chicken being killed without displeasure."[27]

How, in the century that intervened between Montaigne's *Essays* and La Bruyère's condemnation of all spectators who watched with pleasure while other people suffered, did one man's peculiar sensitivity to the suffering of others become, as La Bruyère characterized it, a universal attribute of humanity the lack of which was branded "inhuman"? The progression was by no means a straightforward one; in fact, around the same time that Montaigne was writing his essays, a very different approach to the question of sensitivity and emotions was taking shape around the Flemish scholar Justus Lipsius. Although Montaigne and Lipsius read many of the same classical texts and, in fact, appear to have been admirers of each other, the conclusions that they drew with respect to the question of suffering, and vicarious suffering—or sympathy—in particular, could not have been more different. In the short run at least, Lipsius's views on the subject were to prove much more influential.

Lipsius who, like Montaigne, was writing at a time when the wars of religion were ravaging much of Europe, found solace in the principles of classical stoicism, which privileged cold, level-headed reason over the chaos and unpredictability of the passions. Montaigne's views cannot properly be described as "opposed" to those of Lipsius or those of the "neo-stoics" with whom Lipsius is generally grouped; in fact, Montaigne might be seen to share with them a predilection for rational thought over inflamed passions, and a general attitude of resigned equanimity.[28] But if we are looking specifically at the question of the relationship between the observer and the sufferer, then Montaigne's particular sensitivity, his inability *not* to suffer along with the sufferer, is very much out of step with the neo-stoic leanings of his contemporaries.

In 1584, Lipsius published *De Constantia (On Constancy)*, a text that was enormously popular in its day, going through thirty-two editions in Latin and translated into several European languages.[29] The gist of Lipsius's argument is summarized in the subtitle of the French edition: "the afflictions—primarily public ones—and how one must resign oneself to enduring them." The text itself unfolds as a dialogue between Lipsius and his friend Langius, an admirer of stoicism, for whom pity is "a sickness...the vice of a low and abject soul which allows itself to reach out toward the appearance of something unfortunate in another."[30] Although the stoic devaluation of pity would be much maligned for its insensitivity by future, more sentimental, generations, the injunction to feel no pity was not tantamount to not caring; from a neo-stoic perspective, only dispassionate benevolence had the potential to effect practical change, in contrast to which pity was a meaningless form of self-indulgence.

In the same year that Lipsius's *De Constantia* appeared in French, Guillaume du Vair, an admirer of Lipsius, published his own treatise with the same title.[31] For Du Vair, as for Lipsius, reason and passion were forces at odds with each other, and a state of constancy could only be achieved when the passions were subdued. In his writings, Du Vair portrayed strong emotions and passions as dangerous forces that literally transported the individual away from a reasonable state: "We are hardly out of the cradle when perverse passions [*affections*], like violent winds, overtake us and, filling the sails of our desires with a thousand delightful gusts, take us far away from our proper nature, and [take us] flying from [our] right reason."[32]

More than half a century later, we can still see the influence of stoicism in the writings of René Descartes, who conceived of the passions as potentially dangerous forces that interfered with reason and distorted perception. Throughout *Les Passions de l'âme* (*Passions of the Soul*; 1649), Descartes used the word *émotion* as a synonym for a strong passion, a word that in the context of the day meant something more akin to the current meaning of *emeut*, or uprising, than to the modern meaning of *emotion*.[33] An emotion, for Descartes, was nothing less than an upheaval of the soul. Whereas one might be able to master less keenly felt sensations, one was essentially powerless to ignore stronger passions, or emotions: "[The passions] are nearly all accompanied by a kind of *émotion* [i.e. upheaval] which takes place in the heart, and consequently in the blood and the spirits as well, in such a way that until this *émotion* has ceased, they [the passions] remain present in our thought...."[34]

Although, like the neo-stoics, Descartes considered the passions a kind of disturbance of the soul, he nevertheless regarded them as inherent to human nature. Strong emotions were not, in other words, things that one could decide to indulge or subdue as one saw fit; they were a kind of bodily "storm" that one was powerless to prevent and had to be endured, or at best skillfully circumvented through the clever exercise of the will:

> The most that the will can do, while this *émotion* is in full vigor, is not give in to its effects, and restrain many of the reactions [*mouvemens*] which it demands of the body. For example, if anger raises our hand in order to hit, the will can ordinarily restrain it; if fear incites our legs to run, the will can stop them....[35]

Madeleine de Scudéry, a contemporary of Descartes, and no doubt influenced by his exploration of the passions, made it her life's work to study the emotions, famously mapping them, quite literally, in a *Carte de tendre* (*Map of Tenderness*) that she included in her novel *Clélie*, the first volume of which was published in 1654. Gathering around her a number of like-minded individuals in her Paris salon, Scudéry exerted an important influence on contemporary conceptions of emotions and feelings, and has been regarded by many scholars as one of the most important figures in the rise of sensibility in seventeenth-century France.

Like Descartes, Scudéry considered the passions to be an essential part of human nature, but in marked contrast to him, Scudéry did not regard them as forces that distorted one's perception of the world—forces, in other words, to be struggled against and contained. On the contrary, Scudéry believed that the passions harbored the potential to *heighten* our senses, to give us access to things invisible to reason and the mind's eye. As the literary scholar Joan DeJean has phrased it, Scudéry replaced Descartes' soul with the heart as the "control center" of emotions.[36] What the heart could feel was not a distortion of reality, Scudéry insisted, but rather an enhanced perception of it. The passions were powerful forces that could be harnessed by individuals hoping to expand and deepen their relationship to the world, and most importantly, their connection to other people. In contrast to Du Vair who had compared the passions to "violent winds, [which]...take us far away from our proper nature, and [take us] flying from [our] right reason," Scudéry was suggesting almost the opposite: that one could overcome the limitations of cold reason and discover one's proper nature by riding the winds of passion.

The valorization of deeply felt sentiments was a clear repudiation of neo-stoicism and, as both DeJean and Frank Baasner have shown, the culture wars of the day were fought out by proxy through the dialogue of the characters in Scudéry's novels. As early as 1654, Scudéry imparts a defensive tone to the neo-stoic character of Cleocrite, who bristles at being branded as "indifferent" in her relations with others:

> "It is true that I do not despair [in my friends' absence], and in losing sight of them, I do not go out of my mind. But, gracious me...what great pleasure would my friends take if I did experience the greatest sorrow in the world at their absence?...But because I do not give my whole heart, because I am not sensitive to the utmost of sensibilities, and because I do not interject in all my conversations words of tenderness, ardent friendship, and other such things, I come across as indifferent.... That is what I can't stand. In effect," she continued, laughing, "is it not true that the Sages...make wisdom consist of a detachment from all things?"[37]

Not only can we see neo-stoicism on the defensive here, but we can also see in Cleocrite's caricature of sentimentality—of giving one's "whole heart" to one's friends, of being "sensitive to the utmost sensibilities," and of interjecting into conversations "words of tenderness, ardent friendship and other such things"— evidence that these were already established ways of behaving, at least in certain circles, by 1654.

Baasner suggests that in Scudéry's writing keen sensitivity, or *sensibilité*, was not considered a general trait, but rather was seen as "a quality to be found only in morally outstanding, virtuous individuals," and lauded above all was the friendship that could develop between two such sensitive individuals, who could practically speak to each other from the heart.[38] Although Montaigne had espoused a similar view of friendship,[39] his view of sensitivity, his ability to feel what others were feeling, had been more of an abstract quality inherent in *him*, something he was just as likely to feel for his best friend as for a nameless stranger whom he observed crying. For Scudéry and her circle, however, the ability to feel what others were feeling was restricted to close personal relationships: a kind of communication between two sensitive souls.

In the sense that Scudéry's form of *sensibilité* was clearly much more of a special gift than the peculiar weakness it had been for Montaigne, Scudéry might be seen as a conceptual stepping stone between Montaigne and those who, in the last decades of the seventeenth century, began to look upon *sensibilité*—and specifically a sensitivity to the suffering of others—as not only a good thing but as a universal and instinctive reflex of the human race. In the late 1660s a character in a novel by Madame de Villedieu would deride the "ridiculous philosophy" of stoicism for not recognizing that sensibility was "an attribute of mankind as inseparable from his very nature as is reason."[40]

In the final decades of the seventeenth century, the ideal of the ability to control one's emotions was gradually replaced, as a desirable trait, by the ability to feel deeply; and, conversely, the sin of giving in to one's passions was replaced by the sin of insensitivity. By 1690, a dictionary illustrated the usage of the word *insensibilité* by referring to the Stoics as "That arrogant sect which decked itself in *insensibilité* [and which] was faulted by all others for wanting to turn all men into statues."[41] By the turn of the eighteenth century, sensibility had become an essential human trait, the absence of which was the sign of a moral defect. For many, it was no longer the passions that were a problem, but rather the people who were incapable of feeling them.

After this brief foray into contemporary conceptions of feeling and sympathy, we can begin to understand the seeming contradictions that Tocqueville had noted with respect to Madame de Sévigné, who was a member of Scudéry's extended circle and steeped in the same *sensibilité*, but who, as we have seen, could be so callous in her descriptions of the suffering of others. Her letters to her daughter are dripping with the kind of expressions of tenderness and feeling that were fast becoming a staple of fashionable circles. As DeJean notes, in a letter that Sévigné wrote to her daughter in 1671, she included "in a single sentence, in a veritable affective paroxysm, *sentiments, tendresse* (twice), and *sensibilité*, acccompanied by 'to love' and 'to feel' (twice)."[42] This was no literary affectation; Sévigné confessed to being unable to read letters from her daughter, who lived a great distance away, without dissolving into tears, defending herself to her daughter as follows: "Love my moments of tenderness, love my weaknesses; as for me, I find they suit me quite well. I like them much more than the conceptions of [the Stoic writers] Seneca and Epictetus."[43] Yet, as we have seen, her sensitivity and her tears did not extend to those whose death she delighted in watching on the scaffold. While one catches the occasional glimpse of something resembling pity, Sévigné can hardly be said to have experienced the same immediate and reflexive sympathy for the suffering of strangers that Montaigne claimed to feel. Her circle of tenderness and sympathy was limited to friends, family, and acquaintances (unless we count the fictional characters who also seemed capable of bringing her to tears).[44]

The affective range of sensibility was very much in play over the course of the sixteenth and seventeenth centuries. If Montaigne, in the 1580s, had included strangers and even chickens in his sympathies, and if La Bruyère, in 1688, seemed to think that one should suffer at the sight of anyone who was suffering, and that it was "inhuman" not to, others seemed to feel that sympathetic suffering was something reserved for one's circle of intimacy.

"NEITHER SHAME, NOR HORROR IN ATTENDING"

Perhaps there is no better place to observe the range of emotional responses to the suffering of others around the turn of the eighteenth century than in the variety of reactions to the execution of Madame Ticquet in 1699, only a decade after La Bruyère had leveled the first indictment of watching executions. Madame Ticquet had been accused of hiring two accomplices to murder her husband, a counselor at the parlement of Paris, and although she herself at first denied any involvement in the crime, her two supposed accomplices confessed under torture, as she also did eventually. Her husband, who had only been injured in the attack, begged the king to pardon her, but Louis XIV refused.[45] No doubt because of her high social standing, Parisian society was as consumed and intrigued by Madame Ticquet as it had been by Madame la Brinvilliers and La Voisin before her—and if Madame de Sévigné had still been alive, she would not have missed the spectacle of Madame Ticquet's execution for anything in the world.

On the day of Madame Ticquet's execution in 1699, spectators of every class crowded the streets between the prison of the Conciergerie and the Place de Grève, and all the windows overlooking the scaffold had been rented out well in advance. Anne Marguerite du Noyer, who was herself an acquaintance of Madame Ticquet, but who was nevertheless a spectator that day, ventured to guess that some houses with a view of the execution "brought more money to their owners [that day] than they had ever cost them," and for those who had missed the opportunity to rent a window, or who could not afford one, a number of platforms had been erected on the square itself.[46] And Madame du Noyer was far from being the only friend or acquaintance of Madame Ticquet who had come to watch her be put to death. As du Noyer noted, "The entire court and the city ran to see this spectacle."[47]

Despite having been personally acquainted with Madame Ticquet, du Noyer's account of the execution dwells far less on whatever emotions she might have experienced at the sight of watching her friend die than on the feelings of excitement she felt at watching the spectacle of execution. At times, du Noyer compares Ticquet's "performance" to the experience of watching a dramatic production, recalling Rosset's blurring of the theatrical and the real in his peculiar brand of tragic realism:

> I was in the windows of the Hôtel de Ville, and I saw poor Mme Ticquet arrive around five o'clock in the evening, dressed in white.... One would have said that she had studied her role, because she kissed the chopping block and attended to all the other particulars as if it were simply a matter of performing in a play. In the end, one had never seen such self-possession [*confiance*], and the curé of Saint-Sulpice said that she died a true Christian heroine. The hangman was so moved [*troublé*] that he missed [her head] and had to repeat his job five times before he managed to behead her.... Thus ended the beautiful Mme Ticquet, who was the ornament of all Paris....[48]

Only for a brief moment, toward the end of her account, does du Noyer turn her attention from the spectacle itself to her own emotions as a spectator:

> One never saw anything as beautiful as her head when it had been separated from her body; they left it for a time on the scaffold so that the People could see it. Her face was turned in the direction of the Hôtel de Ville, and I assure you that I was dazzled by it. In the end, I was so touched by her death, that it took me more than six months to recover from it, and it is with pain that I recall these thoughts....[49]

So, finally, we have the reassurance that Madame du Noyer was "touched" by the death of her friend. Nowhere, however, do we get any indication that she thought it might be inappropriate to watch her friend die; on the contrary, she seemed to revel in the execution as if she were watching the premiere of a new tragedy. If she insists that she experienced "pain" in witnessing or in recalling the events, then it was a delightfully painless pain. Overall, it would seem that she not only took pleasure in witnessing the event but believed that others would take pleasure in reading about it. As she wrote to her correspondent (i.e. the reader, as the supposed correspondence was published with readers in mind), "but what would one not do to give you pleasure?"[50]

If du Noyer along with Madame Ticquet's other erstwhile friends and acquaintances saw nothing wrong with watching the spectacle of her death and renting out windows with the best view of the scaffold, the shifting tides of sensibility were such that now, at the turn of the eighteenth century, others were beginning to feel differently. In fact, du Noyer notes that the king himself "found it very bad that ladies had been to see this execution; he even expressed this sentiment to several of them."[51] Along the same lines, the Marquis de Sourches spoke of "an appalling multitude of people" who were on hand to witness the event, but he seemed particularly appalled by the presence of Madame Ticquet's acquaintances:

> Windows had been rented up to seven and eight pistoles, and they were filled with people of the court and the robe, to the point that one saw many men and women who had for a long time been in social contact with madame Tiquet: a monstrous effect of the curiosity of the French, which makes them overlook all sorts of proprieties.[52]

The Comte de Saint-Simon, too, found it extraordinarily distasteful that Madame Ticquet's friends and acquaintances would have numbered among the spectators:

> All the windows of the Hôtel de Ville, all those on the square and on the streets that led to it from the Conciergerie of the Palais, where she was [being held], were filled

with spectators, men and women, many with titles and many of distinction. There were even friends of both sexes of this unfortunate who had neither shame nor horror in attending. In the streets, the crowd was so thick that one could not pass. In general, people pitied her and wished for a pardon, and this was what made people go see her die. Such is society, so unreasonable and so at odds with itself.[53]

For both Sourches and Saint-Simon, an irresistible curiosity was driving people to attend the execution and this was "at odds" with something else, something that was just beginning to be felt: a sense that it was improper, shameful, and horrible to watch the death of an acquaintance as a form of spectacle. Unlike La Bruyère who, a decade earlier, had seemingly condemned the spectacle of all executions, the criticisms here are directed primarily at those who knew Ticquet and should have been feeling not the kind of tragic pity in which one could delight, but the kind of sympathy that would normally preclude watching without pain.

We should also note that Sourches and Saint-Simon mentioned the fact that spectators "of both sexes" were present, and that the king seemed particularly disturbed by the presence of "ladies." Of course, these references may simply be a way of alluding to the fact that many of Ticquet's, presumably mostly female, friends were in attendance. But it seems likely that this is the beginning of an assault on female spectatorship in particular, which would become more pronounced as the eighteenth century progressed, reaching an apex with the execution of Damiens in 1757. While aristocratic women had been attending executions for more than a century and a half by this point without provoking much in the way of comment, by the turn of the eighteenth century their presence, and the delight they often took in executions, was beginning to clash uncomfortably with the idea that was gaining currency at the time that women were naturally more sensitive and sympathetic than men, and that they were inherently incapable of taking pleasure in the suffering of others.[54]

The question inevitably arises: What were Saint-Simon and Sourches themselves doing watching the execution, these two men who found the presence of others so distasteful? Neither suggests that the details of the execution were reported secondhand, and readers are left with the distinct impression that both personally witnessed what they related in their memoirs. Why was watching the execution so shameful and inappropriate for others, but not for them? One answer might simply be that they did not see themselves as acquaintances of Ticquet, and were therefore outside her affective circle. Or perhaps, as men, they saw themselves as less beholden to the dictates of contemporary sensibilities. While both of these answers are plausible, I think that Saint-Simon and Sourches were among the first of a different, somewhat conflicted, breed of spectators, who managed to combine a voyeuristic interest in spectacular punishment with newer, more sympathetic sensibilities. This new type of spectator would continue to seek out executions, but their sensibilities would demand that they criticize the presence of others, as if their very criticism put them above the moral fray; they managed to see themselves as objective witnesses, almost as journalists, watching and judging the spectators who were seated at windows, who themselves were watching the suffering of others. As time wore on, however, it would become increasingly difficult for those who offered first-hand, disparaging accounts of executions to explain their own presence. Some, as we will see, would act as if they were simply recording events for posterity; others would style themselves as observers of their fellow men, proto-anthropologists, recording the (despicable) habits of others; still others would claim to have stumbled on executions accidentally, so that they could both give accounts of what transpired and condemn the spectacle of executions with impunity.[55]

Madame Ticquet's execution in 1699 therefore stands at the intersection between an established tradition of watching executions as a form of entertainment and a rising sensibility that was beginning to include an ever-expanding circle of individuals within its range. If it was inappropriate for friends of the victim to watch the spectacle of her suffering without themselves suffering, a revolution in sensibilities would soon make sympathetic suffering a natural characteristic of human beings as a whole, regardless of their personal attachment to the sufferer.

THE NATURALIZATION OF SYMPATHY: SENSIBILITY AS HUMAN NATURE

From the second half of the seventeenth century onward, even as spectators of all classes still rushed to watch executions, a succession of philosophers, public intellectuals, and novelists began to take it as a fundamental truth that human beings were endowed with a kind of natural goodness making them predisposed toward kindness and love for their fellow human beings and instinctively sympathetic to their suffering. In the words of the historian Norman Fiering, the seventeenth and eighteenth century witnessed the rise of a "doctrine of irresistible compassion" that would prove instrumental in the construction of modern humanitarianism, a term Fiering defines as "the widespread inclination to protest against obvious and pointless physical suffering."[56]

The wave of optimism about human nature, which swept over both sides of the English Channel near the turn of the eighteenth century, was in marked contrast, and indeed in conscious opposition, to the pessimistic ideas about human nature that Thomas Hobbes had expressed in *The Leviathan* (1651). While Hobbes was not unique in his pessimism, and was by no means the last prominent writer to take a dim view of human nature, he nevertheless expressed his views with such forcefulness and clarity that he had the effect of galvanizing those with opposing viewpoints. In Hobbes's wake, the vast majority of those writing on the subject of human nature would accept human goodness and kindness toward others as an article of faith.

Perhaps no writer from the second half of the seventeenth century was a greater champion of the fundamental belief that human beings were born with an innate predisposition to love one another than the philosopher and theologian Nicolas de Malebranche. Writing in 1674, Malebranche, whose ideas would prove influential in both France and Britain, insisted that God "has connected us in such a way with everything that surrounds us, and especially with the beings of our own species, that their ills naturally cause us distress, their joy makes us rejoice, and their greatness, their abasement, their diminution seem to enhance or diminish our own [sense of] being."⁵⁷ Taking up the idea of the time that the passions were forces that heightened our perceptions of the exterior world and deepened our connections to others, Malebranche understood *sensibilité* to be a communal force that connected every human being to every other human being. If physical senses enabled the individual to feel sensations within the body (heat, cold, pain), then the passions enabled individuals to feel sensations outside the body (love, hate, other people's pain): "[I]t is principally by the passions that the soul travels outside itself, and by which it feels that it is effectively connected to all that surrounds it...."⁵⁸

Drawing upon the ideas of Descartes, Malebranche claimed that the human body, not unlike the animal body, could be regarded as a kind of machine that was, so to speak, pre-programmed to respond in certain ways to certain stimuli. Foremost among these instinctive responses was a natural predisposition to respond to other human beings in distress:

> At the sight of something bad which surprises us, or which we perceive to be insurmountable on our own, we utter, for example, a great shout; this shout, which often escapes us without our realizing it, and [which] by the predisposition of the machine [i.e. the human body], enters without fail into the ears of those who are near enough to render us the aid we need. This shout penetrates them, and makes itself heard by them, no matter of what nation or social condition they may be, because this shout exists in all languages and all social classes, as it must, in effect, necessarily be. It agitates the brain and transforms in a moment the entire disposition of the body of those who are struck by it. It even makes them run to the aid [of others] without their realizing it. But it is not long before it acts on their mind [*esprit*], and before it obliges them to want to help, and to think of the means of helping, the individual who has uttered this natural prayer.⁵⁹

For Malebranche, *sensibilité* was no longer the gift of a special few but rather a natural reflex, a basic human instinct that transcended social class.

One finds a similar characterization of the reflexive need to rush to the aid of others in distress in Abbé Gamaches's *Système du coeur* (1704). Although, in contrast to Malebranche's theory of human benevolence, Gamaches's altruism is not quite so selfless:

> Nature is not mistaken in not relying very much on our reason in matters involving the mutual obligations which we are obliged to render to one another, and it is with wisdom that she makes us come to one another's aid by the pressing appeal to our own interests; she makes us suffer when those with whom we have some attachment find themselves in distress, so that seeking, as if by instinct, to deliver ourselves from the troubles she has visited upon us, we seek at the same time to relieve their pain.⁶⁰

Gamaches accords much more of a place to self-interest than did Malebranche, and in this respect he seems to anticipate the writings of Bernard Mandeville, who only a year later would put forward a very similar argument about how seemingly virtuous behaviors were grounded in self-interest.⁶¹ But we should note that Gamaches characterizes the reflexive impulse of human beings to rush to the aid of others as reserved for those "with whom we have some attachment." Nature, in other words, had made human beings in such a way that they cannot help suffering when they see their friends or family suffering, causing them to want to relieve the pain of others as a means of relieving their own (sympathetic) pain. Gamaches's idea of sympathy may have been somewhat more restrictive in terms of the object of sympathy, but both he and Malebranche considered the instinct to sympathize as a universal attribute of human nature. As Baasner astutely points out, "what for Mlle de Scudéry was the quality of only a few aristocratic souls becomes a basic anthropological value in Gamaches's text..."[62]

We can take note of some interesting parallels between what was being debated in the philosophical literature of the day on the nature of sympathy and the variety of opinions that existed at the turn of the eighteenth century with respect to spectatorship and executions. Malebranche's belief that human beings were naturally sympathetic to other human beings in distress seems very much in accord with La Bruyère's universal indictment of the "inhuman curiosity" that drove spectators to watch other people suffer. Gamaches's explanation of sympathy as a natural instinct that one feels for someone "with whom one has some attachment" might be viewed as corresponding to Saint-Simon's and Sourche's criticisms of those friends of Madame Ticquet who attended the spectacle of her death.

The fact that La Bruyère's and Malebranche's universal principles of sympathetic suffering predated by more than two decades those who, at the turn of the century, conceived sympathy as a feeling restricted to one's intimate circle, shows how the path from stoic insensitivity to universal sympathy was by no means a straightforward, linear trajectory. At the turn of the eighteenth century, a variety of opinions existed as to whether sympathy and sensitivity were the province of a few uniquely gifted individuals or a universal trait of mankind, and whether such sympathy was naturally restricted to one's circle of personal acquaintance or extended to all of one's fellow human beings, or even, as some were suggesting, to all living beings, regardless of species.[63]

At the turn of the eighteenth century, the British philosopher Anthony Ashley Cooper, the third Earl of Shaftesbury, offered a comprehensive and systematic analysis of sympathy that managed to reconcile the apparent contradictions between a conception of human nature as innately altruistic and one that regarded human beings as inherently self-interested. For Shaftesbury, the beauty of nature was that it had ensured that individual desires were so often in harmony with the collective good. Human beings and animals alike may be guided by their own self-interested appetites, but these appetites were designed by nature in such a way that they tended toward the preservation of the species as a whole—the desire to procreate being the most obvious example.[64]

Unlike Hobbes, whom he saw as advocating the suppression of "kindness of every sort, indulgence, tenderness, compassion, and in short, all natural affection" in favor of "a steady and deliberate pursuit of the most narrowly confined self-interest" (281–2), Shaftesbury insisted that the common interest and self-interest were not mutually exclusive. In fact, he argued, to experience compassion for someone else and other such "natural affections" was invariably more pleasurable than satisfying one's own, selfish appetites:

> The very disturbances which belong to natural affection, though they may be thought wholly contrary to pleasure, yield still a contentment and satisfaction greater than the pleasures of the indulged sense.... For thus when by mere illusion, as in a tragedy, the passions of this kind are skillfully excited in us, we prefer the entertainment to any other of equal duration. (297)

Shaftesbury makes the remarkable claim, in other words, that those passions or feelings that "draw us out of ourselves, even to the point where we are "disregardful of our own convenience and safety" (281), are actually *more* likely to satisfy us and make us happy than the satisfaction of our own, baser self-interest. He effectively turns Gamaches on his head: We are not motivated by self-interest to feel and act altruistically towards others; altruism, benevolence, pity, and sympathy *are* in our self-interest because they are means to "self-enjoyment." (293)

Anticipating Rousseau, however, Shaftesbury maintained that human beings' entry into civilization had estranged them from their natural state, and had led them to act in ways that were "inhuman", in contrast to which animals, who still existed in a state of nature, might almost be seen as behaving more decently:

> In the other species of creatures around us, there is found generally an exact proportionableness, constancy, and regularity in all their passions and affections; no failure in the care of the offspring or of the society to which they are united; no prostitution of themselves; no intemperance or excess in any kind.... Whilst man... is often found to live in less conformity with Nature, and... is often rendered the more barbarous and inhuman.... So that 'tis hard to find... a man who lives naturally and as a man. (290–1)

The further that human beings were removed from their natural state, the more the natural harmony between self-interest and natural affection deteriorated, the more individuals took pleasure in things that were foreign to their nature. Those who lived in cities "where numbers of men are maintained in lazy opulence and wanton plenty" were particularly susceptible to these unnatural behaviors, in contrast to the "hardy remote provincials" whose "honest and due employment" kept them in greater harmony with nature. (313) Among the "unnatural passions" in which the former indulged was "that unnatural and inhuman delight in beholding torments, and in viewing distress, calamity, blood, massacre and destruction, with a peculiar joy and pleasure." For Shaftesbury, the act of taking delight in watching another living being, whether human or animal, suffer, was not, as it was for Montaigne, something that he alone found unbearable; the act itself was "unnatural": "[T]o delight in the torture and pain of other creatures indifferently, natives or foreigners, of our own or of another species, kindred or no kindred, known or unknown; to feed as it were on death, and to be entertained with dying agonies; this... is wholly and absolutely unnatural, as it is horrid and miserable." (331)

Over the next decade or so, the idea that sympathy was a natural instinct of the human race as a whole increasingly became an article of faith on both sides of the

English Channel. In 1719, Abbé Jean-Baptiste Dubos suggested that this compassionate instinct lay at the very foundation of society itself:

> Nature wished to place in [the human heart] this sensibility, so prompt and so sudden, as the first foundation of society.... Nature decided to construct us in such a manner...that those who have need of our indulgence or our aid can easily move us. In this way, their emotions alone touch us immediately, and they obtain from us, by moving us to tears, that which they would never obtain through reason and argument. The tears of someone we do not know move us even before we know what they are crying about. The cries of a man with whom we have nothing in common but his humanity make us fly to his aid by an automatic [*machinal*] movement which precedes all deliberation.[65]

For Dubos, there is no longer any need, as there had been for Gamaches, to have any kind of connection to the suffering individual. The suffering of *all* human beings automatically elicits our sympathy.

Writing in 1722, William Wollaston, whose book *The Religion of Nature Delineated* was translated into French in 1726, similarly argued that this automatic sympathy was a fundamental trait of human nature, and that human beings could not help sympathizing with the suffering of others, even animals:

> There is something in *human* nature resulting from our very make and constitution, while it retains its genuin form, and is not *alterd* by vitious habits; not *perverted* by the transports of revenge of fury, by ambition, company or false philosophy [i.e. stoicism]; nor *opprest* by stupidity and neglecting to observe what happens to others: I say, there is *something*, which renders us obnoxious to the pains of others, causes us to sympathize with them, and almost comprehends us in their case. It is grievous to see or hear (and almost to hear of) any man, or even any animal whatever, in *torment*.[66]

Suggesting that this capacity to sympathize was a human trait and that "nothing of it appears in brutes," (258) Wollaston maintained, as had Shaftesbury before him, that the lack of this reflexive trait was inhuman: "It is therefore according to *nature* to be affected with the sufferings of other people," and those, on the contrary, who "delighted" in the suffering of others, were partaking in the "most insolent and cruel of all cruelties." Such behavior was, he insisted, "*inhuman* and *unnatural*." (259–60)

In 1725, the Irish-born Scottish philosopher Francis Hutcheson, who saw himself as a disciple of Shaftesbury, similarly spoke of "some Instinct, antecedent to all Reason from Interest, which influences us to the Love of others."[67] To Hutcheson, this "disposition to compassion" was more pronounced in women and children because they were less influenced by "custom, education, or instruction," all of which distorted one's natural sensibility.[68] We can already see here the philosophical underpinnings of a viewpoint that would regard female spectators at executions as betraying the natural instincts of both their species and their sex.

By the mid-eighteenth century, the belief that human beings were naturally and instinctively compassionate reached a kind of apogee in the writings of Jean-Jacques Rousseau, who made it a cornerstone of his world view and the basis for his refutation of Hobbes:

There is... a principle that Hobbes missed entirely and which... tempers the ardor which [man] has for his own well-being by an innate repugnance in seeing another human being suffer. I fear no contradiction in according to man the only natural virtue which the most outrageous detractor of human virtues [Hobbes] was forced to recognize. I am speaking of pity, an attribute suitable to beings as weak and susceptible to so many evils as we are; a virtue even more universal and more useful to man because it precedes all reflection, and so natural that even animals sometimes give clear signs of it....[69]

In Rousseau's view, this natural pity prevented human beings in a state of nature from behaving as Hobbes had claimed they had:

It is [natural pity] which, in a state of nature, takes the place of laws, morals and virtue, with the advantage that no one is tempted to disobey her sweet voice; it is [natural pity] which prevents the strong savage from taking from a weak child or an infirm old man the sustenance that they have acquired with difficulty, if he has hope of providing for himself otherwise.[70]

For Rousseau, in fact, most modern virtues in the last analysis derived from mankind's innate, natural pity: "In effect, what are generosity, clemency, humanity, if not pity applied to the weak, to the guilty, or to human kind in general? Even benevolence and friendship, if you look at them closely, are the product of pity applied with constancy upon a particular object: for, to desire that someone not suffer at all—is it any different than desiring that he be happy?"[71]

From this perspective, self-interest and self-love were not, as Hobbes and Mandeville had suggested, the true nature of mankind, but rather a perversion of natural instincts:

It is reason that engenders our self-love, and it is reflection which strengthens it; it is [reason] that turns man in on himself; it is [reason] that separates him from everything that disturbs him or afflicts him. It is philosophy that isolates him, and according to which he says to himself in secret, at the sight of a suffering man: "Perish if you will; I am safe."[72]

Here, a century and a half after the heyday of neo-stoicism, the valorization of reason at the expense of the passions was turned on its head. Now, for Rousseau and so many others, the natural instinct to commiserate with others was the surer guide than the selfish dictates of reason.

From the late sixteenth to the mid-eighteenth century, the peculiar trait of being automatically sensitive to the suffering of others gradually became something that was commonly believed to be natural to the human race as a whole. While the transformation did not follow a clear, linear trajectory, nevertheless the trend over time was toward a gradual extension of the affective barrier between oneself and the outside world, with an ever-expanding circle of beings within one's range of sensitivity: from one's close family and friends to all human beings, and even, for some, to animals. If Montaigne had considered himself unusual in this respect, by the time Shaftesbury and Rousseau were writing, those who did not experience

Montaigne's automatic sensitivity to the suffering of others were the ones who were unusual, if not downright unnatural.

To a certain extent, we can see attitudes toward the spectacle of execution roughly tracking this shift in sensibility. La Bruyère's condemnation of all who watched spectacles of suffering, on the one hand, and Saint-Simon's and Sourche's condemnation of spectators who could watch the suffering of those whom they knew, on the other, reflect the variety of contemporary conceptions of sensibility and its range of affect, from Malebranche's conception of universal and automatic sympathy to Gamaches's more narrow understanding of sympathy. The trend over time, however, both in conceptions of sensibility and on the specific question of the appropriate emotions of penal spectators, was clearly toward an ever-expanding circle of affect, such that it eventually became inappropriate and, in fact, inhuman to watch *anyone* suffer.

While this shift in sensibilities was taking place, the privileged pastime of watching executions as a form of entertainment was gradually becoming a national pastime, common to all classes of society. With hindsight, it may be obvious that these two cultural trends—the rising spectacularity of executions and the naturalization of automatic sympathy to all human beings—did not fit very well together. At the time, however, while both sensibility and spectatorship were in a state of flux, the looming crisis was not yet apparent.

Indeed, at any given point during this period, one might have found examples of all sensibilities and all forms of spectatorship, both new and old, at the same execution. Surrounding the scaffold itself, individuals weeping with compassion might have stood side by side with those who felt the patient was unworthy of redemption, and who therefore shouted for vengeance. Up above the crowd, in the windows overlooking the square, spectators who had paid for the privilege would have been looking down on the entire scene below them either with a kind of tragic delight or voyeuristic insouciance, taking in the whole scene—the crowd as well as the principal actors, executioner, the patient, and the confessor—as if it were an elaborate spectacle staged for their viewing pleasure. Next to these penal voyeurs, perhaps even in the same room, one might have found those newly sensitive souls who were just beginning to look on in disgust at everyone else, both those down below as well as those in the windows, although they had not yet begun to question what they themselves were doing there.

If some were beginning to question the spectacle of capital punishment, however, almost no one was yet questioning capital punishment itself. The sentimental revolution that was re-imagining human beings as automatically and reflexively sympathetic had, at this point in time, virtually nothing to say about the act of maiming and killing people in public, only about the act of watching it. *Sensibilité*, at least in its early elaboration, had more to do with the *sight* of suffering than with suffering itself.

7

A Spectacular Crisis
Watching Executions in the Age of *Sensibilité*

In the first half of the eighteenth century, the act of watching executions as a form of entertainment spread to all classes of French society, as spectators vied with one another to secure the best vantage point they could afford from which to see the spectacle unfold. At the same time, the seventeenth-century ideal of *sensibilité*, which had originally been conceived of as the unique gift of the privileged few, was increasingly being understood as a kind of automatic predisposition to compassion, a natural human reflex that made it impossible for one human being to witness the suffering of another without suffering themselves. Several eighteenth-century philosophers struggled to reconcile these two seemingly contradictory truths: that human beings could not help gawking at and even taking delight in the suffering of others and, at the same time, that they, at least in theory, could not bear to watch other human beings suffer.

The execution of Robert-François Damiens in 1757 was to mark a profound crisis in several respects. This execution, in which Damiens was to be more or less flayed alive and torn limb from limb by horses for the crime of having attempted to kill the king, was intended to be the most terrifying and impressive spectacle that French justice could stage. To the hundreds of thousands of people who lined the streets of Paris on the day of his execution, however, and to those crowding into every inch of the Place de Grève, filling every window and every seat on the viewing platforms hastily erected where roofs had been, Damiens' execution was to be nothing less than the greatest spectacle of the century. On one level, this eagerness and enthusiasm was difficult to square with contemporary theories of exemplary deterrence. On another level, the desperation of hundreds of thousands of spectators to watch another human being be flayed and quartered alive gave the lie to contemporary theories of natural and automatic sympathy.

Within days of the execution, commentators were expressing their horror, not so much at the execution itself, but at those spectators, and those female spectators in particular, who could watch Damiens die without a trace of the natural compassion that was, by this point in time, assumed to be a defining trait of humanity itself. By the eve of the Revolution, the wealthier classes had largely forsaken the penal spectacle, abandoning the now "horrible" spectacle of public executions to the masses who continued to watch, as yet unaware that it was a perversion of natural human sensibilities to do so. This vulgarization of the penal spectacle would provoke a crisis in its own right, as the very individuals who were now the only ones taking delight in the penal spectacles were precisely the ones to whom exemplary deterrence was meant to be teaching a lesson.

The following pages trace what, with hindsight, we can see as an almost inevitable crisis, as a rising penal spectacularity, a sensibility of automatic compassion, and the logic of exemplary deterrence ran headlong into one another.

PENAL SPECTATORS AND THE FIRST GLIMMERINGS OF SELF-CONSCIOUSNESS

Although the popular aristocratic pastime of watching executions was beginning to be the object of scattered criticism toward the very end of the seventeenth century, the cream of French society continued to attend, eagerly renting out windows overlooking the scaffold, still oblivious to these criticisms. We can see, for example, in the correspondence of the Marquise de Balleroy that in the first decades of the eighteenth century she and her relatives and friends traded accounts of executions in a manner not all that different from Sévigné and her cohort in the preceding century. In March of 1720, Balleroy's brother, Caumartin de Boissy, sent her the following note:

> They burned two men at the Grève yesterday, after having cut off their tongues and fists.... They had uttered blasphemies so shocking and new that the judges who condemned them said that they had never heard anything so terrible.... One was twenty-one or twenty-two, and the other eighteen. The older one looked right and left as they were preparing the pyre, as if he was merely a spectator. The younger one was not as steadfast.[1]

Just eight days later, he followed up this account with another letter that mentions the roughly simultaneous execution of the Comte de Horn and the Marquis de Pontcallec. The former was broken on the wheel in the Place de Grève, despite his noble standing, for having committed an act of premeditated murder, and the latter was executed, along with his conspirators, for having led an uprising in Nantes. In referring to these executions, Caumartin de Boissy strikes a tone so flippant that it seems worthy of Sévigné herself: "Last Tuesday, while the comte de Horn was giving his performance [*représentoit*] at the Grève, another [dramatic] tragedy was going on at the chateau de Nantes."[2] In December of that same year, another of the Marquise's correspondents informed her, sandwiched in between comments about the impending death of the Pope and various banking difficulties, that "They broke a Jew on the wheel at the place de Grève for having killed one of his associates.... He asked to be baptized [before the execution], and the jailer was his sponsor. One has never seen a criminal die so resolute, so repentant, kissing the cross with an abundance of tears."[3]

By the early eighteenth century, however, the voyeuristic viewing habits of the privileged classes, who attended executions more as a diverting pastime than as a ritual that possessed great meaning, was no longer confined to rarefied society, and spectators from across the social spectrum were flocking to the penal spectacle as a form of entertainment. All of this was taking place, of course, at the same moment that a revolution in sensibilities was sweeping across France and Britain, predicated on the conviction that human beings were automatically and reflexively compassionate, and incapable of witnessing the suffering of others without suffering themselves. We have already seen how Saint-Simon described court society of 1699, which flocked to the execution of Madame Ticquet and was torn between feelings of pity and a desire to see her die, as being "at odds with itself." By 1717, the playwright Pierre de Marivaux was making a similar observation about the Parisian crowds who rushed toward the scaffold:

> They were going to put two highwaymen to death one day. I saw a crowd of people who followed them, and I took note of two impulses [*mouvements*] that belong, I think, uniquely to the populace of Paris. This [crowd of] people ran to this sad spectacle with a curious avidity which was joined together with a feeling of compassion for these unfortunates. I even saw a woman who, with a tear in her eye, ran as fast as she could in order to miss nothing of the execution, the thought of which was causing her in advance an instinctual [*machinale*] sadness [*douleur*].... I'd bet that the people could, at the same time, pity a man destined for death, experience pleasure in watching him die, and heap a thousand curses on him.[4]

One can read Marivaux as suggesting that "the people," as a collection of individuals, were watching executions in a variety of different ways. But his description of the woman running as fast as she could with a tear in her eye points to something different: the conflict between voyeurism and sympathy *within* each individual. By 1719, the aesthetic theoretician (among other things) Jean-Baptiste Dubos was putting forward the argument that while compassion for the suffering of others might well be a human instinct, there was another, perhaps equally strong instinct, that impelled individuals to gawk at that same suffering:

> The natural emotion that is automatically [*machinalement*] excited within us when we see fellow human beings in danger or in distress... possesses charms capable of making it sought after, despite the sad and troublesome thoughts that are associated with it and which result from it. An impulse which reason cannot entirely repress makes many individuals seek things that have a tendency to be heartrending. People flock in droves to see the most horrible spectacle that men can watch. I mean the punishment of another man who suffers the rigor of the laws on a scaffold and who is put to death by terrible torments. An individual ought to be able to foresee... that groans of his fellow man, would make a lasting impression on him which would torment him for a long time before being entirely erased; however, the lure of the emotion is stronger for many people than [considered] reflections and the counsels of experience. People [*le monde*] in all countries flock to see these horrible spectacles.
>
> It is the same attraction that makes [people] love the anxiety and alarm caused by perils, in which one observes other men being exposed to dangers in which one does not oneself take part. It is moving, says Lucretius, to see from the shore a vessel struggling against the waves that wish to engulf it, as it is to watch a battle from on high, where one can watch safe from the melée.[5]

In contrast to Saint-Simon and Marivaux, who marveled at the peculiarity of the spectators they saw, Dubos saw the conflict between compassion and gawking as a universal human condition, common to people "in all countries" and of every century.

While social commentators like Marivaux and Dubos struggled to reconcile the idea of natural compassion with the popularity of the penal spectacle, those who attended these spectacles were, for the moment, still relatively unaware of these contradictions, much less the need to explain them. In what might be seen as the first glimmerings of a new self-consciousness, however, there emerged, in the second quarter of the eighteenth century, a relatively new kind of penal spectator: the objective, bourgeois diarist who, although he availed himself of any opportunity to watch an execution, did so with little trace of enjoyment. Quite possibly unknown to one another, the following individuals began recording their detailed impressions of executions around the year 1715: Jean Buvat, who composed his journal from 1715 to 1723; Mathieu Marais, *avocat au parlement*, who wrote from 1715 to 1727; Edmond-Jean-François Barbier, a prolific diarist who was *avocat consultant au parlement de Paris*, and who wrote from 1718 to 1763; and Thomas-Simon Gueullette, who in contrast to the others never wrote a proper diary, but who, in his capacity as deputy royal prosecutor, recorded his reflections on various executions, and amassed an extraordinary collection of documents, drawings, and pamphlets relating to crime and punishment from 1709 until his death in 1766.[6] To this group, one might also add two diarists who began chronicling executions somewhat later: Pierre Barthès, who kept an account of daily life in Toulouse from 1738 to 1780, and Siméon-Prosper Hardy, who recorded all aspects of daily life in Paris between the years 1764 and 1789, but for whom executions seemed to hold a particular attraction.[7]

Although most of the bourgeois diarists chronicled executions within the context of a broad range of topics that caught their attention, Hardy and Gueullette seem to have had a more pronounced interest in executions than the others. Above all, Gueullette stands out as someone who was obsessed with executions, recording his impressions whenever and wherever he had the opportunity to witness them, and always saving the printed *arrêts*, with the details of the crime and the sentence, very often scribbling his personal thoughts in the margins.

Rather than being mere spectators, all of these bourgeois diarists saw themselves as engaged in a kind of "scientific" study of executions and of the spectators who watched, recording all the facts as objectively as possible. As Buvat wrote in his preface, "Since this journal is strictly speaking a simple collection of facts...one has avoided making any reflections on the various events which presented themselves...."[8] Buvat and the other bourgeois diarists saw themselves as performing an important task for posterity (rather than merely gawking at the condemned on the scaffold), and indeed they were; as we will see throughout this chapter, all of these authors provide us with a wealth of information about executions and the people who watched them in the eighteenth century.

COLLISION COURSE: SPECTACULARITY, SENTIMENTALITY, AND EXEMPLARY DETERRENCE

One of the greatest penal "events" in the first quarter of the eighteenth century, drawing the attention not only of our bourgeois diarists but of the country as a whole, was the arrest, trial, and conviction of the notorious Cartouche, along with several hundred of his co-conspirators in 1721. Cartouche was convicted of masterminding an enormous criminal enterprise in Paris, and the sheer number of his crimes, together with his uniquely jaunty and irreverent attitude, combined to create the eighteenth-century equivalent of a media circus. Even in the weeks prior to Cartouche's execution, before his trial had officially begun, Parisians seem to have had a voracious appetite for all things Cartouche, and it was no doubt with the intent of cashing in on the Cartouche craze that the actors of the *Comédie française* had the idea of putting on a play based on his life and his crimes. Thinking that they might lend their play an aura of authenticity, the actors arranged a visit with Cartouche and with members of his gang as they waited in prison for their trials to begin, hoping to learn more about their mannerisms, their argot, etcetera. As the chronicler Marais reported, the actors showed up at the prison dressed "in fine wigs and in gold-braided coats," and by all accounts something of a spontaneous party took place, with Cartouche's gang teaching the actors how to sing and dance like criminals, aided by several bottles of wine. The end result of this research was, as Marais recounts, "a musical comedy, which was scandalously performed at the theater under the title of *Cartouche: or The Thieves*."[9]

The actors no doubt thought that the idea of creating a show based on the life of Cartouche was perfectly natural, given the intense interest in the criminal mastermind at the time. In what was undoubtedly a sign of changing sensibilities with respect to crime and punishment, however, Marais was by no means the only one who was scandalized by the idea of celebrating and making light of the exploits of a man who, truth be told, had killed and robbed quite a number of people. Gueullette found the concept very distasteful, noting that the *comédiens italiens* were putting on a Cartouche play of their own, and remarking that it "proves very well the depravity of morals in this century."[10] Barbier similarly noted that "People of good sense found it very unfortunate that it was permitted to represent on the stage a man who exists in reality, who is being interrogated every day, and whose end will be to be broken alive on the wheel; this is not at all becoming."[11] With reference to *Cartouche* the musical comedy, the *Mercure* fretted: "How will posterity judge the taste of our century...?"[12]

When outraged individuals asked the Regent, the Duc d'Orléans, to ban the play's performance, he apparently replied that there was a precedent, since Louis XIV had allowed the performance of *La Devineresse ou Madame Jobin* while La Voisin, upon whom the play was based, was being tried and executed.[13] Despite the misgivings of many, therefore, the show did go on, and enjoyed a good deal of success. Barbier tells us that, "A surprising number of people are going to [see] it."[14] The *Mercure*, which had been so worried about what future generations might think, nevertheless reluctantly admitted that the playwright had "extracted from its subject matter—itself base and unpleasant—everything good that it was possible to extract."[15] Even Gueullette, who had complained about the moral depravity of his century, could not help admitting that the one-act play that the *comédiens italiens* had put together based on the life of Cartouche was "very funny."[16]

Despite the popularity of *Cartouche* the musical, or perhaps because of it, the play abruptly ceased its run on 11 November 1721, just as Cartouche's trial was getting underway, and some two weeks before his execution took place. If *La Devineresse* had been performed while La Voisin was being tried and executed, some forty years earlier, times had apparently changed. By 1721, it was beginning to seem inappropriate that the actors of the *Comédie française* could blithely sing and dance their way through the days leading up to Cartouche's breaking on the wheel.

As soon as Cartouche's guilty verdict was handed down by the court, crowds of people began flocking to the Place de Grève. He would spend the better part of two days being debriefed by the authorities, who hoped he might denounce his accomplices. During this time, spectators stood vigil on the square, fearful that they might miss the actual moment of execution. (Fig. 8) Here is Barbier's account:

> Thursday 27 [November 1721], the famous Cartouche was submitted to questioning [by torture].... He admitted nothing. In the afternoon, he was supposed to be executed on the wheel along with four others [from his gang], as well as two others who were to be hanged, all at the same time. The [Place de] Grève has never been so full of people as on that day. Most of the rooms [on the square] had been rented.... As night falls early [this time of year], the four wheels were removed, and only his [wheel] remained. He arrived at the [Place de] Grève around five o'clock. He was annoyed at seeing only one wheel. As it was necessary that there be something extraordinary in his end, he gave up the names of an infinite number of people [as accomplices], one after the other, and he stayed [in the Hôtel de Ville] until two o'clock in the afternoon on Friday.... All night long, they did nothing but cart people in [to answer to his denunciations], and the [Place de] Grève was still filled with people who waited....

As everyone stood by, awaiting his execution with great anticipation, even the most trivial details about what Cartouche was up to inside the Hôtel de Ville proved to be of interest:

> He dined Thursday evening and had breakfast on Friday morning. His *rapporteur* asked him if he wanted a *café au lait* that others were having. He said that it wasn't his beverage [of choice], and that he would much rather have a glass of wine with a bread roll. It was brought to him, and he drank to the health of his two judges.[17]

Gueullette, who had connections to the penal establishment, and who prided himself on being able to ascertain almost every detail about important cases, obligingly fills in some of the gaps in Barbier's account: ".... [He] dined Thursday at ten in the evening on a chicken and a bottle of wine, and had another glass or two on Friday morning.... [T]he Grève never emptied of people all night long."[18]

Although some people had expressed misgivings about the appropriateness of the play *Cartouche*, it is difficult to find anyone who spoke out against the air of celebration and frenzied anticipation and excitement that surrounded the spectacle of the execution itself. Curiously, one of the only exceptions was the eleven-year-old Louis XV. When his ten-year-old companion informed the young king that he was intending to watch the execution of Cartouche, little Louis XV apparently replied "If you go, I will never see you again in my life."[19]

A Spectacular Crisis 171

Fig. 8. Cartouche à l'Hôtel de Ville avant son supplice, reproduced in Paul Lacroix, *XVIIIe siècle, Institutions, usages et costumes* (Paris, 1875), 311.

In the days and weeks after Cartouche's execution, French society, even at the highest levels, could talk of little else. The Duchesse d'Orléans, mother of the Regent of France, wrote that "I ran into the comte d'Hoïm and the chevalier de Schaub. They told me about Cartouche's having been executed yesterday; this detained me for quite a while."[20] On 29 November, Caumartin de Boissy wrote to his sister that "For several days, no one has spoken of anything but Cartouche."[21] One even gets the impression that there was almost a sense of loss, shared by members of all social classes. Gueullette called Cartouche "the most clever, adroit, intrepid and determined scoundrel that one had ever heard tell of."[22]

With all Paris having been primed for spectacle, Cartouche's death left people wanting more. This craving was partly satisfied by the ongoing executions of the remaining members of Cartouche's extensive gang, but what people really wanted was more of Cartouche himself, and several entrepreneurs did their best to fill the void:

> The body of Cartouche was brought to St. Cosme and the clerk of the surgeons made more than three hundred livres in exhibiting him to the public. Today we can see the head of this illustrious scoundrel in wax.... [The figure] was molded on the real head of Cartouche, and is the perfect likeness.[23]

Cartouche's reputation lived on long after his execution, serving as a yardstick by which the notoriety of all future criminals would be measured. According to Barbier, a highwayman who had been involved in the murder of more than thirty people was heard to lament the fact that his own celebrity would never match that of Cartouche: "He was overheard to say that it was his great sadness that, two days after his execution, no one would speak of him, whereas people were still talking about Cartouche, who was nothing more than a miserable house burglar."[24]

The interest with which the public followed Cartouche and his execution rivaled, and perhaps even surpassed, the interest that earlier generations had taken in the crime and punishment of Mesdames Ticquet, Voisin, and Brinvilliers. In Cartouche's execution, however, certain nagging questions were beginning to be raised: Was it appropriate to put on a musical comedy about someone who had killed so many people and was himself about to be put to death? How much spectacle was too much spectacle?

The 1720s would seem to mark the very beginning of a new self-consciousness about executions—not yet a condemnation of them, but simply the posing of questions that had never really been asked before. When, for example, members of a ring of sodomites were punished in Paris in 1726, Barbier reports that the authorities struggled to find a way to punish the culprits without "advertising [*illustrer*] this crime and rendering it more common, the majority of people not knowing what it is."[25] In certain cases, apparently, the rationale for exemplary, spectacular punishment seemed less clear. Or perhaps the way people were watching was beginning to seem less appropriate.

Nevertheless, public interest in executions continued unabated through the 1720s and 1730s, and spectators of all classes continued to flock to them in search of excitement, novelty, and entertainment. In 1729, Barbier tells us that the execution of a thief named Nivet, whose crimes were far worse than anything Cartouche had ever done, "attracted the curiosity of all those who love grand spectacles. All the windows on the Grève found brokers to rent them out."[26] And in 1737, when a nobleman was sentenced to be decapitated—a punishment that had not been performed in Paris for quite some time (the Comte de Horn having been broken on the wheel)—the novelty of the spectacle drew, according to Barbier, "a surprising number of people, both in the windows and in the street." Even more interesting than the size of the crowd, however, was their reaction to the performance of the execution: "Everyone applauded in order to compliment [the executioner] on his skill."[27]

Applause at an execution? What about the natural pity that human beings could not help but feel when they witnessed a spectacle of suffering? What about the very premise of exemplary deterrence and the idea that these clapping spectators were supposed to be learning a lesson and perhaps even be terrified by the sight of an execution? It is, I suspect, no coincidence that one year later, when the next decapitation of a nobleman, Louis Moiria, was to occur on the Place de Grève, city officials, for the very first time, endeavored to limit certain spectacular aspects of the execution. Here is Gueullette's account of what happened:

> Mr. Turgot, who was then *prévôt des marchands*, ordered that for Moiria's execution as well as for all such future spectacles, there will be no open windows in the Hôtel de Ville, and [he] gave as his reason that they should be [open] only for happy spectacles and not for those of this nature. His orders were followed exactly, to the great discontent of those who could [not] enter.

Gueullette, perhaps the foremost spectator of executions of the entire eighteenth century, was not about to let over-zealous municipal officials prevent him from witnessing the relatively rare spectacle of a beheading. He snuck inside the office of the king's prosecutor, inside the Hôtel de Ville, "from which location, by detaching three or four little diamond-shaped panes of glass from their leading, we were easily able to see the execution of the unfortunate...."[28]

What prompted this decision on the part of municipal authorities to restrict access to windows looking out from the Hôtel de Ville onto the Place de Grève? Judging by the reported words of Turgot, there was clearly a sense that it was inappropriate to watch the spectacle of execution as a form of entertainment. Applause and appreciation were appropriate for "happy spectacles," but spectacles of "this nature" seemingly called for a different reaction on the part of spectators. Pity? Terror? A combination of the two? What seems clear is that the authorities were anticipating the same sort of applause that had greeted the beheading a year earlier, and they were doing whatever they could to prevent it. Spectator access was not restricted on the square itself, however, presumably so that those who were interested in watching in a more appropriate fashion could do so.

We should carefully note the fact that the idea of executions themselves and the concept of public corporal punishment were still beyond reproach. Very shortly—within the next five to ten years—the first direct criticisms of contemporary penal practice would be made.[29] For the moment, however, it was simply the practice of voyeuristic watching that was just beginning to come under increasing scrutiny.

Turgot's tenure as *prévôt des marchands* ended the following year, and the restrictions on watching from windows apparently did not outlast his time in office. In Paris, as in the rest of France, public executions continued to attract crowds of spectators looking for entertainment. In 1744, when a surgeon was condemned to be broken on the wheel, and crowds jostled to get a good look at him on the eve of his execution, he was reported to say, "Hey, gentlemen, no shoving. You'll have a chance to see me at your leisure tomorrow."[30] And when, in May of 1755, the famous smuggler Louis Mandrin was broken on the wheel in the southeastern town of Valence, some six thousand people crowded into the town on very short notice, filling the Place des Clercs and the surrounding rooftops. An enterprising individual even managed to hastily erect stands from which spectators could have a prime viewing spot for the price of 12 sols.[31]

Two months after Mandrin's execution, in July of 1755, an execution took place in Paris that was to reach new heights in its celebration of the convicted criminal and the eager anticipation with which spectators awaited the execution. Madame Lescombat had been tried and convicted of having convinced her lover to murder her husband, but she had managed to postpone the date of her execution by claiming to be pregnant. When it turned out that she was not, in fact, pregnant, and a date was set for her execution, throngs of spectators flooded into the center of Paris to witness the execution of a woman who was, by all accounts, very beautiful. As Barbier described the scene:

> [T]here was an extraordinary confluence of people in the [Place de] Grève, as well as in all the adjacent streets so that people could at least catch sight of her passing by. There were even people all the way up in the towers of Notre Dame. The rooms were rented out on the Grève, and there were a number of people in carriages in the Place as well as the passages....[32]

The author of a pamphlet devoted to Lescombat's crimes and execution referred to the "infinity of people who were witnesses to her punishment" and included in the pamphlet a song, written to commemorate the event, that begins by marveling at the number of spectators present:

> Quelle nouveauté est-ce aujourd'hui!
> Quel bruit entend-on dans Paris!
> L'on voit le monde qui s'amasse
> Dans les Carfours & dans les Places,
> Qui s'entredisent, allons vois ça,
> L'on va pendre la Lescombat.[33]

While other celebrated criminals had received their fair share of attention, one cannot help getting the impression that Lescombat's execution reached even greater heights of spectacularity. Contemporary pamphlets treat her more as if she were a celebrity than a criminal, and almost without exception dwelled on her remarkable beauty: "All Paris ran to the Prison to see her.... [H]er bust, as well as her arms and hands are beautiful, her skin of a dazzling whiteness."[34] Parisians had an insatiable appetite for her likeness. Her portrait was sold in the streets, which Barbier insisted was "not as pretty as she was in real life."[35] A piece of enameled jewelry was designed, depicting her in the arms of her lover as well as in prison, and a wax figure of her was made, and displayed "to all of Paris."[36] To many observers, the occasion of her execution seemed more like a thrilling stage debut than the execution of a criminal. Barbier tells us that "When she came out of [the Hôtel de Ville] in order to proceed to the ladder [of the scaffold], people clapped their hands as if they were watching a show [*comme à un spectacle*]."[37]

We have already seen how Turgot had attempted to limit the voyeuristic aspects of executions fifteen years earlier with his short-lived efforts to exclude spectators from the windows of the Hôtel de Ville. It would seem that the authorities had similar intentions in mind when they made the decision to cover Lescombat's face during her appearances before the crowd of spectators in her final hours. According to Gueullette, "her face was very hidden by a kind of *bagnolette* [a small, hooded cape]" when she entered the Hôtel de Ville to have her final interview with authorities. When she finally emerged, and was led toward the scaffold, she was wearing a handkerchief over her face. Barbier tells us that the crowds, whose excitement had reached a kind of frenzy, experienced a great sense of disappointment at not being able to see Lescombat's face: "This crazed public was all the more miserable for having seen nothing. This woman's face was covered with a handkerchief, and she was hanged at seven thirty in the evening with this handkerchief."[38] According to Gueullette, the handkerchief caused the public to "murmur quite a bit, and say that it was not La Lescombat, but another woman."[39]

Not Lescombat, but another woman? Our first reaction might be to smile at the suspicions of the crowd; and yet, in many respects, the crowd's reaction was perfectly logical. Wasn't the entire purpose of spectacular justice that people actually witness it? There were only two plausible explanations. The first, and the one that spread through the crowd that evening, was that the person being executed was not, in fact, Lescombat. Why else cover her face? The other explanation, too complicated and too dimly understood probably even by those who had hatched the plan to cover her face, was that the authorities were hoping to carry out an execution that might serve the traditional purposes of deterrence while at the same time minimizing those sensational, spectacular elements, that voyeuristic fascination, which detracted from the lessons the spectacle was supposed to teach. The authorities hoped, in other words, that if they could prevent the crowds from gawking at Lescombat's famous beauty, they might be able to perform an execution that would result in sober edification rather than entertainment. The excited applause that ran through the crowd upon first seeing her, however, would seem to indicate that their efforts were to no avail.

A crisis point had clearly been reached. Spectacular elements of executions were now overshadowing everything else and the very principle of punishment as exemplary deterrence was not only being compromised, it was being largely ignored. Moreover, the eagerness with which spectators were flocking to executions to watch their fellow human beings die a painful death was giving the lie to contemporary conceptions of human nature and the supposed instinct for compassion. Within two years after Lescombat's execution, France was to witness the most spectacular execution to take place in living memory when Damiens was punished for attempted regicide. This execution would bring the most graphic elements of corporal punishments into play at a time when spectators could only process them as the biggest, most extraordinary show in several generations. The eagerness, avidity, and desperation with which spectators anticipated Damiens' death would prove to be impossible to reconcile with contemporary views on the purpose of punishment and with contemporary sensibilities.

THE EXECUTION OF DAMIENS: "THE MOST HORRIBLE AND DISGUSTING PUNISHMENT THAT JUSTICE HAS EVER DARED TO IMAGINE"

As anyone who has read the first section of Michel Foucault's *Discipline and Punish* is well aware, an extraordinary number of painful, graphic punishments were performed on the body of Damiens, the would-be regicide. Contemporaries were themselves struck by the extraordinary nature of the event. When the official *arrêt* was published, stipulating the punishments to which Damiens would be subjected, Barbier recopied the entire judicial sentence into his journal, as if he were trying to take in the enormity of the impending spectacle. Although the array of punishments that Damiens was sentenced to suffer was not entirely new—it was based on the punishment of the regicide Ravaillac in 1610—Damiens' punishment was certainly unique in its time:

> .... [T]he said Damiens [is] condemned to perform the *amende honorable* before the principal door of the church of Paris, where he will be led and conveyed in a tumbrel, naked but for a shirt, carrying a torch of burning wax of a weight of two pounds; and there, on his knees, will say and declare that maliciously and treacherously he committed the said very-malicious and very-abominable and very-detestable parricide, and wounded the King with a knife blow to his right side, of which he repents, asks forgiveness of God, of the King and of justice; this done, [he will be] led and conveyed in said tumbrel to the Place de Grève, and on a scaffold which will be erected there, maimed in the breasts, arms, thighs and calves of the legs, his right hand, holding in it the knife with which he committed the crime, burned by fire and sulfur, and on the places where he will be maimed, thrown molten lead, boiling oil, burning resin, wax and sulfur melted together, and then his body will be pulled and dismembered by four horses, and his limbs and body consumed by fire, reduced to ashes, and these ashes scattered to the winds.[40]

This was to be *the* execution of the eighteenth century. The *Gazette d'Amsterdam* enthused more than two months in advance of the execution: "Never has a spectacle had as many spectators as [Damiens'] punishment will have."[41] Those who could afford it procured individual windows or entire rooms overlooking the Place de Grève long in advance of the execution, and prices were not cheap. Gueullette reported that "My wife's shoemaker rented his [room], which had three windows and the possibility of putting tables seating twelve to fifteen people behind them, for 300 livres."[42] The shoemaker apparently got a very good deal for his room with three windows, as another source reports that in the days before the execution the price had risen as high as 360 livres *per window*, and that demand for viewing spots was so intense that owners of houses were prompted to "uncover their houses, and in place of a roof they built amphitheaters and balconies with seats for rental. They went even further: where there was a separation between the roofs of houses, they built canopies from one roof to the other in order to make room for balconies between them."[43]

On the morning of 28 March 1757, the date of Damiens' execution, Paris was filled to bursting with eager spectators. Although many thousands of people had managed to secure viewing spots on the Grève itself, many thousands more were forced by lack of funds or foresight to catch a glimpse of him as he performed his amende honorable, his public act of contrition, at Notre-Dame, or as he made his way from Notre-Dame to the Place de Grève. The Duc de Croÿ wrote in his journal that "there was *un monde affreux* everywhere that he passed," and Barbier noted that, as Damiens made his way toward the Place de Grève, "all the boutiques and windows were filled with people [hoping] to see him pass by."[44]

A century and a half earlier, in 1610, spectators had similarly lined the streets to witness Ravaillac pass by, and had subjected him to a variety of insults. L'Estoile had reported that the crowd "would have thrown themselves upon him if it hadn't been for the archers who kept order."[45] Were the bystanders who lined the streets to watch Damiens pass by similarly united in their hatred for the would-be regicide? Apparently not: "The Parisians seemed only like gawkers [*badauds*], behaving in an ordinary manner, and even indifferent. They showed neither hatred nor pity."[46]

Those who had managed to secure a spot on the Place de Grève itself or in one of the prized windows overlooking the square awaited Damiens' arrival "with great impatience."[47] Descriptions of the Grève on that early spring day make it sound as if there was not an inch of space left unoccupied: "The roofs of all the houses on the Grève and even the chimneys were covered with people. There were even a man and a woman who fell from one of them onto the Place and who injured others [below]."[48] A contemporary pamphlet said, quite simply, that "One cannot express the number of people who were at the Place de Grève during the execution. All the houses, roofs, and every spot with a view was filled, and one could see, no matter which way one turned, nothing but an incalculable number of people."[49]

Every credible primary source gives the impression that the people who massed on the Place de Grève that day could barely contain their excitement as the fateful hour neared. Terror could not have been further from their minds, unless of course we count the "terror" of missing even a minute of the spectacular show that was about to take place: "Many people came to spend the night in the rooms that they had rented for fear of not being able to make it [to the square] the following day."[50] As for Gueullette, the consummate penal voyeur, he had left nothing to chance, and had arranged for the perfect viewing spot from the windows of the hospital of the Saint-Esprit, right on the Place de Grève. On that special day, he arrived bright and early to see the show, and brought along with him the eighteenth-century equivalent of movie popcorn:

> ....I showed up at 7 in the morning and found a good many of the windows of the rooms on the Grève already filled with spectators of both sexes. I was placed by Madam Superior of the establishment at a window on the first floor...and I had as companions in curiosity three gentlemen....I added my little store of provisions to theirs, and around noon, we dined together with a fine appetite.[51]

Damiens did not arrive at the Grève until a quarter past three, by which time Gueullette had been waiting for more than eight hours. Those who had arrived at their seats the night before had, of course, been waiting far longer. When Gueullette finally caught sight of him, we can almost hear the excitement in Gueullette's voice as he narrates Damiens' entry onto the penal stage: "He was placed at first on the ground, next to the table upon which he was to suffer his punishment...; it happened then that, when he was made to sit up, we got a very good look at him, especially me who was equipped with a good pair of binoculars."

Damiens' punishments were meted out exactly as the *arrêt* had stipulated. They began with his hand, into which was placed the knife with which he had attempted to commit regicide. Bouton, the officer of the watch, gave an account of the proceedings, which Foucault excerpted at length:

> The sulphur was lit, but the flame was so poor that only the top skin of the hand was burnt, and that only slightly. Then the executioner, his sleeves rolled up, took steel pincers, which had been especially made for the occasion, and which were about a foot and half long, and pulled first at the calf of the right leg, then at the thigh, and from there at two fleshy parts of the right arm; then at the breasts. Though a strong, sturdy fellow, this executioner found it so difficult to tear away the pieces of flesh that he set about the same spot two or three times, twisting the pincers as he did so, and what he took away formed at each part a wound about the size of a six-pound crown piece.
>
> After these tearings with the pincers, Damiens, who cried out profusely, though without swearing, raised his head and looked at himself; the same executioner dipped an iron spoon in the pot containing the boiling potion, which he poured liberally over each wound.... [A]t each torment, he cried out, as the damned in hell are supposed to cry out, "Pardon, my God! Pardon, Lord." Despite all the pain, he raised his head from time to time and looked at himself boldly.[52]

When it came time for the executioners to quarter Damiens, they encountered difficulties. As this punishment had not been performed in living memory, the executioners were understandably not skilled at the procedure:

> The horses tugged hard, each pulling straight on a limb, each horse held by an executioner. After a quarter of an hour, the same ceremony was repeated and finally, after several attempts, the direction of the horses had to be changed, thus: those at the arms were made to pull towards the head, those at the thighs towards the arms, which broke at the joints. This was repeated several times without success. He raised his head and looked at himself. Two more horses had to be added to those harnessed to the thighs, which made six horses in all. Without success. Finally, the executioner, Samson [sic], said to Monsieur le Breton that there was no way or hope of succeeding, and told him to ask their Lordships if they wished him to have the prisoner cut into pieces. Monsieur Le Breton... ordered renewed efforts to be made, and this was done; but the horses gave up and one of them harnessed to the thighs fell to the ground.[53]

In the end, the executioners were permitted to help the process along by partially severing the thighs, after which the horses were successfully able to tear Damiens' body apart, limb by limb.

Throughout all of this, it would seem that no one shouted or cried or involved themselves directly in the spectacle in any way. In fact, even if they had wanted to, spectators could not get close enough to the action to be a part of it, as the authorities had taken the precaution of erecting a barrier between the scaffold and the spectators.[54] The barrier did an effective job of keeping the thousands of spectators

A Spectacular Crisis

at bay, although one of the officers on duty would later report that "we were unable to prevent some curious people from slipping through."[55] One of these individuals was apparently Charles Marie de La Condamine. Why had La Condamine breached the barriers? To tear at Damiens' clothes and shout things in his face, as spectators had done to Ravaillac a century and a half before? No. La Condamine had pushed through to the scaffold not so he could partake in the ceremony but so he could be a better spectator, so that he could see and hear the show without obstacles. Here is Grimm's account of the incident:

> [La Condamine's] insatiable curiosity about every subject, combined with a great deafness makes him a bit wearisome to others; as for me, I've always found him interesting. This curiosity drove him...to attend the execution of the unfortunate Damiens. He broke through [the crowd] right up to the executioner, and there, notebook and pencil in hand, at each application of the pincers or strike of the iron bar, he asked, shouting at the top of his voice, "What did he say?" The aides of... [the executioner], thinking him an intruder, wanted to get him out of the way; but the executioner said to them, "Leave him be. The gentleman is an *amateur* [i.e. admirer of the spectacle]."[56]

Apart from La Condamine's lone breeching of the barriers, everyone else was content to stay back and watch. But how did they watch? Were there tears or shouts or gasps of horror? According to the Duc de Croÿ, people watched without showing any emotion at all. Only when the executioners, after struggling valiantly for quite some time, finally managed to separate one of Damiens' limbs from his body, did people apparently respond in any way: "Finally after an hour and a half of these sufferings without precedent in their length, the left thigh took off first, at which the people applauded. Up until that point, they seemed only curious and unmoved [*indifférents*]."[57]

We are, at this precise moment, at the apogee of spectacularity—at the highest point of a pendulum of cultural attitudes that was almost immediately about to come swinging back very swiftly in the other direction. We have already heard Gueullette's remark about having arrived early in the morning only to find "a good many of the windows of the rooms on the Grève already filled with spectators of both sexes." A statement of fact, surely, but also something that he thought worthy of mentioning: Women, as well as men, had come to watch Damiens die. As we have seen, women, particularly well-to-do women, had been watching executions from windows for nearly two centuries by this point in time, and apart from a few criticisms at the turn of the eighteenth century, very few people had found anything wrong with women or anyone else coming to watch people die.

But there seems to have been a sense that Damiens' execution was different. It was one thing for women to watch a famous and beautiful female poisoner be hanged, or for women to watch the rakish and naughty Cartouche die on the wheel, but Damiens had nothing rakish about him; there were no actors meeting him in prison, preparing a musical comedy based on his life. There was nothing, in short, amusing about Damiens. And the molten lead, the sulfur, and the drawing and quartering smacked of something that was much more unpleasant and less diverting than the ordinary execution—something that seemed to make the presence of female spectators less appropriate. But even more inappropriate than their presence was their reaction, which Barbier described as follows: "People noticed that there were many women, and even some of distinction, and that they never left the windows, and that they were better able to stand the horror of the punishment than the men, something that did not do them honor."[58] And there, put very simply, is the sound of the pendulum reversing direction.

We have seen scattered criticisms of executions before, but this is different. Here was Barbier, something of a connoisseur of executions, perhaps not obsessed with them like Hardy or Gueullette, but not—at least not up until now—someone who turned his nose up at them either. But here, in this one sentence, we can see two very important things: the expression of "horror" at an execution and the expression of disdain for those—or at least *some* of those— who witnessed it. As far as I have been able to ascertain, Barbier had never used the word *horror* before in reference to an execution, and he had never before criticized those who had come to watch. But these first criticisms by someone who had hitherto enjoyed the spectacle of execution as much as anyone is evidence of a watershed in sensibilities with respect to executions. From this moment onward we will see executions increasingly referred to as "horrible" and those who came to watch them increasingly viewed as doing something that was unnatural, if not downright inhuman.

But hadn't Barbier *himself* come to watch the spectacle of Damiens' execution? And what about the thousands of other people of both sexes who had showed up to watch Damiens die, the thousands who had rented windows and seats in balconies or lined the streets, and the many others who had rushed to accommodate and profit from all those spectators by constructing temporary amphitheaters on the rooftops from which to watch the show? Why single out the women? Barbier was not alone. In the days after Damiens' execution, all Paris was buzzing with the rumor that many female spectators had looked on blithely while Damiens suffered unparalleled horrors. The playwright Charles Collé wrote in his journal:

> I have been told, in the past few days, that during the punishment of Damiens, which lasted a whole two hours, none of the women who were present (and there were a great many of them and some of the prettiest in Paris) stepped away from the windows, whereas the majority of men could not stand the spectacle and moved to the interior of the rooms, and that many fainted; it's a remark that has been widespread. It is also rumored to be true that the young Madame Préandeau ... who rented some windows, remarked, while watching the difficulties that they were having in quartering the unfortunate: "Oh, Jesus! The poor horses—how I pity them!" I did not hear this remark, but all Paris attributes it to little Madame Préandeau, who is one of the prettiest, and one of the most stupid, creatures that God created.[59]

Was it plausible, as both Barbier and Collé claimed, that women were somehow less affected by the spectacle of Damiens' suffering, less susceptible to the "horror of the punishment," than male spectators? It seems hard to believe that Gueullette, for example, put down his binoculars for even a second, much less move away from the window. What I suspect was bothering Barbier, Collé, and the others was not so much that the women were behaving differently from the men, but rather that the women were behaving differently from the way in which women might have been expected to behave. The fact that they could watch such profound suffering dispassionately not only contradicted the idea of instinctive compassion but the widespread assumption, by this point in time, that women were *particularly* sensitive to the sufferings of others.

Over the course of the eighteenth century, the idea had gradually become nearly axiomatic that if human beings were reflexively compassionate, then women were the paragons of this instinct. In 1713, Marivaux was suggesting that women's propensity to cry at the theater was a reflection of the fact that they, more than men, possessed an "interior sense [*sentiment*] which is by itself capable of distinguishing between false and truthful emotions [*mouvemens*] affecting the heart."[60] Women, in short, could be used as a kind of litmus test for the verisimilitude of emotions represented on the stage: if they were realistic, women could not help crying reflexively. A decade or so later, as we saw in the previous chapter, Hutcheson was arguing that women's "disposition to compassion" was more pronounced than men's because they, like children, were less influenced by "custom, education, or instruction," all of which distorted the natural instinct for pity and compassion.[61] Women, in short, still felt the natural pity that had once been common to human beings as a whole, but which, as Shaftesbury and Rousseau would argue, had begun to disappear in men the further they became estranged from their natural state. For others, however, women's propensity to tears was biological rather than cultural. As the entry "Sensibilité" in the *Encyclopédie* insisted, women were more susceptible to tears because of "the suppleness, the freshness, and thinness of the mucous membrane" of women compared to that of men.[62] By the 1770s, in fact, women were seen as crying so readily that Denis Diderot declared that a single tear shed by a man "touches us more than all the tears of a woman."[63]

Given these preconceptions about women and reflexive compassion, the dry-eyed female spectators at Damiens' execution could mean only one of two things. Either human beings were not as automatically sensitive as public intellectuals had been claiming for more than half a century and women were not the paragons of this uniquely human sensitivity, the natural barometer of other people's suffering; or, much less problematic to admit, there must be something wrong with *these particular women*, who had chosen to come and watch Damiens die a horrible death.[64] Overwhelmingly, commentators opted for the latter choice. After all, what sort of woman could enjoy a spectacle like that?

In the wake of Damiens' execution, the trope of the heartless female spectator became a kind of anti-paragon, a symbol for everything that was base and unnatural in human nature and, no less important, everything that was wrong with spectacular punishment for appealing to those baser instincts. The pretty (and stupid) Madame Préandeau served so well as the iconic heartless female spectator because her prettiness implied a kind of self-centered vanity that made her oblivious to others, and to their suffering in particular. For those who had attended Damiens' execution, and who would later find themselves on the wrong side of contemporary norms of sensibility, the negative example of the female spectator would serve to reassure them of their own humanity. If they too had watched Damiens die a horrible death, then at least they had done so—or they would later recall having done so—fully cognizant of the horrors of what they saw.

Time and again, over the next several decades, those who had been witness to Damiens' execution would recall the insensitivity of female spectators with a degree of shock that never seemed to wane, almost overshadowing their horror of the execution itself. Hardy, for example, would claim twelve years after the fact that he had been very much affected by the way women had behaved on that fateful day: "It was in the month of March 1757, when they executed Robert-François Damiens on the Place de Grève; a great many men fainted, and all the women showed themselves absolutely insensitive to the long punishments of the unfortunate who endured torments as horrible as they were justly deserved." To Hardy, this behavior was "far from honorable for a sex that is otherwise so quick to be moved."[65] Writing around the same time, also more than a decade after the fact, Voltaire seemed to recall the spectators at Damiens' execution as having been predominantly women: "I remember being in Paris when Damiens was forced to undergo the most elaborate and the most ghastly death that one could imagine, that all the windows that looked out on the Place were rented at steep prices by women."[66] And Louis-Sébastien Mercier, writing in the 1780s, recalled that "Women came in droves to Damiens' execution; they were the last to look away from this horrible scene.... Our women, whose souls are so sensitive and whose nervous systems [are] so delicate that they faint before a spider, attended the execution of Damiens! I repeat, they were the last to detach their gaze from the most horrible and disgusting punishment that justice has ever dared to imagine...."[67]

The legend of the heartless, pretty women found its way into several memoirs of varying degrees of authenticity that were published toward the end of the eighteenth century. The Comte Dufort de Cheverny prided himself on the fact that he and his wife had had too much *délicatesse* even to think of attending Damiens' execution, unlike the innumerable women of their acquaintance: "The prettiest women made a party out of going, as if it were a show [*spectacle*]. My *délicatesse* as well as my wife's was repulsed by these sorts of conversations.... I did not understand how that which one calls *la bonne compagnie* could savor a pleasure that belongs only to the vilest scum."[68] In a similar fashion, the supposed memoirs of the Duc de Richelieu recalled that on the day of Damiens' execution "The most delicate, the most sylphlike women of the court rented windows up to the price of twenty-five louis per window,"[69] and the memoirs of Madame du Hausset contain a version of the story of Madame de Préandeau:

> Many people, women even, had the barbarous curiosity to attend [Damiens'] execution, among them Madame de P***, the wife of a farmer general and very pretty. She had rented a window or two at twelve louis, and they played [cards] in the room while they waited. This was recounted to the King; and he put his two hands over his eyes and said: "Fi la vilaine! [Oh, the vile woman!]."[70]

Last but not least, Casanova would claim in his memoirs that, although he himself "was forced to avert my eyes and plug up my ears when I heard [Damiens'] heartrending cries, having only half his body left," his female companions were largely unmoved.[71]

As with many of the sins of the ancien régime, vain, aristocratic women would serve as convenient scapegoats for the sin of callously watching people die as a form of entertainment, when in truth it had been a widely practiced cultural habit that was by no means exclusive to any gender or class. The image of pretty, vapid, courtly women who were entirely insensitive to the sufferings of another human being flayed alive before their eyes would prove an enduring trope (and an interesting counterpoint to counter-revolutionary caricatures of ugly, old, and lower-class *tricoteuses* of the Terror, who would later be accused of knitting or cackling as human beings were guillotined only a few feet in front of them).[72]

THE 1750s: A WATERSHED OF SENSIBILITIES

Why, after some two centuries in which spectators had been watching executions as a form of entertainment with few, if any, moral qualms, did the act of watching suddenly become problematic in 1757? Rather than pointing to Damiens' execution as the direct cause of this shift in cultural sensibilities, it seems more plausible to suggest that the extraordinary nature of his execution made certain tensions that had been lingering beneath the surface become suddenly and glaringly apparent. Exemplary deterrence, contemporary sensibilities, and a culture of avid penal spectatorship had been on a collision course for quite some time, and Damiens' execution brought the crisis to a head.

As we have seen, sensibilities had been gradually changing, as the doctrine of automatic, natural human compassion gained wider credence, not only in France but in other countries as well. While the execution of Damiens might have precipitated what appeared to be an abrupt shift in sensibilities, similar changes were taking place more gradually in the Netherlands and Britain at roughly the same time.[73] These changes, however, were decidedly more complex than a simple shift from a culture of insensitivity to one of caring and compassion. The new "horror" of executions, which came to be expressed in the wake of Damiens' execution, would have less to do with compassion for the criminal than with a kind of squeamishness at witnessing the suffering of others.

While Marivaux, Dubos, and others had spoken of the "conflicted" emotions of the Parisian crowd earlier in the century, the years on either side of Damiens' execution were characterized by a sudden flurry of philosophical pronouncements on gawking and sentimentality, reflecting broader turbulence in the culture at large, as contemporaries struggled to reconcile the popularity of the penal spectacle with the ideal of automatic compassion. Only two years before Damiens' execution, Rousseau had published his *Discourse on Inequality*, in which he had made the argument, not unlike Shaftesbury, that the more educated one was, the more likely one was to have become estranged from the instinct of natural pity. Rousseau argued that "one could blithely slit the throat of a fellow human being underneath the window [of a philosopher, who]... had only to put his hands over his ears and argue with himself a bit" in order to keep his natural instincts in check; the "savage man," by contrast, was incapable of repressing his instinct for natural pity and, by corollary, the uneducated masses were similarly incapable of being insensitive to the sufferings of their fellow human beings.[74] These comments provoked the naturalist Charles Bonnet to challenge Rousseau publicly: "Why does the populace, to whom Monsieur Rousseau accords such a great dose of pity, go with such avidity to feast its eyes on the sight of an unfortunate expiring on the wheel?"[75] Rousseau, never one to let someone else have the last word, replied: "For the same reason that you go to cry at the theater and go to see [Voltaire's] Séide slit the throat of his father, or Thyestes drinking the blood of his son. Pity is such a delicious sentiment that it is not surprising that one seeks [an opportunity] to feel it."[76] The "populace" that flocked to the penal spectacle, he argued, were not gawking; they were suffering along with the condemned, indulging their natural instinct for pity.

Two years after Rousseau's interchange with Bonnet, and thus in the very same year as Damiens' execution, Edmund Burke offered a rather different explanation for why people found it pleasurable to watch executions, suggesting that it had nothing to do with natural pity. Pain, Burke suggested, was an extraordinarily powerful feeling—stronger even than pleasure, so strong, in fact, that human beings would forego an enormous amount of pleasure if it meant that they could avoid pain, and Burke cited Damiens' very recent execution as a case in point: "Nay I am in great doubt whether any man could be found who would earn a life of the most perfect satisfaction, at the price of ending it in the torments, which justice inflicted in a few hours on the late unfortunate regicide in France."[77] Although human beings would avoid pain at all costs, the close proximity to pain, provided one did not feel it oneself, and precisely *because* one did not feel it oneself, was, Burke suggested, perversely delightful: "When danger or pain press too nearly, they are incapable of giving any delight, and are simply terrible; but at certain distances, and with certain modifications, they may be, and they are delightful, as we every day experience." (60) It was for this reason, Burke argued, that people went to see tragedies in which the characters suffered; not, as Rousseau had suggested, because one wanted to feel pity for the sufferer, but rather, because "we have a degree of delight, and that no small one, in the real misfortunes and pains of others." (72) The more realistic the spectacle, Burke argued, "the more perfect is its power;" (76) consequently, no theatrical tragedy could hold a candle to the delight of watching the real-life tragedy of an execution:

> Chuse a day on which to represent the most sublime and affecting tragedy we have; appoint the most favourite actors; spare no cost upon the scenes and decorations; unite the greatest efforts of poetry, painting, and music; and when you have collected your audience, just at the moment when their minds are erect with expectation, let it be reported that a state criminal of high rank is on the point of being executed in the adjoining square; in a moment the emptiness of the theatre would demonstrate the comparative weakness of the imitative arts, and proclaim the triumph of the real sympathy. (76–7)

Although what Burke termed "real sympathy" in the above quotation was, in essence, a delight in witnessing the pain of others, he was careful to stress that the spectator's delight in the suffering of others was not the same thing as wishing misfortune on others:

> We delight in seeing things, which so far from doing, our heartiest wishes would be to see redressed. This noble capital [London], the pride of England and of Europe, I believe no man is so strangely wicked as to desire to see destroyed by a conflagration or an earthquake, though he should be removed himself to the greatest distance from the danger. But suppose such a fatal accident to have happened, what numbers from all parts would croud to behold the ruins, and amongst them many who would have been content never to have seen London in its glory? (77)

Not unlike Dubos before him, Burke was endeavoring to reconcile basic human benevolence (or at least a predisposition not to be "strangely wicked") with a kind of natural gawking instinct.

But it was Adam Smith, writing two years after Burke, who would embark upon the most serious and sophisticated analysis of sympathy in his day. Smith accepted the basic concept of a natural tendency toward compassion, beginning his *Theory of Moral Sentiments* (1759) with the following line: "How selfish soever man may be supposed, there are evidently some principles in his nature, which interest him in the fortune of others, and render their happiness necessary to him, though he derives nothing from it except the pleasure of seeing it."[78] Unlike others who had traced the natural tendency to pity back to a kind of emotional contagion in which sorrow spread from one individual to another, Smith argued that the mechanics of sympathy were decidedly more complex:

> Though our brother is upon the rack, as long as we ourselves are at our ease, our senses will never inform us of what he suffers. They never did, and never can, carry us beyond our own person, and it is by the imagination only that we can form any conception of what are his sensations.... By the imagination we place ourselves in his situation, we conceive ourselves enduring all the same torments, we enter as it were into his body, and become in some measure the same person with him, and thence form some idea of his sensations, and even feel something which, though weaker in degree, is not altogether unlike them. (2–3)

Here was a less altruistic, more selfish conception of compassion than others had expressed. In fact, Smith is careful to distinguish between what others called "pity" and "compassion" from what he calls "sympathy." To him, the former terms implied an ability to feel what others were feeling, a kind of "fellow feeling." But sympathy, he insisted, had nothing to do with feeling the emotions of others; rather—and the difference was a crucial one—sympathy was the process of imagining what we ourselves might feel if we were to find ourselves in the shoes of the sufferer. When we see someone in pain, we "enter as it were into the body" of the sufferer and imagine what we would feel in his place:

> His agonies, when they are thus brought home to ourselves, when we have thus adopted and made them our own, begin at last to affect us, and we then tremble and shudder at the thought of what he feels. For as to be in pain or distress of any kind excites the most excessive sorrow, so to conceive or to imagine that we are in it, excites some degree of the same emotion, in proportion to the vivacity or dulness of the conception. (3)

Other people's pain elicited a kind of phantom pain in our own bodies. The person we are watching may be suffering, but it is we who, "by changing places in fancy with the sufferer," flinch:

> When we see a stroke aimed and just ready to fall upon the leg or arm of another person, we naturally shrink and draw back our own leg or our own arm; and when it does fall, we feel it in some measure, and are hurt by it as well as the sufferer. The mob, when they are gazing at a dancer on the slack rope, naturally writhe and twist and balance their own bodies, as they see him do, and as they feel that they themselves must do if in his situation. (3)

Although he was ostensibly writing on the same subject as Dubos and Burke before him, Smith's argument was subtly and yet profoundly different. Whereas they had struggled to explain the delight in gawking at the suffering of others, Smith was verging on something new. He was among the earliest theorists of "horror":

> Persons of delicate fibres and a weak constitution of body complain, that in looking on the sores and ulcers which are exposed by beggars in the streets, they are apt to feel an itching or uneasy sensation in the correspondent part of their own bodies. The horror which they conceive at the misery of those wretches affects that particular part in themselves more than any other; because that horror arises from conceiving what they themselves would suffer, if they really were the wretches whom they are looking upon, and if that particular part in themselves was actually affected in the same miserable manner. (3–4)

Smith had put his finger on a new kind of sensibility that was just beginning to make itself felt. From the 1750s onward, a new generation of philosophers, public intellectuals, and ordinary individuals would find it increasingly difficult to feel compassion for those on the scaffold, not because they were incapable of feeling pity but because they were too horrified to watch. To these newly squeamish spectators, equally as horrifying as the penal spectacle itself was the sight of other spectators who did not share their sensibilities.

IN THE WAKE OF DAMIENS: A "HORROR" OF THE PENAL SPECTACLE

On a certain level, the shift in sensibilities after the execution of Damiens is difficult to see. Spectators of all classes continued to flock to the penal spectacle in great numbers, particularly if the criminal or the crime was noteworthy. At the execution of the Comte de Lally, for example, who was beheaded for treason in 1766, Hardy reports that "all the windows on the Grève were rented at insane prices, the roofs of many houses were uncovered in order to build scaffolds, and one could see men even on the chimneystacks. It was said that there were at least as many people as at the execution of Damiens in 1757"[79] (Fig. 9). When Hardy added that, "I was a witness to this sad spectacle from a window on the third floor in the house of a wine merchant," it is unclear whether he is betraying something of the new sensibilities with respect to executions, or whether he is referring to the fact that the executioner had required several strokes to sever Lally's head from his body. In the following stanza from a poem by Gilbert, however, we can clearly see the expression of the new horror, both of the spectacle and the spectator, the latter personified by yet another heartless, pretty woman who, like Madame de Préandeau, cared more about the suffering of animals than human beings:

> Shall I speak of Iris? everyone praises her and loves her.
> Her heart is... it is... it is humanity itself.
> If, with a careless foot, some young lout
> kicks, while running, her dog who yaps in fright
> You'll see her die of tenderness and alarm;
> A suffering butterfly makes her shed tears:
> It is true; but also, if condemned to die,
> Lally should be in a spectacle dragged to the scaffold,
> She will be the first to go to this horrible festival,
> Buying the pleasure of watching his head fall.[80]

In the wake of Damiens' execution, individuals who could watch executions dispassionately—individuals who, in other words, would have been utterly unremarkable a very short time before—were now the object of the withering glare of the newly horrified. It is no accident that Rosset's *Histoires tragiques*, which had titillated readers with scandalous tales of criminals and executions for nearly a century and a half, was published for the very last time in 1758, the year after

Fig. 9. Thomas Artur de Lally, condamné par Arest du Parlement d'avoir la tête tranchée en Place de Grève, le 8 May 1766.... Bibliothèque Nationale de France.

Damiens' execution. From now on, the idea of delighting in the tragedy of executions was not something that readers would be able to do unselfconsciously.

At first, the new horror of public executions was expressed at particularly "horrible" kinds of execution, rather than at the general concept of spectacular punishment itself. In 1760, for example, one individual proudly declared that "I have never been able to bring myself to see an [execution by] breaking on the wheel; my compassionate pity does not allow me to do it."[81] Suddenly, the execution of suicides, which was usually done by dragging their corpses through the streets, became a spectacle that many found difficult to witness, lending credence, perhaps, to Smith's analysis of sympathy as imagining oneself in the position of the sufferer, rather than literally feeling their feelings. Pierre Barthès, a chronicler of daily life in Toulouse, reported in 1768 with respect to the execution of a cadaver that "The horror of this execution turned the stomachs of many witnesses, causing them to look away in disgust and heartache."[82] In 1772, Hardy, who had been attending executions for decades by this time, suddenly admitted that he found the execution of suicides distasteful.[83]

Partly in response to changing sensibilities, but no doubt also as a reaction to a general lack of confidence in the deterrent value of these and other executions,[84] a new reticence came to characterize penal practice. Hardy mentions a variety of different pretexts by which those who had committed suicide were spared postmortem executions,[85] and several scholars have noted what amounts to a general caution—one might almost say an *embarrassment*—in the last decades of the ancien régime when it came to executing crimes that had traditionally called for capital punishment.[86]

All of this is not to say that the spectacularity of executions ended overnight. We have already seen how the execution of Lally in 1766 attracted huge crowds. The executions of the poisoner Desrues in 1777 and of the murdering "pederast" Pascal in 1783 also drew an enormous number of spectators, and prompted the inevitable comparison to Damiens' execution.[87] The difference, however, was that even as observers commented on the spectacular nature of these executions, many felt increasingly compelled to stress the "horror" of it all. As Bachaumont wrote with respect to the execution of Desrues, "A preponderance [*concours*] of distinguished spectators wished to enjoy this hideous spectacle [*spectacle affreux*], and the rooms at the Grève were rented out at very expensive rates."[88] In nearly identical terms, Hardy described—and criticized—this same execution: "In order to enjoy the horrible spectacle of his punishment, a great number of people of all ages, of all sexes and condition, rented windows at insane prices in the various houses on the Place de Grève."[89]

Hardy, from the 1770s onward, seems to use the word "horrible" with considerable frequency with respect to executions, as if he is bearing witness to the horror of it all, rather than simply attending out of sheer curiosity. In this awkward position of being the observer and reporter of something that had become problematic for polite company to see, Hardy was by no means alone. Through the 1770s and 1780s, observers like Bachaumont, Mercier, and Nicolas-Edme Rétif de la Bretonne, all of whom were drawn to the spectacle of execution and all of whom wrote for a public audience, scrambled for alibis to justify their presence at what had become, in the eyes of public opinion, a morally repugnant pastime. Although they bent over backwards in their attempts to give some reason for their attendance other than plain curiosity, they nevertheless managed to provide detailed descriptions for their readers who were apparently as eager as they to know about—and, of course, condemn—the spectacle of execution that so horrified them.

Rétif is an interesting case in point. Despite the fact that, as he confessed to his readers, "I can't see blood without fainting,"[90] he nevertheless managed not only to witness but to describe quite a number of executions. Invariably, and predictably, he claimed never to have attended one on purpose, but rather to have stumbled across them "accidentally." (Never mind the fact that almost all executions in Paris in the 1780s took place on the Place de Grève, and it would have been very difficult to happen upon one unintentionally.) Rétif expressed his horror at what he saw, and he condemned the inhumanity of executions. But his horror did not prevent him from watching; in fact it demanded that he watch, so that he could bear witness:

> I was headed home by way of the rue Saint-Antoine and the [Place de] Grève. They had broken three murderers on the wheel the day before. I did not think I would see this horrible spectacle which I had never dared to witness. But, as I was traversing [the Place de Grève], I caught sight of an unfortunate individual, pale, half dead, suffering the pains of having been questioned under torture for the preceding twenty-four hours, who was coming down from the Hôtel de Ville, held up by the executioner and the confessor.... I asked myself: "Do men have the right to give death, even to [a murderer]?" I thought I could hear Nature herself giving me a pained "no" in response. "And what about [giving death as a punishment for] theft?—No! No! Nature cried out."[91]

Mercier's solution to the problem of reporting an execution while not offending contemporary sensibilities was to be ostensibly more interested in the crowd of spectators than in the execution itself. In the following description, which at least initially seems to focus on the composition of the crowd, Mercier ends up giving a very detailed, almost lurid, description of the action on the scaffold:

> The populace leaves the shops and workshops and masses around the scaffold in order to observe in what manner the condemned will accomplish the great act of dying in the middle of public torments.... [T]he executioner strikes with a large iron bar, crushes the unfortunate under eleven blows, spreads him out on the wheel, not with his face turned to the sky as the sentence prescribed, but horribly slumped over; broken bones show through the flesh. The hairs that stand on end from pain give off a bloody sweat. The condemned, throughout the ordeal, asks in turn for water and for death. The people look at the clock on the Hôtel de Ville and count the hours that ring out; they tremble in dismay, they contemplate and they are silent. But the next day another criminal will mount the scaffold, and the hideous spectacle of the day before will not have prevented the claiming of another victim. The populace comes back to contemplate the same spectacle; the executioner washes his bloody hands...[92]

Here, Mercier gives the impression that it is primarily "the populace" that has a taste for the penal spectacle. As he added a few pages later: "The lowest class of people is well acquainted with the face [of the executioner]; he is the great tragic actor for the vulgar populace, who mob these horrible spectacles...."[93] Along similar lines, Hardy implied in 1786 that it was primarily spectators from the poorer fauxbourgs who were most "keen" on watching the penal spectacle: "[T]he condemned was executed in the middle of a prodigious multitude assembled from diverse quarters of the capital and especially from the fauxbourgs, whose inhabitants show themselves today to be more keen than ever for these sorts of spectacles."[94] While it is possible that by the 1780s, the poorer classes were the only ones who were still watching executions as a form of spectacle, we should not forget that the reports by Mercier and Rétif, although they dutifully condemned the "horror" of executions, nevertheless enabled more privileged readers to experience the thrill of watching vicariously.

As the socio-economic character of penal audiences changed, so too did the iconic heartless spectator who, by the 1780s, was more likely to be much lower down the socio-economic ladder than the likes of Madame de Préandeau. The following account is by Rétif who, in his usual fashion, "accidentally" stumbled onto an execution in Paris on the eve of the Revolution:

> We were making our way toward the [Place de] Grève. It was late, so we thought the execution was over already. But the gaping crowd told us otherwise. I saw... the first of the three condemned prisoners who were about to meet their end. When the punishment is too great for the crime, or atrocious, one misses the [intended] effect. One does not frighten: one creates indignation. The man was broken [on the wheel], along with his two partners. I could not bear the sight of this execution: I moved away. While the unfortunate was suffering, I examined the spectators. They chatted and laughed, as if they were watching a comedy skit [*parade*]. But what revolted me more than anything, was a young girl, very pretty, who was before me with her lover. She exploded with laughter, she joked about the demeanor and the cries of the unfortunates. I could not believe it. I looked at her five or six times. In the end, without thinking of the consequences, I said to her: "Mademoiselle, you must have the heart of a monster; and from what I've seen of you this evening, I would believe you capable of any crime. If I had the misfortune to be your lover, I'd get away from you for good." A few moments later, I noticed a few steps away, another young woman, who had broken down in tears. She came to me, leaned on my arm, hiding her face, and said to me: "Here is an honest man who pities the unfortunate!"[95]

Rétif tells us that when the punishment is excessive, it "misses the mark," and that, in essence, it backfires, creating indignation among the assembled crowd. Yet, if we read Rétif's passage closely, the story that he actually tells is a very different one. The crowd is not indignant; it is completely unfeeling. The spectators "chatted and laughed, as if they were watching a comedy skit," while a human being lay dying before their eyes. More than anything, however, what "revolted" Rétif was the sight of, yes, a woman, or "young girl, very pretty" rather, who, instead of feeling compassion or sympathy for those suffering on the scaffold, laughed and joked at his expense.

For Rétif, the horror of the execution lay both in the spectacle itself and in the spectators who were capable of taking delight in the sufferings of others. While the behavior of these spectators certainly offended and horrified newer sensibilities, there is no doubt that it also called into question, for contemporaries, the very logic of spectacular punishment. In Rétif's account above, we have an audience not of society ladies but of common people—exactly the target audience one might hope for if one were staging a spectacle intended to deter. And yet, they were neither horrified by what they saw, nor terrified. Instead, it would seem that the only people who were in any way affected by the suffering of the condemned were precisely the ones who did not need to be taught a lesson. The young woman who broke down in tears, the horrified Rétif: these were the sort of upstanding, compassionate people whom the authorities had no need to deter. As the writer Jean-Baptiste-Antoine Suard would perfectly summarize the paradox of the penal spectacle, "Unfortunately, it's not on the wicked people, but rather on the sensitive souls, that the spectacle of punishments leaves the strongest impressions. The man whom one should most fear meeting in the forest, he's the one who likes attending executions of criminals."[96]

Far from epitomizing capital punishment in the ancien régime, the execution of Damiens took place within the context of a cultural crisis. The excitement and enthusiasm of penal spectators, desperate to see a man be flayed alive, proved too difficult to reconcile with contemporary conceptions of natural human compassion, and no less problematic for the logic of exemplary deterrence. Damiens' execution marked a turning point in the history of spectacular punishment in France, as public opinion gradually turned against the penal spectacle, seeing both the practice itself and those who came to watch it as "horrible." While similar transformations were taking place elsewhere in Europe around the same time, Damiens' execution served as a kind of cultural lightning rod, precipitating a relatively abrupt shift, and marking the beginning of a movement to reform penal practice.

PART IV

A DEATH PENALTY FOR THE MODERN AGE

8

Theorizing a New Death Penalty
Penal Reform on the Eve of the Revolution

Perhaps the most surprising thing about the movement to reform the practice of capital punishment in France is how late it made its appearance. Although Montaigne had, in the late sixteenth century, expressed an abhorrence of spectacular justice, his views had been intended not as a criticism of the practice itself but an expression of his unique sensibilities. Inquisitional torture had been criticized by many, Montaigne included, well before the eighteenth century, but torture was never understood to be a form of punishment, only a method of obtaining information for prosecution. If, as we have seen, scattered critiques of spectacular justice had been voiced around the turn of the eighteenth century, they had failed to attract much attention, and had been directed only at the act of *watching* executions, at deriving pleasure from the spectacle of another human being's suffering, and not at the practice of capital punishment itself.

In France, as in Europe as a whole, there was a long tradition of utopian texts that expressed vaguely humanitarian sentiments, opposing the penalty of death, at least in most cases, out of a respect for the sanctity of life. But none of these texts ever discussed contemporary penal practice, contenting themselves with imagining how things might be different among a fictional people in a land that did not exist. Only in the 1740s were the first serious efforts made, most notably by Montesquieu, to explore punishment from a rigorously theoretical perspective, and to suggest ways of reforming contemporary penal practice with the ultimate aim of making it more efficient. In 1764, Cesare Beccaria would combine these two separate, humanist and utilitarian, strands of penal criticism in his treatise *On Crimes and Punishments*, which ultimately became the most widely read text on penal reform in the western world.

Although Beccaria proposed replacing the penal spectacle of death with a spectacle of forced laborers, he nevertheless retained a kind of emergency death penalty of last resort, which Montesquieu and others had proposed before him, for those individuals who posed a danger to society. If Beccaria's vision of spectacular forced labor never quite caught on, the idea of an entirely new kind of death penalty, which had less to do with the spectacle of exemplary deterrence, and more with ridding society of dangerous individuals, would percolate through the reformist literature.

UTOPIAN PENAL REFORM

While works that called explicitly for the reform, much less the abolition, of capital punishment did not appear in Europe until the middle of the eighteenth century, there was a long tradition of leveling oblique criticisms through utopian texts that hypothesized the existence of imaginary peoples who had found alternatives to the penalty of death. For the most part, this subject was dealt with only briefly, within the context of a much larger work that explored all the different customs and beliefs of a mythical civilization.

Perhaps the earliest mention of an imaginary society in which capital punishment had been abolished can be found in Filarete's *Treatise on Architecture*, written between 1461 and 1464. This text, which describes the architecture of the ideal city of Sforzinda as well as the culture and laws of its mythical inhabitants, contains a description of a large "prison of slaves" to which all those who had committed crimes were sent, including those who had been sentenced to death. Instead of being killed, however, the latter had their sentences "represented" symbolically, after which badges were affixed to them, signifying their crime and "the sign of their death." In contrast to those who had not been sentenced to capital punishment and could hope to be released from the prison one day, those sentenced to "death" had their names written in a black book, and were forbidden to leave the prison. These prisoners suffered a kind of living death; their spouses in the outside world would be entitled to remarry if they chose. Those incarcerated were required to work inside the prison walls, according to their trade or, if they had none, at a variety of odd jobs. "Anyone who came here was so worked and driven that there is no doubt that many persons took care not to commit an evil act, since these [prisoners] were half dead from punishment and half dead from work."[1]

Here, even in this very early sketch of a penal system without death, incarceration combined with forced labor are seen as a natural alternative. Filarete's prison was, in a sense, the inversion of capital punishment as it was practiced in his day. Instead of the spectacular display of death, Filarete proposed hiding prisoners away for life; instead of exerting force on the bodies of the condemned, labor was extracted from their bodies. For the next three hundred years, with minor variations, Filarete's vision would be repeated throughout the reformist literature.

A half century after Filarete's treatise, Thomas More published his *Utopia* (1516), which contains some of the most pointed criticisms of contemporary penal practice to be found in utopian literature. More's fictional traveler, Raphael Hythloday, boldly criticizes capital punishment as an affront to the sanctity of human life: "It seems to me a very unjust thing to take away a man's life for a little money, for nothing in the world can be of equal value with a man's life.... God has commanded us not to kill, and shall we kill so easily for a little money?" But he also criticized the practice of putting thieves to death from a somewhat utilitarian perspective: "[I]f a robber sees that his danger is the same if he is convicted of theft as if he were guilty of murder, this will naturally incite him to kill the person whom otherwise he would only have robbed...."[2] As an alternative, he suggested that a lesson could be learned from the Romans who "condemned such as they found guilty of great crimes to work their whole lives in quarries, or to dig in mines with chains about them."[3]

Although the Romans had indeed sentenced individuals to the mines, this punishment existed alongside many others, including capital punishment. For More, however, as for most of the utopian reformers, the mines were meant to be a substitute for and an improvement over the penalty of death. From his vantage point, the mines not only respected the sanctity of life, but they also promised a very effective means of exemplary deterrence: "[T]he sight of [the convicts'] misery is a more lasting terror to other men than that which would be given by their death." At the same time, the convict's forced labor promised "a greater benefit to the public than their death could be," allowing criminals to repay their debt to society.[4]

Interestingly, the citizens of Utopia did not entirely abandon the penalty of death. If, for example, adulterers had served their time in forced labor, or slavery, and had been pardoned by the prince, but once again committed adultery, they were punished with death. And if those condemned to forced labor rebelled, and refused to play their role in the penal system, "they are treated as wild beasts that cannot be kept in order, neither by a prison nor by chains, and are at last put to death."[5] Capital punishment is reserved, therefore, for those who do not or will not "bear their yoke."[6] This death penalty, we should be careful to note, is very different from the capital punishment that was being practiced in More's day. Whereas the latter was primarily about the spectacle of punishment that endured *until* the death of the patient, More's death penalty is about death itself. There is no spectacle, no attempt to justify the practice in terms of example or deterrence. Instead, recidivist and recalcitrant criminals for whom the penal system is not effective are simply dispensed with. Here, death essentially plays the same role as banishment, except that the condemned are pushed beyond the border of the living world rather than beyond a geographical border; they are exterminated, in the original meaning of the word: *ex* (beyond) *terminus* (border or boundary).

If More's criticisms of contemporary penal practice were leveled by a fictional character, and if his suggestions for alternatives were modeled on the practices of a civilization that did not actually exist, the implications could not have been lost on his readers. As one character commented with respect to the narrator at the beginning of *Utopia*, "he told us of many things that were amiss in those new-discovered countries, so he reckoned up not a few things from which patterns might be taken for correcting the errors of these nations among whom we live...."[7]

Filarete's and More's visions of a different way of punishing significantly predate the first French utopian criticisms of capital punishment. Arguably the earliest such critique can be found in Denis Vairasse's *Histoire des Sevarambes* (1675)—arguably, because the book was actually published in English and in England, where Vairasse was residing, rather than in his native country and language.[8] Nevertheless, his book was reissued in French in 1677, and as we can see in the following passage, in which the narrator describes the penal customs of the mythical Sevarambians, Vairasse raised many of the same themes as Filarete and More, but with certain, added novelties:

> They never punish with death, unless it is for some sort of heinous crime, but they sentence [criminals] to several years of imprisonment according to the nature of the crime. In these prisons, one is obliged to work a lot, and one is often punished, and from time to time the condemned are promenaded in the streets to be publicly whipped near the Palace.... When I asked the Sevarambians why crimes were not punished with death, they told me that it would be [an act] of inhumanity and folly to do so—inhumanity to put to death a fellow citizen and take away from him something that cannot be given to him; and folly to destroy a person who could expiate his crime by [performing] useful services for the public. They added that a criminal is punished enough when he is made to work for a long time in a prison where he suffers a long death, and from whence he is taken from time to time to give an example to others and to put before their eyes the punishment that one suffers from crimes that are committed. They said, furthermore, that they had found by experience that men feared long punishments more than they did a quick death, which would release them all at once of their miseries. Often, miscreants were sent to work in the Mines, other times they were kept under guard in a house of correction, depending on whether their employment was needed.[9]

Here, we see the same combination of humanist and utilitarian themes that we saw in More's *Utopia*. The penalty of death had been abolished not simply because it was an act of "inhumanity" but also because forced labor promised certain advantages over death, both from the perspective of deterrence and because of the potential benefit to society. But there is one new twist: the idea that convicts would be taken from the mines and prisons from time to time to "give an example to others" and paraded "before their eyes," in an effort to preserve the spectacular aspects of exemplary deterrence.

Thirty-five years later, many of these same themes are reprised in another utopian novel, the *Avantures de Jaques Massé* (1710), written by Tyssot de Patot. Here we encounter the, now familiar, story of a narrator who sets off on a journey to parts unknown and encounters a lost, utopian civilization where capital punishment does not exist, and dangerous criminals are instead condemned "for their life to work at the bottom of an obscure mine where the light of the sun never reaches." More fully than previous utopian authors, Tyssot fleshed out some of the logic according to which the death penalty was at odds with natural law, at least in the eyes of the citizens of his utopia:

> Crimes are forbidden here, and criminals are punished, but not with the death penalty. They believe that the life of a man is only for God, who gave it to him in the first place, to decide upon. It is not in our power to take it from him, for any cause whatsoever, not even for having killed his father or mother. It was in vain that I explained to them that this was a rule that nearly the entire human race observed.... [They believe that]... each man... can transfer to another, such as to a Prince or Sovereign, the right and authority which Nature has given him over himself, but he cannot give them any power over his life.... According to these principles, they limit themselves to imposing on each individual the punishment which they believe to be most in proportion to his crime....[10]

In 1727, when Tyssot published his *Lettres choisies*, he admitted that this utopian fantasy of a world without the penalty of death was the expression of deeply held humanitarian views. Declaring himself to be "a true partisan of life," he wrote "I esteem it above all that one might imagine; I would never willingly take [life] from even the puniest creature on earth & it is certain that if I were Sovereign, I would never put anyone to death in my realm."¹¹ But, like those utopian authors who came before him, Tyssot was quick to add that his respect for life did not mean that he was somehow soft on crime; forced labor, for him, was clearly no walk in the park:

> ...criminals would have a bad time in my hands: I would send some to the mines, I would force others, in leg-irons, to clean out wells, fountains, and canals, and to keep the streets clean, to grade the highways, to build fortifications, & to work for the public good, in proportion to the crime that they had committed, in such a manner that there would not be the slightest peccadillo that would not be subject to punishment.¹²

For more than two centuries, therefore, a succession of authors had imagined a utopia in which a respect for the sanctity of life had given rise to a penal system that substituted forced labor for the penalty of death. For many, this labor was meant to be performed in "the mines," a concept that More had apparently borrowed from ancient Rome. But there were certain differences: Vairasse, unlike the others, had offered the prospect of a new kind of spectacle in which convicts were paraded around as a public example; and More had retained a non-spectacular form of the death penalty in his utopia, to be applied as a last resort for those malefactors who could not be adequately dealt with otherwise. Beginning in the 1740s, these utopian visions of penal reform were reprised in several philosophical texts that dispensed with the conceit of utopia, and openly began to propose these same ideas as concrete alternatives to the current penal system.

THE END OF UTOPIA: MONTESQUIEU'S *L'ESPRIT DES LOIS*

The year 1748 witnessed the publication of two different texts that touched on the question of capital punishment: François-Vincent Toussaint's *Les Moeurs* and Montesquieu's *Esprit des lois*. Each of these texts represented what was shaping up to be the opposite poles of a debate about capital punishment. Toussaint's position was humanist, arguing that human life was sacred and that society simply did not have the right to kill. Montesquieu's position was utilitarian, approaching capital punishment from the vantage point of efficiency and efficacy rather than morality. Both of these texts, however, mark a moment in time at which penal reform moved from a utopian fantasy to a coherent call for reform that was backed not by the example of a nonexistent far-flung civilization, but by reasoned argument.

At the beginning of *Les Moeurs,* Toussaint makes clear to his readers that this would be no utopian fantasy or vague sketch, but rather a straightforward analysis of contemporary manners and morals, "those that we have as well as those that we should have."¹³ If previous writers had feigned objective impartiality as they described utopian customs, Toussaint made no bones about the fact that the ideas contained in his book were "the sincere expression of the sentiments of my heart."[14]

The section of the book in which Toussaint deals with the question of capital punishment is relatively short and to the point:

> People do not waver in judging [murderers] as deserving of death, by virtue of the law of talion, which they see as coming from natural law—I have no idea on what basis. Because I do not believe that this sacred law...entitles us to punish evil with evil, and punish homicides with murder. I have never been persuaded that God permitted men to kill one another. If a citizen troubles the order [*police*] of the State, prevent him from doing it; this you can do without stringing him up to a gibbet.
>
> For thieves, who do not kill, we know deep down that they do not deserve death.... Put them to work as forced laborers at some sort of useful employment: the loss of their liberty will punish them rigorously enough for their crime, will sufficiently assure public tranquility, will at the same time benefit the State, and will spare you from being accused of [committing an act of] unjust inhumanity.[15]

We have, of course, seen all of these ideas before. The idea that forced labor could replace the penalty of death in such a way that it could deter crime while allowing the criminal to be useful to society had been appearing in the utopian literature for nearly three centuries by this point. But Toussaint's straightforward expression, combined with his bold assertion that his morals were grounded in natural law, somehow made his ideas seem new and different. As Barbier noted in his journal in May of 1748, the book caused a sensation: "I have finally gotten hold of the *Livre des moeurs* which the *arrêt* of 6 May 1748 [condemning the work to be burned] has rendered very expensive and very rare.... Everyone is asking, 'Have you read *Les Moeurs*?' A single copy rapidly finds its way into fifty hands."[16] Barbier, who was himself a great believer in the power of executions to deter crime, found the principles contained in *Les Moeurs* to be "very dangerous," and seemed particularly struck by Toussaint's thoughts on the abolition of the death penalty, which he carefully summarized in his journal.[17]

Several months after the appearance of *Les Moeurs*, Montesquieu's *Esprit des lois* was published, a book that contains what is arguably the most extensive discussion of penal logic and reform in pre-Revolutionary France. In general, the book calls for a legal system based upon clear, known, established laws so that individuals could live their lives in relative security, free from the whims of rulers and legislators. The themes of constancy, fixity, certainty, and predictability run throughout Montesquieu's text, as he was convinced that the physical world was governed by invariable laws, and that political states neared perfection in the extent to which their laws mirrored the invariable laws of the natural world. (Book 1, Chapter 1)

Although Montesquieu divided political states into three general categories—republican, despotic, and monarchical—he was concerned primarily with the monarchical form of government, whereas republican and despotic states served more as abstract counter-examples. With respect to penal law and the assurance of public order, Montesquieu saw the three types of political regimes acting in different ways: republics relied on the virtue and the probity of their citizens; despotic states kept their subjects in a state of perpetual fear; and monarchies existed by the rule of law, relying on the honor of their citizen/subjects to respect the law while assuring that they did so by the potential shame of punishment. One did not have to read very closely between the lines to understand that his argument essentially implied that one could differentiate between a despotism and a lawful monarchy on the basis of penal practice:

> Severe punishments are more appropriate to a despotic government, which is based on the principle of terror, than to a monarchy or a republic, which have recourse to honor and virtue. In moderate States, love of country, honor, and the fear of disapproval, are the corrective measures which are well suited to preventing crimes. The greatest punishment for a bad act would be to be convicted of such an act. (Book 6, Chapter 9)[18]

Moderate states, in other words, punished less frequently and less severely because the "fear of disapproval" prevented people from committing crimes in the first place. Despotic states, by contrast, relied on brutal force applied to the offender after the fact, in the hope that this spectacle might instill fear in others. For Montesquieu, effective crime prevention was clearly superior to ex post-facto punishment: "A good legislator would be less interested in punishing crimes than in preventing them; he would apply himself more to giving morals [*moeurs*] than to inflicting physical punishments [*supplices*]." (Book 6, Chapter 9)

At first glance, Montesquieu's ideas on punishment would seem to have a humanist bent in the sense that he argued it was better to punish humanely (through fear of disapproval) rather than inhumanely (through terror). On closer inspection, however, one realizes that Montesquieu did not prize moderate punishments because of their humane character; rather, he prized the humane character of moderate punishments because of their greater practical efficiency. Despotic governments, with their spectacular outlays of physical pain, were, he argued, constantly forced to increase the severity of punishments in order to assure deterrence:

> If a problem crops up in a state, a violent government wants to correct it immediately. And instead of thinking to execute long-standing laws, a cruel penalty is established which puts a stop to the evil right away. But one uses up the [last] resort of the government: the imagination gets accustomed to this greater penalty just as it had to the lesser one; and as fear is diminished for the latter, one is soon forced to establish the former in all cases. Highway robbery was common in certain States; they wanted to put a stop to it; they invented the penalty of the wheel, which put a stop to [these crimes] for a while. Since that time, one robs just as before on the highways. (Book 6, Chapter 12)

Montesquieu feared, in short, a kind of penal inflation in which the state would necessarily be forced to up the ante over time, constantly battling to stay one step ahead of the public's imagination.

Apart from the practical inconvenience of a penal system based on terror, the prospect of a government that was forever trying to stay ahead of its subjects' fears violated Montesquieu's ideals of certainty, predictability, and invariability. It was far better, thought Montesquieu, to have a system of carefully graduated punishments that did not change over time, and he believed that the best way to accomplish this was to have punishments that arose naturally from the crime itself, so "the punishment does not come from the caprice of the legislator, but from the nature of the thing [itself]; and it is not man who does violence to man." (Book 12, Chapter 4) Crimes of property would be punished by the confiscation of property; crimes against public tranquility, by depriving the offender of his own tranquility, and so on. In this way, a government would avoid all appearance of despotism, and the penal system would be seen as rational and invariable. Moreover, because of this natural connection between the crime and the punishment, potential criminals might be reminded of the punishment before they committed the crime and, ideally, be deterred from going through with it.

Just as Montesquieu criticized the inefficiency of punishment in despotic states, so too did he regard as impractical the idea that a republic could rely on the virtue of its citizens. Far more efficient, and no doubt far more realistic than relying on virtue, was a monarchical model of punishment that functioned in accordance with each citizen's natural desire to avoid shame and dishonor: "In monarchies, the political system makes great things happen with the least amount of virtue possible, just as the art [of constructing] the most elegant [*belles*] machines makes use of the fewest possible movements, springs, and wheels." (Book 3, Chapter 5) Anticipating Jeremy Bentham's Panopticon by nearly half a century, Montesquieu envisioned a penal system that functioned almost effortlessly, with each citizen-subject acting as a self-monitoring cog in an "elegant machine."

If Montesquieu believed that corporal punishments were actually less efficient at deterring crime than more moderate punishments, he nevertheless believed that there were certain circumstances when bodily punishments were necessary. One such circumstance was if someone had committed a crime against property but had no property of his or her own to sacrifice as punishment, a solution that recalls the compensation in flesh provided for in Salic law.[19] But if the crime was of such magnitude that it posed a serious threat to the safety and security of others, then Montesquieu saw no alternative but to deprive the offender of his or her own safety and security:

> The punishments for crimes [that attack public security] are those that we call *supplices* [i.e. physical punishments]. It is a kind of talion which results in society refusing security to a citizen who has deprived, or who has wanted to deprive, another of [such security]. This punishment is derived from the nature of the thing, drawn from reason and from the very foundations of good and evil. A citizen deserves death when he violates [public] security to the point that he has taken life, or has planned to take it. This death penalty is like medicine to a society that is ill. (Book 12, Chapter 4)

This is not the traditional form of capital punishment, but rather a kind of penalty of last resort, when the elegant machine of justice confronts a threat that refuses to be a self-regulating cog, and the only choice is to kill the offender to protect society as a whole.

This new kind of death penalty of last resort was an idea that we have already seen in More's *Utopia*, and it was an idea that had surfaced in the writings of philosophers of natural right, who theorized that the greater good of humanity itself might, on occasion, require the death of the individual if that individual were seen to threaten the safety and security of the social body as a whole.[20] As early as the thirteenth century, Aquinas had argued in the *Summa Theologica* that:

> ...if it be expedient for the welfare of the whole human body that some member should be amputated, as being rotten and corrupting the other members, the amputation is praiseworthy and wholesome. But every individual stands to the whole community as the part to the whole. Therefore, if any man be dangerous to the community, and be corrupting it by any sin, the killing of him for the common good is praiseworthy and wholesome.[21]

Similarly, Grotius, in his *De iure belli ac pacis* (1625) spoke of individuals who commit "grievous Violations of the Law of Nature or Nations" as having sacrificed their humanity, making themselves liable to slaughter: "For of such Barbarians, and rather Beasts than Men, may be fitly said...the justest War is that which is undertaken against wild rapacious Beasts, and next to it is that against Men who are like Beasts."[22] Perhaps most famously, John Locke had spoken of a right of individuals in a state of nature to ensure self-preservation and, as individuals entered society, he had argued, they conferred that right on the magistrate who was empowered to preserve the whole of society by exercising such penalties "as may tend to the preservation of the whole, by cutting off those parts, and those only, which are so corrupt, that they threaten the sound and healthy...."[23] Finally, only a year before the publication of Montesquieu's *Esprit des lois*, the Genevan theorist of natural law Jean-Jacques Burlamaqui's *Principes du droit naturel* had been published, in which the author had insisted that the sovereign right to kill was "nothing other than the Natural Right which human Society and every individual originally had to execute the Laws of Nature, and to ensure their own security, and which [right] they ceded and placed in the Sovereign...[which punishes] in the last resort, in the interest of the security and tranquility of Society."[24]

For Montesquieu, as for the others before him, this form of the death penalty, which was conceived on the basis of a kind of sovereign right of self-defense, had little to do with deterrence. Here, death is executed as an act of desperation, undertaken regretfully, almost shamefully. But because, as Montesquieu had said, the punishment of death was derived "from the nature of the thing [itself]; and it is not man who does violence to man," society could hold itself blameless, almost as if it were merely allowing nature to take its course. The fault lay squarely with the criminal who had initiated an inevitable chain of events. In this vision of the modern death penalty, there is little call for spectacle. In fact, the logic of spectacle is entirely at odds with the logic of a death penalty of last resort. There is nothing to be advertised here; on the contrary, there is much to be hidden. For this penalty represents, in large part, the failure of the system: the failure to correct citizens and prevent crimes before they occur.

Montesquieu referred to his death penalty as "a kind of talion." But, in truth, its logic is less that of the law of talion, an eye for an eye, than that of a kind of permanent banishment, updated for a world of nation states in which exile was proving less practicable.²⁵ The purpose of Montesquieu's death penalty is, quite simply, to get rid of dangerous people. Montesquieu had suggested that it was a form of social "medicine," but perhaps Aquinas and Locke had the most apt analogy when they compared the death penalty to a kind of emergency surgery or amputation, the aim of which was to protect the social body as a whole.

In the decade after the publication of *L'Esprit des lois*, Montesquieu's views on penal efficiency, and his subtle advocacy of society's right to use a discreet form of the death penalty to defend itself against dangerous individuals, found their way into Diderot's *Encyclopédie* through the articles of Montesquieu's admirer Louis de Jaucourt, who availed himself of any opportunity to invoke, paraphrase, or straight-out copy ideas contained in *L'Esprit des lois*.²⁶ Jaucourt's article "Crime," for example, repeats word for word Montesquieu's description of the death penalty as a medicine for a society that is ill.²⁷ Even Diderot himself, in his article "Droit naturel," maintained that those whose individual wills were at odds with the general will might be branded "enemies of the human race" and legitimately "suffocated [*étouffé*]."²⁸

But it was Jean-Jacques Rousseau who, more than anyone in his generation, would offer the most forceful articulation of the sovereign right to kill dangerous individuals. In *Du Contrat social*, Rousseau insisted that the sovereign collective had not only the right but the obligation to make war on those individuals who posed a threat to the general welfare:

> [E]very malefactor, in attacking the rights of the social [collective], becomes as a result of his misdeeds, a rebel and a traitor to the fatherland; he ceases to be a member in violating its laws, and even makes war upon it. Then the survival of the State is incompatible with his own; one of the two must perish, and when one puts the guilty party to death, it is less as a citizen than as an enemy.... He must be severed [*retranché*] [from the collective] through exile as a violator of the pact, or through death as a public enemy.²⁹

For Rousseau, as for Montesquieu before him, the death of the "public enemy" should be seen as the fault of the criminal himself, who "as a result of his misdeeds" has effectively waged war against the sovereign. Interestingly, Rousseau makes the common logic of banishment and the new death penalty explicit, by describing both as a kind of severing of the offending member from the social body. Also like Montesquieu, he believed that the death penalty should only be used as the last resort of a society acting in a kind of collective self-defense: "One does not have the right to kill, even for the sake of [setting an] example, anyone other than someone whose life poses a danger [to society]."³⁰

By the middle of the eighteenth century, therefore, two distinct strands of penal reform were taking shape. One criticized existing penal practice for its inhumanity, and proposed that the death penalty be replaced by forced labor, which might serve the interest of deterrence without violating the sanctity of human life; the other criticized penal practice for its inefficiency, and proposed that harsh penalties be replaced by moderate correction, except in those extreme cases when public safety necessitated the death of the criminal as a matter of collective self-defense. In 1764, a relatively obscure Italian nobleman by the name of Cesare Beccaria managed to combine all of these, somewhat contradictory, ideas into a reasonably coherent and eminently readable polemic against contemporary penal practice. Although none of Beccaria's ideas were original, the single focus of his work, its forceful presentation, its skillful combination of humanitarian and utilitarian themes, would make his treatise the most influential and widely read eighteenth-century text on the subject of penal reform in the entire western world.

BECCARIA'S *ON CRIMES AND PUNISHMENTS*

In 1764, Cesare Beccaria was only twenty-five years old and virtually unknown outside his small circle of aspiring *philosophes* in Austrian-occupied Lombardy, when he published a treatise entitled *Dei delitti e delle penne* (*On Crimes and Punishments*), a book that would go on to achieve enormous success throughout much of the world, and has often been regarded as the seminal text of the modern penal age. Perhaps it was the rhetorical force of Beccaria's impassioned plea for the cause of humanity; perhaps it was the fact that his text was, as Lynn Hunt has aptly described it, "punchy" and "short."[31] No doubt his timing had something to do with the favorable reception of his treatise, particularly in France where, ever since Damiens' execution in 1757, it had become almost a cliché to express one's "horror" of the penal spectacle. Whatever the precise reasons for the extraordinary success of Beccaria's text, all of enlightened Europe seemed to nod in agreement with him when he asked the rhetorical question: "Who does not shudder in horror when seeing, throughout history, so many barbarous and ineffective torments invented and coldly used by men who called themselves Sages?"[32]

Within a year of its publication, Beccaria's treatise fell into the hands of Jean le Rond D'Alembert, who brought the text to the attention of his fellow *encyclopédiste* the Abbé Morellet, who in turn decided, almost on a whim, that he would undertake a French translation of the text. Not only would the translation of the treatise into French assure Beccaria of a much wider readership, but Morellet took the liberty of completely overhauling the book's organization, making the text much more accessible to readers.[33]

In many ways, Beccaria's expression of "horror," quoted above, at the "barbarous and ineffective torments" employed in contemporary penal practice epitomizes his approach to the question. What bothered him was both the "barbarous" nature of existing punishments as well as—and one almost misses the word on a first reading—the fact that these practices were "ineffective." For Beccaria, the "useless profusion of corporal punishments"[34] both offended contemporary sensibilities and failed at the one task that everyone seemed to agree was the raison d'être of punishment: deterring crime.

A great admirer of Montesquieu and an avid student of political economy, Beccaria was concerned, above all, with the efficiency of punishment. To him, the great penal spectacles of his day were barbarous not simply because they inflicted pain, but because they inflicted more pain than was necessary. The best punishments, he wrote, were those "which are proportional to the crime, which make the most effective and lasting impression on the minds of men, and which are at the same time the least cruel to the body of the criminal." (90) Anything more than the precise level of punishment that was needed to deter crime was as cruel as it was useless: "In order for a punishment to produce its effect, it suffices that the bad that it causes outweighs the good that can be had from the crime.... All severity that goes beyond this limit is useless, & therefore tyrannical." (93)

Not only was excessive pain cruel and useless, Beccaria argued, it was also counterproductive. If the punishment was too great, then criminals would commit *more* crimes in order to escape it: "The very atrocity of the punishment means that one takes greater risks to avoid it, and that one commits many crimes to avoid the punishment that is due for a single crime." (92) More importantly, he wondered whether excessive punishments did not actually *incite* criminal behavior rather than deter it by setting "an example of atrocity." (109) Consequently, Beccaria proposed a very different kind of penal spectacle, one that he insisted would be much more effective as a deterrent, while forgoing all excessive physical violence that might set an inappropriate example:

> The death of a scoundrel...is less of a powerful brake on crime than the long and enduring example of a man deprived of his liberty and become a beast of burden [*animal de service*] so that he might spend his life repairing the damage that he has done to society. The frequent, forced reflection of the spectator, "If I were to commit a crime I would be reduced to this unhappy condition for my entire life," makes a much stronger impression than the idea of death which men always see [as occurring] at some distant point in the future. (100–1)

To Beccaria, the spectacular potential of a man reduced to being a "beast of burden" for a lifetime offered enormous advantages, in terms of exemplary deterrence, over the traditional spectacle of capital punishment, which only lasted a few hours.[35] For him, the contemporary penal spectacle, if it did anything at all, tended to evoke either pity or horror in the spectator. Instead, he proposed a new kind of spectacle—one calculated to evoke fear:

> The death penalty inflicted on a criminal is, for the great majority of men, nothing but a spectacle, or an object of compassion or indignation. These two sentiments occupy the soul of spectators much more than the salutary terror that the law claims to give rise to. But for he who is witness to a continuous and moderate punishment, the feeling of fear is the dominant one, because it is the only one. (101–2)

Comparing the contemporary penal spectator to the spectator at the theater who forgets the moral lesson of the play the moment he leaves, Beccaria argued that no sooner was the spectacle of capital punishment over than "the violent and unjust man returns to his injustices." (102) In a kind of cost-benefit analysis, he suggested that, for all the effort that society expended on an execution, it seemed to get too little in return—a one-shot deal. Perpetual slavery, however, because it had "the advantage for society of being more frightening to those who witness it than to those who suffer it," held out the promise of a never-ending didactic spectacle, an unlimited return on the penal investment. (105) If Beccaria's idea of a lifelong spectacle of forced labor sounded just as cruel as the spectacle it was replacing, he offered the following in the way of (cold) comfort:

> Some might say that perpetual slavery is a punishment as painful as death & consequently just as cruel. I respond that if one were to gather together all the unhappy moments in the life of a slave, his pain would be perhaps even more terrible than the greatest punishment; but these moments are spread out over his entire life, whereas the death penalty exerts all its force in a short span of time. (105)

One cannot help being surprised to hear the man, whom Bentham would describe as having been "received by the intelligent as an angel from heaven would be by the faithful,"[36] a man who is universally credited with sparking the modern movement for humane penal reform, describe his vision of ideal punishment as "even more terrible than the greatest punishment." Such passages make clear, however, the extent to which Beccaria was a true student of Montesquieu, striving for the most efficient means of deterring crime with the least societal effort and expense. In fact, one could argue there was little that Beccaria had to say that Montesquieu had not already said two decades earlier. As for his idea of replacing capital punishment with a spectacle of forced labor, Vairasse, as we have seen, had suggested something very similar nearly a century before.

Perhaps the one thing that sets Beccaria apart from almost everyone else writing on the subject, both his contemporaries and his predecessors—even Montesquieu, whom he seemed to follow in everything else—was his apparent support for the complete abolition of capital punishment: "What *right* do men give themselves by which they can slaughter their fellow man?" (97) His answer was that the death penalty was "authorized by no *right*" and was "nothing other than an act of war on the part of the nation against a citizen." (97) And he added: "If I can therefore show that, in the ordinary state of Society, the death of a citizen is neither useful nor necessary, I will have won the cause of Humanity." (97–8)

It is comments such as these that have allowed Beccaria to go down in history as one of the first to support the abolition of the death penalty. Yet, he grudgingly concedes that there were certain exceptional situations, outside the "ordinary state" of affairs, when the sovereign might be left with no other choice but to kill:

> [T]he death of a citizen might be necessary in the case when, deprived of his liberty, he still has connections and a power that might disturb the tranquility of the nation; when his existence might produce a revolution in the form of the established Government. Such a case can exist only when a nation loses or recovers its liberty, or in times of Anarchy when disorders take the place of laws.... [Otherwise], there is no necessity to take the life of a citizen. (98–9)

Interestingly, Morellet had taken the liberty of cutting the last sentence short. Perhaps hoping to fashion Beccaria into more of an abolitionist than he actually was, the abbé had removed from the treatise the following qualifying phrase from the original Italian version: "unless his death is the true and only brake to prevent others from committing crimes, the second case in which the death penalty may be considered just and necessary."[37]

We, perhaps like Morellet, might well ask: What kind of abolition is this? Is Beccaria's stance on the death penalty really all that different from either Montesquieu's or Rousseau's, both of whom had allowed for the sovereign to kill when it was a matter of collective self-defense? Beccaria's supposed abolitionism would seem to amount to a ban on the death penalty except in such cases when it was necessary. But few individuals in Europe by the 1760s were arguing that people should be killed unnecessarily. The crucial difference between those in mid-eighteenth-century Europe who supported the death penalty and those who seemingly called for its abolition would seem to be their definition of what constituted its "necessary" use, which ultimately boiled down to differing conceptions of the fragility of public safety.[38]

BECCARIA'S RECEPTION AND LEGACY

Beccaria had known nothing of Morellet's French translation until it had already been published, but whatever concerns he may have had at the translator's heavy hand were no doubt allayed when Morellet wrote to him, informing him not only that the translation had appeared in print but that its "success is universal, and even apart from the value that everyone places on the book, they have conceived feelings for the author himself that might flatter you even more, which is to say: esteem, gratitude, interest, and friendship."[39] Beccaria must have been as flattered as he was stunned to learn that Morellet had taken it upon himself to recommend the book to some of the most illustrious representatives of the European Enlightenment, and that individuals whom Beccaria had hitherto known only as part of a magical, faraway pantheon of great thinkers were now to be counted not only as his readers but as his admirers, eager to meet the young author.

In September, Voltaire himself published a "commentary" on Beccaria's book (although, in fact, it seemed more a platform for Voltaire's own ideas on the subject of punishment than anything having to do with Beccaria's book). Nevertheless, in future editions, it became customary to publish Voltaire's commentary together with the treatise, and with the imprimatur of the great Voltaire, Beccaria's text became required reading across the enlightened world. It was soon translated into all the major languages of Europe and would be closely studied and praised by everyone from Thomas Jefferson to Catherine the Great.[40]

Beccaria made a brief appearance in Paris, but quickly returned to Italy, having apparently had his fill of Parisian intellectual society. He turned down an invitation from Catherine to visit Russia, and eventually joined the reforming administration of Lombardy, going on to write books on a variety of subjects, none of which came close to enjoying the notoriety and success of his treatise on crimes and punishments.[41] If Beccaria quickly exited from the center stage of the European Enlightenment, his treatise became ever more famous and important over time. Jeremy Bentham, the great penal reformer and future founder of utilitarianism, would later write, after reading Beccaria's treatise, "Oh, my master, first evangelist of Reason, you who have raised your Italy so far above England, and I would add above

France...you who have made so many useful excursions into the path of utility, what is there left for us to do?—Never turn aside from that path."[42]

Beccaria's treatise was not simply an international bestseller; it is often regarded as *the* seminal text of modern punishment. At the end of the century, reflecting back on the years before the Revolution, the politician, lawyer, and economist Pierre-Louis Roederer wrote the following in a letter to Beccaria's daughter:

> ....[T]he *Treatise on Crimes* so changed the spirit of the old criminal courts in France that ten years before the Revolution they had become unrecognizable. All the young magistrates of the courts—and I can attest to this because I was one myself—judged more in accordance with the principles of this text than according to the laws. It is in the *Treatise on Crimes* that the likes of Servan and Dupaty derived their ideas, and it is possible that it is to their eloquence that we owe the new penal laws which France is honored to have.[43]

Although there is no question that Beccaria's treatise had a galvanizing effect on European public opinion, the fact that so much of what he had to say had already been said by others would seem to suggest that his influence had less to do with his ideas themselves than with the way he packaged them. For, perhaps the only truly novel feature of Beccaria's *Treatise* was the way in which it mixed two different, hitherto largely separate, strands of penal reform: practical efficiency and heartfelt humanism. This combination was, however, less a skillful merging than a kind of naïve embrace of two things that were, in the end, largely incompatible. Beccaria decried the inhumanity and cruelty of capital punishment, and yet insisted that his new penal spectacle would be just as cruel. He deplored the death penalty as an inhumane violation of natural law and nevertheless supported it, in certain vague circumstances, as a fundamental principle of natural law. In the end, one suspects that Morellet's pruning and rearrangements were attempts to make Beccaria's treatise not only more readable but less obviously inconsistent.

Despite its flaws, appearing in France only a few years after the execution of Damiens, when sensibilities were primed to abhor the horror of capital punishment, Beccaria's treatise reprised old ideas in a rhetorically exciting, comprehensible, and straightforward manner. After its publication, the penal landscape would never be the same. Whether they acknowledged him or not, subsequent penal reformers were indebted to him for the energy of his conviction if not directly for the novelty of his ideas.

THE GREAT (NON-)DEBATE ON CAPITAL PUNISHMENT FROM BECCARIA TO THE PENAL CODE OF 1791

In the quarter century after the publication of Beccaria's *Treatise on Crimes and Punishments*, countless reformers took up their pens to condemn the barbarism and inhumanity of the existing system of punishment, and waxed eloquently and enthusiastically about a new, more humane, and infinitely more rational penal regime. They saw themselves as intellectual warriors at the forefront of a great battle to be waged against the defenders of the penal status quo, those who championed barbarism and cruelty over reason and humanity.

In the first decade after Beccaria, many of the texts urging penal reform seemed to be in dialogue with his treatise, but by the late 1770s and early 1780s, such was the palpable sense of excitement that a new penal age was dawning that Beccaria began to seem as if he belonged to a different time when ideas for reform had been treated as abstractions. Several academic institutions proposed essay competitions on the subject of how best to enact practical reforms of the existing penal system. The winner of one of these competitions, organized by the academy of Châlons-sur-Marne, was the young lawyer and future leader of the Revolutionary Girondins, Jacques-Pierre Brissot de Warville, who took it upon himself to publish not only his own essay, but a ten-volume set of essays that, in his view, had made an important contribution to the question of penal reform over the preceding decades. Beginning with a new translation of Beccaria's treatise, the compilation included everything from Catherine the Great's penal code and the Constitution of Pennsylvania of 1776, to works by Voltaire, Servan, and, of course, several texts by Brissot himself.[44] (Not included, was an essay on penal reform which had been written by a young lawyer from Arras by the name of Maximilien Robespierre and had been submitted to an essay competition sponsored by the academy of Metz, as the essay had failed to rise past the second tier in that competition).

Such is the sense of excitement that pervades all of the reforming texts produced in the decades after Beccaria that one might easily conclude every author was pushing the boundaries of penal theory, expressing ideas that were radically new and revolutionary. But this was not the case. One struggles in vain to find anything new in the entire corpus of texts produced on the subject of penal reform in the decades before the Revolution. Not only had all of the arguments been made many times before, but each author puts forward nearly identical arguments, almost as if they were reading from the same script, as perhaps they were. While some openly expressed their admiration and indebtedness to Beccaria, nearly all mustered the very same arguments against current penal practice and an identical vision of forced labor as an alternative to the death penalty.

If there is one characteristic attribute of post-Beccarian writings on penal reform, it is the endurance of Beccaria's tendency to consider the *humanity* of punishment as bound up with and entirely inseparable from the question of *useful* punishment. It was not simply a question of punishing less harshly, but of punishing both less harshly *and* more effectively. As the reforming jurist Joseph-Michel-Antoine Servan remarked in his speech before the parlement of Grenoble in 1766, "the spirit of all good criminal law is the reconciliation, as much as possible, of the least punishment of the guilty party with the greatest public utility."[45] Indeed, the questions posed by the various essay competitions for which many of these texts were initially written seemed to assume, as a matter of course, that the purpose of reform was to combine humanitarianism and utilitarianism. The competition at Châlons-sur-Marne, which had inspired Brissot's essay and, ultimately, his ten-volume compilation, had asked: "Indicate the penal laws which are the least severe and nevertheless the most effective in preventing and reprimanding crime by prompt and exemplary punishments, while respecting the honor and the liberty of citizens?"[46]

The most common example used to illustrate the point that harsher punishments were not necessarily the most useful ones, cited by nearly every pamphlet written on the subject of penal reform, was that of the hypothetical highwayman who, for fear of being put to death for the crime of highway robbery, ends up murdering his victims rather than simply robbing them.[47] The death penalty for domestic theft was another favorite example of those who sought to illustrate how the excessive severity of the current system actually incited crime rather than deterring it. In the words of the inimitable Voltaire:

> What is the effect of this inhumane law which equates a precious life with eighteen [stolen] napkins? Because what master of a household would dare to forswear all feelings of honor and pity to the point that he would hand over his servant guilty of such a petty crime in order to be hanged on his doorstep? One contents oneself with discharging [the servant]; he goes to steal elsewhere and often becomes a murdering brigand.[48]

Alongside highway robbery and domestic theft in the list of crimes that were "inhumanely" and "uselessly" punished by death were the crimes of counterfeiting, smuggling, desertion, and suicide, all of which countless authors condemned as inhumanely, but more to the point, *needlessly* punished by death.[49]

Beyond the concerns expressed about the excess punishment of particular crimes, there was a general sense that repeatedly resorting to the death penalty had the effect of both eroding its impact and accustoming spectators to the sight of violence. Just as Montesquieu had expressed a fear of penal inflation, so too did Jean-Paul Marat worry that "punishing with rigor a light infraction of the laws is to squander the [last] resort of authority; because if [the law] inflicts great punishments on petty delinquents, what will be left for it to punish great criminals?"[50] And just as Beccaria had wondered whether the oft-repeated spectacle of graphic physical violence did not give rise to a kind of taste for cruelty, so too did Brissot express his concern that such punishments "familiarize people's eyes with the effusion of blood."[51]

Voltaire might be seen as summarizing the position of everyone writing on the subject when he offered the maxim: "Punish, but don't punish blindly. Punish usefully."[52] What precisely did this mean? In part, it meant that punishments should in every case have the effect of deterring crime. But it also meant something else. As Voltaire was fond of reminding readers, "A hanged man is good for nothing."[53] He added, by way of explanation, "It is clear that twenty hardy thieves condemned to a lifetime of labor in the public works serve the State by their punishment, and that their death does no good for anyone but the hangman whom one pays to kill men in public."[54]

Almost as if Beccaria and the utopian reformers before him had never mentioned the idea, author after author touted the virtues of forced labor as if they were the first to have hit upon the idea. For many, the concept simply appealed to common sense, for it allowed the criminal, as Brissot put it, to "expiate his crime no less severely" than by death, but in a manner that would prove "nevertheless useful for society."[55] Voltaire went so far as to suggest that condemned criminals might become the personal slaves of those they had wronged by their actions: "As regards to your brother's murderer, he will be your slave for as long as he lives. I will render him useful to you, to the public, and to himself."[56]

Just as the story of the highwayman who killed in order to avoid the death penalty was a seemingly obligatory part of the literature on penal reform, so too was the shining example of the tsarinas Catherine and Elizabeth of Russia who had suspended the death penalty and replaced it with forced labor. Beccaria himself had written of Elizabeth's moratorium as giving "a more beautiful example than the most brilliant of conquests," and Voltaire, Brissot, and others all followed suit.[57]

Among all of the authors, Brissot's vision of a post-abolition penal society is perhaps the most elaborately sketched. He imagined a world in which hordes of forced laborers went forth to tame nature and build great things: "We demand useful punishments! Do not France and England have their colonies, Sweden and Poland, their mines... Russia, the wastelands of Siberia, Spain, the mines of Potosi and of California, Italy its marshes and galleys, and every country its empty lands to people, its fields to cultivate, manufactures to perfect, buildings, and public roads to construct?"[58] But Brissot also imagined that the abolition of the death penalty might solve two great problems at once. On the one hand, the state would no longer be guilty of murdering its own citizens, and would instead "throw [the guilty party] into slavery, [and] make him useful to the fatherland whose laws he has violated."[59] On the other hand, the existence of criminal slaves offered the possibility of ending another great injustice that was near to his heart: "Replace those unhappy negroes who are guilty only of having a languid look and of absorbing all the rays of light in their epidermis; replace those negroes in your plantations, your sugar factories, and your mills with the condemned whom you judge deserving of being deprived of a liberty which is dangerous to the human race."[60]

Apart from the value of criminal labor, there was an entirely different kind of worth that many writers attached to the concept of forced labor. Once again following Beccaria, many subsequent penal reformers were particularly impressed by the spectacular potential of penal servitude. As one author put it, "the example [of forced laborers], constantly before the eyes of *all classes* of citizens, will necessarily keep them in line," adding, with a breathlessness signified by multiple periods, or full stops, in the text: "Prison is useful only to hold the guilty during the discovery phase of their trial.... A life sentence in prison is idiotic.... every penalty must set an example.... As soon as a man is put away [in prison] he no longer sets an example, because one does not even know whether he exists.... public works are certainly a much better idea."[61] Not unlike Vairasse, a century before, Brissot thought that a kind of spectacular preview to forced labor might help to augment its exemplary potential:

> I would like it if, before being enclosed in the mines or put out to perform public works, [the criminal] were to appear publicly and on several occasions, so that one

could read his crime [aloud, or on a placard?] and reproach him with it, so that exposed to the view and indignation of his fellow citizens, one could see him only with horror, and so that everyone cries out: *let us flee from him; he is a monster*.[62]

But then, seemingly changing his mind in mid-paragraph, Brissot suggested that there was perhaps even greater spectacular potential in bringing spectators to the penal spectacle rather than vice versa:

> I would like that from time to time, after having prepared [people's] minds in advance with a reasoned speech on the conservation of the social order, and on the utility of punishment, that young people and even [grown] men be led into the mines, and to the public works, in order to contemplate the horrible fate of these outlaws. These patriotic journeys will be far more useful than those the Turks undertake to Mecca.[63]

Marat also embraced the didactic potential of the spectacle of forced labor, but stipulated that the jobs undertaken by criminal laborers ought to be "disgusting, unhealthy, and dangerous."[64]

Although most of these reforming texts give the impression that their authors were breaking new theoretical ground, there was, at the same time, a somewhat contradictory sense that what was being proposed was consistent with universal, trans-historical truths, and that, in the end, the choice to be made was between barbarism and Reason. Only a few years after Beccaria published his treatise, Jean-Baptiste Claude Delisle de Sales related the story of Sabacon, the emperor of ancient Egypt who, according to Herodotus, had abolished the death penalty in his time. In the following passage, de Sales imagines that Sabacon came to this decision by heeding the advice of an "infinitely enlightened and infinitely sensitive" young advisor who, if we did not know better, we might mistake for the young Beccaria, transported some three thousand years back in time. Not only was the young advisor extremely sensitive: "my blood becomes agitated at the sight of my fellow man in peril, my heart tightens, my tears flow,"[65] but he was also very concerned about the efficacy of capital punishment: "The death penalty does not prevent attacks on public order; on the contrary, in incessantly providing horrible spectacles it incites them;...Let us punish, as we must, those who disturb the social order; but let us punish in a manner that it useful...."[66] And his proposal to replace capital punishment with a new kind of spectacle sounds awfully familiar: "Let the permanent spectacle of the guilty who...leads an arduous and painful existence serve as a brake on the multitude who might be tempted to imitate him [in his crimes].... Put them to the task of all the public works, which are not made for the free hand of the citizen.... Let them erect pyramids."[67] Only with the mention of pyramids is the reader suddenly reminded that the historical context of this speech is ancient Egypt, rather than eighteenth-century France. But such is the presumed universality of these penal truths (and the sensibility that informs them) that de Sales imagined there was little difference between civilized societies and naturally sensitive individuals, separated as they may have been by three thousand years.

Despite the rhetoric of self-evident universality, there were those who disagreed in whole or in part with these ideas. Perhaps the most well-known, outspoken, and intractable critic of these ideas for reform was Pierre-François Muyart de Vouglans, who in his rebuttal to Beccaria's *Treatise* fired the opening salvo in what many, both at the time as well as subsequently, have considered to be a great battle between those, on the one hand, who supported the abolition of the death penalty and its replacement by forced labor, and those on the other, who defended the status quo. Bristling at the idea that any opponent of the penal reformers was necessarily inhumane, Muyart insisted "I pride myself on my sensibility as much anyone." Nevertheless, he simply could not accept the "host of dangerous assertions" that were being leveled by "our modern criminologists."[68] He accused Beccaria directly of making "imputations as gratuitous as they are indecent" and of "taking it upon himself to sketch the Laws of all Nations from the depths of his office."[69] Above all, he took issue with Beccaria's idea to replace capital punishment with a kind of spectacular slavery:

> At the very least we must agree that it would be a sovereign injustice not to make murderers suffer the same penalty that they inflict on others.... But the system of the author does not simply sin against *natural* law and the law of *nations* [*Droit des gens*], it is also contrary to all sorts of *positive* laws, which is to say civil and canon Law, the common Law of all Nations, and to the Experience of all the centuries, which authorize at the same time as they justify the necessity of the establishment of the death penalty.[70]

In response, the penal reformers gave as good as they got; as Brissot wrote in rebuttal, "To cite canon law in this century would seem like a joke had I not seen in the various treatises by M. Muyart, otherwise estimable, that he still belongs to a century in which one believed in the infallibility of the pope, in the existence of ghosts, and in the excellence of inquisitorial torture."[71] When it came time to assemble his *Bibliothèque philosophique*, which was to include, as the subtitle proclaimed, a "Selection of the best speeches, dissertations, essays, [and] fragments composed on [the subject of] criminal legislation by the most celebrated writers," Brissot adamantly refused to include anything by Muyart, or indeed by anyone whom he saw as steadfastly insisting on the preservation of the status quo. He did, nevertheless, include Bernardi's essay, which expressed some skepticism about the idea of forced labor as an alternative to the death penalty: "To hold that the death penalty is less efficacious than the penalty of slavery is to contradict nature which has given us a vivid [sense] of horror at the destruction [of life] and which, by the sweet sensation of existence renders misfortunes tolerable which would otherwise not be."[72]

On the one side, then, we have those who proposed to abolish the death penalty, or who at the very least proposed that it be used in only the most exceptional cases; and on the other, we have someone like Muyart, who believed that forced labor was a poor substitute for the unique spectacular deterrence of the death penalty. Somewhere in the middle were individuals like Gabriel Bonnot de Mably and Bernardi who, while they objected to the overuse of the death penalty and recognized the value of replacing it in most instances by forced labor, nevertheless advocated retaining the death penalty in cases of premeditated murder.[73]

But there is something wrong here; for, in fact, almost no one actually proposed abolishing the death penalty altogether, and almost no one insisted on its wanton usage, without restrictions. Upon closer examination, the great debate between abolitionists and those who supported traditional capital punishment seems more like a general agreement, among all parties, that the death penalty should be made significantly more rare, but that it should be retained as a last resort for criminals who posed a threat to society.

This basic idea that society had the right to get rid of dangerous individuals, which we saw in Montesquieu and Rousseau, and which Beccaria preserved in his penal system, Morellet's translation notwithstanding, was a constant refrain throughout the post-Beccarian reformist literature. It can be found across the spectrum, even among those authors who, at least ostensibly, seemed to support the idea of replacing the death penalty by forced labor. In 1766, Servan had suggested that the "irrevocable death penalty be allowed to subsist, at least as a last resort; it must be relegated to the extremity of our criminal laws, so that inexpiable crimes might be abandoned to it in order to rid us of rare scoundrels who cannot be preserved without danger."[74] In 1770, Delisle de Sales put the following words in the mouth of his Becarrian advisor to the ancient Egyptian pharaoh, who paused in the middle of his speech about forced laborers building pyramids to remark that "If by a coincidence of infinitely rare, unhappy circumstances, it should happen that the blood of a lone individual can prevent the dissolution of a state, it is necessary that an individual be sacrificed in the interest of all."[75] Voltaire wrote that Beccaria had been right to suggest that one did not teach an abhorrence of murder "by killing a man in a great spectacle"; nevertheless, he insisted that the death penalty was permissible in the case of "someone for whom there would be no other means of saving the lives of a greater number; this is the case in which one kills the rabid dog."[76] And, in 1781, the article "Punishment" in the *Répertoire universel et rasionné de jurisprudence*, which insisted that the death penalty should never be used in cases of theft, nevertheless insisted that it was "useful and therefore necessary for the maintenance of order."[77]

Nearly every penal reformer in the decades before the Revolution retained some sort of provision for the death penalty, whether for the crime of premeditated murder or as an emergency last resort to save the state in time of crisis. There are, however, two partial exceptions to this general rule. One was Brissot himself, who came very close to advocating complete abolition. Even he, however, who praised Catherine of Russia as the "benevolent legislator of the north" for having instituted a moratorium on the death penalty, was quick to excuse her for having abandoned the idea when confronted with the Pugachev rebellion in the early 1770s and decapitating, drawing, and quartering Pugachev himself in 1775: "If the tsarina of Russia strayed from the law of not sentencing [people] to death in the Pugachev rebellion, it is because this rebel, more an executioner than a warrior, had fleeced more than five hundred families."[78] Moreover, in his essay for the Châlons competition, Brissot, the abolitionist of capital punishment, came very close to sounding like everyone else when he wrote:

> It is possibly for [crimes of high treason] alone, for Regicides above all, that it is permissible to be implacable. It is for them alone that cruelty is authorized, even mandated by humanity. Because can one regret that the art of the executioner is expended on the likes of Chatel, Ravaillac, Damiens, these monsters vomited up by hell in order to plunge our nation into mourning?

Apparently the answer to the question was "no": "Let this monster be pitilessly extracted from the midst of men; [and] delivered over to everything that is terrifying and terrible in human justice, let the horrible image of his punishment go forth through the ages to terrorize the frenzied individuals who may be tempted to imitate him."[79] If Brissot was an abolitionist, he wasn't a very consistent one.

One of the rare supporters of abolition who does not seem to contradict himself was Nicolas Pinel, who in his "Dissertation sur la peine de mort," which Brissot included in his collection, presents his categorical opposition to the death penalty:

> The atrocity of any crime cannot alter the maxim that a man cannot, in any case, give to another man or to several men together a right which he does not have: this [maxim] permits no exceptions....
>
> Let us conclude, then... that the right to punish with death does not exist; that the laws which inflict this punishment are as invalid as they are horrible [atroces], and that each time [these laws] undergo their terrible execution, an attack on the human race is committed.[80]

Pinel stands out as a rare exception to the general rule that nearly all the penal reformers, abolitionist or not, supported the death penalty in some form or other.

If there was no great division between the so-called abolitionists, on the one hand, and supporters of capital punishment, on the other, and if they shared much more in common than is often assumed, there was, nevertheless an important line that divided all of these individuals in the decades before the Revolution; this dividing line was not, however, where the historical actors seemed to think it was, or indeed where subsequent historians have often posited it. The division lay between those, on the one side, who were primarily interested in punishment as didactic spectacular deterrence, and those, on the other side, who were beginning to formulate an entirely new conception of the death penalty that had little to do with deterrence or with teaching lessons, and everything to do with getting rid of dangerous individuals as unspectacularly as possible.

As we have seen, the idea of a kind of non-spectacular death penalty of last resort had made an occasional appearance in the utopian literature, and it had been alluded to by the likes of Grotius, Montesquieu, Rousseau, and Burlamaqui. In the decades after the publication of Beccaria's treatise, the idea slowly changed from an abstractly theorized concept on the right of the sovereign to kill in self-defense to a practical principle of a reformed penal system. While Beccaria was to become the most celebrated penal reformer, his idea for a never-ending spectacle of criminal slave laborers never really came to pass. Rather, it was the vision of a new kind of death penalty—a penalty that had nothing to do with spectacle, but was instead discreet, hidden, almost abashed—a vision that is to be found throughout the writings of penal reformers and even within Beccaria's treatise itself, that would soon become common practice throughout much of the modern world.

In marked contrast to the long-standing idea that capital punishment should serve the purpose of exemplary deterrence through the extravagant spectacularization of pain, this new conception of capital punishment posited a death penalty that was intentionally insipid, and utterly devoid of extravagance and passion. As Servan declared in his 1766 speech before the parlement of Grenoble: "Vengeance is a passion and the laws are exempt from [passion]. [The laws] punish without hatred and without anger; they even punish with regret, and it is not without pain that they consent to lose a citizen by punishment...."[81] A decade later, Mably suggested that the death penalty should be used only rarely, but if it were used, "that the most gentle death is the cruelest punishment that a prudent legislator can permit. Father of the country, he must punish as a father; he will punish with regret."[82] And Marat wrote that, instead of the spectacle involving "the most horrible physical punishments," the death penalty should ideally be a punishment in which the offending criminal was simply "excised from the number of the living."[83]

The spectacle of capital punishment that had existed for half a millennium was soon to be regarded as the barbaric vestige of another age. It would ultimately be replaced by an unspectacular death penalty, which, even if it was often justified by the rhetoric of deterrence, had less to do with sending a message than with simply getting rid of people. If there is any predecessor to this new punishment, it was not the spectacular capital punishment of old, but rather the logic of banishment that was similarly predicated not on exemplary deterrence but, as Marat had put it, on the excision of the criminal from society. Capital punishment, which had traditionally been a spectacle *until* death, was to become the penalty *of* death. As for punishment in general, all of the myriad ways in which justice had been done would eventually be replaced by two non-spectacular forms of exclusion from the social body: imprisonment and death.

9

Legislating the New Death Penalty
The Simple Deprivation of Life

By the eve of the French Revolution, almost everyone writing on the subject of punishment had come to accept the idea that the death penalty should be used much more rarely, that it should involve as little pain as possible, and that the bulk of crimes should be punished by some sort of incarceration or forced labor. There remained some disagreement as to whether the death penalty should be applied for all egregious crimes, or whether it should be used only as a last resort, when the state itself was in danger. There was also significant disagreement as to whether punishment, capital or non-capital, should retain elements of spectacle. For many who saw exemplary deterrence as the raison d'être of punishment, some form of spectacle was indispensable. For others, who were beginning to think that the ultimate aim of punishment was to remove criminals from society, either temporarily or permanently, such spectacles were less necessary.

As the representatives to the new, Revolutionary political body, the National Assembly, debated the future of punishment in France, they struggled to reconcile exemplary deterrence with a newer understanding of punishment as exclusion. The resulting legislation would put in place a new kind of death penalty, one that, although it was meant to be vaguely deterrent and therefore necessarily public, was first and foremost predicated on the excision of offending individuals from the social body, as discreetly and unspectacularly as possible.

GUILLOTIN'S PROPOSALS FOR REFORM

In the last years of the ancien régime, scattered bits of legislation were aimed at making the death penalty somewhat rarer. In 1775, for example, the death penalty for desertion was made applicable only in times of war, and in May 1788, Louis XVI increased the number of judges required to render a death sentence, and instituted a mandatory waiting period of one month between a sentence of death and its execution.[1]

In 1787, when it was announced that the Estates General was to be called for the first time in more than a hundred and fifty years, individuals throughout the country gathered together to draft *cahiers* containing their grievances and suggestions for reform. In the assessment of the nineteenth-century historian Albert Desjardins, who undertook a thorough analysis of the regional cahiers with respect to criminal legislation, "there was no general demand for the abolition of the death penalty, but rather a sense that it was applied in too many cases, and out of proportion to the crimes committed."[2] Public opinion had not turned against exemplary punishment—in fact, several of the cahiers reiterated the need to set spectacular examples by means of alternatives to the death penalty[3]—but the clear consensus was that the the death penalty itself should no longer involve the spectacularization of pain. As the cahiers of the nobility of Dourdan urged, the death penalty should "be executed in only one manner: the least painful."[4] The spectacle of suffering was to be replaced by a kind of targeted surgical precision, excising the condemned from the social body as neatly as possible.

The suggestion, which can be found in several of the cahiers, that beheading should become the sole means of executing the death penalty reflects a general consensus that executions should not only be relatively brief and painless, but that they should no longer impart the infamy traditionally associated with capital punishment. Beheading, because it had traditionally been the exclusive privilege of the nobility, would spare the condemned the stigma of being handled by the executioner, while at the same time sparing surviving family members from the traditional "national prejudice which stains the families of the condemned."[5] As a relatively obscure provincial lawyer by the name of Maximilien de Robespierre had observed a few years before, in an article on the subject of "infamous" punishments, "whereas the gallows stigmatize the relatives of a commoner forever, the iron which fells the head of a great man imprints no stain on his posterity."[6] Furthermore, several cahiers urged that the taint of execution not follow the condemned into the afterlife. The third estate of Paris suggested that "the cadaver receive an ordinary sepulcher and that there be no mention in the death certificate of the cause of death."[7] As much as possible, the death penalty should resemble a natural death. In the words of the cahiers of the nobility of Beauvais, the new death penalty ought to be nothing more than the simple "deprivation of life."[8]

Before the delegates who gathered in Versailles for the meeting of the Estates General were able to have a substantive discussion about the penal reforms that had been suggested in the cahiers, a political Revolution had taken place, and they were no longer delegates to the Estates General, bound to represent the views of the localities that they represented, but had been transformed into representatives of a new National Assembly, more or less free to present the views they imagined to be in the interests of the nation at large. When Joseph-Ignace Guillotin, a physician, and delegate of the third estate of Paris, raised the issue of capital punishment for the first time on the floor of the National Assembly in October of 1789, the views that he expressed were, nevertheless, very much in keeping with those that had been expressed in many of the cahiers, and reflected a broad-based call for a new, relatively painless and unspectacular death penalty.

Guillotin could have chosen a better moment to propose radical reforms. Only a few days before, thousands of individuals, with a complex and confused agenda, had marched on Versailles and "escorted" the king and his family back to Paris, where they would remain de facto prisoners until their disastrous attempt to flee the country two years later. As the National Assembly awaited word as to whether it ought to remain in Versailles or follow the king to Paris, the representatives did their best to conduct business as usual, "in order to show," as Mirabeau put it, "that the ship of State is not in danger."⁹ As the storm raged around them, those who steered the "ship" pressed on with the order of the day, which included debating such relatively mundane issues as the national debt, the formal nature of the king's consent to legislation, criminal jurisprudence, and penal legislation.

The first, relatively straightforward articles for the reform of criminal justice were presented on the evening of 8 October and the morning of the 9th, and were passed by a voice vote. Toward the close of the morning session, the representatives received a note from the king, informing them that he had "decided" to stay in Paris, and he invited the representatives, who had declared themselves to be "inseparable" from the king, to send an advance team to Paris in order to scout out possible locations for the Assembly's future seat in Paris. In the evening session of 9 October, during a relatively dry discussion of procedural issues relating to criminal trials, Guillotin stood up to propose several articles related to trial procedures, all of which were passed by a voice vote.

Perhaps emboldened by his success, Guillotin proposed six additional articles that touched directly on the subject of the execution of capital punishment. The first two of these articles, in themselves, proposed to revolutionize contemporary penal practice:

> Art. 29 The same crimes will be punished by the same penalty [*supplice*], regardless of the rank and estate of the guilty party.
>
> Art. 30 In all cases in which the law shall pronounce the death penalty against the accused, the method of punishment [*supplice*] will be the same, regardless of the nature of the crime for which he has been found guilty. The criminal will have his head severed.¹⁰

Here, in three short sentences, Guillotin proposed, in effect, the complete obliteration of the traditional penal spectacle. The multiplicity of different ways in which individuals had been put to death in France for several centuries—hanging, burning, drowning, boiling, etcetera—each of which had been attached to particular kinds of crimes, and had been a function of the age, sex, and status of the offender, were now to be reduced to one form of punishment, regardless of the criminal or the crime: beheading. Moreover, Guillotin proposed additional articles reflecting the wish expressed in many of the cahiers, that the death penalty excise individuals as "simply" as possible from the social body: no stain would be imprinted on surviving family members, who would be entitled to inherit the estate of the condemned, and the latter would be buried in an ordinary grave, with no mention of the penalty being made either on the gravestone or the death certificate.

No sooner had Guillotin proposed his articles for reforming the death penalty than Louis-Marie Guillaume, a representative of the Parisian suburb of St. Cloud, rose in support of Guillotin's proposed reforms. Speaking of the need for "men to be equal in the eyes of the law" and of the need to "erase uselessly barbarous punishments [*supplices stérilement barbares*]" from the penal code, Guillaume urged that the death penalty be pronounced "only for the most atrocious crimes," such as murder, poisoning, and arson, and that all other crimes previously punishable by death instead be punished by a life sentence in the galleys. He further proposed that various corporal punishments, including whipping and branding, be abolished and that banishment be replaced by imprisonment.[11]

Together, Guillotin's and Guillaume's proposals amounted to nothing less than a sketch for punishment in the modern age: all crimes were to be punished by various forms of exclusion, whether by confinement in a prison or in galley ships, for a period of time or for life, or by the ultimate exclusion from the social body: death. If, however, the National Assembly had been more than happy to pass twenty-eight articles relating to criminal procedure by a voice vote, they seemed to balk at Guillotin's and Guillaume's proposals, tabling them for discussion at a later date.

A month and a half later, Guillotin, undaunted, presented his proposals to reform capital punishment to the Assembly yet again.[12] This time, however, there was a novel twist. Here is how the *Mercure de France* reported his speech to the Assembly:

> M. Guillotin gave a speech on the reform of the penal Code. He proposed a draft of decrees according to which 1) All crimes of the same type will be punished with the same penalty. 2) The [punishment] of death will be decapitation by mechanism. 3) The punishment of a criminal will leave no stain on his family. 4) Confiscation of estate is abolished. 5) The corpse of the offender [will be] given over to his family.[13]

Another journal lingered slightly longer on the subject of Guillotin's proposed "mechanism": "He wishes to call for the equality of punishments for guilty parties of all ranks and estates; the same kind of punishment for all crimes carrying the penalty of death; DECAPITATION, not by an executioner, whose existence and duties in the midst of men are [a source] of great dread and a great disorder for humanity, but by an instrument put into motion by a simple mechanism."[14] Last but not least, the most extensive and the most colorful account of Guillotin's speech was given in the *Journal des Etats Généraux*:

> Painting...a portrait, which was as picturesque as it was sensitive, of the terrifying punishments which have endured even in the century of humanity—gibbets, wheels, scaffolds, burnings at the stake, barbarous punishments invented by barbarous feudalism—he concluded by [suggesting] that there should only be a single punishment of the same type for all crimes. No matter who the criminal, he was punished enough by death [itself], and society was sufficiently avenged by vomiting him from its breast. He proposed the following article: "In all cases in which the law pronounced the death penalty against the accused, the punishment will be the same, no matter the nature of the crime for which he has been found guilty: decapitation, and the execution will take place by the effect of a simple mechanism."
>
> Here, M. Guillotin went on and on about those punishments which make mankind worse than ferocious beasts, torture with red-hot pincers, etc. I pass over them in silence. It is to be hoped that we will soon forget even the names [of these punishments]. He described the horror inspired by those beings known by the name of hangmen [*bourreaux*]...
>
> M. Guillotin gave a description of the mechanism. I will not follow him in all the details; in order to give a picture of its operation, he forgot for an instant that he was

a legislator, in order to say as an orator: the mechanism falls like thunder, the head flies off, the blood spurts, the man is no more.[15]

Subsequent reports, of somewhat dubious credibility, would claim that Guillotin had addressed the following words to his colleagues in the Assembly: "Gentlemen, with my machine, I will make your head fly off in the blink of an eye without your feeling the slightest pain," or, alternatively, "The punishment that I have invented is so gentle that one would not know what to say if one had not expected to die and one would think that one had felt but a light breeze upon the neck."[16]

Whatever the precise words Guillotin may have used when he presented his idea for a "simple mechanism," his colleagues in the Assembly seemed reluctant to debate the idea. To no avail did the Duc de Liancourt rise in support of Guillotin's proposals, reminding his fellow representatives that there were many individuals awaiting the execution of death sentences and that it was therefore "indispensable" that they not delay even one day. The Assembly decided, once again, to postpone further discussion of Guillotin's articles, although the representatives did, perhaps by way of concession, allow themselves to discuss and to pass the first and least controversial of his proposed articles: that punishments would henceforth be meted out equally to all people, regardless of rank and status.[17]

More than three months after he had originally made his proposals, and after significant attention had been paid to them in the press, the bulk of Guillotin's articles were finally debated in the Assembly on the evening of 21 January 1790. Among his reforms, those that garnered the most support from his fellow representatives were the ones that emphasized the "personal" nature of capital punishment, and that would leave surviving family members comparatively untouched by the infamy of punishment. For the Abbé Papin, who spoke in support of Guillotin's reforms, while the death penalty should still serve in some vague sense as an example, it should neither be a spectacle nor a source of infamy, but simply a means of removing an individual from society: "[If criminals] deserve death; let them suffer it. Avert your gaze. Reparations are necessary, examples are necessary; let them serve as such. But do not allow their transitory torments to reflect endlessly on their families."[18]

Most of Guillotin's articles were debated and approved by the Assembly that January evening. Not debated, however, and adjourned yet again for discussion, was Guillotin's proposal that all sentences of death be executed by a "simple mechanism." This proposal was referred to the Committee on Criminal Legislation (otherwise known as the Comité des Sept) for further review, and it would be another year and a half before the Assembly would again take up the subject of the death penalty. In the meantime, executions of capital punishment continued to be practiced as they had been for centuries: as a protracted spectacle of pain and suffering, performed before a crowd of spectators.

One cannot help wondering whether the representatives' reluctance to discuss, much less adopt, Guillotin's proposals was itself a consequence of the very sensibilities that gave rise to the new, more discreet death penalty. Just as the Abbé Papin had accepted the regrettable necessity of capital punishment, while urging his fellow representatives to "Avert your gaze," so too did the National Assembly repeatedly stress the importance of the subject of capital punishment, while betraying a clear aversion to discussing its practical execution.

Public opinion, however, was not nearly as reticent. Guillotin's proposals were discussed in several journals, and his idea for a decapitating mechanism garnered particular attention. Soon after Guillotin had first made mention of his "simple mechanism," Louis-Marie Prudhomme reported in his *Révolutions de Paris* that the device had already been dubbed the "guillotine" and that "someone has written a song about this subject to the tune of *Menuet d'Exaudet*."[19] The song was published shortly thereafter in *Actes des Apôtres*, a journal that found much humor in Guillotin's novel idea, speculating whether the machine might continue to be named after Guillotin, or whether it might not instead be named, in homage to Mirabeau, the *Mirabelle* [i.e. plum].[20]

The *Moniteur*, by contrast, expressed outrage that anyone could find humor in the subject, insisting that the matter ought to be taken very seriously and that Guillotin himself deserved praise for raising the subject:

> Regarding Dr. Guillotin's motion with respect to the selection of a *mechanism* whose action would sever the head of criminals in the blink of an eye, indecent and trivial remarks can be found in several public papers. The French people also have something to lose in the Revolution: namely, base habits... among the most despicable of which is joking about punishments [*supplices*]...
>
> ... M. Guillotin... is perhaps the first who, in an assembly of legislators, has spoken of punishments with humanity, and of the ignominious suffering [that they cause] with a genuine concern.
>
> The innovation of putting a *mechanism* in the place of an *executioner* who, like the law, separates the sentence [of death] from the judge [who pronounces it], is worthy of the century in which we will live, and of the new political order in which we are entering.[21]

Even at this early stage, when the concept was barely more than a dream in Guillotin's head, we can see how part of the appeal of a decapitating machine was the way it allowed society to distance itself from the act of killing. As it was originally understood, the guillotine would be used "in the place of an executioner," making the death penalty a pure transaction between the law and the condemned. It was as if the commission of a criminal act put into motion a chain of events leading to the necessarily regrettable consequence of death, with judges and legislators acting almost as bystanders to a process in which they played no direct part. This, at least, was the theory. Practically speaking, someone would still be needed to set the machine in motion, and to maintain it and ensure its proper functioning. In the end, the machine would not so much replace as upstage the executioner, relegating him to the role of a bit player in what was to be left of the penal spectacle.

In December of 1789, the executioner was still very much a creature of the ancien régime, still the object of enormous prejudice, and still required in many places to wear the multicolored outfits, both on and off the scaffold, that broadcast his profane status.[22] The mere presence of this untouchable pariah on the scaffold could not fail to draw the attention of spectators, at a time when sensibilities were demanding that everyone "avert their eyes." What the new, more discreet death penalty demanded was a technician, a bureaucratic functionary, not someone who reeked of infamy. Some three weeks after Guillotin first proposed the idea of a decapitating machine to the National Assembly, the representatives of that body, who had been so reluctant to discuss the matter, nevertheless found themselves debating the civil status of the executioner, and ultimately decided to strip him of his infamy, and to welcome him as an equal member of society. The "naturalization" of the executioner was presented as the logical consequence of humanitarian values and the rights of man, which perhaps it was. But it was also a necessary precondition to the delivery of death with discretion.

THE NATURALIZATION OF THE EXECUTIONER

In late December of 1789, the National Assembly took up the question of the civil eligibility of three groups that had been denied a civil status in the ancien régime: actors, executioners, and Jews.[23] Because the possession of a civil status in the new régime necessarily implied eligibility for public office, the debates in the Assembly touched not only on whether individuals from all of these hitherto marginalized groups would henceforth be regarded as French citizens, but also on whether they would be eligible for elected office. All three groups had their critics, but the idea of making executioners into ordinary citizens struck many as disturbing, and the idea that they might be entrusted with public office, patently absurd. As Prudhomme wrote in *Révolutions de Paris*:

> [W]hen everything is in anarchy, when everything demands immediate repair, the National Assembly devotes several sessions to discuss...a great question which in the last analysis boils down to determining whether the hangman of Paris, for example, can sit down as a municipal [representative] in between M. M. Bailly, and La Fayette.... [I]f the national assembly decides that the hangman can be mayor, judge, and commander, one doesn't dare affirm that nineteen-twentieths of the nation would not look upon their representatives as lunatics....[24]

Within the Assembly itself, the most vocal opponent of extending a civil status to executioners was the Abbé Maury who insisted that "The exclusion of Executioners of justice is not founded upon prejudice. It is in the soul of all good men to shudder at the sight of someone who murders his fellow man in cold blood."[25] In response, the executioner of Paris, Charles-Henri Sanson, dashed off a letter to the representatives of the National Assembly on behalf of all executioners in France, informing them that Maury's comments had "troubled and alarmed our hearts," and that he, for one, would tender his resignation if executioners were not granted a civil status.[26]

For Stanislas de Clermont-Tonnerre, however, the infamy did not lie in the executioner, but rather in the current methods of execution that could not help tainting the executioner who practiced them. The task at hand was to find a method of execution that allowed the executioner to distance himself from the ignoble act, and here he hinted at Guillotin's machine:

> It would be humane and maybe even politic and befitting a sound legislation to find methods of execution that do not spread infamy...onto the agent of judicial power, onto the man of law. An honorable member [M. Guillotin] has made a motion on this subject which has been adjourned.... In order to pull the executioner from infamy, it is simply a question of making him a less immediate agent, of changing the nature of punishments.[27]

Punishment in the old régime had involved a kind of slathering of infamy, extending not simply over the intended victim but, as the reformers had pointed out so often, over the victim's extended family as well. It seemed increasingly the case that even spectators risked at least a modicum of infamy merely through the act of watching, rather than averting their gaze as contemporary sensibilities were demanding. But Clermont-Tonnerre was mistaken in thinking that the act of making the executioner a "less immediate agent" of punishments would suffice to "pull the executioner from infamy," for the source of that infamy was not the instruments of punishments, as he suggested. Rather, several centuries of mangling bodies, not to mention wallowing in sewers, trafficking in offal, and herding prostitutes and lepers, had rendered the very person of the executioner a fount of infamy, tainting his entire family and indeed everything he touched. In this respect, the idea for a decapitating machine was not all that different from the tin spoon that executioners had been required to use in many localities for the purpose of claiming their allotted due in the marketplace; both were instruments intended to mediate between the profanity of the executioner's touch and its intended target, allowing him to take what was his, while sparing everything in close proximity.

The efforts of the National Assembly to "naturalize" the executioner—in the sense not only of making him a citizen but also making him normal, natural, and unremarkable—was not simply the result of a humanitarian desire on the part of the representatives to eradicate the unjust prejudices of the ancien régime. These efforts were also intended to rescue capital punishment from the infamy of the executioner, to make it a more straightforward, automatic, and, in the end, less spectacular process. The mere presence of this profane being on the penal stage was incompatible with the execution of a discreet death and the simple deprivation of life.

Perhaps the clearest indication that the representatives of the Assembly were driven more by practical penal concerns than by heartfelt humanitarian values was the obvious displeasure that the representatives took in having to raise executioners as a subject for discussion. While actors and Jews had their share of supporters, no one wanted to appear to be the friend of executioners, and even those who supported granting them a civil status did their best to avoid mentioning them by name. This studious avoidance was pointed out in the middle of a speech by Clermont-Tonnerre, who was proposing that actors and members of "other professions" should no longer be excluded from society, when an individual interrupted, calling out: "And what about the hangman [*bourreau*]?" To which, Clermont-Tonnerre had felt compelled to say: "Yes, and the hangman."[28] When, finally, Clermont-Tonnerre came around to discussing the executioner explicitly, he could not help expressing his discomfort: "The professions which the adversaries of my position would hope to mark with infamy can be reduced to two: the execution of criminal sentences, and the actors who occupy our theater.... I blush at having to put the children of the arts side by side with the instrument of penal law; but the objections [which have been raised] force me to do so."[29]

Although Clermont-Tonnerre did indeed speak of executioners by name, he clearly seemed to prefer referring to them by such euphemistic phrases as "the agent of judicial power" and "the instrument of penal law." When it came time for the Assembly to decree the granting of a civil status to executioners and to legislate their inclusion in the new social order, they were not mentioned by name. The law stated simply that "No motive for exclusion can be invoked against the eligibility of any citizen other than those that result from constitutional decrees."[30] In other words, unless they were explicitly excluded from eligibility, any citizen was presumed to be eligible. But, as Maton de la Varenne, the executioners' legal advocate, would later observe in a pamphlet that called for a clearer law, "This decree does not say that we must regard [executioners] as citizens."[31] It was hardly a glorious welcome into the new socio-political body, but that was entirely the point: to naturalize executioners without calling attention to them, to complete the process of their "deprofanation" as discreetly as possible.

A NEW PENAL CODE?

In May of 1791, a lengthy report on the project to draft a new penal Code was submitted to the National Assembly by Louis Michel Lepeletier de Saint Fargeau, acting on behalf of the Comité de Constitution and the Comité de Législation Criminelle. In a variety of different respects, the report is an extraordinary document. It is deeply philosophical, the worthy heir of Montesquieu and Beccaria; surprisingly ambitious in its desire for sweeping change; and utopian, both in the sense that it voiced many of the themes already raised by utopian reformers for centuries, as well as in its unbounded optimism that existing penal practices could be completely and profoundly transformed with the stroke of a pen.

The report assumed, as a matter of course, that the representatives to the National Assembly "will no doubt banish from your code... all those legal horrors which are detested both by humanity and by [public] opinion," and would put an end to those "cruel spectacles [which] degrade public morals and [which] are unworthy of a humane and enlightened century".[32] Like Beccaria and the penal reformers who came after him, the report combined a humanist critique of "barbaric" punishments with more practical criticisms concerning the efficacy of traditional, spectacular punishments. As the report suggested, not only did such spectacles fail to teach any moral lessons, but they appealed to the basest instincts of the populace:

> Consider the immense crowd which is drawn to the public square in the hope of [seeing] an execution. What sentiment draws them there? Is it the desire... to allow oneself to be penetrated by a religious horror of crime? On such a day, is the good citizen any better when he returns home? Does the perverse man abandon the plot he was contemplating? No, gentlemen, it is not for the lesson [*exemple*], but for the spectacle that all these people come running. A cruel curiosity calls them there. (8:535)

For Lepeletier and those who collaborated with him on the report, it was not even a question whether brutal forms of capital punishment would continue to be practiced: "Everyone agrees that the death penalty, if it is maintained, must be reduced to the simple deprivation of life, and that the infliction of physical pain [*usage des tortures*] must be abolished" (8:534). If it is maintained? It is with this phrase that the report takes a turn toward the utopian. The vast majority of penal reformers had, as we have seen, retained the death penalty in egregious cases or when the individual posed a threat to society as a whole. But Lepeletier's report went further than most reformers of the day in its willingness to consider a world without a death penalty.

For the authors of the report, deterrence was the raison d'être of punishment (as opposed to the myriad other functions that might be served by punishment, such as vengeance, recompense, simply getting rid of people, etcetera). As they stated at the beginning of the report, if they "succeeded in preventing the execution of a single crime, they would be well rewarded for the thankless and arduous task to which... they had for so long devoted their thoughts and attention" (8:526). Judged from the perspective of deterrence, however, "The simple death penalty, the only [one] which humanity will permit us to maintain, is a very inefficient penalty for the prevention [*repression*] of crimes" (8:534–5). A criminal knew that he would die some day, and simply hastening the hour of his death would do little to deter him: "His last hour approaches; he suffers the fate common to all, and in his peaceful countenance you will find no expression of fright or horror of death. Criminals also have their philosophy.... 'No,' they say, 'the idea of the gallows has never dissuaded us from committing a single crime; only the wheel disturbs our unbridled courage'" (8:534).

The task at hand, therefore, was to find a humane method of non-capital punishment that would succeed in deterring individual criminals from committing crimes, and which at the same time might serve as an example to others. What the report ended up suggesting was that the death penalty be abolished, and replaced by an extraordinarily complex system of punishments involving careful gradations, not of afflictive punishments, but rather of deprivations of pleasure, or what the report termed "a progression of successive alleviations" in deprivation (8:544).

Although the rhetorical tone of the report recalled Beccaria's treatise, published three decades earlier, the complexity of the penal system that it proposed and the carefully detailed carceral scheme that it presented, seemed to have more in common with the utopian fantasies sketched out by Filarete more than three centuries earlier. The report envisaged three different stages of punishment. The most severe stage of punishment was intended to replace the death penalty, and was reserved for murderers, poisoners, and those who were guilty of *lèse-nation*, or an attack on the head of state (8:544). This stage would deprive criminals of light and human company except for two days a week when, hoping to associate the idea of labor with a positive good, the criminal would be permitted, but not forced, to leave the cell to work and would be allowed to see the light of day, but no other human beings (8:544). Criminals who completed this stage of punishment would graduate to a stage of punishment involving less severe deprivations, and here they would be joined by criminals who had been convicted of less heinous crimes. In this middle stage of punishment, criminals would have sunlight, but they would be chained by an iron belt. Five days a week, prisoners would be allowed to work alone, and two days a week they would be accorded the privilege of gathering with other prisoners in order to work together; on those two days, the chains would be removed (8:573). Finally, the last stage of punishment, the "prison," was the one in which the deprivations would be fewest. Here, the only real deprivation was to be the "deprivation of liberty." Although criminals would still be confined alone, they would be permitted to gather together with others every day of the week in common labor.

In marked contrast to Beccaria's and to many other penal reformers' interest in the idea of the spectacle of forced labor, with an eye toward exemplary deterrence, the authors of the report were decidedly opposed both to force as well as to the spectacularization of labor. Work was to be a positive good rather than a punishment, and the idea of parading prisoners in public would disturb a prisoner's solitude, which the report regarded as "one of the truly essential qualities of the punishment." Moreover, the cost and effort involved in guarding prisoners outside prison walls seemed prohibitive (8:573).

The authors of the report did not entirely abandon the principle of exemplary deterrence, however. Annexed to each stage of punishment was a form of spectacle, beginning with the exposition of the criminal prior to incarceration:

> ... the condemned will be exposed for three days upon a scaffold erected in the public square.... He will be attached to a post; he will be seen fettered with the same chains which he will wear for the duration of his punishment. His name, his crime, his sentence will be detailed on a placard placed on top of his head. This placard will also present the details of the punishment he must suffer. (8:536)

Even after incarceration, the report suggested that spectators be allowed to enter into the less restrictive areas of the penal system where "prisoners will be exposed to their gaze in chains. Their name, their crime, their sentence will each be inscribed above the door of their cell" (8:573).

Lepeletier and the members of the two committees, who had collaborated on the report with him, no doubt put in a vast amount of time and effort to conceptualize such a complex penal system, which seemed to satisfy many different penal purposes at once. At the level of individual deterrence, the Committee members assured the Assembly, echoing Beccaria's justification for his own penal reforms, that the new system of punishment would be a far greater deterrent than the old: "Some claim that the death penalty is the only [penalty] which can frighten [sufficiently to deter] crime; the situation we have just described will be worse than the cruelest death...." (8:544). Furthermore, through the various spectacles, both before and during incarceration, the new penal system promised a form of exemplary deterrence that did not risk setting an example of violence. Finally, by endeavoring to establish a penal system that aimed "both to punish the guilty party and to render him better" (8:527), Lepeletier and his colleagues hoped to effect a different kind of deterrence: one that might prevent crime by correcting prisoners, and by producing law-abiding citizens rather than recidivist criminals.

As confident as they may have been in the advantages of their new penal system, the authors of the report nevertheless retained two "fail-safe" options. Although they derided banishment as an "absurd and fatal exchange which relocates the criminal without suppressing or punishing the crime," (8:533–4) the authors of the report nevertheless proposed deportation in cases of recidivism:

> Whosoever is apprehended...and condemned a second time, will suffer the penalty stipulated by the law for the crime; but when he has thus satisfied this exemplary purpose, he will be conducted to the established place for deportation. In such a way, you will satisfy the dual goals of punishing recidivism and of ridding society of an incorrigible malefactor. (8:574)

But when the state itself was threatened, Lepeletier and his colleagues seemed prepared to forget about setting examples, and instead opted for the solution of getting rid of the offender more quickly and more permanently:

> As attached as we are to the purity of the principle of the abolition of the death penalty, the death penalty is [nevertheless] called for on one occasion in the law that we are presenting to you.
> That is relating to the head of a party which has been declared in rebellion by a decree of the legislative body. This citizen must cease to live, less in order to expiate his crime than for the safety of the state. (8:545)

So, even here, in this earnestly abolitionist vision for a new penal system, a system that endeavored to replace active punishments with careful gradations of deprivation, and insisted that punishment made no sense without individual and exemplary deterrence, a system that strove to remake criminals into better citizens—even here, in the last instance, the death penalty remains. Even if the authors of the report insisted on the exceptionality of their death penalty, Prudhomme wasn't so sure, writing in his *Révolutions de Paris*: "If such a law were decreed and put into execution, there would soon be no liberty; despotism would not hesitate to sanction it and make use of it."[33]

While the report presented to the Assembly by Lepeletier did not unequivocally abolish the death penalty, it was nevertheless a wildly ambitious project that sought completely and radically to remake the practice of punishment in France. In the National Assembly's ambivalent reception of the report, however, and in the ensuing debate on the legitimacy of capital punishment, we can see both a guarded excitement at the dawn of a new penal era as well as a certain reluctance to abandon traditional penal theories and practices.

DEBATES ON CAPITAL PUNISHMENT

On 23 May 1791, as the representatives sat listening to Lepeletier present the report for a projected new penal code, one wonders what must have been going through their minds. No doubt some listened patiently and sympathetically to the extraordinarily complex scheme to replace all forms of capital and corporal punishment with "a progression of successive alleviations" in deprivation. Others were undoubtedly mystified, as much by the complexity of the system, with its peculiar mix of voluntary but invisible labor, as by the arcane terminology it employed to describe the three levels of deprivation. By listening to the representatives respond to the plan, almost person by person, and by watching as the debate[34] slowly turned to the very legitimacy of capital punishment itself, we can literally see the transition to a new penal epoch; we can witness radical historical shifts in a kind of slow motion, as individuals struggled to balance their desire for change with long-held preconceptions about the nature of punishment.

One week after the report had initially been submitted to the Assembly, the matter finally came up for debate. Lepeletier opened the discussion with a brief statement in which he said that the committees had "nothing to add for the moment," but he nevertheless proceeded to frame the ensuing debate: "We will content ourselves with asking you to open the discussion with this single question: Should the death penalty be retained or not?"[35]

Jean-Baptiste Charles Chabroud was the first to speak. He noted the extraordinary efforts that the members of the committees had put into the project, but he nevertheless clearly felt that the tenor of the report was somehow strangely out of sync with the practicalities of the task at hand: "In making my way through this project, I noticed many infinitely felicitous details, very philosophical details.... But gentlemen, I do not believe that it is in such details that we should occupy the attention of the legislative Assembly" (26:617). As far as Chabroud was concerned, lurking beneath the mass of minute details, there was a very strange penal principle:

> It seems to me...that there should be a kind of correlation between the crimes and the punishments.... Well, the Committee takes a completely different tack, so that, [for example,] if I betray my country, I am put away; if I have killed my father, I am put away; all crimes imaginable are punished in the exact same manner. (26:618)

In fact, Chabroud had seized upon the essential element of the proposed new penal code. Despite a nod to exemplary deterrence, it essentially reduced the multiplicity of different punishments in the old code—branding, whipping, banishment, death by various methods, etcetera—to one punishment: removing criminals from society. Stripped of its thin veneer of spectacle, it was a plan that punished by getting rid of people, whether through confinement for a period of years or more permanently.

Louis-Pierre-Joseph Prugnon took the podium next. For him, too, the code seemed strangely impractical, almost utopian: "If ever it should please the Eternal [being] to form a new people, and to set them up on a completely new island, the

Committee could propose its code to them" (26:622). But for France in 1791, he argued, the death penalty was not something that could safely be abolished; it was, rather, "a sad necessity" (26:620). Noting that the traditional form of capital punishment had actually worked at cross purposes with deterrence because it "familiarized the multitude with the spectacle of cruelties and the sound of pain and encouraged a kind of ferocity more likely to multiply crimes than to prevent them," Prugnon concluded that "The cruelest punishment that the legislator can and must inflict is, therefore, the gentlest death" (26:620–1). He did not, however, agree with the report that a "simple" death penalty was ineffective as a deterrent, or that it should be applied only to those guilty of lèse-nation. He therefore proposed that the penalty of a simple death be extended to murderers, poisoners, and arsonists (all of whom the new penal code would have sentenced to the most restrictive level of deprivation), as well as to those who forged *assignats*, the new paper currency.

The next speaker was an eloquent young man who had only just begun to make his mark on the Assembly: Maximilien Robespierre. And it was Robespierre who, ironically enough, delivered the most eloquent plea to the members of the Assembly in favor of abolishing the death penalty:

> When the news came to Athens that the citizens were condemned to death in the city of Argos, people ran to the temples and entreated the gods to make the Athenians abandon such cruel and deadly thoughts. I come to beg not the gods, but the legislators who must be the organs and interpreters of eternal laws which divinity has dictated to mankind, to erase from the Code of the French the blood laws which call for juridical murders. (26:622)

Robespierre's speech was briefly interrupted by the Abbé Maury who implied that he was being unrealistically utopian, and snidely suggested that he should try delivering his speech in the forest of Bondy, a well-known haunt of dangerous criminals. In the end, Robespierre's speech was greeted with applause, and the discussion was adjourned for the day.

The following morning, 31 May 1791, the first speaker was Jean-Joseph Mougins de Roquefort who confessed that it was "a painful sentiment to present an opinion that seemed to contradict the rights of humanity," but who nevertheless insisted that "public tranquility and safety demand that one balance penalties against the atrocity of crimes, and that human beings [i.e. victims of crimes] not be sacrificed in the name of humanity" (26:637). Citing Montesquieu, Rousseau, and Mably, he urged his colleagues: "Punish with regret, but punish. It is the common interest which orders you to do so. I conclude that murderers be punished with the penalty of simple death" (26:640).

Next to speak was Jérôme Pétion de Villeneuve, who agreed with the authors of the report that the death penalty in and of itself could never deter the average criminal. Here he cited the famous Cartouche, who reportedly scoffed at the prospect of his own death: "A bad quarter hour passes quickly" (26:641). Addressing his colleagues in the Assembly, and urging them to reject the death penalty, Pétion declared "Like you I want [the murderer] to be punished, but not by cutting short his life by [another] murder, but rather by prolonging his penalty, and applying it to all the moments of his existence" (26:642). To Pétion, long-term penalties had the advantage both of "intimidating by example those men who might be tempted to give themselves over to crime" as well as offering the possibility of "correcting the man [who committed the crime] and making him better" (26:641). But this last point was immediately challenged by Jean Anthelme Brillat-Savarin, who asked "But in these prisons, will these men become better?" and answered his own question: "On the contrary, they will establish a kind of school for crime there.... My work has often called me to these places where crime awaits its punishment; I have seen how much the death penalty is superior to all other [punishments].... No penalty can replace death" (26:643).

At this point, sensing that the representatives were straying from the recommendations contained in the report, Adrien Duport stood up and reminded the Assembly that "both your Committee on the Constitution and your Committee on Criminal Legislation, which include a rather considerable number of men, were unanimously in accord with respect to the project that they have presented to you." Duport assured his colleagues that the committees had not been afraid to resort to the death penalty when "the security of an entire society" might be in danger; in such cases the death of the offender was "both indispensable and legitimate." In all other cases, however, when the state was not in danger, then the only plausible reason for the penalty of death might be exemplary deterrence. But, once again citing Cartouches's euphemism for capital punishment as "only a bad quarter hour," Duport insisted that such punishments failed to deter; on the contrary, he claimed, spectacles of execution had the potential to be "dangerous and corrupting for the spectator" (26:643–6).

The following day, when the very existence of the death penalty would be put to a vote, the first speaker harped on the traditional exemplary function of spectacular capital punishment: "[T]he father of a family, the school teacher, the master of a workshop, would bring his children, his pupils, his workers to these sad spectacles, profiting from the punishment of crime in order to give them lessons in virtue." In apparent contrast to this very point, however, this same speaker urged his colleagues to replace the penal spectacles of the old regime with a relatively unspectacular death penalty: "Let us hasten, beginning today, to banish from our books the terms *stake*, *wheel*, and *torture*. Let us do more. Let us reduce to the smallest number of possible cases, the application of a simple death." To him, somehow, the rare execution of a simple death might actually "become more frightening... more effective" (26:684).[36]

Shortly after this speech, a voice vote was taken, and the Assembly decided that "the death penalty will not be abolished." Although, on the surface, the representatives might be described as having maintained capital punishment, in truth they supplanted the death penalty of the ancien régime with an entirely different kind of death penalty. Over the next few days, as they discussed the precise manner in which executions might be performed, they revealed many of their aspirations and their fears concerning the role of the death penalty in the new penal age.

A SPECTACULAR DEATH VS. THE SIMPLE DEPRIVATION OF LIFE

On the subject of how the new death penalty was to be executed, Lepeletier once again framed the debate with a leading question: "Shall the death penalty be reduced to the simple deprivation of life?" (26:685).

For Dominique Garat, the problem with the simple deprivation of life was that it was too uniform to allow differentiation between more or less atrocious crimes. He proposed, therefore, that an exception be made for those who committed parricide, who might be differentiated from all others by having their hands cut off prior to suffering a simple death (somewhat clouding the very notion of a simple death). But Bertrand de Barère, who spoke next, insisted that the concept of a simple death ought to have no exceptions and that executions "be reduced to the simple deprivation of life, without any kind of [physical] torture" (26:687).

It was at this moment that Adam Philippe, Comte de Custine, stood up and made an astounding proposal. And one can almost hear the tectonic plates shifting:

> The Assembly has maintained the death penalty for the sole reason that a dangerous man must be removed from society. I demand therefore not only that this penalty not be accompanied by [physical] tortures, but that it not be aggravated by the frightening spectacle [*appareil effrayant*] which renders it more terrible to the individual who suffers it, and that executions be performed behind closed doors (*murmurs in the house*). The legislator must not go beyond that which is necessary for the conservation of society. (26:687)

Custine's proposal was revolutionary in every sense of the word. It was radically modern, rejecting the very principle of spectacle, and acknowledging that the death penalty was primarily about "removing" people from society. Deterrence was secondary, if indeed it factored into the equation at all. The murmurs interrupting Custine's speech are a testament to the fact that his contemporaries were not ready to move so quickly from the old to the new. (In fact, it would take another century and a half, during which time successive measures would reduce the spectacular nature of capital punishment to something just barely visible, before the French state could finally bring itself to embrace Custine's vision fully.) In 1791, few could yet conceive of capital punishment without spectacle, even if the laws they were in the process of enacting were making enormous strides in that general direction.

Immediately after Custine, Jérôme Legrand took the podium and proposed what seemed to be a compromise between Garat's position, that there be some gradation in the punishments, and Barère's position, that simple death be the only form of capital punishment. Legrand wondered "whether it might be possible to put a gradation in the death penalty itself, which is to say in its spectacle [*appareil*] rather than in its degree of pain, which corresponded to the different kinds of crimes and to their [level of atrocity]." He was suggesting, in other words, that the spectacular nature of the execution could be augmented or diminished in relation to the crime, and even if all capital offenses were punished by simple death, certain criminals might nevertheless be "exposed for several days to the gaze of the public at the place of punishment in order to impress upon the people the horror of the crime with which [the criminals] have sullied society" (26:687). Legrand's spectacular appendage to the death penalty almost recalls the earliest days of spectacular punishment, when the pillory was used as an appendage to spectacularize otherwise non-spectacular punishments.[37]

But before anyone could take up Legrand's proposal, Lepeletier rushed to the podium and demanded, in the name of the Committee, that Custine's proposal for non-visible executions be rejected. "The principle of every punishment," he insisted, "is that it deter through example [qu'elle soit repressive par l'exemple]; it must therefore not be secret" (26:687). Sharing the same views, the next speaker, Antoine Dufau, encouraged his colleagues to consider the ways in which simple death might be made *more* spectacular (like Garat, somewhat complicating the notion of a simple death):

> Do you want the death penalty, reduced to the simple deprivation of life, to lose nothing of its effectiveness as an example?...Let the punishment of the guilty individual present an imposing spectacle; associate the most lugubrious and the most touching form of spectacle with the punishment; let this terrible day be a kind of day of mourning for the fatherland....Let the magistrate, dressed in a funeral crape, inform the people of the crime and the sad necessity of a legal vengeance. (26:688)

In opposition to Lepeletier's and Dufau's proposals to maintain or even increase the degree of spectacle, Charles Malo François de Lameth stood up in support of Custine: "Since I am convinced that a man [who is] destroyed by the order of society, massacred in cold blood, can only render the morals of the people ferocious and barbarous, I demand that the amendment of Custine, which seeks to destroy the element of spectacle [apareil], which is to say, the publicity, be sent to the Committee [for consideration]." Several individuals in the Assembly shouted their support, and Lameth continued, urging his colleagues, to find a method of execution that "would not accustom the people to the [kind of] abominable spectacle, which creates more murderers than it dissuades from crime" (26:688).

At this moment, Pierre Joseph Lachèze-Murel stepped forward to decry Custine's and Lameth's proposals to de-spectacularize executions. Their proposals, he insisted, had "the air of reducing the action of the law in criminal matters to an act of vengeance. If it is only a question of putting [the criminal] in a state in which he can cause no harm, certainly, Gentlemen, you would not have made use of the death penalty; you would have made use of incarceration [reclusion]" (26:688). Without realizing it, Lachèze had put his finger on the secret of the modern penal age: incarceration and the new death penalty were conceptual cousins, differing more in the permanence with which they removed individuals from society than in their intended purposes. Surely, Lachèze insisted, the representatives had retained the death penalty "solely for the purposes of example." Custine's and Lameth's proposal for a non-spectacular death penalty therefore made no sense, and he urged the Assembly to reject them out of hand, which indeed it proceeded to do.

Rather than embracing spectacle entirely, however, the Assembly settled on a position along the lines of what Legrand had suggested, decreeing: "Without aggravating [physical] torments in any case, there will be gradations in the spectacle [*appareil*] of the punishment corresponding to the different types of crime and proportionate to their severity" (26:689). In many ways, it was the perfect compromise, allowing for executions that were spectacular, in the sense that they were able to signify the gravity of the crime through "gradations in the spectacle," and yet relatively unspectacular, in the sense that they would ideally dispatch offensive individuals with as little pain as possible, avoiding the spectacle of suffering.

KILLING HUMANELY

After more discussions, on the practice of branding criminals, which the Assembly formally rejected, and on the merits of forced labor, which it embraced, the Assembly again took up the question of capital punishment on 3 June 1791. Once again, Lepeletier set the stage for the discussion, focusing on how, precisely, the simple deprivation of life might best be executed:

> Gentlemen, you have established the principle that the death penalty will exist, but that it will be exempt from [physical] torture, and reduced to the simple deprivation of life; your Committee had therefore to seek out a kind of death which caused the least suffering to the condemned. It was torn between the [penalty] of the gallows and that of beheading. The gallows seemed to [the Committee] to be the most prolonged of the two and, consequently, the cruelest. (26:720)

Adding that beheading had a greater potential to spare surviving family members the taint of infamy, Lepeletier proposed that the Assembly declare: "All those sentenced to death will have their heads cut off."

Chabroud was the first to speak. He pointed out that beheading "requires a great amount of skill" and that, performed poorly, it threatened "to expose the condemned to horrible sufferings." But he also made the telling admission that "I would prefer that there would be no blood spilled in any of the punishments." With the sensibilities of the spectator (more than the suffering of the condemned) uppermost in his mind, he expressed a preference for the gallows over the "horrible spectacle" of beheading. No sooner had he finished than Joseph Golven Tuault de la Bouverie objected, seemingly unable to comprehend Chabroud's point: "A terrible spectacle is necessary to keep the people in their place." Like so many others, he failed to understand what possible purpose could be served by a death penalty that did not aim to terrify by example.

Faced with something of a deadlock between the supporters of beheading and the supporters of hanging, Le Pelletier proposed the following: "In order to put an end to this sad discussion, a friend of humanity has just relayed to me an idea which might break our stalemate. The [effusion] of blood associated with beheading, and the horrors associated with the gallows might both be avoided if the condemned were attached to a post and strangled with a tourniquet" (26:721). This suggestion was greeted with murmurs. Feeling that the discussion was becoming a bit too graphically detailed for a legislative body, Chabroud urged that the matter "be sent to the Committee... so that it is not in the Assembly that we dwell on this sad discussion" (26:721). Shortly afterward, Tuault de la Bouverie suggested to his fellow representatives that their quest for the holy grail of a painless death was in vain: "Gentlemen, no matter what you do, you will never come up with a kind of death that is gentle or exempt from pain; that is where your error lies." But rather than leaving it at this astute observation, Tuault cast his lot with those who believed that the answer to the stalemate lay in returning to the traditional logic of exemplary deterrence: "It is in the interest of society that a great example be given. It is extremely important that a man exposed to all the passion of humanity return to his home after the punishment with a heart filled with terror and fear" (26:721).

In the end, although the representatives were divided on the question of whether exemplary spectacle was fundamental to capital punishment, they nevertheless managed to find consensus around a few basic points. They agreed that the death penalty should be executed solely by beheading, as this method seemed most likely to satisfy the requirement that capital punishment involve as little pain as possible. They also agreed that executions would take place in public, in the main square of the town in which a case was adjudicated.

Some three months later, the Assembly returned to the question of the penal spectacle, hoping to resolve how executions might involve gradations of spectacle without aggravating punishment beyond simple death. How, in short, could they stage a relatively unspectacular spectacle? Lepeletier framed the debate, by presenting the following proposed article, drafted by the Committees of Constitution and Criminal Jurisprudence:

> Whosoever has been condemned to death for the crime of murder, poison, or arson shall be attached to a post on the public square; he will remain there, exposed to the gaze of the people for three hours prior to the execution.
> Those condemned for murder or poison will wear a red shirt.
> The parricide will be exposed for 6 hours prior to the execution. He will have his head and face veiled with black fabric. He will be unveiled only at the very moment of execution. (31:81)

Chabroud, for one, objected that these elements of spectacle violated the very principle of a simple death: "[O]ne aggravates the penalty.... The [article] which is being proposed to you is therefore, as I see it, very barbaric. I believe that a man who is exposed and who knows the very hour that he will be put to death, will be exposed to the most abominable torments that a man can suffer." He wondered, moreover, whether this sort of spectacle might not "replace the just horror of crime in the hearts of the people with the sentiment of pity" (31:81). In the end, a compromise was struck. The exposition of the condemned was dropped, while the red shirt and the black veil were retained.

The new criminal code was passed by the Assembly on 25 September and enacted into law on 6 October 1791. Here is how the relevant articles were worded in the final version:

> Article 2: The death penalty will consist of the simple deprivation of life, without any [physical] torture ever being permitted to be executed upon the condemned.
>
> Article 3: All condemned [to the death penalty] will have the head cut off.
>
> Article 4: Whosoever will be condemned to death for the crime of murder, arson, or poison will be led to the place of execution dressed in a red shirt.
>
> The parricide will have his head and face veiled with black fabric; he will be unveiled only at the moment of execution.

Fig. 10. Ecce Custine, 1794. Carnavalet Museum/Snark Archives. © Photo12/The Image Works.

Article 5: The execution of those condemned to death will be performed in the public square of the city in which the grand jury will have been convened. (31:326)

Together, these articles express the competing and conflicting desires for a discreet and simple deprivation of life that nevertheless, however vaguely, carried the burden and the aspiration of exemplary deterrence. Here, in other words, is the ancestor of the death penalty that still exists today in those countries continuing to practice it.

Anyone looking to write an ironic history of the Revolution would certainly find plenty of material in these debates on capital punishment. Several of the representatives who most enthusiastically supported the death penalty as a fundamental tool for protecting society from dangerous individuals would themselves suffer the penalty within three years' time. Lepeletier, who had expressed his strong opposition to the death penalty, would nevertheless vote in favor of Louis XVI's execution a year and a half later, and would himself be assassinated by a royalist on the eve of the king's death. Custine, the deputy who proposed the idea that the death penalty might be truly discreet and executed behind closed doors, would himself become one of the most recognizable icons of the spectacularity of the guillotine, his head thrust out toward spectators in an oft-reproduced graphic print (Fig. 10). Of course, most ironically of all, Robespierre, who had spoken so eloquently in favor of the complete abolition of the death penalty, would go down in history as an individual renowned for its unbridled practice.

Beneath these multiple ironies, however, beneath the contrasting positions of all those who spoke against or in favor of the death penalty, a vague consensus was nevertheless emerging. The vast majority of representatives had come to the conclusion that the spectacularization of pain was not simply offensive to contemporary sensibilities but was also ineffective and perhaps even counter-productive, as likely to incite a lust for blood as an aversion to shedding it. If, however, they were opposed to the idea of making a spectacle of pain, they were equally opposed to that of performing executions behind closed doors; the overwhelming majority clung to the belief that public, relatively unspectacular executions could still, in a vaguer and more abstract sense, deter by example. The only question that remained was the practical one of how to stage a public execution with a minimum of spectacle—how, in short, to kill criminals in public while at the same time restricting what spectators could see.

10

Executing the New Death Penalty
The Invisible Spectacle of the Guillotine

With the Revolutionary penal code of 1791 the French nation turned its back on centuries of spectacular capital punishment in which the suffering of the condemned was meant, at least in theory, to deliver a powerful message to would-be miscreants and a sober lesson to everyone else. Of course, it is not entirely clear whether that message had ever been received by the enormous crowds who had flocked to the penal spectacle, eager to watch the show. From 1791 onwards, a new logic would govern the death penalty in France, one predicated less on spectacular and exemplary deterrence than on a need to remove dangerous individuals from the social body. While legislators insisted that executions remain public, the overwhelming consensus was that the penalty of death should be as painless as possible, not only for the victims who suffered it but for the spectators who watched.

As legislators endeavored to decide upon a new method of executing the death penalty "humanely," much of the legislative debate and administrative correspondence reveals that the overriding concern was less the suffering of the condemned than the sensibilities of the general public, for whom the act of watching other human beings suffer was now profoundly problematic. Acting upon medical advice as well as on the advice of the executioner of Paris, legislators settled upon the idea of a decapitating machine. This machine, almost immediately dubbed the guillotine after the lawmaker who had first proposed the idea, promised to "dispatch" offenders quickly and discreetly. Although executions would continue to be performed in public, the speed of the guillotine's blade was such that the actual moment of death would be practically invisible to the spectator's eye, satisfying the aspirations of lawmakers to devise a death penalty that was, at one and the same time, both public and unspectacular.

If the public was initially curious to see the new guillotine in action, it quickly became apparent that these executions were extraordinarily different from the traditional spectacle of capital punishment. While, at first, there was a good deal of fascination with the speed at which the guillotine could transform a living human being into a lifeless head, over time it would seem that the spectacle of the guillotine proved somewhat disappointing to spectators, for the simple reason that a process which used to unfold over a period of time, sometimes several hours, was now reduced to an almost invisible moment. If the public still came to watch, there was, in truth, little that remained to be seen. The executioners of France, much like the spectacles they had overseen for generations, were themselves, in the end, a casualty of the new machine. Their complex craft, handed down from father to son, was now reduced to the simple act of pulling a cord.

THE SEARCH FOR A HUMANE KILLING MACHINE

The passage into law of the new penal code in 1791 precipitated a crisis in the execution of the death penalty. Beheadings had been an exceedingly rare form of punishment, practiced exclusively on members of the nobility who had been convicted of a capital offence. They had required all the skill that an experienced executioner could muster, and even then they had not always gone as planned. The botched execution of the Comte de Lally in 1766, during which the executioner had taken several tries to fully separate Lally's head from his body, still lived on in people's memories as one of the more gruesome spectacles that had taken place in the ancien régime (see Fig. 9, Chapter 7).

As we have already noted, some members of the National Assembly had objected to the idea of beheading, both because of the amount of blood involved as well as because of the "horrors" that might ensue if things went wrong. It was no doubt with such thoughts in mind that a citizen by the name of Girardet took it upon himself to submit a proposal to the Committee on Legislation entitled "Idea for a means of publicly giving death to criminals without spreading blood and fulfilling the aims of moderation." Girardet's idea was to build an asphyxiation "booth" [*guérite*], and although it had little chance of being adopted because the Assembly had already declared beheading to be the sole means of executing the death penalty, his proposal is nevertheless a fascinating document that deserves our careful attention. For, in a few short lines, Girardet managed to distill those conflicting aspirations for a death that was public and yet caused no (visible) pain, aspirations that would soon give rise to the guillotine.

Girardet proposed that a scaffold be erected 6 or 7 feet high, with a wooden post in the middle to which "the servant of death [i.e. the executioner] would attach the condemned by the neck, feet, and hands behind the back, all of which he would cover or enclose in a kind of booth, 5 feet square, equipped with panes of glass on all four sides and with a tight-fitting cap on top." Underneath the scaffold, at a given signal, "charcoal, sulfur, and other materials that cause asphyxiation could be introduced into the booth by means of an inverted funnel in such a way that the condemned would suffocate and expire instantaneously." But the beauty of the device, for Girardet, was not simply the delivery of a quick death; equally important was the way that the device prevented spectators from actually seeing the spectacle of suffering: "One will see through the panes of glass, notwithstanding the thickness of the smoke, *death by suffocation*; horrors will be concealed; and justice will be done promptly. The cadaver will be removed from the booth, it will remain for a quarter hour in the public gaze, and then carried to the *field of sleep*."[1] Girardet's asphyxiation booth was almost like a magic trick. A live criminal would be introduced into the glass booth, smoke would momentarily obscure the view, and then presto: a cadaver of a criminal emerged. The corpse would be briefly exhibited, and then quickly taken to the "field of sleep." What could be more gentle? Girardet's booth seemed to promise a public death without the "horrors" of a spectacle.

Undoubtedly, there were no individuals in France more familiar with the risks and problems associated with beheadings, and the need to find an alternative to the current method of performing them, than the executioners themselves. In a memorandum aptly entitled "Observation on the execution of beheading, with the nature of different problems it poses and to which it is truly susceptible," none other than Charles-Henri Sanson, the executioner of Paris, sought to make both legislators and government administrators aware of the potential difficulties facing him and his colleagues, and of the "dangerous scenes" that might take place, if they attempted to execute the law according to existing methods of beheading. As he wrote in the memorandum, "When there shall be several condemned [criminals] who will be executed at the same time, the terror created by this [form of] execution, because of the immensity of blood which it produces and which it spreads out, will give rise to fright and weakness in even the most intrepid of those who remain to be executed." Sanson was concerned, in short, that the execution "would become a struggle and a massacre." In contrast to other forms of capital punishment in which "it was easy to conceal the [patient's] weaknesses from the public, because one did not need the condemned to remain firm and without terror in order to finish," beheading was entirely dependent on a calm patient: "... [I]f the condemned loses his nerve [*fléchit*], the execution will be botched."[2]

Observing that the National Assembly must have decided upon beheading as a means of avoiding the "lengthiness" of executions as traditionally practiced, and recognizing that they had been guided by "humanitarian views," Sanson felt it his duty to warn the representatives that beheading, if executed by sword, would most likely result in a spectacle that was the very opposite of what the Assembly had intended. He concluded his memorandum by stressing that it was "indispensable" to find a method of beheading that could "fix the condemned in place" in such a way that it might "avoid lengthiness and assure certainty." Doing so, he noted, would not only "fulfill the intention of the legislator" but it would also protect executioners from "the effervescence of the public," which had traditionally taken out its frustration at a botched execution on them.

Sanson sent copies of his memorandum to several of his colleagues in the provinces, who in turn addressed letters to the Minister of Justice, echoing Sanson's concerns.[3] Meanwhile, there were criminals who needed to be executed, and the reluctance of executioners throughout the country to carry out beheadings according to current procedures had the effect of bringing the wheels of justice to a halt. In March of 1792, nearly six months after the Assembly had decreed beheading as the sole means of executing the death penalty, but had not yet stipulated how such executions were to be carried out, one frustrated official wrote to Roederer, the *procureur général syndic* of Paris:

> You promised me, Sir, a response by noon yesterday... on the method of execution to be employed against those condemned to death. I gather from your silence that you have not yet decided on this matter. I believe I must therefore directly address the president of the National Assembly. It is time that the public had an example before its eyes; murders are on the increase, and good citizens are complaining and bemoaning the inertia and negligence that are characterizing the execution of the law.[4]

As we can see, the movement toward a humane and less spectacular form of capital punishment did not seem to lessen the belief or the desire that the death penalty could still function as a powerful means of exemplary deterrence.

On the day after the above note was written, responding to the growing level of frustration on the part of judicial administrators as well as to the growing backlog of condemned criminals slated for execution, the administrators of the Directory of Paris as well as Louis-François Duport-Dutertre, the Minister of Justice, sent letters to the National Assembly, apprising them of Sanson's memorandum and asking them to determine a solution to the problem. Duport's letter begins by apologizing to the representatives for having to bring such unpleasant matters to their attention. He assured them of his own "repugnance" of the subject, but insisted that "humanity" and the growing number of individuals who had been condemned but not executed made it necessary for them to address the issue and, one hoped, "never return to the subject." Citing Sanson's report, Duport suggested that the representatives had been "mistaken" in selecting beheading, at least as it was currently practiced, as the sole means of executing the "simple deprivation of life." He warned that either "the punishment of beheading will be horrible for spectators" or, perhaps worse, "it would show them to be atrocious if they could stand [to watch] the spectacle."[5] Upon receipt of Duport's letter, the Assembly immediately decided to remit the matter "which is so important for humanity" to the Committee of Legislation for review.[6]

Seizing the moment, a citizen by the name of Thomas—a schoolmaster, of all things—thought that the time was ripe to propose his idea for a strangulation machine to the National Assembly. In the belief that it was "as impolitic as it is revolting to subject a gentle people and a regenerated Frenchman to the spectacle [of a beheading]," Thomas proposed a device that, much like Girardet's asphyxiation booth, promised to kill with little (visible) pain. The patient was to be led up to the scaffold, seated on a chair, and attached to a post. Above the patient, suspended in the air, would be a veil or curtain, and around the patient's neck a cord attached to a winch. And then: "At the agreed upon signal for the moment of punishment, one of the executioners would drop the suspended veil onto the body [of the condemned] down to the waist, while another [executioner], turning the winch, and stopping it at the necessary point...would leave the patient in a state of constant suffocation for at least an hour."

To Thomas, the advantages were numerous. In the first place, it was foolproof, and executioners would therefore not be at risk of botching the execution and incurring the wrath of the crowd. In the second place, "one would not see anything hideous, either blood spilled, or a man shaking indecently." Making clear it was the spectators' sensibilities rather than the suffering of the victim that was uppermost in his mind, Thomas wrote:

> We will finally no longer fear hearing, as we did in the old days, those frightful cries of horror among the spectators, which the horrible spectacle [*appareil*] of punishment involuntarily elicited from [even] the least sensitive, and everyone will leave this distressing spectacle merely sighing deeply and calmly over the deserved misfortune of the guilty, and the just severity of the law.

As a finishing touch, perhaps recalling the wishes of the Assembly to imbue executions with gradations of spectacle, Thomas suggested that the color of the veil that fell over the condemned at the moment of execution might represent the crime: red for traitors and parricides, violet for arsonists and murderers, and black for all other criminals.[7]

Like Girardet's asphyxiation booth, Thomas's strangulation machine promised a public execution that masked the pain from spectators. With the veil only covering the top half of the victim's body, one could see that justice was being done without seeing the expression on the victim's face as he or she died. Thomas hoped, not unlike the officials who had decided to veil Madame de Lescombat back in 1755, to perform a relatively unspectacular public execution. Spectators could watch, but there would be little to see. Moreover, the winch would serve to mechanize the process, not only ensuring its success but mediating between the victim and the executioner, sparing the former the taint of the executioner's touch, and sparing the latter the direct responsibility for the victim's death.

INVENTING THE GUILLOTINE

Unbeknownst to Thomas, the Assembly had not turned its back on beheading, but merely on the method by which it had traditionally been performed. From the very moment that the Assembly had referred the matter to the Committee on Legislation, plans were in the works to develop a new method of beheading, one that, like Thomas's strangulation machine, would promise both mechanized certainty and a relatively invisible spectacle. The Committee immediately consulted Dr. Louis, permanent secretary to the Academy of Surgery, who promptly drafted a report in which he agreed with the executioner's assessment that traditional beheading practices would result in a spectacle that was "horrible for the patient as well as for spectators." Recalling the botched execution of the Comte de Lally, Louis remarked that "One watched this hatchetry, if it may be permitted to coin this term, with horror." After a dutifully scientific paragraph in which Louis analyzed the efficiency of different kinds of blades slicing at different angles, and another, in which he detailed the bones that composed the vertebral column, he finally concluded that "it is not possible to be assured of a prompt and perfect separation [of the head from the body] by confiding [the task] to an agent susceptible to variation in performance due to mental or physical causes." In other words, the job needed to be entrusted to a machine: "For the certainty of the procedure, it is necessary that [the task] rely on invariable mechanical methods.... Decapitation would take place in an instant, in accord with the spirit and the will of the new law."[8]

A decapitating machine? The concept had, of course, been suggested more than two years before by Guillotin, but few had taken the idea seriously. What, in 1789, had seemed like a very odd suggestion and had been the butt of countless jokes, was now beginning to seem like a logical, humane, and rational method of executing people. On 10 March 1792, Roederer invited Guillotin to come "at your first free moment" to his office: "The Directory will unfortunately be in the process of determining the mode of decapitation which will henceforth be used.... I am charged with asking you to communicate the important ideas that you have gathered and evaluated for softening a penalty which the law does not intend to be a cruel punishment."[9]

Roederer's need to stress the unfortunate nature of the business at hand, just like Duport's need to assure the representatives of his "repugnance" at discussing the matter, is typical of a general sensibility among legislators, public officials, as well as journalists, many of whom took pains to stress the unpleasant nature of capital punishment. It was as if they would have preferred to have nothing to do with it, but duty or "humanity" demanded their involvement. This general reluctance to approach the subject directly—or at least to avoid giving the appearance that they actually *wanted* to discuss it—mirrors, in many respects, the ideal image of the new spectator. The idea was that people would not flock to the new death penalty as they did to the old, but they would—in theory, of course—reluctantly attend almost as a civic duty; or as Thomas, the inventor of the strangulation machine, had put it, that they would leave "sighing deeply and calmly over the deserved misfortune of the guilty, and the just severity of the law."

This strange ambivalence between humane sensibilities, which precluded one's watching or at least wanting to watch, and the dictates of exemplary deterrence, which made it essential that the execution be performed in public before an audience, can be seen very clearly in an image that must have been produced at some point after Guillotin's first mention of his machine in December of 1789, but before the deployment of the actual machine in April of 1792, as it portrays the executioner slicing the cord of the machine with a sword, rather than pulling it, as he would do (Fig. 11). In the illustration, the machine is standing on a large scaffold or courtyard, with only the victim, the confessor, and the executioner in close proximity. At some distance, two guards stand by, and behind them is a barrier, keeping spectators at bay. Undeterred, several spectators seem to be hoisting themselves up, craning their necks in an attempt to see something. But the ideal participant/spectator would seem to be the executioner himself who, at the moment of execution, averts his gaze (one wonders how this was supposed to work in practice). The caption reads as follows:

> Executions will take place outside of town, in a place designated for this purpose; the machine will be surrounded by barriers to prevent the people from approaching; the interior of these barriers will be manned by soldiers carrying firearms, and the signal of death will be given to the executioner by the confessor at the instant of absolution; the hangman, averting his eyes, will cut the cord with his saber, at the end of which will be suspended a drop-hammer armed with an axe.

Here, we can see the conflicting aspirations for a form of execution that was meant to be both public and discreet. At one and the same time, people were bidden to watch but prevented from seeing anything. The executioner, almost a personification of the state, kills without looking.

When the Committee on Legislation presented its report along with Dr. Louis' assessment of the situation to the Assembly on 13 March, the Committee thought that it might be too "distressing" for the representatives if the report were read aloud. Sparing their sensibilities, the report was printed instead, allowing them to read it on their own. Within the report itself is yet another textual deferral: "[Y]our committee thought that it could dispense with presenting the methods of execution to you. It was convinced that a discussion of such a subject would be repugnant to your sensibilities, and would be too painful [*pénible*] to its rapporteur."[10] The report therefore referred the representatives to Dr. Louis' letter as well as to the letters from Duport and Roederer. The representatives, in other words, had to dig down to a report within a report to find any mention of a decapitating machine.

Fig. 11. Machine proposée à l'Assemblée nationale pour le supplice des criminels par Mr. Guillotin, 1789. The Getty Research Institute, Los Angeles, CA (2682-320).

Was this a reluctance to speak of unpleasant things? Or did it reflect an effort to hide the idea of the machine from a public that had, two years earlier, greeted Guillotin's proposal with ridicule?

On 20 March, having had a week to read the report, the representatives decided not to discuss it but simply to decree that:

> article 3 of the penal Code [i.e. beheading] will be executed according to the manner indicated and the mode adopted in the signed consultation with the permanent secretary of the academy of surgery [Dr. Louis]...; consequently, [the Assembly] authorizes the executive power to make all necessary expenditures to arrive at this method of execution, in such a manner that it will be uniform throughout the kingdom.[11]

One would have to have been familiar with both the penal Code as well as with the contents of Louis' report to know that the Assembly had just authorized the construction and deployment of decapitating machines throughout France.

Almost immediately, there followed an urgent, almost frenzied effort to build a decapitating machine as quickly as possible. It took only about a month from the Assembly's decree ordering its construction until the first guillotine was ready for use. Judging from the various letters between government officials, administrators, and judges, however, a month was far too long. As one judge complained, the delay was not only cruel to the condemned for whom "each instant" of waiting "must be [like] a death" but it was also dangerous for society as it "compromises the security of citizens."[12]

By mid-April, after some initial difficulties in finding a carpenter/machinist who would take on such an odious task without charging an exorbitant fee, the machine was finally ready. With the help of Dr. Cullerier, chief surgeon at the hospital of Bicêtre, Louis arranged for a trial run to be performed on several cadavers at the hospital on 17 April. Writing beforehand to Dr. Cullerier, Louis thanked him for the "zeal [with which] you have seized upon the general will in this sad affair."[13] Cullerier replied:

> Sir,
> You will find at Bicêtre all the facilities that you desire for the trial of a machine that humanity cannot see without shuddering, but which justice and the welfare of society make necessary. I will keep the corpses of those unfortunates who die between today and Monday. I will arrange the amphitheater... [and if] the ceiling does not accommodate the height of the machine, I can make use of a little isolated courtyard situated next to the amphitheater. The honor that you are bestowing on the House of Bicêtre, Sir, is a very nice gift that you are giving me, but it would be even more so if you wished to accept a simple and frugal meal, such as a bachelor can offer.[14]

Cullerier's letter betrays obvious excitement and enthusiasm, just barely tempered by the obligatory nod toward the regrettable nature of the business.[15] One wonders whether the need for strict privacy, and the choice between an enclosed amphitheater and an "isolated" courtyard, resulted more from the desire not to reveal the guillotine until it was absolutely ready for its first performance or from the self-consciousness of those involved in the act of decapitating corpses.

THE GUILLOTINE IN ACTION

On 17 April the first trial of the guillotine took place. On hand to witness the event were: Sanson, the executioner of Paris, along with his son and an aide; the carpenter who built the machine and his aides; and several members of the medical establishment including Drs. Louis, Cullerier, and Pierre Jean George Cabanis, the prominent physician and friend of Mirabeau. Reportedly also in attendance that day were several members of the National Assembly, and last, but certainly not least, an individual who was both a politician and a physician: Dr. Guillotin himself.[16] By all accounts, the trial was a wonderful success. As Dr. Louis enthused in his report to Roederer, the machine decapitated three cadavers "so neatly that one was astonished by the force and celerity of its action."[17] Dr. Cabanis would later describe the blade's descent as having "severed the heads faster than one could see, and the bones were cleanly cut."[18]

After the successful trial, preparations were made for the first execution of a living person by guillotine, which would take place eight days later. On the morning of the execution, Roederer sent off a letter to General Lafayette, Commander of the National Guard, expressing his worries about the crowd of spectators that was likely to show up: "The new method of execution...will certainly attract a considerable crowd to the [Place de] la Grève, and it will be important to take measures so that no one damages the machine."[19] Most likely, Roederer feared that the excitement and curiosity of spectators might get the better of them and that they might unintentionally harm an instrument that had been developed and constructed at great expense and effort.

At half past three in the afternoon of 25 April 1792, Nicolas-Jacques Pelletier, who had committed armed robbery in October of the previous year, and who had been awaiting the execution of his death sentence since his conviction in December, became the first person to be executed by guillotine. As it turns out, Roederer had been right about the size of the crowd. The *Chronique de Paris* reported that "The novelty of the punishment considerably augmented the crowd of those who are drawn to these sad spectacles by a barbarous pity."[20] The very phrase "barbarous pity" reveals the conflicting sensibilities and emotions surrounding even this new, supposedly humane, form of punishment. Even if one felt pity for the condemned, the desire to see an execution remained, at least in the view of this journalist, barbarous.

If Roederer had been right to anticipate a large crowd, it would seem that he may have been mistaken about their enthusiasm. Very far from being carried away with excitement, spectators appear to have been startled, almost stupefied, and in the end, disappointed. The *Courrier Extraordinaire* gave the following account of the crowd's reaction, witnessed by proxy, as the editor Joseph Duplain was too sensitive to witness an execution at first hand:

> I have never in my life been able to get close to a hanging victim, but I confess that I have even more repugnance for this sort of execution; the preparations make one shudder, and aggravate the mental punishment, and as for the physical punishment, I had someone else go watch, who reported to me that it was over in the blink of an

eye [*en un clin d'oeil*]. The people seemed to call for M. Sanson [the executioner] to return to [the methods of punishment of] the ancien régime, and said to him:

> Give me back my wooden gallows,
> Give me back my gallows.[21]

Here, as in other reports,[22] spectators appear to have been initially confused and disappointed by the speed of the guillotine. After centuries of being accustomed to the penal equivalent of a three-act play, it was as if they had been invited to attend a new kind of performance, one that was finished almost at the same moment as it began. While Guillotin had reportedly envisioned a machine that would execute "in the blink of an eye," it was perhaps Cabanis who described the experience of watching the guillotine most aptly when he said that its blade acted faster than one could see, or literally "at the speed of sight [*avec la vitesse du regard*]." The guillotine promised, for all practical purposes, a spectacle that was impossible to see. In the words of René-Georges Gastellier, who was, like Guillotin, both a representative to the National Assembly and a physician, the speed of the guillotine was such that "from the first point of contact to the last, there is no distance; it is an indivisible point; the blade falls, and the patient no longer exists."[23] Like Girardet's asphyxiation machine, which obscured spectators' view with smoke, and like Thomas's strangulation machine, which obscured their view with a veil, the guillotine also obscured the view of spectators—but through speed rather than through obstruction. In many ways it would offer the perfect solution to the dilemma of how to produce a non-spectacular public spectacle, one that allowed spectators to watch without being able to see.

Although the public was not immediately taken with the new method of execution, bureaucrats could not have been more thrilled. Orders were placed for eighty-three guillotines, so that each department might have its own. The wait proved frustrating to many, however, and the Ministry of Justice was besieged with letters from departments throughout France, begging for a guillotine to be sent "as instantaneously as possible."[24] One official from Falaise apparently could wait no longer, and took the liberty of having a guillotine constructed on the basis of a drawing he had seen. He informed the Minister of Justice of the "incalculable rapidity with which the head of [the condemned] was separated from his body" and enthused: "This rapidity was like a lightning bolt which foreshadows or is a precursor to thunder. The blink of an eye cannot see the separation of a head leaping forward seventeen or eighteen inches from the body…"[25]

A spectacle that was over in "the blink of an eye" or that took place "at the speed of sight" precipitated a great change not only in the spectator's experience of the event, but also in narrative accounts of executions. What could one write about, specifically, if executions had been reduced to an invisible moment? As we have seen, public executions had been attracting the attention of chroniclers for centuries, from the relatively laconic accounts of the *Journal d'un bourgeois de Paris* in the fifteenth century to the more colorful accounts of Felix Platter and Madame de Sévigné in the sixteenth and seventeenth centuries, and the more detailed, almost punctilious, accounts of Gueullette and Hardy in the eighteenth century. But there would be no chronicler of executions by guillotine. As the historian of the guillotine G. Lenotre lamented:

> One can scarcely imagine how rare accounts of these sad scenes are.... I cannot recall reading a single account in the journals of the day which is worth mentioning; usually the newspapers give the names of the victims which the guillotine devoured each day and the hour of the punishment. That's all!... [N]o spectator thought to keep a daily record of his impressions and remembrances. Ah! If only we possessed a *Journal of a Parisian during the Terror*, written by some obscure individual, without preconceived opinions, without the preoccupation of posing for posterity! But, unbelievably, no such journal was written.[26]

In many respects, accounts of executions during the Revolution bear a strange resemblance to accounts written prior to the sixteenth century, when narrators were also unwilling or unable to describe what they saw, and confined themselves to transcribing the court sentence, followed by the words *ce qui fut fait*, with little or no description of what had taken place on the scaffold.[27] One Revolutionary pamphlet, which purported to give an account by "Lady Guillotine" herself of the many individuals "upon whom she has bestowed passports to the other world," detailed the interrogations of the victims as well as the court sentences, but when it came to the executions, simply declared, time and again, "The execution took place" followed by the date and time.[28]

Just as chroniclers before the sixteenth century had focused on the procession to the scaffold, the clothes worn by the victim, and the disposition of the corpse after the execution, so too did many accounts of execution by guillotine similarly narrate "around" the execution. As Daniel Arasse observed, these accounts "substitute the before and after for the narrative poverty of the instant of the guillotine."[29] If there was very little that one could write about the actual moment of death, then it made sense to emphasize ancillary aspects of the execution: the procession to the scaffold, the brandishing of the head afterwards, and the fate of the victim's remains. If we take, as an example, an account of the most symbolically and politically charged execution of the Revolutionary period, that of Louis XVI, now Louis Capet, we can see how the actual execution itself almost disappears in a narrative that, by necessity, focuses on the prelude and the aftermath:

> At five o'clock in the morning, the call was given in all the sections [of Paris]. Between seven and eight o'clock, the entire armed forces had their weapons ready, and all battalions were at their respective battle posts. Capet left the Temple [prison] at eight forty-five; he was in a green carriage with his confessor; the horses of the carriage were at a walk. The greatest calm reigned along the route. He arrived at ten o'clock at the Place de la Révolution. The scaffold was placed more or less at the foot of the pedestal where formerly stood the statue of the second to last tyrant, in such a way that the criminal could face the palace of the Tuileries.
>
> Capet remained for some time before descending from the carriage. Finally, he got out with the minister of religion, who was dressed simply in black. He mounted the scaffold with a firm step, in a white shirt, his hands tied. He approached the edge, his head raised, and looked from right to left. The greatest silence reigned. He offered only these words: "I pardon my enemies." Then he was brought back and [his body] placed [in position], and the execution did not even last eight seconds. But scarcely was the weight of the guillotine detached, when a universal cry of *Vive la république* was heard, and all hats were thrown in the air on top of bayonets and pikes.

The executioner of justice took his head and showed it to the people; and his body, according to custom, was put in a basket and transported to the church of the Magdelaine....Capet died at ten twenty-four. The greatest tranquility reigned in Paris. No joy was expressed, but no sadness, expressing regrets.[30]

In a similar manner, Prudhomme's *Revolutions de Paris* devoted several pages to describing Louis' final hours: his putting his affairs in order, his last meeting with his family, his meeting with his priest, his last dinner on the eve of the execution, his rising on the fateful day, his dressing, his last mass, his last communion and last confession, his departure from the prison, and his ride toward the place of execution. Louis' last moments on the scaffold are dealt with in one short paragraph, at the end of which the actual moment of execution almost disappears: "At ten minutes past ten o'clock his head was separated from his body and then shown to the people: instantly, shouts of *vive la République* were heard from all quarters." Then, echoing other reports, Prudhomme noted "the calm that reigned in the city" and added: "Work was suspended for a moment, but soon taken back up as if nothing had happened."[31]

Indeed, judging from the narrative accounts of Louis' execution, Prudhomme was right: it was almost as if *nothing had happened*. The king had been put to death, and yet, in contrast to the spectacles of the ancien régime, there had been very little to see. The brandishing of his head had not allowed anyone to see anything other than the fact that he was already dead, as if somehow the show was already over (Fig. 12). Arasse has suggested the narrative tendency to elide the moment of death may not simply be a function of the comparative invisibility of the spectacle, but a result of the fact that, in some ways, the guillotine showed too much rather than too little: "In the instantaneity of its action, the guillotine allows to be seen very precisely the invisibility of death at the exact and [yet] indeterminate moment that it is taking place.... [T]his public display of the sacred moment in which an individual dies will be perceived as a monstrous obscenity...."[32] In other words, although the guillotine makes the precise moment of death invisible, it paradoxically makes that same moment public in a way that it never had been before by fixing the otherwise irreducible nature of death into a finite fraction of a second.

Arasse makes an interesting point, but I am tempted to put it slightly differently. By distilling death into a moment so brief that it was invisible, the guillotine did not so much display death as it removed, with startling ease, the dividing line between life and death. By dispatching, for example, twenty-one Girondins in the space of thirty-eight minutes,[33] the guillotine seemed as if it were repeatedly opening and shutting a window onto the hereafter. Perhaps Arasse is right that it profaned a "sacred moment," but more than that, the guillotine routinized it; it took an exceptionally rare thing and essentially allowed for its mass production. I would go so far as to suggest that once spectators overcame their initial confusion and disappointment over the brevity of the spectacle, the very rapidity and repeatability of the instantaneous transformation from life to death would prove to be its own source of fascination, and a primary reason for the guillotine's popularity.

Death by guillotine took place so quickly that it hardly seemed like a death at all.[34] Spectators marveled at the now-you-see-them-now-you-don't quality of executions, and euphemisms abounded for a transformation that seemed much less tragic, much less consequential than deaths by execution in the ancien régime: "passing through the little window,"[35] "a passing out of passports to another world,"[36] or "the dropping of apricots"[37]—all of which describe a process whereby society had been conveniently "delivered"[38] of its inconvenient individuals. As Mona Ozouf has noted, even the execution of the king was repeatedly referred to euphemistically, as if he had been made to disappear rather than killed.[39]

Whereas the hallmark of executions in the old régime had been their unique character and their unpredictability (in the sense that no two executions were ever alike, and one never knew how long the spectacle might last), executions by guillotine were more or less identical and predictable. One of the few variables in

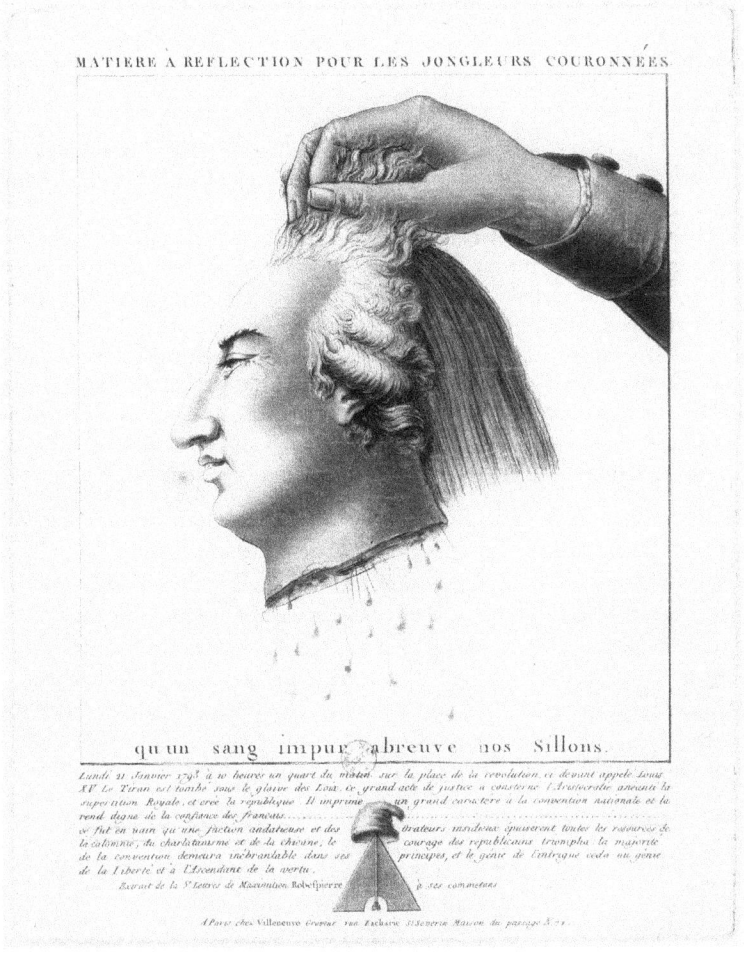

Fig. 12. Matière à réflection pour les jongleurs couronnées, 1793. Bibliothèque Nationale de France.

execution by guillotine was related not to quality but to quantity. Multiple executions, when several individuals were guillotined in rapid succession, proved especially novel and interesting to spectators, at least in the period before the so-called Great Terror, when such executions would become commonplace. In June of 1793, for example, even comparatively well-to-do spectators rushed to watch the execution of twelve men and women, convicted in the so-called Brittany conspiracy, with a lighthearted curiosity that recalls the behavior of spectators of earlier times: "They were running at great speed, for fear of missing the spectacle of the tragic scene that was taking place. Almost all of them had elegant opera glasses [*lorgnettes fines*], and kept moving around in order to find the vantage point which would afford them the best view."[40]

These words were written by a police observer, who confessed to finding the spectacle of execution very difficult to witness, but who nevertheless felt that it was his duty to report on the entire proceedings:

> Around three o'clock the fatal cortege arrived. I got up on a carriage near the square. I thought I could see before me all the inhabitants of Paris. I look and I see twelve unfortunates, entire families whose members seemed to me well-born in general....
>
> I wondered to myself how, after such a heartrending spectacle, I could manage to watch the rest of it. Well! I saw everything, and I must give you an account, as this is my duty....
>
> The people said nothing. They attentively watched the demeanor and gestures of the unfortunates. [The victims] were brought down [from the cart], and soon one was brought up [onto the scaffold], who turned around and greeted the people; three or four men preceded the women; in ten minutes it was all over.
>
> ...As for any rapport that there might have been between the executed and the spectators, I believe I saw a lot of indifference, because one must differentiate between something that arises only out of simple curiosity at such a striking spectacle and that which comes directly from the heart. As for the heart, a good two thirds of the spectators would have spared [the victims], especially [sparing] the women.

If some of the spectators had initially been excited at the prospect of seeing the novelty of a mass execution, their ultimate reaction was less enthusiastic. Instead of spectators screaming "Vive la Révolution!" and throwing their hats in the air, the police reporter saw "indifferent" spectators who would just as soon have pardoned the victims. In fact, it almost seems as if the spectators were not quite sure what they were supposed to be looking at. Reporting on conversations that took place among spectators after the execution was over, the observer noted: "The people, and women especially, remarked, in speaking of the great lady [who had been executed], 'Ah, what nice skin she had, what white thighs she had.'"[41]

GAUGING THE GUILLOTINE'S POPULARITY

There is no denying that, for a time, the guillotine achieved an almost cult-like status in certain circles. Innumerable images and ornamental objects were produced commemorating noteworthy executions, the king's and queen's especially.

There were also quite a number of engravings and objects—including plates, enamel boxes, and earrings—which represented nothing but the guillotine, all by itself. Sometimes these representations of the guillotine sported captions such as "The Good Pillar of Liberty," "Traitors: Look and Tremble. She won't stop working until you have all lost your lives," or simply "She Awaits the Guilty." Sometimes, the guillotine was entirely unadorned with words, as if the image spoke for itself.[42] There were, as well, countless songs and poems written in the guillotine's honor, including several in which the "Sainte Guillotine" was lauded as an object worthy of veneration.[43]

If executions by guillotine were all nearly identical, the guillotine itself was nevertheless special. It had a peculiar character all its own that seemed to capture the public imagination in ways that no other form of capital punishment ever had. One could argue, for example, that shooting people might be as fast, if not faster, than guillotining them, but as one prosecutor confessed to a colleague in a neighboring department, "Recently, lacking an executioner, I was reduced to have a former *seigneur* shot.... It would have had a better effect if he had been guillotined instead."[44] There was something special about the guillotine, and I do not think it is too far-fetched to suggest that the iconography of heads being removed from bodies must have had a special resonance in a nation that for centuries had regarded its king as the literal head of its social and political bodies, but which had recently come to regard the nation as a body unto itself, and the head as entirely expendable.[45]

Although references to and representations of the guillotine abounded in the years 1792 to 1794, it is unclear to what extent this reflects the popularity of actually watching executions. No one seems to have taken much of an interest in ordinary criminal executions after the first use of the guillotine on the armed robber Pelletier in April of 1792. As for political executions, which began in August of 1792, while spectators were initially curious about multiple executions, and although they turned out in large numbers for certain executions—those of the king and queen, of Charlotte Corday, and of Père Duchesne, for example—it is difficult to tell with any degree of certainty how well attended less noteworthy executions may have been. Likewise, as public expression became more constrained, from late 1793 through the summer of 1794, it is extraordinarily difficult to gauge the attitudes of spectators.

There is no doubt that many individuals during this period sang the praises of the guillotine, and expressed the opinion that executions were necessary. As one undercover police observer reported overhearing: "The aristocrats, people say, are like a multitude of pigeons who are ravaging a field. You need a scarecrow, and that scarecrow is the guillotine." Or: "The people are saying that one guillotine is not enough; you need at least four of them in Paris."[46] We should not discount, however, a certain element of "bluster" inherent in such comments. As another police observer reported, "A citizen whom I ran into at the moment when a prisoner was being led to his execution, said to me that the guillotine was not yet ready to rest and that there were still twenty thousand more [people to be executed]. 'What!' I said, a little startled, 'In Paris alone!' 'Oh, no,' he answered, a little taken aback, 'in the various departments [of France].'"[47]

But do these sorts of comments necessarily translate into an interest in watching executions themselves? One could, conceivably, detest enemies of the Revolution and have a deep respect for Revolutionary justice without necessarily harboring any particular desire to see people be put to death. While sources do indeed suggest that crowds of people lined the streets, jeering prisoners on their way to the guillotine, and that spectators gathered around the scaffold, cheering enthusiastically as heads rolled, the politically skewed nature of many of these reports call their credibility into question. As Dorinda Outram has pointed out, descriptions of both "ghoulish" and "enthusiastic" crowds tend to have been produced, respectively, by post-Thermidorian authors with a political axe to grind, or by officials of the Terror and sympathetic journalists eager to show the people's desire for vengeance.[48]

On one end of the political spectrum, we have heartfelt and tragic accounts like the one written by the Abbé Carrichon (purportedly, and seemingly years after the fact), detailing his experience in July of 1794 as he followed a procession toward the guillotine, attempting surreptitiously to give absolution to the Maréchale de Noailles and her daughter. He recalled the "shouts of cannibals" uttered by spectators who massed at various spots along the route, "tormenting" the victims with rude comments. Arriving at the scaffold, he reported seeing it surrounded by soldiers, behind whom were a number of spectators, the majority of whom "were laughing and enjoying this depressing spectacle." Mercifully, each execution took only a moment: "The master hangman takes the left hand, the head valet takes the right, another the legs; in an instant [the victim] is lying prone, the head cut off, thrown along with the clothed body into a vast cart in which everything swims in blood." But the crude disposition of the body's remains could not diminish what, for the abbé, was a martyr's death: "She offered herself like a gentle and tender lamb to slaughter. I felt like I was attending the martyrdom of one of those young virgins or holy women, such as are represented in the paintings of Correggio or Domenico."[49]

At the other end of the political spectrum, we have accounts like the following description of the execution of Marie-Antoinette offered by the inimitable Hébert, otherwise known as Père Duchesne:

> I saw the head of the female *veto* fall into the bag. I'd like, you fuckers, to be able to express to you the satisfaction of the Sans-Culottes, when the arch-tigress traversed Paris in a cart.... The bitch was audacious and insolent up to the end.... Her damned head was finally separated from her spindly neck, and the air reverberated with shouts of "Long live the republic."[50]

Although for the Abbé Carrichon righteousness lay on the side of the victim, and for Père Duchesne it lay with the sans-culottes, one might very well argue that, despite their very different political vantage points, both are describing enthusiastic and attentive spectators. Yet, it is difficult to ignore the fact that both writers would have had compelling reasons to give the descriptions that they did. A world descended into hell or, conversely, a world in which the justifiable anger of the sans-culottes had taken center stage, would seem to demand the presence of numerous, engaged, and attentive spectators.

Along the same lines as the Abbé Carrichon's account, there were several sources that were "discovered" and published in the nineteenth century, purporting to give authentic descriptions of the crowds that attended executions at the height of the Terror. These post-Revolutionary accounts, of dubious credibility, would seem to be the basis for the oft-cited "furies," women who unleashed their hysterical fury on the victims of the Revolution as they mounted the scaffold, and of the "*tricoteuses*," women who, perhaps even more perversely, knitted without emotion and without sympathy as their fellow human beings passed, one after another, under the blade of the guillotine. The following, somewhat lyrical description is from the *Mémoires de Fleury*, supposedly based upon notes written by the actor Fleury and published posthumously in 1836:

> ...[The radical] females, [were] more unkempt than [the men] were disheveled, and were perhaps even more ferocious than they. These shrews had the work of surrounding the scaffolds, exciting people, and letting loose shrill cries during the spectacles. If they were old, they were called *tricoteuses*; if they were young, they had the name *furies of the guillotine*. As for me, when I saw them assemble for the first time, the women and the men...it seemed to me that I was watching...uncoil a horrible legion of the damned, screaming, yelling, throwing their tangled hair into the wind, turning, ever turning...[51]

Countless novelists and historians have drawn from accounts such as these, painting a picture of large, almost frenzied crowds, dominated by hysterical or entirely emotionless women. The following passage, from P. J. B. Buchez and P. C. Roux's history of the Revolution, published in 1837, attempts to shunt responsibility for mass guillotining from the French people onto a radical fringe and a few crazed harpies in their pay:

> We must also say that more than six months before the 9th of Thermidor, the public no longer applauded guilty verdicts, but very much showed their joy and satisfaction at all acquittals. If the furies of the guillotine, led astray, corrupted, and paid by the faction of murderers, often insulted the victim who, calmly and innocently, made their way toward their execution, we must declare that this was never the people of Paris. The people never called for blood. They called only for just laws and for the tranquility of the state and the happiness of all.[52]

Stories like this were picked up by Thomas Carlyle, and in turn by Charles Dickens, who in his *Tale of Two Cities* described women like Madame Defarge and her friend "The Vengeance" who sat with their fellow "knitting-women" in chairs directly in front of the scaffold "as in a garden or public diversion...busily knitting," while they patiently, methodically, and without emotion, counted the heads that fell.[53]

Do these stories have any basis whatsoever in reality? In some sense, they may. An undercover police observer named Pourvoyeur filed this report to his superiors on 25 January 1794: "People are saying that they've noticed that women have become bloodthirsty, that they speak of nothing but blood, that there are a number of women who never leave the guillotine or the Revolutionary Tribunal; that most of these women have a grudge against and criticize true patriots."[54] The same observer filed a similar report some three weeks later: "On the place de la Révolution [i.e. the site of executions], people gathered in a little group were saying this afternoon: 'When will the guillotine be over with? They don't seem to get tired of guillotining every day.' 'It's surprising,' someone said, 'how ferocious women have become. They attend executions every day.'"[55]

But before we take Pourvoyeur's accounts at face value, we would do well to remember the criticisms of female spectators who had come to watch the prolonged and gruesome execution of Damiens in 1757 or Rétif's indictment of the female spectator with the "heart of a monster" a few years before the Revolution.[56] As I have suggested, this focus on and criticism of female spectators may have had more to do with the particular discomfort at seeing women watching executions without apparent sympathy, than with any real preponderance of female spectators or anything unique about their reactions or emotions. I would venture to guess that the case was no different during the Terror. Undoubtedly, there were women who, just like men, made a point of attending executions, but there is little evidence to suggest that they attended in hordes, much less violent, dancing, turning hordes. There is ample evidence to support the fact that individuals of both sexes sometimes shouted "A la guillotine!" and jeered victims on their way to the scaffold, and that spectators screamed "Vive la République!" at the execution of important political figures. But beyond this, the mood and the emotions of spectators at executions is very difficult to access, particularly during the Terror, when individuals clearly did not feel free to express their opinions and feelings honestly and openly.

Perhaps the best window that we have onto spectator reactions to executions during the Terror are the accounts written by police observers, but these are not exactly transparent sources, as they were no doubt skewed by the political leanings of the men who wrote them as well as by the temptation to report things that their superiors might want to hear. Furthermore, it is abundantly clear that even undercover observers would have had only limited access to people's honest reactions, as spectators were clearly constrained in their expression of thoughts and emotions during this period. In contrast to expressions of sympathy and pity that had been expressed prior to the Revolution, and even, as we have seen, as late as June 1793, any demonstration of sympathy or even horror at the height of the Terror, however involuntary or spontaneous, laid one open to the charge of being a political sympathizer of the aristocracy and the Counter-Revolution. Consider, for example, the following account of an incident that took place in March of 1794:

> They were putting away the instrument, which had just purged the Republic of some new traitors and scoundrels. The girl was passing with her mother: "Oh, God!" she screamed, "I didn't think the guillotine would be set up today!" and no sooner had she said these words than she fainted. She was brought to, she uttered another cry and fainted yet again. "Oh! My dear daughter!" said the mother, holding her to her breast. She'll be like this for seven hours straight! This problem has been happening ever since the day when she was inconvenienced by female menstruation, and she found herself inadvertently in front of an execution. Ever since that time, she hasn't been able to see the scaffold without turning white and feeling sick.

While we might think that the mother was providing more information than any stranger would want to know, we begin to understand her motivation in blaming her daughter's fainting spells on menstruation and a nervous temperament when we read what happened next:

> Among the citizens who witnessed this affecting spectacle, some thought that this young citizeness must have had relatives or friends who had been guillotined. Others [thought] that she was an aristocrat. No one [thought] that it was the natural effect of the sensibility of certain temperaments.
>
> "How is it," said the mother, whom I approached while men were carrying her daughter, whom they had lifted up in their arms, "that people interpret my daughter's illness in such a shameful manner?" "Citizeness," I answered, "your daughter is not the only one who has been so severely judged for her natural fears. One day, I carried in my arms a young mother. She had encountered the fatal cart [filled with victims on their way to the guillotine], grew white, and fell into my arms. The cavalry that followed caught sight of the accident. "Look!" said one to another, "look how that woman turned white! These must be her relatives or friends whom she ran into without wishing to."

The police observer proceeded to offer the following explanation for those who were suspicious of expressions of sympathy:

1) Their hearts are embittered by the long misfortunes that the enemies of the republic have brought upon them. Their minds, clouded by suspicion, see aristocrats everywhere and think that only bad citizens could be interested in the fate of these scoundrels to whom the nation has accorded a just punishment.

2) Everyone is not susceptible to this exquisite sensibility which swoons at the sight of misfortune, no matter what the object [of suffering], nor to that philosophy which, casting a general eye upon mankind, pities them equally for the evil that they do onto one another....

At the conclusion of his report, the observer added the following note for the benefit of his superiors: "People are demanding that the executioner's cart have an invariable route, so that the weak can avoid it."[57]

Automatic compassion, after enjoying its heyday in the decades before the Revolution, had seemingly become, at the height of the Terror, once again the gift (or curse) of a few sensitive souls, as it had been in the seventeenth century, rather than the reflexive instinct of human beings in general. In some sense, these overly sensitive women might be seen as representing a kind of mirror image of the Thermidorian trope of the unfeeling *tricoteuse*: women feeling inappropriate emotions, depending on one's political point of view.[58]

One wonders, though, how this police observer thought that he could express an appreciation for the young woman's "exquisite sensibility" without falling under suspicion himself for sympathizing with the Revolution's enemies. Perhaps he had second thoughts; in a report written the very next day, he stressed that the idea to fix the executioner's route had not been his own opinion, but rather the opinion of others. He felt compelled, moreover, to explain how fixing the route might foil the malevolent intentions of aristocrats who "make use of the kind of incidents that I reported yesterday in order to skillfully draw the people's attention to the number of executions and to make them pity... the fate of their enemies...."[59]

Apart from the few who expressed horror, on the one hand, and the fervent patriots who saw any expression of horror or sympathy as a sign of disloyalty, on the other, there appear to have been quite a few individuals—and one cannot help wondering whether they may have been the majority—who were neither in favor of nor opposed to executions, but rather did not seem to have much of an opinion about them at all. Here, for example, is a report from February of 1794 in which the police observer could not make head or tails of remarks he overheard about executions:

> The day after seventeen guilty persons had been executed, a few people in the group that ordinarily forms at the place where the guillotine is mounted were pushing away with the ends of their canes the water from the little puddles which are left behind from the washing that follows an execution. [They] were saying that this place had been well washed so as not to conserve the trace of so much blood. "Bah!" said someone. "It doesn't cost any more, when the machine is going, to guillotine seventeen instead of only one." "Only," said another, "You need more horses."
>
> The semi-serious, semi-joking manner of those who used this language did not allow one to confirm whether they were expressing criticism, approval, or indifference.[60]

By the winter of 1794, the novelty of the guillotine had worn off, and spectator's fascination would seem to have followed suit. As another police observer reported, people had become so accustomed to the spectacle of the guillotine, that they had begun to doubt whether it was terrifying enough to serve the purposes of exemplary deterrence:

> A lot of people think that instead of leading conspirators and others to the punishment [of the guillotine], they should be shackled with irons and made to labor on public works and on draining swamps. The passage from life to death without any kind of pain, any kind of torture, has nothing frightening about it, whereas the fear of living in an arduous slavery would be a punishment they would fear....[61]

Writing a year later, in the wake of Thermidor, and looking back on the mass guillotinings of the Terror, the physician Cabanis wondered whether the guillotine's simplicity, its comparative lack of spectacle, had made mass killings possible, and he suggested re-spectacularizing capital punishment:

> If the death penalty is to be maintained, then at least it should be imbued with a more imposing spectacle. The death of a man ordered in the public interest is without a doubt the greatest act of social power. It is necessary that the spectacle itself should render the punishment more rare and more difficult; it is necessary, in short, not to habituate people to the sight of blood.
>
> When a man is guillotined, it is over in a minute. The head disappears and the body is thrown immediately in a basket. The spectators see nothing. There's no tragedy for them. They have no time to feel emotions. They only see blood flow, and if they derive any lesson from this sight it is only to harden themselves to spilling [blood] themselves with less repugnance than [if they were] drunk with furious passions.[62]

These calls for a more spectacular form of execution reflect what we might consider a general "aesthetic" dissatisfaction with the spectacle of executions by guillotine. Beyond the obligatory cries of "Vive la République," spectators who showed up to watch the guillotine in action were often confused about what, precisely, they were supposed to be looking at. They undoubtedly understood, from the abundance of rhetoric about "purging" the republic, that the guillotine was about getting rid of the nation's enemies, but they could not seem to help wanting executions by guillotine to be more satisfying.

In no context was the inadequacy of the guillotine as a spectacle more palpably felt than in the execution of Hébert. Here was someone who, as his alter ego Père Duchesne, had made a career out of calling for people's heads, and who had amused himself by devising a variety of affectionate nicknames for the guillotine.[63] He had heaped so much abuse and so many expletives on those he portrayed as the people's enemies that, when he himself was cast in that role, he found himself the target of all the anger and bile that he had spewed on others. The public mocked him, wondering whether he was "fucking angry" as he sat in prison, awaiting his fate.[64] When it came time for him to meet "the national razor" or "the holy guillotine," as he had called it so many times, people were desperate for something more than a simple execution by guillotine. As a police observer reported about a week prior to his execution:

> The conspiracy of Hébert and his accomplices is still the subject of every conversation. General opinion is very much against them; the people are so indignant about their wickedness, that the guillotine seems to them too gentle a punishment for such great criminals. In a group on the place de la Révolution, many citizens of both sexes were saying out loud that the Convention should declare a special punishment for crimes of this nature. "That would be against the Constitution," retorted one citizen, "the Constitution allows only one method of punishment." "That's true," replied a sans-culotte, but the dangers of the fatherland don't allow us to enjoy all the advantages of the Constitution yet. The Convention was forced to decree a revolutionary government; let it also decree revolutionary punishments for all the scoundrels who want to murder the people." This proposal was applauded....[65]

Many expressed a profound sense of betrayal. As one police observer reported, "Women were saying that the more they had loved the père Duchesne, the more horrified they were."[66] People felt a visceral need to see him suffer, to see him get his just desserts, and anticipating that they would not be able to see much at the execution itself, many planned to watch him on the rue Saint-Honoré, where he would pass in the tumbrel on his way to the scaffold. On the square itself, they would be kept at a distance by rows of soldiers, but on the rue Saint-Honoré they would be able to see him up close, perhaps for a full minute, and they would be able to gauge his expression, and scour his face and the faces of his accomplices for signs of remorse: "Everyone wanted, at the least, to see them pass in order to judge what kind of an impression the sight of an immense crowd and the expectation of the death they would soon suffer might have on a wicked soul."[67] More than a week before Hébert's execution, a police observer reported that "All the windows on the rue Saint Honoré have been rented and spoken for in order to see Père Duchesne pass by."[68]

In the old régime, the most avid spectators had done their best to secure a spot near the scaffold, or better yet, a window overlooking it; those who had missed their chance or those who simply could not afford a window had to content themselves with finding a spot along the route traveled by criminals on their way toward the place of execution. With the advent of the guillotine, however, the situation was the opposite. As the historian Lenotre remarked, "It was there [on the rue Saint-Honoré] that the real drama took place. It was there that you could see close-up the slow agony of those who were being led to slaughter."[69] And it was from one of these windows overlooking the rue Saint-Honoré that Jacques-Louis David sketched his famous portrait of Marie-Antoinette as she sat on the cart, making her way toward the scaffold (Fig. 13).

On the day of Hébert's execution, the crowd was estimated by a police observer to number four hundred thousand.[70] Although many lined the rue Saint-Honoré, many others massed on the Place de la Révolution to see justice done. This once, perhaps, they would not be disappointed. Although the law stipulated that no one could suffer any legal death other than the guillotine, the executioner sensed that on this occasion, the public needed something more, and he did his best to compensate for the guillotine's spectacular inadequacies:

> Upon the arrival of [Hébert] at the Place de la Révolution, he was greeted, he and his accomplices, with boos and expressions of indignation. As each head fell, the people avenged itself with the cry of "Vive la République!" while throwing their hats in the air. Hébert was saved for last, and the executioners, after having put his head in the fatal ring, responded to the wishes which the people had expressed to accord this great conspirator a punishment [that was] less gentle than the guillotine, by keeping the blade suspended for several seconds on the neck of the criminal, and throwing their hats victoriously around him during this time and assailing him with harrowing cries of "Long Live the Very Republic" which he had wanted to destroy.[71]

Hébert had claimed to personify the wrath of the people, and now it was the people who expressed a desire to see that wrath visited on his own head—not figuratively, but literally to *see* it. On this one occasion, the invisible spectacle of the guillotine was made visible.

THE INDUSTRIALIZATION OF CAPITAL PUNISHMENT?

In many ways, the story of the advent and reception of the guillotine was not unlike that of other technological innovations of the modern age: a period of intense fascination and interest, with a relatively rapid half-life. Just as, for example, the novelty of motion pictures, a century later, initially fascinated spectators by the sheer magic of making inanimate images seemingly come to life, so too did the guillotine attract spectators by performing essentially the opposite: transforming living beings into inanimate heads. And just as motion pictures would eventually need to be supplemented by the addition of a story line to maintain spectator interest once the "wow" factor had dissipated, so too did officials of the Terror attempt to embed individual executions within a broader narrative of the triumph

Executing the New Death Penalty

Portrait de Marie-Antoinette, reine de France, conduite au supplice, dessiné à la plume par David, spectateur du convoi et placé à une fenêtre (rue Saint-Honoré) avec la citoyenne Jullien, épouse du représentant Jullien.

Fig. 13. Jacques-Louis David's sketch of Marie-Antoinette on her way to the scaffold, from a facsimile of the original in Hector Fleischmann, *La Guillotine en 1793* (Paris, 1908), 215.

of liberty over despotism in an effort to give spectators a reason to come watch when, in truth, there was little to see.[72]

But there were other respects in which the advent of a decapitating machine mirrored the process of industrialization more generally. If we can imagine executions in the ancien régime to have been a kind of artisanal craft, in which process and performance were as important as product, then the advent of industrialized death had much the same effect on executions as they had on artisanal production in other fields. A means of production that was entirely dependent on the skill of the craftsman was mechanized so that the resulting product was essentially invariable and identical. Not only were the innumerable ways in which one could perform an execution reduced to one perfectly repeatable act, but the ever-present uncertainty of what might happen (Would the crowd express sympathy? Would the executioner botch the job? Would there be a last-second reprieve?) was replaced by one inevitable and invariable ending: a head. Moreover, as Daniel Arasse points out, in the "iconographic treatment" of guillotine victims in portraiture, the heads all look more or less the same (see Figs. 10 and 12).[73]

In this transformation of executions from a process to a product, something else changed as well. Like so many other skilled craftsmen in the modern age, the executioner was entirely displaced by the machine. His gradual derogation in status can be seen in the iconography of the Revolutionary period, which came to focus much more on the machine itself, with the executioner figuratively, and sometimes quite literally, left out of the picture. In the illustration shipped off with each guillotine to departments throughout France, showing what the machine would look like when properly assembled, the condemned stands facing the machine, ready to be executed, with no executioner in sight, almost as if the machine could perform the task without any help (Fig. 14). In the many engravings displaying a brandished head, one can glimpse the executioner's arm, but it might as well be anyone's arm; indeed it might as well have been anyone who pulled the guillotine's cord, for it was an act that required little skill. Even in those images that portray the entire scaffold, the focus is almost always on the machine itself or on the victim and the machine, with the executioner often indistinguishable from his aides, as if he too was nothing more than a servant of the machine.

Executioners, despite their social and civil ostracism, had been among the most privileged individuals of the ancien régime. Although their status had already begun to decline in the years before the Revolution, the advent of the guillotine would reduce many of them to a state of poverty. As guillotines were sent to each of France's eighty-three departments from April of 1792 onward, it gradually became apparent that there was no particular need for more executioners than there were guillotines. On 13 June 1793, the National Convention decreed that there would henceforth be only one executioner per department. As there were many more executioners in the north than in the south, the Convention ordered the preparation of a "Table of Executioners" in France, in the hope of facilitating an equal redistribution of executioners throughout the country. The idea was that all executioners who suddenly found themselves unemployed would be able to relocate to departments without executioners, and if there were any who could not immediately find an available post, the government would pay them 600 livres per year until a post became available. Those who chose not to relocate were, in theory, free to find gainful employment in some other profession.[74]

Although no doubt well-intentioned, the law of June 1793 resulted in the near total devastation of the profession of the executioner. Perhaps unknown to the legislators themselves before the data for the "Table of Executioners" had been compiled, there were far more executioners than anyone had imagined. In the jurisdiction of the former parlement of Nancy alone, which had been subdivided into four departments, there were forty-one official executioners, not including those paid by local seigneurs.[75] In other words, the law of June 1793 put more than thirty-seven executioners out of work in a single jurisdiction. While it is true that sixteen departments, largely in the south of France, had no

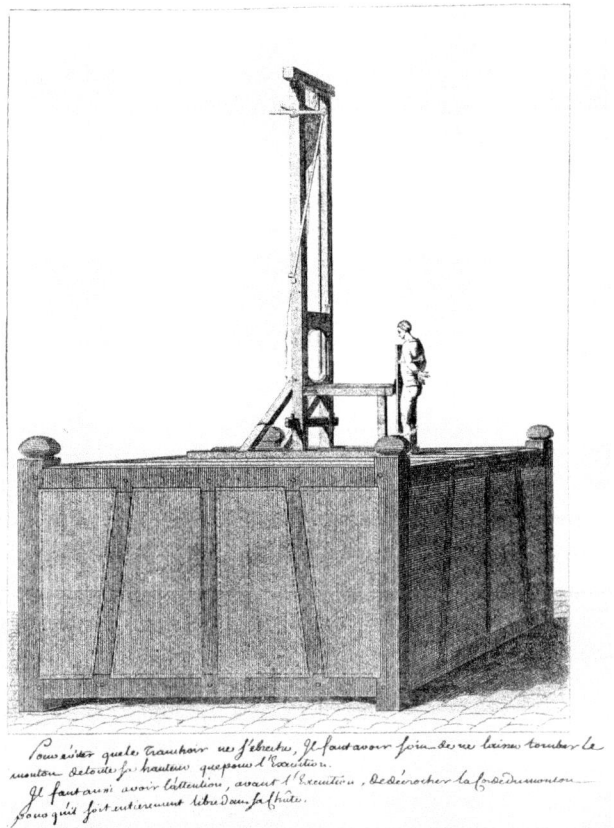

Fig. 14. Illustration accompanying the guillotine in each department, with assembly instructions, from a facsimile of the original in Philippe Maréchal, *La Révolution dans la Haute-Saône* (Paris, 1903), 406.

executioners at all, there were many other regions that, like Nancy, had a great surfeit of executioners.

Even the simple idea that a surplus of executioners in the north would be offset by a scarcity of executioners in the south proved anything but simple. Although executioners in the northern half of the country had always constituted a race of pariahs, they were at least considered indigenous outcasts, reviled but accepted, and even, until recently, possessing rare privileges. In the south, however, multi-generational dynasties of executioners had never taken root, and executions had often been performed by criminals who had volunteered to do the job in return for a commutation of their sentence. Those executioners in the north who were willing to relocate to the south along with their extended families were therefore subjecting themselves to a derogation from their already reviled status to something even worse. If we add to this the fact that the government provided no funds to offset the cost of relocation, and that there were substantial differences between dialects spoken in the north, many of which were related to German, and those in the south, where the *langue d'oc* was still widely spoken, we begin to understand why a great number of executioners simply refused to relocate.[76]

The situation of some executioners was so desperate, however, that they begged to be accepted for any available post, regardless of its location. Laurent Coquellin, who had been executioner in the department of the Bouches-du-Rhône, sent a letter to the Minister of Justice in the summer of 1795, detailing "the sad situation in which he finds himself at this moment, reduced to the utmost indigence, having taken refuge, along with his wife and children, at the home of his colleague," and he begged the Minister to have the "goodness to place him in the first vacant department and [in the meantime] to allow him to enjoy the indemnities accorded… to executioners who have been displaced."[77]

For those who did undertake the long journey to the south of France, the experience was often profoundly unpleasant. The following particularly poignant letter was written in 1803 by an executioner who was descended from a family of executioners in northern France, and who had accepted the position of executioner in the southeastern city of Grenoble in 1796, a decision he later came to regret:

> Citizen minister, my pain is indescribable. I would need a pen filled with blood in order to [do it justice]. Allow me simply, dear citizen, to detail for you in a few words, my succession of misfortunes over the past, nearly seven years….
>
> Arriving in Grenoble, I was put in an isolated house, one league from town, and since executioners in this region before my arrival had been criminals whom judges had plucked from jail to exercise these duties, I was regarded as a wretched individual. Something which in my opinion augments this terrible prejudice, is the fact that… the public prosecutor had just installed two scoundrels in the unhappy house in which I lived: one condemned to chains and the other to deportation. So there I was, confused with the vilest of [people], and ever since then, insulted, scorned and constantly threatened. I live in fear, and I cry into my dinner.
>
> I beg of you, dear citizen minister, have pity on me. I can no longer survive in this monstrous region.[78]

In many ways, the long, slow decline of the executioner as a penal master of ceremony paralleled the downfall of the spectacle they had traditionally overseen. The advent of the guillotine, and the mechanization of the death penalty, spelled the end of a craft that had involved a kind of sculpting of flesh, and of a spectacle that had been more about the process than the final product. But these services were no longer needed in the modern penal age. In 1832, the number of executioners in France would be cut in half. In 1848, their number was reduced to one for each court of appeals, or twenty-eight. Finally, in 1870, the number of official executioners in France was reduced to one: a lone executioner in Paris, accompanied by five aides. Once again, technology was to blame. The railroad had made it possible for a single executioner, based in Paris, to travel to any department that might need him, bringing along with him, or perhaps following, the guillotine.[79]

The invention and deployment of the guillotine fulfilled the dream of penal reformers to develop a method of putting people to death that did not offend contemporary sensibilities, one that was not only painless for the victim but painless for spectators as well, easy to experience and easy to watch. The guillotine managed to accomplish what proposals for a strangulation machine and an asphyxiation booth offered to do, but with infinitely more subtlety. It prevented spectators from seeing pain and the moment of death not by smoke or veils, but by sheer speed.

As Custine had pointed out in the course of the Assembly's debates on the death penalty, there was nothing in the new theory of capital punishment that mandated it be public; if the purpose was to remove people from society as efficiently as possible, then the death penalty might just as well be accomplished behind closed doors. After half a millennium of watching people be put to death in public, however, the French people were not quite ready for the concept of a non-public, invisible death. In the century and a half after the promulgation of the Revolutionary penal code that made the execution of a "simple death" the law of the land, a theory of capital punishment predicated on getting rid of people as discreetly and quickly as possible was to coexist awkwardly with a penal practice that was somehow still predicated on public display. After the brief reign of Terror in which the guillotine basked in the limelight, successive French governments and administrations would find themselves charged with the task of simultaneously staging executions and doing everything in their power to prevent people from watching them.

Epilogue
The Play Over, the Actors (Slowly) Leave the Stage

Spectacular capital punishment died a slowed death. In theory, it was almost killed off in the late eighteenth century, when penal reformers proposed replacing the death penalty with various forms of forced labor and imprisonment. In law, the new penal Code of 1791 did away with capital punishment for all but the most egregious criminals, whom it intended to kill publicly but with as little spectacle as possible. In practice, however, spectacular capital punishment staggered on for another century and a half, not quite dead but not exactly flourishing either. The law insisted that executions be performed in public, as legislators and public opinion still clung to the idea that the death penalty, even stripped of its most spectacular elements, could still serve, however vaguely, as a deterrent. But if the principle of exemplary deterrence necessitated that executions be public, contemporary sensibilities frowned on those who showed up to watch, finding it abhorrent that anyone could derive pleasure in the act of seeing another human being die. Consequently, those who staged these nominally public executions did everything in their power to prevent people from actually coming, and to prevent those who did come from seeing much of anything. Nevertheless, spectators continued to turn up, hoping to catch a glimpse of a vanishing spectacle. Even after government officials removed the elevated scaffold, and insisted that executions be performed at twilight, the executioner and the guillotine soldiered on, like actors deprived of a stage and lights, reluctant to let the curtain come down.

THE GUILLOTINE: A DISAPPEARING ACT

In April of 1793, in his *Révolutions de Paris*, Prudhomme complained of certain spectacular aspects of executions by guillotine that, to him, smacked of the ancien régime:

> The ritual of execution should be perfected and everything that is derived from the ancien régime should be done away with. This cart, in which one puts the condemned...; those hands tied behind the back, which obliges the patient to take an uncomfortable and servile position; that black robe in which we still permit the confessor to dress up...; all these spectacular elements [*appareil*] are not befitting the morals of an enlightened, humane, and free nation....Another reproach one could level at this punishment is that, if it spares the condemned pain, it does not sufficiently conceal the sight of blood from spectators; one can see it flowing from the blade of the

guillotine and spraying out in abundance over the cobblestones near the scaffold. This repulsive spectacle should not be offered to the eyes of the people...as it familiarizes them with the idea of murder, committed, it is true, in the name of the law, but with a sang-froid which leads to a deliberate ferocity.... The people are degraded in seeming to want vengeance rather than contenting themselves with wanting justice done.[1]

The following month, Pierre-Gaspard Chaumette, the Procureur of Paris, who would himself fall under the blade of the guillotine in less than a year, sent a letter to the Procureur of the department of the Seine, complaining, like Prudhomme, about the spectacle presented by executions: "Dogs come to lap up [the blood], and...a crowd of men feast their eyes on a spectacle which leads the soul toward ferocity." The recipient of the letter forwarded it to the carpenter in charge of the guillotine's maintenance, instructing him to do what he could about the blood so that "this spectacle [which] is distressing for humanity no longer presents itself to the gaze of men."[2]

That same month, in the department of the Gers, a member of the General Council urged his colleagues to order that the guillotine be removed from the public square immediately after each execution, basing his views "on the sentiments of humanity, on the collective anticipation of the death penalty's [eventual] abolition, [and] on the danger of accustoming citizens to the terrible spectacle of public vengeance...." His colleagues on the council agreed, and although the guillotine had already been painted red "in order to diminish horror of the spectacle of executions [by masking the blood] as well as to preserve the wood," it was ordered to be removed immediately after each use, so that the sight of it would not offend the sensibilities of the town's citizens.[3]

During the height of the Terror, as we have seen, expressions of similar sensibilities were liable to be construed as sympathy for the victims, and in many places the guillotine was erected *en permanence* without complaint. No sooner did the Terror come to an end, however, than complaints about the visibility of the guillotine began to resurface. Only three months after the fall of Robespierre on 9 Thermidor, year II (27 July 1794), a representative of the people of Dijon ordered the guillotine in that city, which had been permanently on display, immediately dismounted, and put strict provisions in place for its reappearance:

> The representative of the People J. Marie Calés, having just been informed that the instrument of punishment—which must be exposed to the eyes of the people only when the execution of the law demands it and which, in all other circumstances, can only revolt sensitive souls and attack the humanitarian sentiments which must characterize a free people—exists *en permanence* in one of the squares of Dijon, orders, that upon receipt of these presents, this instrument to be removed.... It is prohibited by these presents for all public functionaries to expose [the guillotine], under any pretext whatsoever, before a death sentence has been pronounced. It may be [exposed] only one hour before the execution and will be removed immediately and without delay after the execution....[4]

For those citizens of Dijon who lived in close proximity to the public square where executions were performed, this change, while welcome, did not go far enough. Rather than objecting to the permanent display of the guillotine, they insisted, in a letter to their representative, on the right *never* to see it, suggesting that it be moved somewhere else, farther from the center of town, where it would no longer disturb sensitive souls:

> The inhabitants of the Place du Morimont have recognized your justice and your humanity in having removed from before their eyes the scaffold, where for too long the blade, which must serve only to punish the wicked, was suspended.
>
> They would desire that this apparatus, always terrifying, no longer appear on this square, something which would spare delicate and sensitive souls the spectacle of blood, which the proximity of their domiciles forces them to see despite themselves.
>
> There is a place more suitable for undertaking these sorts of executions, so that no one will any longer have anything to complain about. It is the Place de la Liberté, which is a vast, isolated square, where a little national building has been built which would be suitable for receiving the bodies of the punished as well as the wood for the scaffold and other instruments of punishment, and two steps from there is the cemetery; whereas, from the Place du Morimont, one is obliged to transport the corpses into a nearby building where, during the summer, the blood which spreads out, spreads fetid fumes [which are] always deleterious to health.
>
> Furthermore, the wine market which takes place on this square three times per *décade* [ie. ten days] attracts many non-locals who do not see without discomfort [*peine*] a permanent scaffold which, in any case, should never have been placed at any moment other than that of execution and removed immediately.[5]

We should be careful to note that, as with the comments quoted above, it was not executions in and of themselves that the citizens of the Place du Morimont found so objectionable, but rather the *sight* of them. They pronounced no opinion on the morality or the necessity of the death penalty, but they were certain that the proximity of executions, the sight and the smell of the scaffold, were bad for business, hazardous to health, and offensive to sensitive souls.

Officials in Auch, who had objected to the continuous display of the guillotine before the Terror, renewed their efforts to remove the spectacle of justice from the center of town after the Terror. As a local administrator proclaimed to his colleagues:

> Citizens, the days of the Terror which we have unfortunately endured were the reason why the machine for decapitation was placed on the Place de la Liberté of this commune, in order to make an impression on wicked counter-revolutionaries. But today, when we exist under a gentler and happier government, it is suitable to choose another public square to perform executions....[6]

In Paris, the guillotine's story is somewhat more complicated. It had been erected *en permanence* on the Place de la Révolution (today's Place de la Concorde) from August 1793 until June 1794, at which point it was moved, very briefly, to the Place de la Bastille, before settling at the Place du Trône-Renversé (today's Place de la Nation). There was another guillotine at the Place de Grève, which served to execute ordinary criminals rather than those convicted of political crimes, but this one was mounted and taken down for each execution. With the fall of Robespierre on 9 Thermidor, the guillotine returned to the Place de la Révolution, where it dispatched 103 politicians of the Terror over a three-day period. For a year after that, the only scaffold in Paris was the one at the Place de Grève. With the uprisings of Prairial (May 1795), however, the guillotine once again returned to the Place de la Révolution for a brief period, to execute those who had been associated with the revolt. Finally, in July of 1795, the National Assembly decreed that "the Place de la Révolution will no longer serve as a place of execution," and for the next thirty-five years all executions in Paris took place at the Place de Grève, the traditional site of executions in Paris.[7]

In January of 1832, however, citing the fact that "generous citizens had gloriously spilled their blood for the national cause" at the Place de Grève (in the recent Revolution of 1830), the Prefect of the department of the Seine decreed:

> .... That the place de Grève can no longer serve as a place of execution.... Considering that it is important to designate, preferably, locations which are removed from the center of Paris, and which have easy access; considering, furthermore, that by reasons of humanity, those locations must be chosen which are as close as possible to the prisons where the condemned are detained;... we order that sentences carrying the death penalty will in the future be executed at the location which is located at the extremity of the faubourg Saint-Jacques.[8]

Interestingly, although the Prefect had cited the newly hallowed nature of the Place de Grève and the "humanity" of executing prisoners closer to their place of detention (to spare them a long journey to the scaffold), one suspects that there were other considerations weighing more heavily on the decision to relocate the guillotine. In fact, the new location of the barrière Saint-Jacques was only marginally closer to the prison at Bicêtre, which held condemned prisoners, than the Place de Grève had been (three and a half kilometers as opposed to five and a half, respectively). What the barrière Saint-Jacques did offer, however, was a location far removed from the center of Paris, with easy access by relatively wide roads and comparatively little traffic. The logic in choosing this location can be gleaned from the two other areas that had been considered. One was the Place Vauban, behind the Invalides, which had seemed promising because it was "isolated, and distant from the center of population," but the military had raised objections. The other proposed site was alongside the slaughterhouses of Grenelle, at the western edge of the city, where a different kind of killing was being sequestered out of sight, hidden from the view of sensitive souls.[9] But perhaps the best indication of the motivation of authorities in selecting the barrière Saint-Jacques can be discerned from the nature of the first execution that took place there, as reported by Victor Hugo:

> [The condemned] was put into a kind of basket, dragged on two wheels, closed in on all sides, locked and padlocked, then... with little noise and no crowds, the package was dropped off at the deserted barrière Saint-Jacques. Arriving there at eight o'clock in the morning, the sun scarcely risen, there was a guillotine freshly mounted; as for the public, a few dozen little boys grouped on nearby piles of stone next to the unexpected machine; quickly, the man was taken out of the basket, and without giving him a chance to breathe, furtively, sneakily, shamefully, his head was taken off for him. That is what one calls a public and solemn act of high justice.[10]

The "basket" to which Hugo refers here is an early version of the *voitures cellulaires*, enclosed wagons dubbed *paniers à salade* [salad baskets] that would transport prisoners through the streets, safe from the prying eyes of the public.[11] The procession to the scaffold, which had for a long time constituted its own spectacle, would now disappear as well.

With the Revolution of 1848, the guillotine of Paris was moved yet again, this time immediately outside the gates of the new prison of La Grande Roquette, on the eastern side of the city.[12] With the guillotine now only steps from the prison gates, the journey from the prison to the scaffold had finally been reduced to the shortest distance possible for an execution that was, at least in theory, still public. As Maxime du Camp would later point out, however, executions outside the prison of la Roquette seemed as if they were public in name only: "The high buildings... are an invincible obstacle to the unhealthy curiosity of the population; the trees are numerous, close together, leafy, which prevent one from seeing; the scaffold, erected almost against the walls of the prison, is hidden as much as possible;... [the public]... is pushed away, kept at a distance...."[13] Even for those who were able to catch a glimpse, there was precious little to see: "Fourteen seconds, calculated on a watch with a second hand, went by between the moment when the condemned put his foot on the first step [of the scaffold] and the [moment] when the basket [which received the body] was closed."[14]

The contradictions between a law that mandated executions be public and a succession of governments and administrations that seemed increasingly intent on masking, as much as possible, the visibility of executions, was not lost on contemporaries. Writing in 1855, the jurist Joseph Louis Ortolan observed:

> Our penal law wishes executions of the death penalty to be public, and the progress of morals already makes us ashamed of this publicity, or the evil that it engenders warns us that it is time to put a stop to it. In earlier times, the scaffold, the gibbet, or the wheel were erected in the center of the city, opposite the hôtel de ville; the life of a man was destroyed in plain daylight, with great spectacle, at an hour announced well in advance.... Today, some remote corner of the city, the day kept a secret, the preparations undertaken in cover of darkness, the twilight just barely enough to satisfy the visibility required by law, form [the basis of] our publicity.

For Ortolan, however, there seemed no reason why the function of exemplary deterrence could not be assured by the "intellectual publicity" of the execution, the knowledge that it had taken place, rather than the actual "physical spectacle" itself. He therefore expressed his preference for the methods of execution that had recently been adopted in certain German states, which mandated that executions take place "in an interior courtyard of the prison, in the presence of judicial authorities, twelve citizen witnesses, two doctors and one priest."[15]

But French legislators were as yet reluctant to abandon public executions, and administrators therefore focused on chipping away at what remained of the spectacle of justice. In 1864, administrators drafted a report on the feasibility of building a guillotine on wheels, which could be quickly rolled out for an execution and just as quickly rolled back in again. The idea was to abbreviate drastically the process of putting up and taking down the guillotine for each execution, a process that took several hours and could not fail to announce an impending execution and attract the attention of curious onlookers. "Public morals demand that such a spectacle be cut short," the author of the report declared.[16] The executioner of Paris at the time, when apprised of the report, was skeptical: "Any new system might save a few minutes, but would not diminish the crowds which curiosity constantly draws to the place designated for capital executions."[17]

It would fall to the newly installed government of National Defense, the first administration of the Third Republic, to—quite literally—push both executioners and the guillotine off the public stage. On 25 November 1870, Adolphe Crémieux, recently installed as Minister of Justice, declared the number of executioners to be "excessive" and reduced that number to one: a single executioner in Paris, accompanied by five aides. At the same time, arguing that "the maintenance of the *bois de justice* [i.e. the guillotine], in each jurisdiction of a court of appeals, unnecessarily burdens the budget," he ordered that the number of guillotines in continental France be reduced to two, both of which were to be kept in Paris (one as the primary guillotine, and the other as a backup). Finally, in view of the fact that "no law legitimates the practice of mounting [guillotines] on a platform elevated above ground level," Crémieux ordered the abolition of elevated scaffolds. While he cited, as his justification for this measure, "the great inconveniences in terms of the transport and mounting" of the guillotine, he could not help adding that the scaffold had the effect of "transforming legal expiation into a hideous spectacle."[18]

Stripped of its scaffold, the number of executioners reduced to one, the spectacle of the guillotine persevered, still managing to draw determined spectators. In March of 1879, the administration of President Jules Grévy proposed to put an end to the spectacle of execution once and for all. Addressing the Chamber of Deputies on behalf of the president, the Minister of Justice and Minister of the Interior proposed to amend the penal code requiring public executions, and to mandate that, henceforth, executions would take place behind prison walls. The Grévy administration was essentially advocating a reform that would not only fulfil Custine's vision of nearly a century before, but which would also bring France into line with those European and American states that had already made spectacular capital punishment a thing of the past:

> Gentlemen, according to the provision of article 26 of the penal Code, the execution of the death penalty is performed on one of the public squares of the location designated by the judicial sentence....
>
> Scandalous scenes which occur all too often around the scaffold, dishonor the work of justice. Shameful instincts which appear among the crowd, show the extent to which the law has failed to achieve its ends, in wishing to restrain [those instincts] by the spectacle [*appareil*] of punishment. Society understands that it has nothing to gain in presenting these bloody spectacles to the public; [society] has sought to mitigate, in practice, the unfortunate aspects [*inconvénients*] of publicity. Little by little, the scaffold has been relegated to the least frequented public squares; the earliest hours in the morning have been chosen to execute judicial sentences; the crowd was kept at a distance from the instrument of punishment, [which was] lowered to ground level. We

have sought, in a word, as much as the imperative prescriptions of the law have allowed us, to restrain the legal publicity of executions.

These precautions... are, however, insufficient and do not prevent revolting scenes from accompanying capital executions, particularly in large cities.[19]

Here we have what amounts to a full confession, not simply on behalf of the government of the Third Republic but, arguably, every government and administration since the first attempts to close off the windows of the Hôtel de Ville from curious spectators in 1738 or to veil the face of Madame de Lescombat in 1755. For a century and a half, generations of French officials had been waging a constant battle against spectators who not only seemed unwilling to learn the lessons they were supposed to be deriving from these spectacles but who, to the constant chagrin of government officials and administrators and the embarrassment of enlightened and sensitive public opinion, were actually enjoying the show. The only thing that had changed over time was the social composition of the crowd of spectators, which in the eighteenth century had included all classes of society, but which, by the late nineteenth century, would seem to have been reduced largely to the lower social strata, not including, of course, all the upstanding members of society who watched vicariously through the descriptions provided by Maxime du Camp and other journalists. (And the government had made an effort to hinder even this kind of second-hand "watching" as well.)[20]

As we can see in the above statement, the Grévy administration had drawn a distinction between French "society," which was repulsed by such spectacles, and the French "public," or at least the portion of it that formed the "crowds" around the scaffold. Here, restated, was the same paradox that Jean-Baptiste Suard had expressed a century earlier: "Unfortunately, it's not on the wicked people, but rather on the sensitive souls, that the spectacle of punishments leaves the strongest impressions. The man whom one should most fear meeting in the forest, he's the one who likes attending executions of criminals."[21] To the Grévy administration, the only solution to the problem was to follow the example of "England, Prussia, several States of Germany, Sweden, a considerable portion of the United States of America, [which] have made a point of enclosing the scaffold in the confines of prisons."[22]

Of course, the prospect of abolishing the spectacle of justice raised the perennial issue of exemplary deterrence. What purpose would be served by a capital punishment that no one could see? Rather than acknowledging, as many theorists and some politicians in the late eighteenth century had already done, that the death penalty served a purpose of extermination above and beyond whatever deterrent functions it may have had, the politicians of the Third Republic insisted that exemplary deterrence could still be served by non-spectacular means: "The condemnation produces its exemplary effect by dint of the sole fact that it has been pronounced publicly and that everyone is certain that it has been executed. The sight of the punishment adds nothing to this beneficial impression; on the contrary, it awakens bloodthirsty instincts in the soul of those who witness it." Dismissing the notion that it was proposing "clandestine executions," the Grévy administration argued that the public would still be able to witness the execution virtually, through its representatives: "Instead of the banal and confused publicity of the public square, the proposed law substitutes a publicity [which is] defined and regulated by law. In the presence of its magistrates, its representatives, its witnesses, society will solemnly accomplish an act of high justice."[23] Furthermore, as a means of supplementing the public nature of this non-public spectacle, and to "allay all suspicion," the government proposed to allow certain designated members of the press to attend executions: "Thanks to the press, whose delegates shall be admitted to the execution, one will soon know in the smallest village of France, that justice has been done. The optional presence of representatives elected by the people will take away, furthermore, any pretext for suspicion."[24] To put it somewhat differently: the people and the press, excluded from the spectacle, would be represented by individuals designated to see justice done on their behalf. Spectacular justice would henceforth take place by proxy.

The proposed law contained a complex scheme whereby official witnesses would be divided into three categories: "indispensable," "obligatory," and "authorized." In lieu of a public spectacle, the law proposed a different kind of publicity, insisting that immediately after the execution, a full account of its proceedings "shall be printed and posted in various places." Instead of the spectacle of capital punishment, it was almost as if the authorities were proposing a kind of updated version of the old executions in effigy, except that, instead of an effigy of the execution, the public would be offered an effigy of the spectacle.

In the end, the Chamber of Deputies did not pass the new law. Renewed attempts were made five years later, when Senator Agénor Bardoux proposed yet another ban on public executions to the Senate. In anticipation of the vote, the Minister of Justice circulated a questionnaire to public prosecutors and magistrates throughout the country, asking for their opinion on the publicity of executions. According to the historian Emmanuel Taïeb, respondents to the questionnaire seemed to dwell on the disorderly nature of the crowds that came to watch public executions as a primary justification for ending them. Interestingly, those in the provinces tended to assume that these problems existed for the most part in Paris, and those in Paris seemed to think the disorders in Paris were nothing compared to those in the provinces.[25] Nevertheless, many respondents insisted that the death penalty remain public: "The death penalty must be exemplary in the highest possible degree, which is to say that it must produce terror in the [potential] criminal and intimidation to the point that he will renounce the crime which he has planned."[26] While some respondents insisted that moving executions behind closed doors would give the appearance that capital punishment was somehow "ashamed of itself,"[27] the newspaper *Le Rappel* made precisely the same argument about the current, half-public nature of capital punishment: "It hides itself. It is ashamed. It recognizes its own impossibility in the light of *l'esprit moderne.*"[28]

This divided sentiment—seventeen courts pronounced themselves in favor of abolishing the spectacle of punishment and ten in favor of preserving it—led to a situation in which the proposed law banning public executions was passed by the Senate, but would not be taken up for ratification by the Chamber of Deputies until a decade later. When, in 1894, the law finally came up for a vote in the

Chamber, it was defeated by an odd coalition of staunch supporters of capital punishment and abolitionists. The former insisted that capital punishment without spectacle failed in the task of exemplary deterrence, and the latter thought that any attempt to make the death penalty more palatable to contemporary sensibilities would forestall the day of its wholesale abolition.[29]

In November of 1902, another commission was formed by the Chamber of Deputies, to explore, once again, the question of public executions, and once again the Chamber was divided. Those who opposed public capital punishment dwelled on the disorderly and obscene nature of the crowd of spectators, which was invariably formed from the "dregs of society." Those who supported capital punishment insisted, as always, that it was predicated on exemplary deterrence, and that if executions were performed behind closed doors, then no one would ever know whether the condemned had actually been killed, or perhaps whether someone else might have been substituted in his or her place.[30]

While successive attempts to pass legislation abolishing public executions failed, the long campaign to reduce spectacle to its absolute, bare minimum continued unabated. Despite the oft-cited disorderly nature of crowds as a justification for abolishing the penal spectacle, we can see in the events surrounding a quadruple execution in 1909 in the town of Béthune, that it was less the behavior of spectators, than the very fact of their *seeing* executions, that so disturbed contemporaries.

Although President Armand Fallières, an ardent opponent of the death penalty, had systemically commuted the death sentences of everyone who had been condemned after his election in 1906, the brutality of the crimes committed by a gang in the Pas-de-Calais region led him to abandon his moratorium on death sentences. The execution of four gang members in January of 1909 would be the first execution in France in three years, and the first quadruple execution since 1870.[31] Citing the anticipated large number of spectators as its primary justification, the authorities, in what may have been the first act of cinematographic censorship in France, took the unusual step of forbidding the filming of the execution. Despite their best efforts, however, a film of the event was apparently made, and the Minister of the Interior immediately sent out a notice to all the prefects of France and Algeria instructing them to forbid the showing of the film. Public order was cited as the reason:

> The judicial authority in the interest of order required for the quadruple capital execution in Béthune has proscribed [and declared] its absolute opposition to the use of any apparatus or procedure whatsoever to reproduce the scene of the execution. Despite the vigilance of the police, filmed images [*clichés*] of this scene may have been taken by subterfuge or by surprise with the aim of using them for cinematographic spectacles. It is possible, as well, that with the same goal in mind, companies have created purely imaginary images [of the event]. I believe that it is indispensable to entirely forbid all public cinematographic spectacles of this genre, [which] are liable to incite gatherings of people [*manifestations*] troubling public order and tranquility.[32]

The assurances of the Minister of the Interior aside, it is somewhat difficult to understand how either the filming or the screening of an execution might contribute to disturbances of public order. Nearly impossible to understand is the rationale that banned the screening of "imaginary images" of the execution, unless, of course, what was disturbing was not the behavior of the crowds, but rather the very fact that the crowds wanted to see someone die, whether they witnessed the event in person, saw it reproduced on film, or even if they saw it *simulated* on film.

The anxiety of the authorities in 1909 was the consequence of a struggle that had been playing out for at least a century and a half between competing and contradictory ideas and customs: exemplary deterrence, predicated on the existence of spectators capable of being terrorized or, at the very least, being soberly reflective; sensibilities, which insisted that human beings were naturally incapable of watching other people suffer without suffering themselves and that any other behavior was unnatural; and the curiosity of spectators who, despite the changing socio-economic makeup of the crowd, had been coming to watch executions as a form of spectacle for some four hundred years. What disturbed the authorities was not the crowd; it was the simple fact that people wanted to watch. The reason why 1909 marked a crisis point is that the advent of filmed images brought to naught all the efforts to restrict access to the spectacle. One person with a film camera could allow countless others to watch the event, over and over again, long into the future.

Despite the uproar over the quadruple execution of 1909, public executions in France continued for another thirty years, and did not end until 1939, when the allegedly scandalous behavior of the crowd that had gathered to watch the German serial killer Eugène Weidmann be put to death on the morning of 17 June provoked the authorities into decreeing the end of public executions by fiat, rather than awaiting a legislative act. Weidmann had lured a young American tourist to her death, and subsequently killed several other individuals. The crimes and the trial of this handsome German "vampire" had occupied the front pages of the French press, as France itself slipped inexorably closer to war with Germany.[33] Weidmann was executed at four-thirty in the morning outside the walls of the Saint-Pierre prison in Versailles, in what would prove to be the last public execution in metropolitan France.

There was enormous public interest in the Weidmann case, and many journalists were on hand to witness the execution. In its evening edition, the *Petit Parisien* gave a blow-by-blow, almost minute by minute, account of the hours preceding the execution. According to the paper, spectators had begun to gather the evening before the execution, both outside the prison walls and in neighboring cafés. Shortly after midnight, near the site where the execution was to be performed, the following scene had taken place: "A big American automobile, completely white and filled with women whom one suspected were elegant, although [the car] was crammed full, had already been spotted [a few times]. 'That one again' came the cry from a bench on which the female element dominated, discussing details of the execution."[34] A little after one in the morning, the police had begun erecting barriers about fifty meters from the spot where the guillotine would be set up; there was a brief tussle with the crowd, which resented being pushed back, and a woman was slightly injured, and taken to a nearby café. At two o'clock in the morning, the electric street lights had been extinguished, prompting "howls and whistles from the crowd." At 3.35 a.m., the chief of Versailles police had spotted what he thought was a woman dressed as a man who, in the words of the reporter from the *Petit Parisien*, "had slipped in among the journalists, who were there out of professional duty." She (or he) was brought in for questioning. People were spotted on the roof of an adjacent building, and were made to come down. This, however, would seem to be the extent of any unusual or disorderly behavior on the part of spectators, who were clearly excited and curious, but hardly out of control. Apart from a little jostling of the barriers, nothing untoward seems to have taken place.

Over the next week, however, the reports of crowd behavior would take on a life of their own, and the unruliness of spectators seemed to worsen with each successive retelling. *Paris-Soir* would describe the crowd in its 18 June edition as "A disgusting crowd [which] is squeezed into the cafés, this unruly crowd is devouring sandwiches... there are jostling, clamors, whistling."[35] Eventually, there would be reports of drunken mobs that had caroused through the streets of Versailles, and even of women who had rushed to dip their handkerchiefs in Weidmann's blood.[36] The Rennes newspaper *L'Ouest-Eclair*, which on 18 June had seen fit to remark only that "some murmurs and even whistles arose from the crowd," would characterize the crowd's behavior rather differently ten days later, citing other reports: "What is almost certain is that the crowd showed itself to be particularly hideous, that windows had been rented at exorbitant prices, that women disguised as men—resembling the '*tricoteurs*' of Thermidor—were able to slip in among those who carried a pass, to [see] the prelude to the execution."[37]

The government declared itself to be horrified by these accounts of the crowd's abominable behavior. On 24 June, the Prime Minister, the Minister of Justice, and the Minister of the Interior issued a report along with a proposed decree to the President of the Republic, banning all public executions:

> According to the terms of article 26 of the Penal Code, capital executions must take place on one of the public squares of the location which is indicated by the court sentence.
>
> This article, whose authors intended for it to have a moralizing effect, has had practically the opposite results.
>
> Already, as a result of regrettable behaviors [*manifestations*] which have sometimes characterized capital executions, the publicity [of executions] has been considerably reduced and a proposed law, adopted by the Senate on 5 December 1898, hoped entirely to put an end to the admission of the public at these executions.
>
> It seems to us that the moment has come to achieve this reform, which is desirable in all respects, and that it is with this goal in mind that we have the honor of submitting for your approval the present proposed decree.

The decree was very much in keeping with earlier proposals. Executions would henceforth take place within the prison enclosure, and only certain officials, as well as the defense attorney, a religious minister, and the prison doctor would be allowed to witness the execution. As for the public, the decree ordered:

> The account [*procès-verbal*] of the execution will be drawn up by the court clerk.... Immediately after the execution, a copy of the account... will be posted at

the door of the penitential establishment where the execution has taken place and will remain there for twenty-four hours.

No indication, no document relating to the execution other than the [official] account can be published in the press, under penalty of a fine of one hundred to two thousand francs.[38]

Here, in the last provision of the decree, we can catch sight of the real motivation for the decision to ban public executions. It was not the behavior of the allegedly raucous, disgusting, sandwich-eating crowd that made this the last public execution to take place in metropolitan France. What truly set this execution apart from others was the fact that the newly installed executioner, performing his first execution, either underestimated how long it would take him to prepare or misunderstood the time at which it was supposed to take place. Instead of the execution taking place at the crack of dawn, as usual, it was performed in full daylight. Photographers capitalized on the situation, taking an extraordinary number of startlingly clear still images, which were soon splashed across the pages of widely read magazines, such as *Match* and *Life Magazine* (Fig. 15). The two-page photo spread in the latter featured a dozen sequential pictures, showing the arrival of the condemned, his placement on the guillotine, the executioner with his hand poised on the cord, the blade caught in mid-air, and the corpse of the victim, after the blade had fallen. This sequence of images, taken in rapid succession, had the effect of slowing down the execution, freezing the guillotine in that invisible blink of an eye, so that one could, in fact, see it fall. Indeed, so quick was the succession of photographs, that the blade was caught in mid-descent not once but twice. At the same time, the images almost seemed like a flip-book of pictures, giving the illusion of movement, as if the pictures could both freeze the action and convey it at the same time. Worse yet, as far as the authorities were concerned, someone—perhaps even two people—had managed to film the execution surreptitiously.

Protestations about crowd behavior aside, the government knew that it could do everything in its power to discourage spectators from seeing the spectacle of execution, but that all these efforts were pointless in the face of one individual with a movie camera, which would make possible the endless replaying of the spectacle for the innumerable spectators, present and future, who wished to see someone die.[39] As the columnist for *Paris-Municipal*, a weekly journal of judicial and financial affairs, pointed out, the government's decision to ban public executions by fiat had been an unusual one: "[T]hose interested in the exegesis of constitutional law might ask themselves what relationship there might be, exactly, between this measure and national defense which, alone, gives the government the right to legislate by decree." Nevertheless, the same columnist pronounced the text of the decree "excellent" and added:

> We will no longer see entire columns on the front page of the big daily papers, dedicated to the final moments of the condemned and to the most futile details of the sad process. We will no longer see, as well, a big illustrated weekly ... publish photographs of the victim lying flat on the scaffold. And so much the better, because this indirect publicity was no less unhealthy than the direct publicity.[40]

Fig. 15. Execution of Eugène Weidmann. © Roger-Viollet/The Image Works.

From this moment on, the only visible aspect of executions would be the official *procès-verbal*, posted on the prison door, informing the public that justice had been done. In many ways, these non-public executions would be nearly indistinguishable from life sentences of imprisonment, both of which had the effect of making criminals disappear behind closed doors.

For this final show, the swansong of public executions in France, it is almost as if all the ghosts of spectators past, real and imaginary, had been summoned to witness the event: the desperate spectators who had paid exorbitant sums for windows overlooking the execution, or who massed on the rooftops; the elegant Madame de Sévigné, Madame du Noyer, and Madame Préandeau crammed into a big white American automobile; the *tricoteuses*, muttering on the bench, and the strange woman dressed as a man—all these women, unnaturally interested in seeing the death of a fellow human being. And last, but not least, Gueullette himself, in the guise of a reporter for *Le Petit Parisien*, who chronicled every single minute of the event "out of professional duty."

In the end, if the guillotine had reduced the spectacle of punishment to an invisible moment, if the railroad had helped to whittle down the profane race of executioners and the legion of guillotines to a single specimen of each, then it was the technological innovation of film that proved to be, so to speak, the last nail in the coffin for public executions. An infinity of potential spectators, present and future, who were eager to see another human being die, gave the lie to an unwavering conviction in the natural and instinctive sensitivity of human beings to the suffering of others, as well as to the ability of public executions to "terrify" by example. Short of simply declaring that the primary purpose of capital punishment was simply to get rid of people, which in and of itself would have obviated the need for executions to be performed in public, the only solution was to hide executions behind closed doors. The death of public executions was, it would seem, essential to the survival of exemplary deterrence as a concept.

From 1939 until the abolition of the death penalty in France in 1981, executions would take place behind prison walls in the presence of designated witnesses. The resulting official account, posted for twenty-four hours on the prison wall, was the last vestige of the public nature of executions.

The age of spectacular capital punishment had come to an end.

Conclusion
Punishment Past and Present

This book began with the story of the Sow of Falaise, the tale of a pig that was seized by the authorities in January of 1386, found guilty of having eaten the face of a three-month- old boy (thereby causing his death), and sentenced to be hanged by the official executioner. Although the story strikes the modern reader as odd, even somewhat silly, I think that we can now see how, within the context of its time, the execution of the Sow of Falaise was a perfectly logical act of justice, duly performed by the executioner. A crime, an atrocious crime, had been committed, and the body of the convicted offender was made the subject of a penal ritual, just as it would have been if that body had been human, and just as it would have been if that body had been, in the absence of the actual offender, the representation of a body in the form of an effigy. Justice demanded the ritual of punishment, not only so that someone, or some animal, would "pay" for the crime, but so that those in attendance could overcome the atrocity of the crime—so that they could literally see justice done, and move on.

The only thing truly extraordinary about the case of the Sow of Falaise, then, is what nineteenth-century historians did to the story. The inability to see anything but deterrence in penal practice not only colored their understanding of the pre-modern penal ritual but, in this case, colored the facts themselves, leading them to supply the "missing" details according to which modern historians could read the Sow's execution as a tale of exemplary deterrence mixed with crude retaliation: the forced attendance of the child's father, the sow's owner, and (in the most recent retellings) a "multitude of pigs," all of whom, along with the spectators, were meant to be learning some lesson from the execution.

Even if we can begin to understand the logic of the punishment of the Sow of Falaise within the context of its time on an intellectual level, and even if we strip the tale of its nineteenth-century embellishments, both this story and those of the hundreds of other animal executions in Europe through the medieval and early modern periods still strike the modern reader as odd. The idea that a pig could be sentenced to capital punishment is simply too foreign to our understanding of either animals or the law for us not to find it strange. But what, precisely, is so strange about it?

As the fates would have it, on the very day that I first sat down to draft this conclusion, another tragic homicide took place, some seven hundred and fifty years and four thousand miles away from the events in Falaise. Although the details are a bit murky, it would seem that a sixty-five-year-old librarian, out for a walk near her home, not far from the University of Georgia in the United States, was set upon and killed by a pack of "feral" dogs—eleven dogs and five puppies, investigators would later determine. When her husband, a retired German professor, went out to look for her, he too was set upon and killed by the dogs. Upon being informed of the events by the local sheriff, a superior court judge, citing his concern for public safety, ordered that the dogs be rounded up and remanded to a local humane society until their fate could be determined. The following day, the same judge issued a court order for the dogs and puppies to be euthanized.

These events are undeniably tragic, and my intent here is not to make light of them in any way. But equally as tragic, no doubt, were the events that took place in the town of Falaise in the fourteenth century, although the distance in time makes us perhaps less able to appreciate the tragedy of the death of the three-month-old boy in that case. My intent here is simply to juxtapose a case of animal homicide in the present day with one from the fourteenth century, as a way not only of comparing what we find normal with what we find strange, but perhaps also of allowing us to see our own, present understanding of punishment in a slightly different light—to make the present "strange," as the Russian formalists meant by the term *ostranenie*.

When I first came across the story of the pack of dogs in Georgia in the newspaper, I read it with a certain degree of interest, and then turned the page. Surprisingly, I did not at first make the connection between the dogs in Georgia and the Sow of Falaise, despite the fact that animal executions have obviously been very much on my mind for quite some time. Somehow, what had happened in Georgia seemed perfectly "normal" to me, whereas the events in Falaise, although I now believe that I understand them, still seemed intuitively "strange." It was only as I was going to sleep later that night, that I suddenly became aware of the similarities between the two cases, and, perhaps even more importantly, the stark differences in penal practice that those similarities enable us to see.

The similarities seem fairly clear. In both cases, we have animals who were found guilty of homicide, and who were ordered held for a period of time, before a court order sentenced them to death. But the differences are a bit harder to see at first glance. We do not know enough about the particular details of the Sow's case, but we can, I think, safely extrapolate from the many other animal trials and executions of the time and assume that an investigation was undertaken, and that the Sow was found sufficiently guilty to warrant a death sentence. We know from some of the other cases that guilt was not always presumed, even in the case of incriminating evidence. There was the case, for example, discussed in the Introduction, in which a sow and her six piglets were taken into custody, but the piglets were later provisionally returned to their owner, despite the telltale signs of blood on their snouts, because this evidence, although incriminating, was not wholly sufficient to prove their guilt.[1] In the case of the dogs from Georgia, however, it would seem that a decidedly looser standard of guilt was applied. The authorities reported that no actual blood was found on the dogs, that the dogs had never before shown any signs of aggression, but that the coroner's office determined that the wounds were consistent with dog bites, all of which led the authorities to determine that the pack of feral dogs and puppies living on the street must have been to blame.

In the Sow's case, it is probable that the facts were weighed very carefully before her guilt was determined; in other words, her case was handled in a way that was not substantially different from how it would have been handled if she had been human. The pack of dogs in Georgia, however, although they too had the benefit of legal procedure, were not accorded the same due process as the state of Georgia would have accorded to human beings. Weighing the evidence, a lone judge of the superior court of Oglethorpe County in the state of Georgia determined, in a decision titled, appropriately enough, "State of Georgia v. A Number of Dangerous Dogs," that the "need to protect the public" made it necessary to authorize "any state-certified law enforcement officer...to capture or seize any unrestrained dogs found in or near the area [where the crime took place]...and to impound those dogs and hold them for further legal proceedings."[2] It is conceivable that the same judge might have ordered a human being who was suspected of homicide to be held pending further investigation. But the following day, without the formal inquiry and perhaps even a trial that might have been accorded to an animal suspect in the pre-modern period, the superior court judge authorized "any state-certified law enforcement officer, animal control officer, or animal shelter staff...to euthanize the feral dogs seized at or near the area [of the crime]...and being held in the Madison County Animal Shelter." We can only imagine what an uproar there would have been if human suspects had been placed into custody, held for a day, and then executed on the authority of a single judge, not to mention if other people who just happened to be "at or near the area" of the crime had also been rounded up and executed. Presumably, however, in the mind of the judge, public safety held precedence over whatever rights feral dogs and puppies may be thought to possess.

But there is something else—something about the way the dogs were executed—that begs for further analysis, and this is what I missed when I first read the story. I understood that the dangerous dogs were simply being euthanized as a precautionary measure, and I suppose I did not see the fate of these dogs as being substantially different from when we put our own beloved pets "to sleep." What I was oblivious to, however, was that the manner in which the feral dogs were being euthanized was, in fact, also the most commonly used form of capital punishment in the United States, although we prefer to use the term "lethal injection," rather than "euthanasia" or "putting to sleep" in the latter case. I missed, in other words, the ways in which the "State of Georgia v. A Number of Dangerous Dogs" was, in fact, a modern case of animal capital punishment, albeit with a significantly abbreviated procedure, and no right to a trial, much less an appeal.

I would like to suggest that the punishment of animals, whether in fourteenth-century France, or in Georgia today, affords us an extraordinary window onto pure penal practice. Because animals are usually held to be incapable of criminal intent, all the rhetoric of exemplary deterrence is stripped away, and without any theoretical clothing, so to speak, naked practice is revealed. The Sow of Falaise was forced to take part in a penal ritual, as if she had been human. The Dangerous Dogs of

Georgia were made to disappear, excised from this world in the interests of "the need to protect the public," a need that, we should note with interest, took precedence over the definitive determination of guilt.

What does all this tell us? It shows very clear differences in penal practice that are usually confused and masked by a rhetoric of exemplary deterrence. It also allows us to see some lingering vestiges of the past in the present: the overriding need for someone to "pay" for the crime, even in the absence of anyone, or at least any human being, who is clearly culpable. The authorities in Georgia did apparently explore the possibility of bringing charges against a man who had been feeding the dogs for several years. But no charges were brought, in part because the man had recently moved away, and had returned only occasionally to feed the dogs; he was, moreover, in ill health. One wonders, however, if the chain of culpability had been a bit tighter and the dog-feeder a more constant presence and a less pathetic character, whether the authorities might not have pursued issues of human culpability more than they did.[3] The question that is always retroactively asked on these occasions is whether there was anyone who could have foreseen that this might have happened and who, through their actions, in some way contributed to the events that took place. This ever-present need to stress retroactive foreseeability is the gift that Roman law has given modern penal culture. This, combined with a traditional desire to see someone—anyone—"pay" for a crime (along the lines of what early medieval penal laws stipulated), forms the logical foundation of innumerable cases in which individuals are held not just civilly liable but *criminally* liable for acts that may very well, when viewed objectively, be simple accidents.

The Dangerous Dogs of Georgia were punished, then, not simply to protect the public, but also to make someone or something "pay" for the tragic crime that had taken place, and perhaps also to provide the family and friends of the victims and even the community at large with some sort of "closure," however poor and unsatisfying that closure may have been. One cannot help wondering whether, in fact, the medieval penal ritual was better at providing for a ceremony of overcoming than the modern practice of simply killing the guilty party, whether animal or human.

In fact, modern justice would seem to provide few opportunities for overcoming and "closure." Families of victims interviewed before or after a criminal case very often speak of their need to "see justice done," a phrase which, I have little doubt, is a linguistic vestige of the time when one literally did *see* justice done. In modern society, however, there is hardly any opportunity to see anything at all. Since the early modern revolution in sensibilities, it has been considered inhumane to make a spectacle of the suffering of criminals; and if there is a vague sense that criminals should suffer for their crimes, any desire actually to see them suffer, to witness their suffering, can only strike us as unseemly if not unnatural.

In the modern judicial system, the only time that the public has the opportunity to see (accused) criminals is when they appear at trial. Seating for those who wish to see the trial in person is, of course, limited, and although cameras are sometimes allowed in the courtroom, in many cases the public must content itself with drawings, satisfying our need to see *something*, and perhaps functioning in ways not unlike the drawings and paintings that served as effigies of the condemned in the pre-modern period. In some countries that allow publicity before the determination of guilt, the public may be treated to the sight of accused offenders as they make their way to and from the prison and the courtroom—the so-called "perp walk" in the United States. When crime and punishment are the subject of novels, television, and film, the focus is invariably on the investigation and the trial, with dramatic courtroom scenes serving as modern-day equivalents of Rosset's scaffold scenes, the moment when audiences can appreciate the tragedy of the crime and search the face of the defendant for signs of remorse or the lack of it. But in the modern system, whether in fiction or in reality, punishment itself is, for all practical purposes, invisible. At the moment when punishment begins, the condemned is whisked away, a curtain of opacity descends, and we see nothing more. This is the moment of their casting out, their exile from society, whether temporary or for a lifetime, into the prison system, our own colonies of internal banishment. Or, in those few countries like the United States that still practice the death penalty, they are sent off to be exterminated, a word that originally meant to banish beyond (*ex*) the border (*terminus*).

It may seem unscholarly of me to have juxtaposed, in this conclusion, historical events that took place in France hundreds of years ago with ones that are taking place in the present day in the United States. But it is a fundamental premise of this book that all of Western culture shares a common penal heritage. Through this juxtaposition of penal systems not only across time but across national boundaries, I hope to have made clear what I attempted to express in the introduction: that this is not meant to be a book only about the history of France a long time ago, but a book about the ways in which France's past epitomizes the penal past that is common to Western culture as a whole, and about how France's entry into the modern penal age offers us a window onto our common passage into modernity.

We are, whether we live in France, Britain, the United States, or in the many other countries that share a common cultural genealogy, the heirs of several distinct historical influences, all of which have a say in why and how we punish. My intention, throughout this book, has not been to suggest that deterrence plays no role whatsoever in the logic of punishment, either historically or in the present day; rather, I have simply tried to say that it has not played *every* role. Our preoccupation with deterrence has tended to obscure every other aspect of punishment, past as well as present. If we can, however, just for a moment, look beyond deterrence, we can glimpse the surprising ways in which the past still lives in the present. Even after all these centuries, we too want in some visceral way to see people (or animals) *pay* for their crimes. And despite the demise of the penal spectacle, we still want to *see* justice done.

Notes

INTRODUCTION

1. See J. Berriat-Saint-Prix, "Rapport et recherches sur les procès et jugement relatifs aux animaux," *Mémoires et dissertations sur les antiquités nationales et étrangères* (1829), 8:441–5, and E. P. Evans, *The Criminal Prosecution and Capital Punishment of Animals* (1906; reprint, London and Boston, MA, 1987), 298–303.
2. Evans, *Criminal Prosecution*, 150.
3. The phrase "a new glove" [*un gand neuf*] suggests that Charnage may not have transcribed the receipt exactly as written. Most likely, he mistakenly assumed that the old French *gans*, which referred to the gains or payment to the executioner, was an alternate spelling of glove, and altered the sentence accordingly. I thank Pascal Bastien for this clarification.
4. Claude François Blondeau de Charnage, *Dictionnaire de titres originaux pour les fiefs, l'histoire, la généalogie* (Paris, 1764), 2:72–3.
5. *Suite de la clef, ou Journal Historique* (June 1764), XCV:419, and M. Fréron, *L'Année littéraire. Année M.DCC.LXV* (Amsterdam, [1765]), 3:205.
6. Michel Béziers, *Chronologie historique des Bailles et des Gouverneurs de Caen* (Caen, 1769).
7. "Animal" in *Dictionnaire de Jurisprudence de Brillon* (Lyon, 1786), 5:85.
8. P. G. Langevin, *Recherches historiques sur Falaise* (Falaise, 1814), 146.
9. [P.G. Langevin], *Supplément aux recherches historiques sur Falaise* (Falaise, 1826), 12.
10. Ibid, 12–13.
11. Charles de Vauquelin et al., *Statistique de l'arrondissement de Falaise*, (Falaise, 1826), 1:83–4.
12. See, for example, Berriat-Saint-Prix, "Rapport et recherches," 8:427; Emile Agnel, *Curiosités judiciaires et historiques du moyen âge* (Paris, 1858), 11–12; and Alexandre Sorel, "Procès contre des animaux et insectes," *Bulletin de la Société Historique de Compiègne* 3 (1876–77), 275.
13. Evans, *Criminal Prosecution*, 140–1.
14. One author refers to the case as "One of the most famous examples, for which we have found ample evidence," [Gérard Dietrich, *Les procès d'animaux du moyen-âge à nos jours* (Lyon, 1961), 31–3] and another refers to it as "one of the best documented among the sixty or so known trials" in medieval France [Michel Pastoureau, "Une justice exemplaire: Les procès faits aux animaux" in Claude Gauvard and Robert Jacob (eds.), *Les Rites de la justice: Gestes et rituels judiciaires au Moyen Age* (Paris, 1999), 180].
15. See Michel Pastoureau, *Une histoire symbolique du Moyen Age occidental* (Paris, 2004), 33, and Hélène Grimaud, trans. Ellen Hinsey, *Wild Harmonies* (New York, 2003), 8.
16. Paul Friedland, "Beyond Deterrence: Cadavers, Effigies, Animals and the Logic of Executions in Premodern France," *Historical Reflections/Réflexions Historiques*, 29(2) (2003), 313.
17. Michel Foucault, *Discipline and Punish: The Birth of the Prison*, trans. Alan Sheridan (New York, 1979), 34.
18. Ibid, 24.
19. Ibid, 48.
20. Ibid, 44–5.
21. Ibid, 49.
22. Ibid, 58.

23. Michel Foucault, *Power/Knowledge: Selected Interviews and Other Writings, 1972–1977*, ed. Colin Gordon, trans. Colin Gordon et al. (New York, 1980), 97.
24. "What Calls for Punishment," in Michel Foucault, *Foucault Live: Interviews, 1966–1984*, ed. Sylvère Lotringer, trans. John Johnson (New York, 1989), 283.
25. David Garland, "Death, Denial, Discourse: On the Forms and Functions of American Capital Punishment," in *Crime, Social Control and Human Rights: From Moral Panics to States of Denial*, ed. David Downes et al. (Devon and Portland, OR, 2007), 141.
26. David Armstrong, "Bodies of Knowledge: Foucault and the Problem of Human Anatomy," in Andrew Blaikie et al. (eds.), *The Body: Critical Concepts in Sociology* (London and New York, 2004), 3:112.
27. Foucault, *Discipline and Punish*, 53–4.
28. Pascal Bastien, *L'Exécution publique à Paris au XVIIIe siècle* (Paris, 2006), 12.
29. Pieter Spierenburg, *The Spectacle of Suffering: Executions and the Evolution of Repression: From a Preindustrial Metropolis to the European Experience* (Cambridge, 1984); "Violence and the Civilizing Process: Does it Work?" *Crime, histoire & société/Crime, History & Society*, 5(2): 87–105, and "Punishment, Power, and History: Foucault and Elias," *Social Science History*, 28:4 (winter 2004), 607–36. Lynn Hunt, *Inventing Human Rights: A History* (New York and London, 2007). See also V. A. C. Gatrell, *The Hanging Tree: Execution and the English People: 1770–1868* (Oxford, 1994), which devotes significant attention to the history of emotions and its relationship to capital punishment in Britain.
30. Clifford Geertz, "'From the Native's Point of View': On the Nature of Anthropological Understanding," in *Bulletin of the American Academy of Arts & Sciences*, 28:1 (October 1974), 29. Emphasis added.
31. To cite just the most important monographs (additional articles are cited throughout the book): Esther Cohen, *The Crossroads of Justice: Law and Culture in Late Medieval France* (Leiden, 1993); Robert Muchembled, *Le Temps des supplices: de l'obéissance sous les rois absolus, XVe–XVIIIe siècle* (Paris, 1992); Nicole Gonthier, *Le Châtiment du crime au Moyen Age, XIIe–XVIe siècles* (Rennes, 1998); Michel Porret, *Le Crime et ses circonstances: de l'esprit de l'arbitraire au siècle des Lumières selon les réquisitoires des procureurs généraux de Genève* (Geneva, 1995); Claude Gauvard, *Crime, état, et société à la fin du Moyen Age. 'De grace especial'* (Paris, 1991); Pascal Bastien, *L'Exécution publique à Paris au XVIIIe siècle* (Seyssel, 2006); Richard van Dülmen, *Theatre of Horror: Crime and Punishment in Early Modern Germany*, trans. Elisabeth Neu (Cambridge, 1990), and Richard J. Evans, *Rituals of Retribution: Capital Punishment in Germany 1600–1987* (Oxford, 1996).
32. Michel Bée, "La Société traditionnelle et la mort," *XVIIe Siècle*, 106–7 (1975), 81–130; "Le Spectacle de l'exécution dans la France d'ancien régime," *Annales: Economies, Société, Civilisations*, 38 (1983), 843–62, and "Le Théâtre de l'échafaud à Caen, au xviiie siècle," in Jean-Pierre Bardet and Madeleine Foisil (eds.), *La Vie, la mort, la foi, le temps: mélanges offerts à Pierre Chaunu* (Paris, 1993), 259–72.
33. See Cohen, *Crossroads*, 77–84.
34. James A. Brundage, *Medieval Canon Law* (London, 1995), X.
35. J.-M Hurel, *Le Château de Falaise* (Falaise, 1880), 53–4.

CHAPTER 1

1. Montesquieu, *L'Esprit des lois* (Book 28, Chapter 4).
2. Ibid.
3. Friedrich Carl von Savigny, *Histoire du droit romain au moyen âge*, trans. Charles Guenoux (Paris, 1830), 1:134–7.

4. [Joseph] Ortolan, "Généralisation du droit romain," in *Explication historique des instituts de l'empereur Justinien* (Paris, 1870), 1:536.
5. See Katherine Fischer Drew, "Another Look at the Origins of the Middle Ages: A Reassessment of the Role of the Germanic Kingdoms," in *Speculum*, 62:4 (1987), 803.
6. Paul Viollet, *Histoire du droit civil français* (Paris, 1893), 149–50.
7. P. S. Barnwell, "Emperors, Jurists and Kings: Law and Custom in the Late Roman and Early Medieval West," *Past & Present*, 168 (2000), 9.
8. See Wendy Davies and Paul Fouracre (eds.), *The Settlement of Disputes in Early Medieval Europe* (Cambridge, 1986); Patrick J. Geary, "Extra-Judicial Means of Conflict Resolution," in *La giustizia nell'alto medioevo* (Spoleto, 1995), 1:569–605; and Warren C. Brown and Piotr Górecki (eds.), *Conflict in Medieval Europe: Changing Perspectives on Society and Culture* (Aldershot and Burlington, VT, 2003), 1–35.
9. See Jean Heuclin, "Identité et rôle du clergé à l'époque du Bréviaire d'Alaric," in Michel Rouche and Bruno Dumézil (eds.), *Le Bréviaire d'Alaric: Aux origines du Code civil* (Paris, 2008), 65, and Jean Gaudemet, *Le Bréviaire d'Alaric et les Epitome* (Mediolani, 1965), 9.
10. Gaudemet, *Bréviaire*, 20.
11. See Alan Watson, *The Evolution of Western Private Law* (Baltimore, MD, and London, 2000), 211, and Katherine Fischer Drew (trans.), *The Burgundian Code* (Philadelphia, PA, 1972), 6.
12. Ian Wood, "The Code in Merovingian Gaul," in Jill Harries and Ian Wood (eds.), *The Theodosian Code* (London, 1993), 166.
13. *The Theodosian Code and Novels and the Sirmondian Constitutions*, trans. Clyde Pharr (Princeton, NJ, 1952), 9-7-6.
14. Gaudemet, *Bréviaire*, 30.
15. Ibid, 29–30.
16. On capital punishment for attacks on the royal person in the Visigothic kingdom of the seventh century, see Geneviève Bührer-Thierry, "'Just Anger' or 'Vengeful Anger'? The Punishment of Blinding in the Early Medieval West," in Barbara H. Rosenwein (ed.), *Anger's Past: The Social Uses of an Emotion in the Middle Ages* (Ithaca, NY, 1998), 78–9. I thank Barbara Rosenwein for bringing this article to my attention.
17. See title LXXV of the *Pactus Legis Salicae*; titles LXLV and LXLVI of Capitulary III; and title LXIX of the *Lex Salica Karolina*, in Katherine Fischer Drew, *The Laws of the Salian Franks* (Philadelphia, PA, 1991), 135, 143, and 224.
18. See Elisabeth Magnou-Nortier, "Remarques sur la genèse du *Pactus Legis Salicae* et sur le privilège d'immunité (IVe–VIIe siècles)," in *Clovis: Histoire & mémoire*, vol. 1, *Clovis et son temps, l'événement* (Paris, 1997), 497–8.
19. Viollet, *Histoire du droit civil français*, 95. See also Paul Vinogradoff, who remarks in his classic text that Salic law is "based almost exclusively on Teutonic principles." Paul Vinogradoff, *Roman Law in Medieval Europe* (Cambridge and New York, 1968 [1929]).
20. See Barnwell, "Emperors, Jurists and Kings," especially 16–17 and 24–9.
21. See sections II though VIII of the *Pactus Legis Salicae* in Drew, *The Laws*, 65–73.
22. Ibid, Section XLI, 104–6.
23. Jean-Marie Carbasse, "La Peine en droit français," *La Peine*, 2 (1991), 157–8.
24. Harold J. Berman, *Law and Revolution: The Formation of the Western Legal Tradition* (Cambridge, MA, and London, 1983), 56.
25. Maurizio Lupoi, *The Origins of the European Legal Order*, trans. Adrian Belton (Cambridge, 2000), 291–2.

26. See "Lex Salica Karolina" in Drew, *The Laws*, 224–5.
27. In colonial New England, this retraction or taking back of comments was literally called "unsaying." See Jane Kamensky, *Governing the Tongue: The Politics of Speech in Early New England* (Oxford, 1999), 127–49. I thank Erik Seeman for this reference.
28. See Drew, "Another Look," 810–12, and Carbasse, "La Peine," 158–9.
29. Drew, *The Laws* (section XII), 77.
30. Ibid.
31. Ibid (section XL, no. 5, 102).
32. Ibid (Capitulary VI, section I, no. 2), 157 and (section II, no. 3), 158.
33. See the Burgundian code (section II, 23, and section xxxv, 46); the Ripurian code (section 38, 184); and the laws of the Lombards (section 1, 53; section 13, 55; and sections 211 and 212, 93).
34. "Capitulary of the Emperor Charlemagne (802.ad)," in *Select Historical Documents of the Middle Ages*, trans. and ed. by Ernest F. Henderson (London, 1905), 198–9.
35. Oscar D. Watkins, *A History of Penance* (London, 1920), 2:552.
36. Sozomen, *Historia Ecclesiastica*, quoted in Watkins, *History of Penance*, 1:424.
37. Cyrille Vogel, *Le Pécheur et la pénitence au moyen âge* (Paris, 1969), 17.
38. Caesarius of Arles, Sermon 261, quoted in Watkins, *History of Penance*, 2:553.
39. Ibid, 1:482–3.
40. Concile de Toledo, 589, quoted in Vogel, *Le Pécheur*, 15.
41. Concile de Chalon-sur-Saône, quoted in Ibid, 16.
42. Vogel, *Le Pécheur*, 19–20.
43. Quoted in Watkins, *History of Penance*, 2:702.
44. Council of Chalon-sur-Saône, 813, c.25, quoted in Vogel, *Le Pécheur*, 25.
45. Council of Paris, 829, c.32, quoted in Vogel, *Le Pécheur*, 25.
46. Ibid, 26–7. See Watkins, *History of Penance*, 710–11.
47. Mary C. Mansfield, *The Humiliation of Sinners: Public Penance in Thirteenth-Century France* (Ithaca, NY, 1995).
48. Anselm of Canterbury, "Why God became Man," in Brian Davies and G. R. Evans (eds.), *Anselm of Canterbury: The Major Works* (Oxford, 1998), 283.
49. Thomas P. Oakley, "The Cooperation of Mediaeval Penance and Secular Law," *Speculum*, 7:4 (1932), 518.
50. "Capitulary of 802," in *Select Historical Documents*, 199.
51. Ibid, 190.
52. Ibid, 197.
53. Capitulary of 823–5, cited in Carbasse, "La Peine," 159.
54. See Jean-Marie Carbasse, *Histoire du droit pénal et de la justice criminelle* (Paris, 2000), 94–111.
55. Esther Cohen, *The Crossroads of Justice: Law and Culture in Late Medieval France* (Leiden, 1993), 160. See also her article "Symbols of Culpability and the Universal Language of Justice: The Rituals of Public Executions in Late Medieval Europe," *History of European Ideas*, 11 (1989), 407–16.
56. Jean Gaudemet, "Le Droit romain dans la pratique et chez les docteurs," in Jean Gaudemet, *Eglise et société en Occident au Moyen Age* (London, 1984), section X:366.
57. See Anders Winroth, *The Making of Gratian's Decretum* (Cambridge, 2000), 162–74. Winroth also suggests that because Irnerius's influence has been exaggerated, the renaissance in Roman legal studies has been assumed to have taken place a generation earlier than it actually did.

58. See Charles M. Radding, *The Origins of Medieval Jurisprudence: Pavia and Bolognia, 850–1150* (New Haven, CT, and London, 1988), 8, and Peter Stein, *Roman Law in European History* (Cambridge, 1999), 40–1.
59. See, for example, Stephan Kuttner, "The Revival of Jurisprudence," in *Studies in the History of Medieval Canon Law* (Aldershot and Brookfield, VT, 1990), 3:303–5.
60. Radding, *Origins*, 10. See pages 7–10, 115, and 155–7 for Radding's discussions of Kantorowicz's and Kuttner's arguments.
61. Berman, *Law and Revolution*. For criticism of Berman's thesis, see Radding, *Origins*, 113–16 and 182.
62. See Stein, *Roman Law*, 45–54; Jean Gaudemet, "Bologne, capitale européenne du droit," *Archivio giuridico Filippo Serafini*, 199 (1980), 3–22; Carbasse, *Histoire du droit pénal*, 111–13, and Manlio Bellomo, *The Common Legal Past of Europe: 1000–1800*, trans. Lydia G. Cochrane (Washington, D.C., 1995), 58–65.
63. See "La Vie universitaire à Paris (XIIe–XIIIe s.)," in Jean Gaudemet, *Eglise et société en Occident au Moyen Age* (London, 1984), section IX:120.
64. Stein, *Roman Law*, 54–7 and 67–8. See also Gaudemet, "Le Droit romain," 371–2, Bellomo, *The Common Legal Past*, 82–3, Vinogradoff, *Roman Law*, 77–8, and Thomas Edward Scrutton, *The Influence of Roman Law on the Law of England* (Cambridge, 1885), 67–73.
65. Stein, *Roman Law*, 57.
66. See Winroth, *Making of Gratian's Decretum*. See also James Brundage, *Medieval Canon Law* (London and New York, 1995), 59.
67. Ibid, 59–61.
68. Abbé Metz, "La Responsabilité pénale dans le droit canonique médiéval," in *La Responsabilité pénale. Travaux du colloque de philosophie pénale (12 au 21 janvier 1959)* (Paris, 1961), 85.
69. Alan Watson, *Roman Law & Comparative Law* (Athens, GA, 1991), 182.
70. This subject is discussed in somewhat greater detail at the beginning of the following chapter with specific respect to the concepts of guilt, intentionality, and malice aforethought.
71. While this may have seemed obvious to the Romans, as it is to us in the twenty-first century, the heyday of animal trials in Europe occurred within a century or two of the renaissance of Roman legal studies, casting some doubt on the extent to which the indisputable conquest of Roman legal theory actually influenced penal practice. But, as I discuss in chapter 4, animal trials in Europe had very little to do with questions of intent.
72. *The Digest of Justinian*, trans. and ed. Alan Watson (Philadelphia, PA, 1985), 9, 1, 1, 5.
73. C, 9, 27, 1; quoted in Carbasse, *Histoire du droit pénal*, 65–6. Carbasse also cites a passage from the *Digest* which stipulates that those found guilty of highway robbery would suffer the punishment of the cross on the spot where their crime had been perpetrated so that "by this terrible spectacle, others will be dissuaded from [committing] similar acts" but also, interestingly, so that the relatives of the victims might be "consoled." (D.48, 19, 28, 15]).
74. See Richard M. Fraher, "Preventing Crime in the High Middle Ages: The Medieval Lawyers' Search for Deterrence," in James Ross Sweeney and Stanley Chodorow (eds.), *Popes, Teachers, and Canon Law in the Middle Ages* (Ithaca, NY, 1989), 214ff.; see also his article "The Theoretical Justification for the New Criminal Law of the High Middle Ages: 'Rei publicae interest, ne crimina remaneant impunita,'" *University of Illinois Law Review* (1984), 577–95.
75. Gerd Tellenbach, *Church, State and Christian Society at the Time of the Investiture Contest*, trans. R. F. Bennett (Toronto, 1991), 131.

76. See Brundage, *Medieval Canon Law*, 151.
77. Ibid. Aquinas, in the thirteenth century, might be seen as endeavoring to reconcile the medicinal conception of punishment with deterrence by suggesting that punishment was, at one and the same time, medicine for the individual as well as a "medicine for preventing sin" in society at large. (Quoted in James J. Megivern, *The Death Penalty: An Historical and Theological Survey* [New York and Mahwah, NJ, 1997], 113.)
78. Innocent III, quoted in Fraher, "Preventing Crime," 220. On Innocent III and heresy see chapter 2 (p. 52).
79. Fraher, "Theoretical Justification," *passim*, and Ken Pennington, "Innocent III and the Ius Commune," in Richard Helmholz et al. (eds.), *Grundlagen des Rechts: Festschrift für Peter Landau zum 65* (Paderborn, 2000), 349–66.
80. Durandus de St. Pourçain, quoted in Fraher, "Preventing Crime," 231.
81. Canon 18, "Fourth Lateran Council of 1215," in H. J. Schroeder, *Disciplinary Decrees of the General Councils: Text, Translation and Commentary*, (St. Louis, MO, 1937).
82. Canon 3, in Ibid.

CHAPTER 2

1. On customals in general and the transformation of custom into written law, see Esther Cohen, *The Crossroads of Justice: Law and Culture in Late Medieval France* (Leiden: E. J. Brill, 1993), 8–38; Paul Viollet, *Histoire du droit civil français* (Paris, 1893), 177ff.; Paul Vinogradoff, *Roman Law in Medieval Europe* (1929; reprint, Cambridge and New York, 1968), 78–94. On Norman customals, see Daniel Power, *The Norman Frontier in the Twelfth and Early Thirteenth Centuries* (Cambridge, 2004), 148–9; and Harold J. Berman, *Law and Revolution: The Formation of the Western Legal Tradition* (Cambridge, MA, and London, 1983), 460–3.
2. See *The Coutumes of France in the Library of Congress: An Annotated Bibliography*, eds. Jean Caswell and Ivan Sipkov (Washington, D.C., 1977), 61–4.
3. Philippe de Beaumanoir, *Coutumes de Beauvaisis*, ed. Am. Salmon (Paris, 1899), 1:4–5 (title 7).
4. Cohen, *Crossroads*, 9–10.
5. P. Petot, "Le Droit commun en France selon les coutumiers," *Revue historique de droit français et étranger*, 38 (1960), 414.
6. On the lack of distinction between intentional and accidental homicide in "Germanic" law, see Paul Viollet's comments in the introduction to *Les Etablissements de Saint Louis*, ed. Paul Viollet (Paris, 1881), 1:232–3.
7. *Peter Abelard's Ethics*, ed. and trans. D. E. Luscombe (Oxford, 1971), 41.
8. Virpi Makinen and Heikki Pihlajamaki, "The Individualization of Crime in Medieval Canon Law," *Journal of the History of Ideas*, 65:4 (2004), 532.
9. Stephan Kuttner, *Kanonistische Schuldlehre von Gratian bis auf die Dekretalen Gregors IX* (Vatican City, 1935).
10. Francis Bowes Sayre, *"Mens Rea,"* *Harvard Law Review*, 45:6 (1932), 974–1,026.
11. Guyora Binder, "The Rhetoric of Motive and Intent," *Buffalo Criminal Law Review*, 6:1, 13.
12. Jean Gaudemet, "Il diritto canonico nella storia della cultura giuridica europea," in *La Doctrine canonique médiévale* (Aldershot and Brookfield, VT, 1994), 6. See also Abbé Metz, "La responsabilité pénale dans le droit canonique médiéval," in *La Responsabilité pénale. Travaux du colloque de philosophie pénale* (Paris, 1961), 101.
13. *Le Conseil de Pierre de Fontaines*, ed. M. A. J. Marnier (Paris, 1846), 4.

14. Paul Viollet, *Histoire du droit civil français* (Paris, 1893), 179. See also Gaudemet, "L'Influence des droits savants (Romain et Canonique) sur les textes de droit coutumier en Occident avant le XVIe siècle," in *Actas del II congreso internaccional de derecho canonico....* (Pamplona, 1979), 169.
15. *Li Livres de Jostice et de Plet*, ed. L. Rapetti (Paris, 1850), 277 (chapter XXIV, article 2).
16. Ibid, 280 (chapter XXIV, article 34).
17. Beaumanoir, *Coutumes de Beauvaisis*, 1:433 (article 840).
18. Ibid, 1:430 (articles 826 and 828). A similar distinction can be found in *Livres de Jostice et de Plet*, 290, and in *Le Grand Coutumier de France* (Paris, 1868), 637. On the beginning of the differentiation between premeditated and unpremeditated murder (or murder and homicide), see Viollet, "Introduction," *Etablissements*, 1:236–9. On premeditation in English law, see Frederic William Maitland, "The Early History of Malice Aforethought," in *The Collected Papers of Frederic William Maitland*, ed. H. A. L. Fisher (Cambridge, 1911), 1:304–28.
19. Beaumanoir, *Coutumes de Beauvaisis*, 2:297 (tit. 1575). See also Beaumanoir's related comments on the punishment of animals, discussed in chapter 4 (pp. 112–13).
20. Ibid, 1:474 (article 935).
21. On the absence of punishment for mere criminal intent in customary law, see Viollet, "Introduction," *Etablissements*, 1:234–5; see also Carl Ludwig von Bar, *A History of Continental Criminal Law*, trans. Thomas S. Bell (Boston, MA, 1916), 156–7.
22. Beaumanoir, *Coutumes de Beauvaisis*, 1:434 (article 842). See also 1:446 (article 883) and 1:449–50 (article 887). For a discussion of the influence of Roman law on Beaumanoir, see Gaudemet, "L'Influence des droits savants," and P. van Wetter, "Le Droit romain et Beaumanoir," *Mélanges Fitting* (Montpellier, 1908), 2:533–82. See also Petot, "Le Droit commun en France selon les coutumiers," 418.
23. *Coutumes et institutions de l'Anjou et du Maine* (Paris, 1883), 4:308.
24. Codex 1, 3, quoted in Alexander Murray, *Suicide in the Middle Ages*, vol. 2: *The Curse of Self-Murder* (Oxford, 2000), 408.
25. Pierre de Belleperche, Quoted in Murray, *Suicide*, 410. On the subject of the punishment of mere intent in Roman and medieval jurisprudence, see pp. 397, 408–11.
26. See chapter 1 (p. 43).
27. See Walter Ullmann, "The Significance of Innocent III's Decretal "Vergentis," in *Etudes d'histoire du droit canonique dédiées à Gabriel Le Bras* (Paris, 1965), 1:729–41.
28. The concept had made a very brief appearance in the Capitularies of Charlemagne. See J. G. Bellamy, *The Law of Treason in England in the Later Middle Ages* (Cambridge, 2004), 3. See also S. H. Cuttler, *The Law of Treason and Treason Trials in Later Medieval France* (Cambridge, 1981), 8.
29. See Cuttler, *Law of Treason*, 10. On the mention of the concept of *lèse majesté* even earlier in English legal texts, such as in *Glanvill* (c.1188), see Bellamy, *Law of Treason*, 4 ff.
30. See *Ordonnances des roys de France de la troisième race...* (Paris, 1736), 5:479. On the legal history of *lèse-majesté* in France, see Cuttler, *Law of Treason*, 10–19.
31. Jean Boutillier, *Somme rural ou le grand coustumier général de practique civil et canon* (Paris, 1603 [c. 1385]), 170 (tit. xxviii). For a discussion of *lèse-majesté* in other customals, see von Bar, *History of Continental Criminal Law*, 163–4, and Cuttler, *Law of Treason*, 18–22.
32. Boutillier, *Somme rural*, 278–9 (title xxxix). As Murray rightly points out, this same logic would still be in force in the mid-eighteenth century, when Damiens would be

tried as a "regicide" for having attempted to kill Louis XV, but in fact barely scratching his skin with a knife (Murray, *Suicide*, 396–7).

33. Boutillier, *Somme rural*, 279.
34. See *Theodosian Code*, Book IX, title 14, no. 3, which similarly stipulates that the goods of traitors would be confiscated, that intent alone was punishable, and that the crime was "hereditary."
35. Boutillier, *Somme rural*, 280 (title 39). For other fourteenth- and fifteenth-century examples in which counterfeiting was seen as a crime of *lèse-majesté* and treason, see Hirsch, *The Law of Treason and Treason Trials*, 52. On the punishment of counterfeiters by boiling as early as 1311, see Félicien de Saulcy, *Recueil de documents relatifs à l'histoire des monnaies frappées par les rois de France depuis Philippe II jusqu'à François Ier* (Paris: 1879), 1:180. In Roman law, the *Digest* had treated counterfeiting as part of the Lex Cornelia on falsehoods, and lumped it together with a variety of crimes ranging from giving false witness to tampering with wax seals, etc., and it was only in the late fourth century that anyone suggested that crimes of counterfeiting could be considered a *crimen laesae majestatis*. (See *Digest*, book 48, chapter 10, titles 8 and 9; see also *Theodosian Code*, 9.21.1.)
36. Boutillier, *Somme rural*, 170 (title xxviii).
37. *Britton*, ed. and trans. Francis Morgan Nichols (Oxford, 1865), 1:40–1 (book I, chapter ix).
38. *Livres de Jostice et de Plet*, 290. This same text also includes corrupt lawyers, tavern keepers, and those who use false measures in the category of people who commit treason (p. 280).
39. Beaumanoir, *Coutumes de Beauvaisis*, 430 (chapter xxx, no. 826).
40. Quoted in R. W. Carlyle and A. J. Carlyle, *A History of Mediaeval Political Theory in the West* (Edinburgh and London, 1950), 3:26. (The translation is mine.) For a discussion of the mutually binding nature of the feudal relationship in Ibelin and other contemporary texts, see pp. 25–9 and 52–72.
41. Beaumanoir, *Coutumes de Beauvaisis*, 2:383 (title 1735).
42. Quoted in Reynolds, *Fiefs and Vassals* (Oxford, 1994), 22.
43. The criminalization of suicide might be seen as an example of how a crime against an individual came to be seen as a crime against that individual's lord. To kill oneself was not only a sin, it deprived one's lord of his subject, and attacked the unbreakable bond that united them. By definition, it was a crime of premeditation, and in the eyes of the thirteenth-century jurist Pierre de Belleperche, it was such a serious crime that suicidal intent alone, in the absence of the act, was a capital offense, no different from attempted murder: "Suppose someone has tried to kill himself, and other people come and prevent him. I say he should be hanged, because the law states that if anyone tries to kill someone else and is prevented, he should nevertheless undergo the penalty for homicide. The same should go for someone who tries to kill himself." (Pierre de Belleperche, quoted in Murray, *Suicide*, 413.) This logic would endure through the eighteenth century, with attempted suicides liable to be punished by death, and with actual suicides punished post-mortem. The eighteenth-century jurist François Serpillon declared the crime of suicide to be "a crime of divine lese-majesty." (Quoted in Julius R. Ruff, *Crime Justice, and Public Order in Old Regime France: The Sénéchaussées of Libourne and Bazas, 1696–1789* (London and Dover, NH, 1984), 70.
44. Nicole Gonthier, *Le Châtiment du crime au Moyen Age, XIIe–XVIe siècles* (Rennes, 1998), 112–13. See also A. Giry, *Histoire de la ville de Saint-Omer et de ses institutions jusqu'au XIVe siècle* (Paris, 1877), 213; and *Etablissements*, 2:416 (book II, chapter xxiv).

45. See Gonthier, *Le Châtiment*, 111–12.
46. Jean Carbasse, "'Curant nudi'. La répression de l'adultère dans le Midi médiéval (XIIe–XVe siècles)," in *Droit, histoire, et sexualité*, ed. Jacques Poumarède and Jean-Pierre Royer (Paris, 1987), 83ff.
47. *Ordonnances des roys de France de la troisième race*, ed. D.-F. Secousse (Paris, 1732), 3:130 (item 9).
48. See chapter 1 (p. 44).
49. For a discussion of the logic of banishment in the Middle Ages, see Daniel Lord Smail, *The Consumption of Justice: Emotions, Publicity, and Legal Culture in Marseille, 1264–1423* (Ithaca, NY, 2003), 169–76.
50. The logic of executions in effigy is discussed in chapter 4.
51. See, for example, the fine levied for lesser crimes in the Beauvaisis. As a general rule it was 5 sous; for most (but not all) gentlemen, however, the fine was 10 sous, unless one lived in certain exceptional villages, where the fine was either 12 deniers or somewhere between 7 sous and 6 deniers (Beaumanoir, *Coutumes de Beauvaisis*,1:442 and 446, titles 871 and 882).
52. Jean-Marie Carbasse, "La Peine en droit français," *La Peine*, 2 (1991), 169.
53. On the variation and inconsistency of punishments, see Gonthier, *Le Châtiment*, 170, and von Bar, *History of Continental Criminal Law*, 151–2.
54. *Le Très Ancien Coutumier de Normandie* in *Coutumiers de Normandie, ed.* Ernest-Joseph Tardif (Rouen and Paris, 1903), book 1, part 2, 27. On the inappropriateness of hanging women, see Cohen, *Crossroads*, 97–8. The fact that even a man who had killed his lord accidentally was subject to the aggravated punishment of drawing and hanging may show the extent to which a defense of authority trumped even the new juridical interest in intentionality.
55. Beaumanoir, *Coutumes de Beauvaisis*, 1:429 (title 824).
56. Ibid, 2:340–1 (title 1642).
57. Ibid, 2:342 (title 1646). See also title 1652.
58. "Cas et Esplois de justice fez a Noysi le Grant et ou terrour de Noisi," in *Registre criminel de la justice de St Martin des Champs à Paris au XIVe siècle*, ed. Louis Tanon (Paris, 1877), 226.
59. Beaumanoir, *Coutumes de Beauvaisis*, 1:431, title 833, chapter xxx. See also title 312.
60. Ibid, 1:431, title 834.
61. Robert Estienne, *Dictionarium Latinogallicum* (1552).
62. Bernardino of Siena, quoted in Robert Mills, *Suspended Animation: Pain, Pleasure and Punishment in Medieval Culture* (London, 2005), 83. Mills also suggests (p. 84) that the penalty of burning "seemed designed to hark back deliberately to the burning of the biblical Sodom and Gomorrah."
63. *Livres de Jostice et de Plet*, 279–80. There have been a variety of different translations of this passage in the secondary literature. Some have translated *membre* as penis, a translation that makes little sense with respect to female sodomites. Basing her comments on precisely such a mistranslation, one author has gone so far as to suggest that the excision of a female "member" speaks to contemporary misconceptions about female anatomy (Carolyn Dinshaw, *Getting Medieval* [Durham, NC, 1999], 91). I find it much more plausible that *membre* here means simply *limb* or any portion of the body such as a foot.
64. *Livres de Jostice et de Plet*, 280–2 (chapter xxiv).
65. The earliest mention of hanging on the *fourches* that I have come across is in 1258, when a thief in the vicomté of Rouvroy was displayed in the pillory and then led to

the "*fourkes de le ville et pendus.*" (See the letter reprinted in Ernest Prarond, *La Topographie historique et archéologique d'Abbeville* [Paris and Abbeville, 1884], 3:476.) Various sources suggest that the most famous *fourches*, those at Montfaucon in Paris, were constructed around the same time, circa 1270. Beaumanoir also makes mention of the *fourches,* and writes that anyone found guilty of removing a body on display from the *fourches* should himself be hanged (Beaumanoir, *Coutumes de Beauvaisis*, 1:484 [title 953]).

66. Giry, *Histoire de Saint-Omer*, 213, 389.
67. Charter of 1184 in E. Prarond, *Histoire d'Abbeville. Abbeville avant la guerre de cent ans* (Paris, 1891), 20. See also Beaumanoir, *Coutumes de Beauvaisis*, 1:441 (chapter xxx, title 868).
68. *Registre criminel du Châtelet de Paris, du 6 septembre 1389 au 18 Mai 1392* (Paris, 1861), 1:47.
69. Quoted in Daniel Jousse, *Traité de la justice criminelle de France* (Paris, 1771), 3:262.
70. Article 12, charter of Tournai, in M. Tailliar, *Recueil d'actes des XIIe et XIIIe siècles…* (Douai, 1849), 493. See also the Charter of Abbeville in *Histoire d'Abbeville*, 22.
71. *Etablissements*, art, xxxii, 2:48–9 This same text also states that whoever sets fire to a house at night loses his eyes—more serious, apparently, than stealing clothes, but not quite as serious as stealing a horse or mule. For another case calling for the offender's eyes to be put out, see the *Coutumes et institutions de l'Anjou & du Maine antérieures au XVIe siècle*, ed. C. J. Beautemps-Beaupré (Paris, 1878), 2:505, article 1379.
72. Court sentence, quoted in A. Dubois, *Justice et Bourreaux à Amiens dans les XVe et XVIe siècles* (Amiens, 1860), 8.
73. *Livres de Jostice et de Plet*, 282, art, 55.
74. Jacques Chiffoleau, *Les Justices du pape: Délinquance et criminalité dans la région d'Avignon au quatorzième siècle* (Paris, 1984), 235.
75. *Registre de St Martin des Champs*, 50–1.
76. See the *Coutumes d'Anjou et du Maine*, 2:492.
77. For executions involving the burying and burning of women, see *Registre de St Martin des Champs*, 220; *Registre du Châtelet*, 2:437; and *Coutumes et institutions de l'Anjou & du Maine*, 1:434 and 2:503–5. On beheading see Giry, *Histoire de la ville de Saint-Omer*, 218–19; Jean Roisin, *Franchises, lois et coutumes de la ville de Lille* (Lille and Paris, 1842), 118; and Gonthier, *Le Châtiment*, 151–6.
78. Boutillier, *Somme rural*, 278. The *Chronique* de Philippe de Vigneulles mentions several cases in which a wheel was used for punishment as early as 1364 (See Gonthier, *Le Châtiment*, 166–7). Although Salic law mentions the punishment of a wheel, it is unclear whether the device was the same as that used in the later Middle Ages.
79. *Somme rural*, 278–9 (title xxxix), and *Coutumes et institutions de l'Anjou & du Maine*, 2:502 (title xviii, article 1363). The penalty of quartering was apparently practiced earlier than this, although it is not entirely clear to what extent it was a legal sentence as opposed to the execution of more or less spontaneous vengeance. According to the *Chronique normande* as well as other chronicles of the period, Aimery de Pavie suffered a punishment at the hands of the English in 1355, in the town of Saint-Omer, that may very well have served as a precedent for the later punishments of Ravaillac and Damiens: "[He was] put on a scaffold before the people and with a burning iron poker both of his breasts were ripped off as well as several other parts [*membres*] of his body, and then his two thighs were cut off and his two arms and his head, and the parts were hung outside the city, and the head was put in the middle of the marketplace" (quoted in Gonthier, *Le Châtiment*, 157). In addition to this case, Gonthier

mentions several other fourteenth-century cases of quartering cited by various chronicles (see pp. 158–60).
80. *Grand Coutumier*, 637 (chapter viii).
81. Ibid, 638. D'Ableiges uses the word *gibet* as a plural of *fourche*, meaning that one or more wooden *fourches* sharing a stone pillar would comprise a *gibet*.
82. Ibid.
83. Ibid.
84. *Le Grât coustumier du pays et Côte du Maine* [1535], article lvi. This customal includes a remarkably extensive breakdown of the specific crimes that fell to the various categories of hierarchical justice, explicitly dividing crimes according to the extent of malice aforethought, or *guet-apens* (see article xliiii).
85. See Robert Muchembled, *Le Temps des supplices: de l'obéissance sous les rois absolus, XVe–XVIIIe siècle* (Paris, 1992), 74.
86. Jean-Marie Carbasse, *Histoire du droit pénal et de la justice criminelle* (Paris, 2000), 135.
87. Petot, "Le Droit commun en France selon les coutumiers," 412–29. In contrast to this conception of common law, based upon a perceived underlying unity inherent in customary law, others posited the existence of common law as something that existed where customary law and Roman law agreed. Both Boutillier's *Somme rurale* and D'Ableiges's *Grand Coutumier* speak of common law in this sense (p. 426).
88. Ibid, 412. On the gradual development of the idea of a common law in France, see also Berman, *Law and Revolution*, 470–3, and Cohen, *Crossroads of Justice*, 27–9.
89. See Muchembled, *Le Temps des supplices*, 103–4; and Carbasse, *Histoire du droit pénal*, 177–87.
90. See Bernard Schnapper, "Les Peines arbitraires du xiiie au xviiie siècle," *Tijdschrift voor rechtsgeschiedenis. Revue d'histoire du droit. The Legal History Review*, 42 (1974), 81–112.
91. Quoted in Ibid, 92.

CHAPTER 3

1. Apart from articles or short, often amateur, studies on executioners in specific localities, surprisingly few books have been devoted to the subject of executioners. They include the recent book by Hannele Klemettilä, *Epitomes of Evil: Representations of Executioners in Northern France and the Low Countries in the Late Middle Ages* (Turnhout, Belgium, 2006); the very competent and thorough popular history by Jacques Delarue, *Le Métier de bourreau: du Moyen Age à aujourd'hui* (Paris, 1979), and a fascinating and comprehensive genealogical study self-published by Michel and Danielle Demorest, "Les Bourreaux et leur parentèle." I would like to thank the Demorests for their generosity in sharing with me the fruits of their research. On executioners in Germany, see Kathy Stuart, *Defiled Trades and Social Outcasts: Honor and Ritual Pollution in Early Modern Germany* (Cambridge, 1996). Significant attention is also paid to executioners in Richard J. Evans, *Rituals of Retribution: Capital Punishment in Germany 1600–1987* (Oxford, 1996).
2. Michel Foucault, *Discipline and Punish: The Birth of the Prison*, trans. Alan Sheridan (New York, 1979), 49.
3. I am reminded of Tom Stoppard's play *Rosencrantz and Guildenstern are Dead*, which retells the story of Shakespeare's *Hamlet* from the vantage point of the bit

characters Rosencrantz and Guildenstern offering a radically different take on a very familiar story.
4. See Michel Porret, "Corps flétri—corps soigné: l'attouchement du bourreau au XVIIIe siècle," in *Le Corps violenté: du geste à la parole* (Geneva, 1998), 103–35.
5. Louis-Sébastien Mercier, *Tableau de Paris* (Amsterdam, 1782), 3:273 (chapter 279).
6. J. de Maistre, *Les Soirées de Saint-Petersbourg, ou Entretiens sur le gouvernement temporel de la providence* (Lyon, 1836), 1:39–41.
7. Delarue, *Le Métier*, 60. Stuart, *Defiled Trades*, 25–6. Pieter Spierenburg, *The Spectacle of Suffering: Executions and the Evolution of Repression: from a Preindustrial Metropolis to the European Experience* (Cambridge, 1984), 24–5.
8. Delarue, *Le Métier*, 62–3; Adolphe de Cardevacque, "Le Bourreau à Arras," *Mémoires de l'Académie des sciences, lettres et arts d'Arras*, 24, second series (1893), 167–8.
9. Pagart d'Hermansart, *Le Maitre des hautes œuvres ou bourreau à Saint-Omer* (Saint-Omer, 1892), 7; Delarue, *Le Métier*, 39; Demorest, "Les Bourreaux," 75, 299–300; A. Dubois, *Justice et bourreaux à Amiens dans les XVe et XVIe siècles* (Amiens, [1860]), 4; and Clémont-Janin, *Le Morimont de Dijon: Bourreaux & suppliciés* (Dijon, 1889), 9–10.
10. Stuart, *Defiled Trades*, 27,and Jacques Chiffoleau, *Les Justices du pape: Délinquance et criminalité dans la région d'Avignon au quatorzième siècle* (Paris, 1984), 67.
11. Delarue, *Le Métier*, 62–3; Demorest, "Les Bourreaux," 195–200.
12. Cardevacque, "Le Bourreau à Arras," 177.
13. Comments on the good character and religiosity of candidates for the position of executioner were usually included in their *lettres de provision*, many of which can be found at Archives nationales, V¹ 540.
14. Cardevacque, "Le Bourreau à Arras," 180–7.
15. This estimation of tenure is calculated on the basis of information derived from the biographies of executioners contained in Demorest, "Les Bourreaux."
16. Ibid, 174.
17. G. Lenotre, *La Guillotine et les exécuteurs des arrêts criminels pendant la révolution* (Paris, 1910), 8–9. Demorest, "Les Bourreaux," 95–114, 141–7.
18. See the letters of provision for the executioners of Bar le Duc and Mans; the latter confers the rights of succession on the sons of the named executioner, with the provision that, in the event of his death, his widow would hold onto the office—presumably enjoying its privileges while farming out the actual practice of it to someone else—until his sons had reached the age of majority (A.N. V¹ 540).
19. Demorest, "Les Bourreaux," 58. Delarue, *Le Métier*, 65.
20. See Stuart, *Defiled Trades*, 75–84, 92, 227; Delarue, *Le Métier*, 67–8, and Richard van Dülmen, *Theatre of Horror: Crime and Punishment in Early Modern Germany*, trans. Elisabeth Neu (Cambridge, 1990), 68.
21. Demorest, "Les Bourreaux."
22. This was the case, for example, in Toulouse in 1659, and in Bordeaux in 1674. See G. Brégail, *Les Bourreaux à Auch* (Auch, 1923), 6; Michel Bée, 'Le Bourreau et la société d'Ancien Régime," in *Justice et répression, de 1610 à nos jours. Actes du 107ᵉ Congrès national des sociétés savantes* (Paris, 1984), 1:64; and Delarue, *Le Métier*, 39.
23. André Lachance, *Le Bourreau au Canada sous le régime français* (Quebec, 1966), 61–2. According to Lachance, of the fourteen executioners in Quebec, ten were criminals (p. 53).
24. On the ostracism of actors, see Paul Friedland, *Political Actors: Representative Bodies and Theatricality in the Age of the Revolution* (Ithaca, NY, 2002), 1–7, 17–20.

25. On the definition of high justice, see chapter 2 (pp. 58, 63–5).
26. See, for example, the letters of provision of office for the executioners of Bar le Duc and Nancy, A.N. V¹ 540. See also Brégail, *Les Bourreaux à Auch*, 18–19, and Bée, "Le Bourreau et la société d'Ancien Régime," 62.
27. Clémont-Janin, *Le Morimont*, 13; Nicole Gonthier, "La Violence judiciare à Dijon à la fin du Moyen Age," *Mémoires de la Société pour l'Histoire du Droit et des institutions des anciens pays bourguignons, comtois et romands*, 50 (1993), 31; and Louis Grignon, *La Justice criminelle et le bourreau à Châlons et dans quelques villes voisines* (Châlons-sur-Marne, 1887), 82.
28. Municipal codes reprinted in E.-L. Lory, "Ordonnance concernant les droits qu'avait anciennement l'exécuteur de la haute justice de la ville de Dijon," in *Mémoires de la commission des antiquités du département de la Côte-d'Or* (1885–1888), 2:18–19. See also Clémont-Janin, *Le Morimont*, 3–4, 51–2. For similar provisions in Paris, see Delarue, *Le Métier*, 93.
29. See, for example, the letter of provision of the executioner of Bar le Duc, A.N. V¹ 540.
30. Grignon, *La Justice criminelle*, 98. See also T. Boutiot, *Histoire de la ville de Troyes et de la champagne méridionale* (Troyes and Paris, 1872), 2:285. In Amiens, the executioner was charged with the responsibility of making sure that prostitutes did not stray from defined areas of the city, as well as with the task of lining up lepers along the *grande rue* Saint-Denis on All Saints Day, for which he was paid 20 sous (Dubois, *Justice et bourreaux*, 10–11, 14). See also Cardevacque, "Le Bourreau à Arras," 171–2, and Jean Boca, *La Justice criminelle de l'échivinage d'Abbeville au moyen-âge, 1184–1516* (Lille, 1930), 46. For Germany, see Stuart, *Defiled Trades*, 27, 30; Evans, *Rituals of Retribution*, 56–64; and Lyndal Roper, *The Holy Household: Women and Morals in Reformation Augsburg* (Oxford and New York, 1989), 100.
31. Stuart, *Defiled Trades*, 30. Cardevacque, "Le Bourreau à Arras," 176.
32. Lory, "Ordonnance," 5, 21.
33. See "Les Comtes de Chartres de Chateaudun et de Blois aux IXe et Xe siècles," *Mémoires de la société archéologique d'Eure-et-Loir*, 12 (1895–1900), 202–3; see also Vicomte de Souancé and Charles Métais, *Archives du diocèse de Chartres. 1: Saint-Denis de Nogent-le-Rotrou (1031–1789). Histoire et cartulaire* (Vannes, 1899), 28. The article "exécuteur de la haute justice" in the *Encyclopédie* suggests that the concept of *havage* was descended from the king's *droit de prise*, the right according to which the king and members of his court could requisition necessary provisions from individuals who would theoretically be compensated at a later date (*Encyclopédie, ou dictionnaire raisonné des sciences, des arts et des métiers* [Berne and Lausanne, 1781], 13:481–2).
34. Brégail, *Les Bourreaux à Auch*, 17; [Ferrieres], *Dictionnaire de droit et de pratique...* (Paris, 1769), 671; *Dictionnaire universel françois et latin, vulgairement appelé Dictionnaire de Trévoux* (Paris, 1771), 4:745; and "Havage" in the *Encyclopédie*.
35. Geneviève Aclocque, *Les Corporations, l'industrie, et le commerce à Chartres du XIe siècle à la Révolution* (1917; reprint New York, 1967), 255–6.
36. Ordonnance [1452–3] in Lory, "Ordonnance," 19.
37. Ibid, 20.
38. Ibid.
39. See "Exécuteur de la haute justice" in the *Encyclopédie*, 13:482; Bée, "Le Bourreau et la société," 69, and Brégail, *Les Bourreaux à Auch*,18. Although I have not come across ordinances mandating the use of a spoon, many of the letters of provision of office do refer to a "spoonful" of a particular foodstuff in their detailing of the specific rights of *havage*.

40. See Chiffoleau, *Les Justices du pape*, 244–5, on various prohibitions in Avignon applied to Jews, lepers, and prostitutes on the touching of foods: fruits, bread, meat, and fish on display in the marketplace.
41. On the derogatory nature of half colors, see Ruth Mellinkoff, *Outcasts: Signs of Otherness in Northern European Art of the Late Middle Ages* (Berkeley, CA, 1993). See also Klemettilä, *Epitomes of Evil*.
42. Cardevacque, "Le Bourreau à Arras," 193; Dubois, *Justice et Bourreaux*, 17–31; Lory, "Ordonnance," 19. On robes and insignias in other areas see D'Hermansart, *Le Maitre*, 23; Delarue, *Le Métier*, 45–6; and Emile Desplanque, *Les Infâmes dans l'ancien droit roussillonnais* (Perpignan, 1893), 78–80. In Germany, see van Dülmen, *Theatre of Horror*, 68, and Stuart, *Defiled Trades*, 29.
43. Clément-Janin, *Le Morimont*, 52. Emphasis added.
44. Lory, "Ordonnance," 8.
45. See Bronislaw Geremek, *Margins of Society in Late Medieval Paris*, trans. Jean Birrell (Cambridge, 2006), and Dubois, *Justice et Bourreaux*; Stuart, *Defiled Trades*; Roper, *Holy Household*, and Peter Richards, *The Medieval Leper and his Northern Heirs* (Cambridge, 1977).
46. Stuart, *Defiled Trades*, 29. For an extended discussion of the executioner's costume in both France and the Netherlands, see the chapter entitled "The Hangman's Outfit" in Klemettilä, *Epitomes of Evil*, 109–57.
47. See [Anne Marguerite Petit du Noyer], *Lettres historiques et galantes de deux dames de condition, dont l'une étoit à Paris, & l'autre en Province* (Cologne, 1733), 291–4, and Lenotre, *La Guillotine*, 323–4. In an eighteenth-century twist on the story, a prostitute is horrified to discover that her prospective client is the executioner of Paris, and a spat of mutual recriminations about "ignominious professions" ensues. (Siméon-Prosper Hardy quoted in Pascal Bastien, "Fête populaire ou cérémonial d'Etat? Le rituel de l'exécution publique selon deux bourgeois de Paris (1718–1789)," in *French Historical Studies*, 24:3 (2001), p. 523).
48. Joseph Marie Lequinio, denounced as a *terroriste*, was accused of "having habitually eaten with the hangman" (Lenotre, *La Guillotine*, 62–3). Joseph-Antoine Lebon was similarly accused, in the course of his trial in 1795, of having "habitually" dined with the executioner. Lebon claimed, however, that the latter "came without being invited, and sat himself at the table... despite the repugnance that many felt..." (Ibid, 86).
49. See Cardevacque, "Le Bourreau à Arras," 176, 183–5; *Arrêt de la cour de parlement portant règlement pour l'habitation de l'exécuteur des hautes œuvres* ([Paris], [1709]); see also D'Hermansart, *Le Maitre*, 25; Brégail, *Les Bourreaux à Auch*, 67; Chiffoleau, *Les Justices du pape*, 67; and Lachance, *Le Bourreau au Canada*, 54–5 and 95–6.
50. Cited in Desplanque, *Les Infâmes*, 78.
51. Cardevacque, "Le Bourreau à Arras," 184–5; Lory, "Ordonnance," 9; Bée, "Le Bourreau et la société," 69; and Lenotre, *La Guillotine*, 322–3.
52. See *Mémoire à consulter et consultation pour François-Thomas & Charles Ferey, Exécuteurs des Arrêts, Jugements & Sentences criminelles de Rouen, tant pour eux que pour leurs familles* (Rouen, 1781).
53. Quoted in Grignon, *La Justice criminelle*, 82.
54. Lory, "Ordonnance," 9.
55. On the complexity of municipal, seigneurial, and royal jurisdictions in the fifteenth and sixteenth centuries, see David Potter, "'Rigueur de Justice': Crime, Murder and the Law in Picardy, Fifteenth to Sixteenth Centuries," *French History*, 11:3 (1997), 265–72.

56. Grignon, *La Justice criminelle*, 97–8.
57. Ibid, 98.
58. Ibid, 99–100.
59. Quoted in D'Hermansart, *Le Maitre*, 20.
60. Lory, "Ordonnance," 10. See also H. Forestier, "Le Bourreau à Auxerre et à Sens au XVIIIe siècle," *Annales de Bourgogne; revue historique* 13 (1941), 40.
61. Pierre Lefranc, "Les Exécuteurs des sentences criminelles à Poitiers au xviiie siècle," *Bulletin de la Société des Antiquaires de l'Ouest et des Musées de Poitiers* (1962), 4th series, vol. 6, 344.
62. In seventeenth- and eighteenth-century letters of provision detailing the rights of *havage*, one does not find the same broad exemptions for locals that could be found in earlier times. For references to double levies on execution days, see the letters of provision for Chinon and Nevers, A.N. V¹ 540. See also Delarue, *Le Métier*, 93–6 for references to double levies as well as levies from surrounding localities.
63. The executioner of Nevers, for example, in addition to an impressive variety of foodstuffs, was also allowed to take his due in glasses, bottles, and pottery, and the executioner of Rouen was entitled to his share of cider, A.N. V¹ 540.
64. *Extrait des régistres du conseil d'état* ([Lille], [1758]), 2–3; A.N. BB³⁰ 176; and Delarue, *Le Métier*, 81–2. Payments for individual executions existed throughout the medieval and early modern periods, alongside rights of *havage*. Executioner's bills for services rendered to the city of Dijon in the seventeenth and eighteenth centuries can be found in the Archives Départementales de la Côte-d'Or, C 397, C 2207, C2273. Additional receipts as well as receipts from earlier periods can be found at the Archives communales de Dijon, C43, C44, and C44bis. For other towns see D'Hermansart, *Le Maitre*, 21, 27–8; Brégail, *Les Bourreaux à Auch*, 16–17; Desplanque, *Les Infâmes*, 76–7; Cardevacque, "Le Bourreau à Arras," 167–70, 172.
65. Pierre Lefranc, "Exécuteurs à Poitiers," 334–5.
66. Some of these letters are discussed in this chapter, below, as well as in chapter 10.
67. Michel Bée, "Vivre du métier du bourreau en Normandie au XVIIIe siècle," *Cahiers Léopold Delisle* 32 (1982–83), 101. See also Lefranc, "Exécuteurs à Poitiers," 344; and Clément-Janin, *Le Morimont*, 108–9.
68. Lory, "Ordonnance," 11–16.
69. Archives municipales de Chalon-sur-Saône, CC 122. On Paris see "Mémoire instructif pour l'exécuteur des jugements criminels de la ville de Paris," in Lenotre, *La Guillotine*, 136. The executioner of Paris would continue to collect *havage* in the communities outside the walls of Paris until 1767 (Delarue, *Le Métier*, 97; see also 94–5).
70. Lefranc, "Exécuteurs à Poitiers," 345.
71. *Arrest du conseil d'état du Roi, qui suspend la perception des droits d'Octrois des villes sur les Grains, Farines & Pain: Et qui défend aux Exécuteurs de la Haute Justice, d'exiger aucunes rétributions, soit en nature, soit en argent, sur les Grains & Farines, dans tous les lieux où elles ont été en usage jusqu'à présent. Du 3 Juin 1775* (Lille, [1775]), 3.
72. One can, however, find a letter of provision bestowing the right of *havage* as late as 1790. See the letter of provision of the executioner of Nancy in 1790, A.N. V¹ 540.
73. "Tableau des exécuteurs existans dans le Royaume," A.N. BB³ 206.
74. Letter of Joly de Fleury dated 12 January 1783, quoted in Grignon, *La Justice criminelle*, 104.
75. Ibid, 104–5.

76. Letter from D'Agay, intendant of Picardie, to M. Duflos, subdelegate of Calais (30 June 1775), A.N. BB³ 206.
77. Letter from Pierre Joseph Outredebanque to Duport, A.N. BB³ 206.
78. Michel Benoist to Minister of Justice Duport, 4 October 1791, 21 January 1792, and 10 November 1792, A.N. BB³ 206.
79. Letter from Chesdeville to the Administrators of the Department of the Côte D'Or (28 February 1791), A.D. Côte D'Or, L 1783.
80. Letter from Pierre André Louis Desmorest to Duport (29 October 1791), A.N. BB³ 206.
81. Letters from Nicolas Charles Gabriel Sanson to Duport and to the Members of the Committee of Legislation, A.N. BB³ 206.
82. See the Epilogue for a discussion of the effect of the guillotine on the profession of the executioner.

CHAPTER 4

1. "Loi ou Constitution portant que les condamnés pourront être confessés avant l'exécution," Paris, 12 February 1396," in Isambert et al., ed., *Recueil général des anciennes lois françaises* (Paris, 1824), 6:776.
2. Daniel Jousse, *Traité de la justice criminelle de France* (Paris, 1771), 2: 476–7.
3. See Richard Mowery Andrews, *Law, Magistracy, and Crime in Old Regime Paris, 1735–1789* (Cambridge, 1994), 311. On fines, alms, and other sentences see Jousse, *Traité*, 1:36–7.
4. Andrews, *Law, Magistracy, and Crime*, 311 and 314.
5. For an extensive discussion of the ritual of the readings of the sentence and the involvement of the officers of the court, see Pascal Bastien, *L'Exécution publique à Paris au XVIIIe siècle* (Seyssel, 2006), 114–18, 133–6; see also Robert Anchel, *Crimes et châtiments au XVIIIe siècle* (Paris, 1933), 143–9.
6. Archives nationales, X^{2b} 1334.
7. On the *question préalable*, see Jousse, *Traité*, 2:48, and Andrews, *Law, Magistracy, and Crime*, 467–72.
8. A.N. AD III, 10. See also an account from 1681 in which the condemned fainted at the moment the executioner seized him (*Archives de la Bastille*, ed. François Ravaisson [Paris, 1874], 7:23).
9. *Conduite admirable de Dieu, sur l'Eglise de Sens, dans les moyens miraculeux qu'il a employez pour parvenir à la juste punition de deux Scelerats qui ont volé les Vases sacrez & profané le Corps adorable de Jésus-Christ...* [1737] (contained in A.N. AD III, 6).
10. While it seems fairly clear what the public reading consisted of, the executioner's cry remains something of a mystery. Anchel suggests that his cry "announced to the people the reading of the judgment when the drummers and trumpeters had amassed a crowd" (Anchel, *Crimes*, 149), but it would seem that in most cases, as in the case of Bernard, the executioner's cry came after the public reading rather than before it. The *procès-verbal* of an execution in 1682 states that the judgment was read and then "proclamé par l'exécuteur au peuple assemblée," which seems to suggest that the judgment was either repeated or affirmed somehow by the executioner (see "Procès-verbal d'exécution de Maillard," in *Archives de la Bastille*, 7:88–9).
11. See chapter 2, (pp. 60–2).
12. Nicole Gonthier, *Le Châtiment du crime au Moyen Age, XIIe–XVIe siècles* (Rennes, 1998), 124.

13. For specific sentences and placards, see A.N. AD III, 16. For general information on pillories, placards, and paper hats see Jousse, *Traité*, 1:60–1; Bastien, *Exécution publique*, 111–12; Robert Muchembled, *Le Temps des supplices: de l'obéissance sous les rois absolus, XVe–XVIIIe siècle* (Paris, 1992), 49; and Gonthier, *Le Châtiment*, 122–5.
14. On these and other similar punishments, see chapter 2 as well as Gonthier, *Le Châtiment*, 129; Bastien, *Exécution publique*, 111; and Anchel, *Crimes*, 117–18. See also the very interesting article by Antonella Bettoni, "Fama, Shame Punishment and the Administration of Justice (16th and 17th centuries)," *Forum Historiae Iuris, Erste europäische Internetzeitschrift für Rechtsgeschichte* (http://www.forhistiur.de), 24 March 2010.
15. See Jousse, *Traité*, 1:63–5, and Jean Imbert, *La Practique judiciaire civile et criminelle...* (Paris, 1627), 687ff.
16. Jousse, *Traité*, 4:666.
17. See the discussion of public penance in chapter 1, (pp. 33–8).
18. Jean-Marie Moeglin, "Pénitence publique et amende honorable au Moyen Age," *Revue Historique* 604 (1997), 225–69. See, in particular, pp. 239–40. Rather than focusing on the amende honorable performed by condemned criminals, Moeglin's article focuses exclusively on public acts of contrition performed in lieu of punishment.
19. See chapter 1, (p. 36).
20. On aggravated penalties for those who refused to play their part, see Jousse, *Traité*, 2:540.
21. Ibid, 1:37.
22. See Cyrille Vogel, *Le Pécheur et la pénitence au moyen âge* (Paris, 1969), 208–13.
23. Esther Cohen, *The Crossroads of Justice: Law and Culture in Late Medieval France* (Leiden, 1993), 80.
24. *Loi Salique ou Recueil contenant les anciennes rédactions de cette loi...*, ed. J. M. Pardessus (Paris, 1843), Title LVIII, 32.
25. Gonthier, *Le Châtiment*, 134–40. On banishment, see also Muchembled, *Le Temps*, 36, 39, 48, 50–1, 67, and Jacques Chiffoleau, *Les Justices du pape: Délinquance et criminalité dans la région d'Avignon au quatorzième siècle* (Paris, 1984), 232–4.
26. On the practice of mutilation and branding, see Jousse, *Traité*, 1:55–8; Cohen, *Crossroads*, 166–8; Gonthier, *Le Châtiment*, 140–6; and Muchembled, *Le Temps*, 48–50.
27. "Déclaration concernant la punition des voleurs" (4 March 1724) in Isambert, *Recueil*, 21:260–1. In cases of domestic theft, however, even first-time offenders were subject to a mandatory death penalty.
28. Esther Cohen, "To Die a Criminal for the Public Good," in Bernard S. Bachrach and David Nicholas, eds., *Law, Custom, and the Social Fabric in Medieval Europe: Essays in Honor of Bryce Lyon. Studies in Medieval Culture, XXVIII* (Kalamazoo, 1990), 295, 296, 298. See also Cohen, *Crossroads*, 197–201.
29. It is interesting to note that in the papal state of Avignon the local executioner apparently played the role of Christ's executioner in local Passion plays. See Chiffoleau, *Les Justices*, 239.
30. A.N. AD III, 6 (1736).
31. See Muchembled, *Le Temps*, 115; Esther Cohen, "Symbols of Culpability and the Universal Language of Justice: the Ritual of Public Execution in Late Medieval Europe," *History of European Ideas*, 11 (1989), 410; Cohen, *Crossroads*, 184–5; Chiffoleau, *Les Justices*, 239–40. For a discussion of the route taken in Florence, see Samuel Y. Edgerton, Jr., *Pictures and Punishment: Art and Criminal Prosecution during the Florentine Renaissance* (Ithaca, NY, 1985), 141–2.

32. *Journal d'un bourgeois de Paris sous le règne de François Premier (1515–1536)*, ed. Ludovic Lalanne (Paris, 1854), 306–7. Much like the Filles-Dieu, the Quinze-Vingts also apparently performed the service of offering bread and wine to condemned criminals on their way to execution near the rue Saint-Honoré in the sixteenth century. See Robert Hénard, *La Rue Saint Honoré: des origines à la Révolution* (Paris, 1908), 130. In Evreux, the brothers of charity similarly dispensed bread and wine to condemned criminals on their way to the scaffold. See Michel Bée, "La Société traditionnelle et la mort," *XVIIe Siècle*, 106–7 (1975), 100–1.
33. For a discussion of the various interconnections between rituals of criminal justice and Christ's Passion, and in particular the relationship between medieval paintings of the Crucifixion and contemporary criminal justice rituals, see Mitchell B. Merback, *The Thief, the Cross, and the Wheel* (Chicago, IL, 1999). See also Muchembled, *Le Temps*, 117–19.
34. *Conduite admirable de Dieu* (contained in A.N. AD III, 6).
35. *Relation de la conversion, et de la mort édifiante d'une jeune Fille complice d'un Assassinat, executée à Paris au mois de Janvier 1737* (contained in A.N. AD III, 6).
36. Bée, "Société traditionnelle et la mort," 94. Other articles in which Bée makes similar arguments include "Le Spectacle de L'exécution dans la France d'ancien régime," *Annales: Economies, Société, Civilisations*, 38 (1983), 843–62, and "Le Théâtre de l'échafaud à Caen, au xviiie siècle," in Jean-Pierre Bardet and Madeleine Foisil (eds.), *La Vie, la mort, la foi, le temps: mélanges offerts à Pierre Chaunu* (Paris, 1993), 259–72.
37. *Recueil de journaux caennais*, cited in Bée, "La Société traditionnelle et la mort," 98. As Pascal Bastien has rightly pointed out, this account, first cited by Bée in 1975, has been cited several times in subsequent years in the secondary literature, and has been made to bear perhaps too much of a conceptual burden for those looking to find evidence for the religiosity of executions in the eighteenth century. Bastien cites Julius R. Ruff, *Violence in Early Modern Europe, 1500–1800* (Cambridge, 2001), 104, as well as my own article, "Beyond Deterrence: Cadavers, Effigies, Animals and the Logic of Executions in Premodern France," *Historical Reflections/Réflexions historiques*, 29 (2003), 307. The story is also cited in Giancarlo Baronti, *La morte in piazza, opacità della giustizia, ambiguità del boia e trasparenza del patibolo in età moderna* (Lecce, 2000), 243.
38. Bastien, *Exécution publique*, 96, 143, 189–90.
39. The rise of this kind of spectatorship is explored in the following chapters.
40. In the first decade of the eighteenth century, for example, the municipal authorities in the town of Mont-Saint-Vincent were convinced that in order to "establish public tranquility and to give terror to these criminals and their accomplices it is necessary to have the executions performed in the area [the crime took place] or at least to erect their cadavers on the grand chemin leading to Mont-Saint-Vincent" (A.D. Saône-et-Loire, B691).
41. On the singing of the *Salve Regina* as a matter of rote form, see the eighteenth-century accounts by the court *greffier* in which the singing of the *Salve* is mentioned at the end of each report as follows: "getting up on the ladder [to be hanged] the *salve* sung, the said death sentence was ex[ecuted] fully…" [A.N. X^{2b} 1334]. For more moving and spiritual examples of executions in the eighteenth century, involving singing and prayers, see Pierre Barthès' accounts cited in Robert Schneider, *The Ceremonial City: Toulouse Observed 1738–1780* (Princeton, NJ, 1995), 93–5, and Siméon-Prosper Hardy's account of the execution of an English spy in Brest (2 December 1769), in which "the people…melted into tears," in Siméon-Prosper Hardy, *Mes Loisirs, ou Journal*

d'événemens tels qu'ils parviennent à ma connoissance (1753–1789), eds. Daniel Roche and Pascal Bastien (Quebec, 2008), 1:546 (2 December 1769).

42. Louis Guibert, *Les Confréries de pénitents en France et notamment dans le diocèse de Limoges*, in *Bulletin de la Société archéologique et historique du Limousin*, 27 (1879), 5–193; see especially pages 34, 40, and 126–34; Toussaint Gautier, *Dictionnaire des confréries et corporations d'arts et métiers* (Migne, 1854), 415; and Emile Desplanques, *Les Infâmes dans l'ancien droit rousillonnais* (Perpignan, 1893), 87–8. On the Italian confraternity of Saint John the Beheaded and of Santa Maria della Croce al Tempio, which assisted at executions, see Edgerton, *Pictures and Punishment*, 139–46, 178–98.

43. A.D. de la Haute Vienne, G 731.

44. For occasions when crowds turned against executioners after an execution had been botched, see Desplanques, *Les Infâmes*, 26 and 88–9; A.D. de la Côte d'Or C2203; Michel Bée, "Le Bourreau et la société d'Ancien Régime," in *Justice et répression, de 1610 à nos jours. Actes du 107ᵉ Congrès national des sociétés savantes* (Paris, 1984), 1:72; A. Dubois, *Justice et Bourreaux à Amiens dans les XVe et XVIe siècles* (Amiens, 1860), 25; G. Lenotre, *La Guillotine et les exécuteurs des arrêts criminels pendant la révolution* (Paris, 1932), 315–16; François Lebrun, *Les Hommes et la mort en Anjou aux 17e et 18e siècles* (Flammarion, 1975), 421; Schneider, *Ceremonial City*, 92–3; T. Boutiot, *Histoire de la ville de Troyes et de la Champagne méridionale* (Troyes and Paris, 1873), 3:448 and 492; and Jacques Delarue, *Le Métier de bourreau, du moyen âge à aujourd'hui* (Paris, 1989), 43. For examples outside of France see Pieter Spierenburg, *The Spectacle of Suffering: Executions and the Evolution of Repression: From a Preindustrial Metropolis to the European Experience* (Cambridge, 1984), 13–15 and 33–4; Richard van Dülmen, *Theatre of Horror: Crime and Punishment in Early Modern Germany*, trans. Elisabeth Neu (Cambridge, 1990), 69, 112–18. On the outcast status of actors see Paul Friedland, *Political Actors: Representative Bodies and Theatricality in the Age of the French Revolution* (Ithaca, NY, 2002), 1–7, 17–19.

45. The earliest uses of effigies that I have come across are two cases from Noisy-le-Grand, which was within the jurisdiction of St. Martin, in Paris. In the first case, a female counterfeiter who had already been executed in the royal jurisdiction of Paris, was executed again in effigy within the ecclesiastical jurisdiction of St. Martin des Champs in Paris. The effigy was boiled, the usual penalty for counterfeiters. In the second case, a horse that had already left the jurisdiction was drawn and hanged in effigy for killing a man. Although neither of these cases can be definitively dated, the editors of the collection date them to the first part of the fourteenth century, and their use of the word *figure* rather than *effigie* would seem to suggest that the terminology had not yet been established. See *Registre criminel de la justice de St Martin des Champs à Paris au XIVe siècle*, ed. Louis Tanon (Paris, 1877), 226–8. On the dating of these documents, see pp. cxxx–cxxxi.

46. See the receipt for 20 sols as payment for two effigies cited in Dubois, *Justice*, 9.

47. Boucher d'Argis, "Effigie," in *Encyclopédie, ou dictionnaire raisonné des sciences, des arts et des métiers* (Paris, 1755), 5:407.

48. "Remarques de Jacques le Marchant," in *Bulletin de la Société des Antiquaires de Normandie*, 26 (1908), 48.

49. See, for example, *Arrest de la chambre royale de l'arsenal, Qui condamne Guillaume Valette dit Falgous, Guillaume Broca, & George André Favre, à estre pendus en Place de Grève…* [1736].

50. Michel Porret, *Le Crime et ses circonstances: de l'esprit de l'arbitraire au siècle des Lumières selon les réquisitoires des procureurs généraux de Genève* (Geneva, 1995), 402–3.

51. Arlette Lebigre, *La Justice du roi: la vie judiciare dans l'ancienne France* (Paris, 1988), 135–6. See also the execution of a fully clothed effigy in fifteenth-century Caen, cited in S. H. Cuttler, *The Law of Treason and Treason Trials in Later Medieval France* (Cambridge, 1981), 119; and the execution in the form of a mannequin with a mask of a Greek man condemned for killing a church canon in 1554, in *Félix et Thomas Platter à Montpellier, 1552–1559, 1595–1599. Notes de voyage de deux étudiants Balois publiées d'après les manuscrits originaux appartenant à la bibliothèque de l'université de Bâle* (Montpellier, 1892), 85–6.
52. Cited in Henri Bruno Bastard-D'Estang, *Les Parlements de France* (Paris, 1858), 429.
53. Title XVII, Article 16, in Isambert et al., *Recueil général des anciennes lois françaises* (Paris, 1829), 18:408. See also Jousse, *Traité*, 2:439–40.
54. Julius R. Ruff, *Crime, Justice and Public Order in Old Regime France* (London, 1984), 61.
55. Benoît Garnot, *Justice en France aux XVIe, XVIIe, et XVIIIe siècles* (Paris, 2000), 178.
56. Michel Porret, "Mourir sur l'échafaud à Genève au XVIIIe siècle," *Déviance et société*, 15:4 (1991), 399.
57. See Lebigre, *La Justice du roi*, 136.
58. *Mémoires de Fléchier sur les grands-jours d'Auvergne en 1665* (Paris, 1856), 258–9.
59. On the legal theory behind the criminalization of suicide, see supra p. 292 n. 43.
60. For different interpretations, see Carl Ludwig von Bar, *A History of Continental Criminal Law*, trans. Thomas S. Bell (Boston, MA, 1916), 187, and Gonthier, *Le Châtiment*, 131–4.
61. Cited in Muchembled, *Le Temps*, 50.
62. See, for example, Léon Ménabréa, *De l'Origine, de la forme et de l'esprit des jugements rendus contre les animaux* (Chambéry, 1846), 126, who cites an *arrêt* by the parlement of Paris in 1601, which ordered that the records of a case of bestiality be burned together with the body of the patient. In this case, because the ruling was issued by such a high court, the arrêt itself survived. See also E. P. Evans, *The Criminal Prosecution and Capital Punishment of Animals* (1906; reprinted London and Boston, MA, 1987), 150.
63. Quoted in Dubois, *Justice*, 12–13.
64. Excerpted in Evans, *Criminal Prosecution*, 296–7.
65. On the punishment of animals, in addition to Evans's classic text and Ménabréa's *De l'Origine*, cited above, see the many texts cited in the Introduction.
66. See Evans, *Criminal Prosecution*, 153–4. The full sentence is reproduced on pp. 298–303. For a related case, see pp. 144–5.
67. See, for example, *Registre criminel de la justice de St Martin des Champs*, 227–8.
68. See chapter 2 (p. 57).
69. I suspect we can see the same redressing of an "atrocity" in many of the cases that Cohen mentions in which Jews were hanged upside down. See Cohen, *Crossroads*, 113 and 116–18 for a discussion of executions involving disparities in hierarchy.
70. Philippe de Beaumanoir, *Coutumes de Beauvaisis*, ed. Amédée Salmon (Paris, 1899), title 1944, 2:481. See the excellent discussion of this passage in von Bar, *A History*, 154–5.
71. See Menabrea, *De l'Origine*, 122–7, and Evans, *Criminal Prosecution of Animals*, 108–9.
72. See Donald R. Kelley, *Foundations of Modern Historical Scholarship: Language, Law, and History in the French Renaissance* (New York and London, 1970), 53–85, and Julian H. Franklin, *Jean Bodin and the Sixteenth-Century Revolution in the Methodology of Law and History* (New York, 1963), 18–26.

73. Hotman, quoted in Franklin, *Jean Bodin*, 47, 49.
74. Baudouin, quoted in Ibid, 45.
75. Jean Duret, *Traicté des peines et amendes...* (Lyon, 1610), 37. On Duret's admiration for Budé and Hotman, see Kelley, *Foundations*, 213.
76. Jean Bodin, *La Méthode de l'histoire*, trans. Pierre Mesnard (Paris and Algiers, 1941), xxxii.
77. Pierre Ayrault, *Ordre et instruction judiciaire* (Paris, 1881), 9. The full title of the 1576 edition was, tellingly enough, *De l'ordre et instruction judiciaire, dont les anciens Grecs et Romains ont usé en accusations publiques. Conféré à l'usage de nostre France.*
78. "Des procès faits aux cadavres, à la mémoire, aux bestes brutes, choses inanimées et aux contumax" [1591], in Ibid, 275.
79. Ibid, 277–8.
80. Ibid, 289–90.
81. Ibid, 279, emphasis added.
82. Ibid, 286.

CHAPTER 5

1. Jean de Troyes], "Les Chroniques du très chrestien et très victorieux Louys de Valois...," in *Collection complète des mémoires relatifs à l'histoire de France...*, ed. M. Petitot (Paris, 1826), 14:25.
2. See Esther Cohen, *The Crossroads of Justice: Law and Culture in Late Medieval France* (Leiden, 1993), 182.
3. Claude Gauvard, *Crime, état, et société à la fin du Moyen Age. "De grace especial"* (Paris, 1991), 2:902.
4. *Journal d'un bourgeois de Paris de 1405 à 1449*, ed. Colette Beaune (Paris, 1990), 60.
5. Ibid, 240–2 and 272. See also the description of the execution of Joan of Arc, whose exploits and execution understandably seemed to demand more details than usual. Because of Joan's habit of dressing in men's clothes, the chronicler paid particular attention to the fact that her true sex was revealed when her clothes were burned off her body in the course of her execution (pp. 296–7).
6. Ibid, 34.
7. For other, only slightly less terse, descriptions of this execution, see *Journal de Nicolas de Baye, greffier du Parlement de Paris, 1400–1417*, ed. Alexandre Tuetey (Paris, 1885), 1:292, and *Chronique du religieux de Saint-Denys*, ed. M. L. Bellaguet (Paris, 1842), 4:275–7.
8. *Le Journal d'un bourgeois de Paris sous le règne de François Ier* (1515–1536), ed. V.-L. Bourrilly (Paris, 1910), 186.
9. Ibid, 157–9.
10. [de Troyes], "Chroniques," in Petitot (ed.), *Collection complète*, 14:24–5.
11. See the examples cited below, pp. 134 and 149. See also Cohen, *Crossroads*, 188–9.
12. *Journal d'un bourgeois de Paris (1515–1536)*, 154.
13. Ibid, 363.
14. Ibid, 245. See also the case of Lucas Daillon, who similarly refused to perform the amende honorable in the same year, and about whose execution the author says next to nothing (p. 265).
15. "Chronique parisienne," in *Journal d'un bourgeois de Paris (1515–1536)*, 426–7. On the execution of Berquin, see Ibid, 321–2, and Nicolas Versoris, *Livre de raison de Me Nicolas Versoris, avocat au parlement de Paris, 1519–1530* (Paris, 1885), 119.

16. Jean Crespin, *Histoire des martyrs persecutéz et mis à mort pour la vérité de l'Evangile* .... [1554], ed. Daniel Benoit (Toulouse, 1885), 1:276.
17. See David Nicholls, "The Theatre of Martyrdom in the French Reformation," *Past and Present*, 121 (November 1988), 49–73.
18. "Chronique parisienne," in *Journal d'un bourgeois de Paris (1515–1536)*, 434–5.
19. Crespin, *Histoire des martyrs*, 286–7.
20. Nicholls, "Theatre of Martyrdom," 68–9.
21. Quoted in Ibid, 69.
22. See Ibid, 69–70, for examples of executions in which crowds attacked the condemned in the late 1550s.
23. As an example of the ways in which the intervening years may have influenced Platter's memoirs, he apparently incorporated the language of a text published in 1610 into a passage from his edited journal dealing with the year 1552. See Emmanuel Le Roy Ladurie, *The Beggar and the Professor: A Sixteenth-Century Family Saga*, trans. Arthur Goldhammer (Chicago, IL, and London, 1997), 173.
24. *Félix et Thomas Platter à Montpellier, 1552–1559, 1595–1599* (Montpellier, 1892), 67. References to other religious executions can be found on pp. 49 and 64–7.
25. Ibid, 24.
26. Ibid, 71.
27. Ibid, 84–5.
28. Ibid, 90–1; for details on his body-snatching larks, see pp. 91–7.
29. The Montpellier anatomy theater, built between 1554 and 1556, was one of the first such structures in Europe. This passage, concerning events in 1552, refers to the temporary anatomy theater built in advance of the permanent structure. (See Paul Findlen, "Anatomy Theaters, Botanical Gardens, and Natural History Collections," in Katharine Park and Lorraine Daston (eds.), *The Cambridge History of Science, vol. 3, Early Modern Science* (Cambridge, 2006), 272–89. For a very interesting discussion on the various interconnections between anatomical dissection and public executions, see the article by Florence Egmond, "Execution, Dissection, Pain and Infamy—A Morphological Investigation," in *Bodily Extremities: Preoccupations with the Human Body in Early Modern European Culture*, eds. Florike Egmond and Robert Zwijnenberg (Aldershot, Hampshire, 2003), 92–128. See also Katherine Park, "The Criminal and Saintly Body: Autopsy and Dissection in Renaissance Italy," in *Renaissance Quarterly*, 47 (1994), 1–35.
30. *Félix et Thomas Platter à Montpellier*, 30.
31. Ibid, 107.
32. Ibid, 147.
33. *Mémoires-Journaux de Pierre de l'Estoile*, ed. Brunet, Champollion-Figeac, Halphen et al. (Paris, 1888–96) 2:326.
34. Ibid, 1:10–12.
35. Ibid, 1:8.
36. See Pascal Bastien, *L'Exécution publique à Paris au XVIIIe siècle* (Seyssel, 2006), 216.
37. *Mémoires-Journaux de Pierre de l'Estoile*, 2:74.
38. Joseph Juste Scaliger, quoted in Bastien, *L'Exécution publique*, 215.
39. *Mémoires-Journaux de Pierre de l'Estoile*, 1:314–15.
40. Ibid, 7:136.
41. Ibid, 7:224.
42. On the history of canards, see Jean-Pierre Seguin, *L'Information en France avant la périodique: 517 canards imprimés entre 1529 et 1631* (Paris, 1964), and Maurice Lever, *Canards sanglants: naissance du fait divers* (Paris, 1993).

43. *Histoire sanguinaire, cruelle et émerveillable d'une femme de Cahors*, in Lever, *Canards sanglants*, 85–6. For a discussion of similarly remorseful and didactic gallows speeches in early modern England, see J. A. Sharpe, "Last Dying Speeches: Religion, Ideology and Public Execution in Seventeenth-Century England," *Past And Present*, 107:1 (1985), 144–67.
44. *Supplice d'un frère et soeur décapités en grève pour adultère et inceste*, in Lever, *Canards sanglants*, 109.
45. See Lever, *Canards sanglants*, 9–13.
46. On the *Histoires tragiques*, see the "Introduction" to François de Rosset, *Les Histoires mémorables et tragiques de ce temps* [1619], ed. Anne de Vauchet Gravili (Paris, 1994). (The 1619 edition of Rosset's text is an augmented and revised version of the original 1614 text, with a slightly different title.) See also Maurice Lever, "De l'Information à la nouvelle: les 'canards' et les Histoires tragiques de Rosset," *Revue d'histoire littéraire de la France* (July/August 1979), 577–93.
47. See Lever, "De l'Information," 581.
48. See also the case of the man who was so evil that "everyone ran [to the place of execution] not so much to see the punishment itself, which is so common in this large city, but out of a curiosity to see an individual whose evil nature was so detested...". Rosset, *Histoires tragiques*, 296.
49. For a discussion of executions within Corneille's plays, see Jacques Truchet, "Note sur la mort-spectacle dans la littérature française du XVIIe siècle," *Topique*, 11/12 (1973), 286–7. Perhaps this process whereby the dramatization of real-life executions made powerful real-life moments seem more like fiction is not unlike the way modern-day cinemagoers witness great disasters on the silver screen and then declare real-life disasters to be "surreal."
50. Norbert Elias, *History of Manners* (New York, 1982).

CHAPTER 6

1. Quoted in *Dictionnaire historique et critique de Pierre Bayle* (Paris, 1820), 10:291.
2. Letter from Laffemas to Chancelier Séguier (15 November 1633), in Roland Mousnier (ed.), *Lettres et mémoires adressés au Chancelier Séguier* (Paris, 1964), 1:210.
3. Tallemant des Réaux, *Historiettes*, ed. Antoine Adam (Dijon, 1960), 2:68.
4. Letter from Scarron to Maréchal d'Albret (20 August 1659), in *French Classics: A Selection from the Letters of Madame de Sévigné and her Contemporaries*, ed. Gustave Masson (Oxford, 1868), 4:220. The translation is mine.
5. Letter to Madame de Grignan (7 June 1671), in *Lettres de Madame de Sévigné de sa famille et de ses amis*, ed. Louis Jean Nicolas de Monmerqué (Paris, 1862), 2:234–5.
6. Letter from Madame de Sévigné to Madame de Grignan (24 November 1675), in Ibid, 4:248.
7. Alexis de Tocqueville, *De la Démocratie en Amérique* (Paris, 1864), 3:268. See also Richard Sennett and Jonathan Cobb, *The Hidden Injuries of Class* (New York and London, 1993), 247.
8. Letter from Madame de Sévigné to the Comte de Bussy (20 October, 1675), in *Lettres de Madame de Sévigné de sa famille*, 4:196.
9. Letter from Madame de Sévigné to Madame de Grignan (30 October 1675), in Ibid, 4:206–7. Tocqueville cites this passage in *De la Démocratie*, 3:267.
10. For background on the case, see Anne Somerset, *The Affair of the Poisons* (New York, 2004), 6–40.

11. Letter from Madame de Sévigné to Madame de Grignan (1 May 1676), in *Lettres de Madame de Sévigné de sa famille*, 4:428. See also her letter five days later (4:435).
12. Ibid (12 May 1676), 4:445.
13. Ibid (26 June 1676), 4:504.
14. Ibid (17 July 1676), 4:528–30.
15. Ibid (22 July 1676), 4:533.
16. *La Marquise de Brinvilliers. Récit de ses derniers moments (Manuscrit du P. Pirot, son Confeseur)*, ed. G. Roullier (Paris, 1883) 2:82–3. See also 2:74 and 2:51.
17. See Pascal Bastien's discussion of Pirot and his text in *L'Exécution publique à Paris au XVIIIe siècle* (Seyssel, 2006), 178 and 190–1.
18. [Pirot], *Brinvilliers*, 2:109–10.
19. A similar sensationalizing of tragic sentiment might be seen in Charles Le Brun's portrait of Brinvillers.
20. [Pirot], *Brinvilliers*, 2:174.
21. Letter to Madame de Grignan (23 February 1680), in *Lettres de Madame de Sévigné de sa famille*, 6:278–9.
22. Damase Jouaust (ed.), *Les Caractères de La Bruyère* (Paris: 1881), 2:18.
23. Jacques Truchet suggests that La Bruyère's comment is unique in the seventeenth century in "Note sur la mort-spectacle dans la littérature française du XVIIe siècle," *Topique*, 11–12 (1973), 285.
24. See Lynn Hunt, *Inventing Human Rights: A History* (New York and London, 2007), 38ff.
25. Montaigne, "De la Cruauté," *Essais de Montaigne* (Paris, 1843), 266 (book II, chapter 11). I am grateful to Danielle Trudeau for signaling to me the importance of Montaigne's *Essays* to my subject.
26. Ibid, 266–7. Similar thoughts are expressed in Montaigne's essay "Couardise, mère de la cruauté" (book II, chapter 27).
27. Montaigne, "De la Cruauté," 265. For a more complete discussion of Montaigne's views on cruelty to animals within the context of the time, see Paul Friedland, "Friends for Dinner: The Early Modern Roots of Modern Carnivorous Sensibilities," in *History of the Present: A Journal of Critical History*, 1:1 (Summer 2011), 84–112.
28. On Montaigne and the neo-stoics, see Anthony Levi, *French Moralists: The Theory of the Passions: 1585 to 1649* (Oxford, 1964), 2, and Anthony Long, "Montaigne: The Eclectic Pragmatist," *Republics of Letters: A Journal for the Study of Knowledge, Politics, and the Arts*, 1:2 (3 April 2010), http://rofl.stanford.edu/node/57.
29. John Sellars, "Justus Lipsius's *De Constantia:* A Stoic Spiritual Exercise," in *Poetics Today*, 28:3 (Fall 2007), 341–2.
30. Justus Lipsius, *Traité de la constance* (Tours, 1594), 27 (chapter XII).
31. Guillaume du Vair, *De la Constance et consolation es calamitez publiques* in *Oeuvres* (1641; reprinted Geneva, 1970).
32. Guillaume du Vair, *La Saincte Philosophie* (Paris, 1597), 6.
33. On Descartes' use of the word *émotion* see Joan DeJean, *Ancients against Moderns: Culture Wars and the Making of a Fin de Siècle* (Chicago, IL, 1997), 80–1.
34. René Descartes, *Les Passions de l'âme* (Paris, 1728), part I, 81 (article 46).
35. Ibid, 82.
36. See DeJean, *Ancients against Moderns*, 83–6.
37. Madeleine de Scudéry, *Artamène ou le Grand Cyrus* (Paris, 1656), 676 (part 7, book 3). See the discussion of this passage in Frank Baasner, "The Changing Meaning of 'Sensibilité': 1654 till 1704," in *Studies in Eighteenth-Century Culture*, 15 (1986), 82.

38. Baasner, "Changing Meaning," 80.
39. See Montaigne, "De l'Amitié," in *Essais*, 103.
40. Madame de Villedieu, quoted in Baasner, "Changing Meaning," 83. The translation is mine.
41. Antoine Furetière, *Dictionnaire universel*, quoted in Ibid, 82. The translation is mine.
42. DeJean, *Ancients against Moderns*, 86–7.
43. Quoted in John D. Lyons, *Before Imagination: Embodied Thought from Montaigne to Rousseau* (Palo Alto, CA, 2005), 124.
44. See Anne Vincent-Buffault, *Histoire des larmes, XVIIIe–XIX siècles* (Paris, 1986), 12.
45. For a recent discussion of the case, see Jeffrey Ravel, "Husband-Killer, Christian Heroine, Victim: The Execution of Madame Tiquet, 1699," *Seventeenth-Century French Studies*, 32:2 (2010), 120–36.
46. [Anne Marguerite du Noyer], *Lettres historiques et galantes, par Madame de C**** (1711), 2:64. Although the letters of Madame du Noyer are presented as the semi-fictional letters between two women, they appear to be based largely on events that she herself had witnessed and, according to Anne Duggan, are probably edited versions of letters that she sent to friends between 1688 and 1700. (See Anne E. Duggan, "The Ticquet Affair as Recounted in Madame Dunoyer's *Lettres Historiques et Galantes:* The Defiant *Galante Femme*," in *Papers on French Seventeenth-Century Literature*, 24:46 (1997), 259–76.)
47. [Du Noyer], *Lettres historiques*, 64.
48. Ibid, 64, 68.
49. Ibid, 69.
50. Ibid.
51. Ibid, 67.
52. *Mémoires du Marquis de Sourches sur le règne de Louis XIV*, ed. Gabriel-Jules Cosnac and Edouard Pontal (Paris, 1886), 6:165.
53. *Mémoires de Saint-Simon*, ed. A. de Boislisle (Paris, 1888), 6:436–7.
54. On the greater sensitivity of women and the inappropriateness of their watching the penal spectacle for amusement, see the discussion of Damiens' execution in the following chapter (pp. 179–83).
55. See the discussion of Siméon-Prosper Hardy, Thomas-Simon Gueullette, Louis-Sébastien Mercier, and Nicolas-Edme Rétif de La Bretonne in the following chapter.
56. Norman S. Fiering, "Irresistible Compassion: An Aspect of Eighteenth-Century Sympathy and Humanitarianism," *Journal of the History of Ideas*, 37:2 (1976), 195–6. My discussion, in the following pages, of Malebranche, Shaftesbury, Wollaston, and Hutcheson is very much indebted to Fiering's important article.
57. Malebranche, *De la Recherche de la verité* (Paris, 1762), 2:295–6 (book IV).
58. Ibid, 2:297.
59. Ibid, 2:299–300.
60. [Gamaches], *Systeme du coeur ou La Connoissance du coeur humain* (Paris, 1708), 79–80.
61. Mandeville published his poem *The Grumbling Hive* in 1705, which was expanded in 1714 as *The Fable of the Bees*.
62. I am indebted to Baasner's citation of relevant passages in Gamaches, as well as the discussion in DeJean, *Ancients against Moderns*, 89; and John S. Spink, "'Sentiment,' 'sensible,' 'sensibilité': les mots, les idées, d'après les 'moralistes' français et britanniques du début du dix-huitième siècle," in *Zagadnienia Rodzajów Literackich*, 20 (1977), 43–4.
63. See Friedland, "Friends for Dinner."

64. Anthony [Ashley Cooper], Earl of Shaftesbury, "An Inquiry Concerning Virtue or Merit," in *Characteristics of Men, Manners, Opinions, Times, etc.* (London, 1900), 1:247–8, 280.
65. Jean-Baptiste Dubos, *Réflexions critiques sur la poésie et sur la peinture* (Paris, 1740), 1:38–9. For a discussion of this passage see Baasner, "Changing Meaning," 90–1; Buffaut, *Histoire des larmes*, 41, and David Marshall, "Adam Smith and the Theatricality of Moral Sentiments," in *Critical Inquiry*, 10:4 (June 1984), 593–4. At mid-century, Etienne Bonnot de Condillac would argue that sympathy lay at the origin of linguistic communication. See David Denby, *Sentimental Narrative and the Social Order in France, 1760–1820* (Cambridge, 1984), 85.
66. William Wollaston, *The Religion of Nature Delineated* (London, 1759), 258.
67. Francis Hutcheson, *An Inquiry into the Original of our Ideas of Beauty and Virtue…* (London, 1729), 158.
68. Ibid, 242. On sensibility and women, see also David Hume, *A Treatise of Human Nature* (Oxford, 1896), 370 (part II, book II, section VII).
69. Jean-Jacques Rousseau, "Discours sur l'origine et les fondemens de l'inégalité parmi les hommes," in *Oeuvres de J. J. Rousseau*, 4 (Paris, 1819), 263–4.
70. Ibid, 267–8.
71. Ibid, 266.
72. Ibid.

CHAPTER 7

1. Letter from Caumartin de Boissy to the Marquise de Balleroy (22 March 1720) in *Les Correspondants de la Marquise de Balleroy*, ed. Edouard de Barthélemy (Paris, 1883), 2:140.
2. Letter from Caumartin de Boissy to the Marquise de Balleroy (30 March 1720) in Ibid, 2:149.
3. Letter from an unknown correspondent to the Marquise de Balleroy (7 December 1720), in Ibid, 2:214–15.
4. Pierre de Marivaux, "Pièces détachées," in *Oeuvres complètes de Marivaux*, ed. Pierre Duviquet (Paris, 1830), 9:311–12. See Pascal Bastien, *L'Exécution publique à Paris au XVIIIe siècle* (Seysell, 2006), 190. Marivaux makes use of his observation to support certain theories on crowds behaving like machines, responding automatically and reflexively to a variety of different stimuli.
5. Jean-Baptiste Dubos, *Réflexions critiques sur la poésie et la peinture* [1719] (Paris, 1733), 12–13. For a detailed and very interesting discussion of Marivaux and Dubos, see David Marshall, *The Surprising Effects of Sympathy: Marivaux, Diderot, Rousseau, and Mary Shelley* (Chicago, IL, 1988), 23–4.
6. Guellette's collection forms the bulk of dossiers A.N. AD III, 1 through 11. For much of the information concerning the eighteenth-century chroniclers, especially Hardy and Gueullette, I am enormously indebted to Pascal Bastien, who in many conversations and through his writing has shared the wealth of his knowledge with me, and who has recently published Gueullette's writings in the following volume: Thomas-Simon Gueullette, *Sur l'Echafaud: histoires de larrons et d'assassins (1721–1766)*, ed. Pascal Bastien (Paris, 2010). See also Bastien's discussion of Gueullette, Hardy, and others in *L'Exécution publique*, 59–91.
7. For the Dutch equivalent, see the discussion of Jacob Bicker Raye in Pieter Spierenburg, *The Spectacle of Suffering: Executions and the Evolution of Repression: From a Preindustrial Metropolis to the European Experience* (Cambridge, 1984), 99.

8. Jean Buvat, *Journal de la Régence (1715–1723)*, ed. Emile Campardon (Paris, 1865), 1:35.
9. *Journal et mémoires de Mathieu Marais*, ed. Mathurin de Lescure (Paris, 1864), 2:198–9.
10. A.N. AD III, 4. See also Frantz Funck-Brentano, "Cartouche auteur dramatique," *Bulletin de la Société de l'histoire du théâtre* (1903), no. 5, 5–23.
11. [Edmond-Jean-François Barbier], *Chronique de la régence et du règne de Louix XV (1718–1763)* (Paris, 1858), 1:167.
12. Quoted in Funck-Brentano, "Cartouche," 10.
13. *Journal et mémoires de Marais*, 2:200.
14. Barbier, *Chronique*, 1:167.
15. Quoted in Funck-Brentano, "Cartouche," 10.
16. A.N. AD III, 4.
17. Barbier, *Chronique*, 1:174–5.
18. A.N. AD III, 4.
19. Letter from Caumartin de Boissy to the Marquise de Balleroy, *Correspondants de la Marquise de Balleroy* ([December] 1721), 2:386–7.
20. *Correspondance complète de Madame Duchesse d'Orléans*... (Paris, 1855), 1:352 (29 November 1721).
21. Letter from Caumartin de Boissy to the Marquise de Balleroy, *Correspondants de la Marquise de Balleroy* (29 November 1721), 2:378.
22. A.N. AD III, 4.
23. Ibid.
24. Barbier, *Chronique*, 1:443.
25. Ibid, 1:425. See also 4:441, 447–8, and L. Petit de Bachaumont et al., *Mémoires secrets pour servir à l'histoire des Lettres en France*... (London, 1780–9), 23:204–5.
26. Barbier, *Chronique*, 2:69.
27. Ibid, 2:86–7. See also Gueullette in A.N. AD III, 6.
28. A.N. AD III, 6. Michel-Etienne Turgot was the father of Anne Robert Jacques Turgot, who, as Comptroller General, would abolish the executioner's right of havage in 1775.
29. See the following chapter.
30. A.N. AD III, 7.
31. Frantz Funck-Brentano, *Mandrin: d'après des documents nouveaux*... (Paris, 1908), 463–5.
32. Barbier, *Chronique*, 6:179.
33. From *Complainte et épitaphe de Madame Lescombat* in Gueullette, A.N. AD III, 8.
34. *Lettre d'un françois à un anglois* (Paris, 1755), contained in Gueullette's collection, A.N. AD III, 8.
35. Barbier, *Chronique*, 6:179.
36. Gueullette, A.N. AD III, 8.
37. Barbier, *Chronique*, 6:179. See also the play *La Mort de Lescombat, tragédie* (1755).
38. Barbier, *Chronique*, 6:179.
39. Gueullette, A.N. AD III, 8.
40. Barbier, *Chronique*, 6:502–3.
41. Quoted in *L'Attentat de Damiens*, ed. Pierre Rétat (Paris, 1979), 257.
42. A.N. AD III, 8.
43. *Relation de l'exécution de Robert-François Damiens, dûement atteint et convaincu*... quoted in *L'Attentat de Damiens*, 256–7. The Duc de Richelieu would later claim in his

memoirs that some windows were priced as high as 25 louis, or 600 livres. See *Mémoires du Maréchal duc de Richelieu*, ed. Fs. Barrière (Paris, 1869), 2:203.
44. *Journal inédit du Duc de Croy (1718–1784)*, ed. Le Vicomte de Grouchy and Paul Cottin (Paris, 1906), 1:401; Barbier, *Chronique*, 6:507.
45. *Mémoires-Journaux de Pierre de l'Estoile*, ed. Brunet, Champollion-Figeac, Halphen et al. (Paris, 1888–96), 10:258–9.
46. *Journal du Duc de Croy*, 1:401.
47. Gueullette, A.N. AD III, 8.
48. Barbier, *Chronique*, 6:508.
49. *Relation de l'exécution de Damiens, qui a été faite le Lundi 28 Mars 1757*, 3 (contained in Gueullette's collection, A.N. AD III, 8).
50. A.N. AD III, 8.
51. Ibid.
52. Quoted in Michel Foucault, *Discipline and Punish: The Birth of the Prison*, trans. Alan Sheridan (New York, 1979), 4.
53. Ibid., 4–5.
54. This barrier was apparently something of a novelty, as several of the sources refer to it in detail. See Barbier, *Chronique*, 6:499–500, and Gueullette (A.N. AD III, 8).
55. "Rapport de Bouton," in *Archives de la Bastille*, ed. François Ravaisson (Paris, 1884), 16: 476.
56. *Correspondance littéraire, philosophique et critique…par le Baron Grimm et par Diderot* (Paris, 1813), 4:401.
57. *Journal du Duc de Croy*, 403.
58. Barbier, *Chronique*, 6:508.
59. Charles Collé, *Journal historique, ou mémoires critiques et littéraires…* (Paris, 1807), 2:177.
60. Pierre de Marivaux, *Les Avantures de *** ou Les effets surprenans de la sympathie* (Paris, 1713), 1:ii. See also p. vii.
61. See chapter 6 (p. 162).
62. Quoted in Anne Vincent-Buffault, *Histoire des larmes, XVIIIe–XIX siècles* (Paris, 1986), 52.
63. Denis Diderot, *Paradoxe sur le comédien* (Cambridge, 1922), 311.
64. There was a third option: One author tried to suggest that it was because of women's unique sensitivity that they had been so deeply affected by the crime itself and consequently felt no pity for the condemned. (See Louis Berger, *L'Almanach historique nommé le postillon de la paix et de la guerre…* transcribed by Gueullette in A.N. AD III, 8.)
65. Siméon-Prosper Hardy, *Mes Loisirs, ou Journal d'événemens tels qu'ils parviennent à ma connoissance (1753–1789)*, ed. Daniel Roche and Pascal Bastien (Quebec, 2008), 1:441(24 March 1769).
66. "Curiosité," in *Dictionnaire philosophique II, Oeuvres complètes de Voltaire* (Paris, 1878), 18:308. See also Voltaire, *Dialogues et entretiens philosophiques*, ed. André Lefèvre (Paris, 1878), 2:124–5.
67. Louis-Sébastien Mercier, *Tableau de Paris* (Hambourg, 1781), 2:129, 132–3.
68. Quoted in *L'Attentat de Damiens*, 301.
69. *Mémoires du marechal duc de Richelieu*, 2:203.
70. Quoted in *l'Attentat de Damiens*, 301.
71. *Mémoires de J. Casanova de Seingalt, écrit par lui-même…* (Paris, 1880), 3:400.
72. See chapter 10 (p. 255).

73. See Spierenburg, *Spectacle of Suffering*, 189ff, and V.A.C. Gatrell, *The Hanging Tree: Execution and the English People: 1770–1868* (Oxford, 1994), 225–41.
74. Jean-Jacques Rousseau, *Discours sur l'origine et les fondemens de l'inegalité parmi les hommes* (Amsterdam, 1755), 73–4.
75. Quoted in Jean-Jacques Rousseau, "Lettre à M. Philopolis [1755]," in *The Political Writings of Jean-Jacques Rousseau*, ed. C. E. Vaughn (Cambridge, 1915), 1:226.
76. Ibid.
77. Edmund Burke, *A Philosophical Enquiry into the Origin of our Ideas of the Sublime and Beautiful* [1757] (London, 1764), 59.
78. Adam Smith, *The Theory of Moral Sentiments* (London, 1774), 1.
79. Hardy, *Mes Loisirs*, 1:156. (9 May 1766).
80. Nicolas-Joseph-Laurent Gilbert, *Oeuvres complètes de Gilbert* (Paris, 1788), 88.
81. Quoted in Michel Bée, "La Société traditionnelle et la mort," in *XVIIe Siècle*, 1975, 106–7, 107–8.
82. Quoted in Robert Schneider, *The Ceremonial City: Toulouse Observed 1738–1780* (Princeton, NJ, 1995), 86.
83. Hardy, *Mes Loisirs*, 2:575 (31 May 1772).
84. It was around this same time that some began to question the usefulness, in terms of deterrence, of hanging domestic servants convicted of theft (see chapter 8, p. 211).
85. See Hardy's journal entries for 11 March 1771, 18 May 1772, 31 May 1772, and 20 January 1774. I am grateful to Pascal Bastien for providing me access to a prepublication online transcription of Hardy's journal entries (at: http/www.mesloisirs.uqam.ca). Hardy's journals will be published in successive volumes as: Siméon-Prosper Hardy, *Mes Loisirs, ou Journal d'évènemens tels qu'ils parviennent à ma connoissance (1753–1789)*.
86. See Benoit Garnot, "Les Peines corporelles en Bourgogne au xviiie siècle," in *Beccaria et la culture juridique des lumières*, ed. Michel Porret (Geneva, 1997), 220–2, and Michel Porret, "Effrayer le crime par la terreur des chatiments: la pédagogie de l'effroi chez quelques criminalistes du XVIIIème siècle," in *La Peur au xviiie siècle: discours, représentations, pratiques*, ed. Jacques Berchtold and Michel Porret (Geneva, 1994), 52.
87. See Bachaumont, *Mémoires secrets*, 10:126 and 23:204–5.
88. Ibid, 10:125–6.
89. Hardy, *Mes Loisirs* (6 May 1777).
90. Retif de la Bretonne, *Les Nuits de Paris* (Paris, 1978), 34.
91. Ibid, 34–5.
92. Mercier, *Tableau de Paris*, 2:103.
93. Ibid, 2:105. See also Helvétius, *De l'Esprit* (1773; reprinted Paris, 1961), 20.
94. Hardy, *Mes Loisirs* (3 July 1786). For a similar characterization of crowds in the Netherlands, see Spierenburg, *Spectacle of Suffering*, 193–4.
95. Retif de la Bretonne, *Les Nuits de Paris*, 211–12.
96. J-B. A. Suard, *Mélanges de littérature* (Geneva, 1971), 3:150.

CHAPTER 8

1. *Filarete's Treastise on Architecture: Being the Treatise of Antonio di Piero Averlino, known as Filarete*, trans. John R. Spencer (New Haven, CT, and London, 1965), 1:282–5.
2. Thomas More, *Utopia* (New York, 1891), 18–19.
3. Ibid, 20.
4. Ibid, 80–1.
5. Ibid, 81.

6. Ibid.
7. Ibid, 9.
8. For details on Vairasse and the various editions of his book, see J. Rivers, "A French Utopia," in *The Library* (1905), s2-VI (23):265–73. See also Frank E. Manuel and Fritzie P. Manuel, *Utopian Thought in the Western World* (Cambridge, MA, 1979), 367–81.
9. [Denis Vairasse], *Histoire des Sevarambes...* [part iv] (Amsterdam, 1702), 49–50.
10. [Simon Tyssot de Patot], *Voyages et avantures de Jaques Massé* (Bordeaux, 1710), 148–50.
11. Simon Tyssot de Patot, *Lettres choisies* (La Haye, 1727), 1:378.
12. Ibid, 379.
13. François-Vincent Toussaint, *Les Moeurs* (n.p., 1748), viii–ix.
14. Ibid, vi.
15. Ibid, 350–1.
16. [Edmond-Jean-François Barbier], *Chronique de la régence et du règne de Louix XV (1718–1763)* (Paris, 1858), 4:300–1.
17. Ibid, 305, 308.
18. These ideas are very similar to ones that had been expressed three years earlier in Diderot's "Essai sur le mérite et la vertu," a loose translation of Shaftesbury's turn-of-the century *Inquiry Concerning Virtue or Merit*. See Denis Diderot, "Essai sur le mérite et la vertu," in *Oeuvres complètes de Diderot* (1875; reprinted Liechtenstein, 1966), 1:56.
19. See chapter 1 (pp. 31–2).
20. I am very much indebted, in this discussion of the sovereign right to kill, to Dan Edelstein who, both in person and in several chapters of his excellent book *The Terror of Natural Right* (Chicago, IL, 2009), has made me deeply aware of the connections between the logic of natural right and the modern death penalty.
21. *Aquinas Ethicus: or, the Moral Teaching of St. Thomas. A Translation of the Principal Portions of the Second part of the Summa Theologica*, ed. Joseph Rickaby, S.J. (London, 1892) (Question LXIV: Of Homicide).
22. Hugo Grotius, *Of the Rights of War and Peace* (London, 1715), 2:509 (book II, chapter XX).
23. John Locke, *Second Treatise of Government* (chapter XV).
24. Jean-Jacques Burlamaqui, *Principes du droit naturel* (Geneva and Copenhagen, 1762), 107. See also *The English Works of Thomas Hobbes of Malmesbury*, ed. Sir William Molesworth (London, 1839–45), 2:113–14.
25. See Hobbes's statement that "a banished man is a lawful enemy of the Commonwealth that banished him," *English Works of Thomas Hobbes*, 3:304.
26. According to the ARTFL database, Jaucourt cited Montesquieu's *L'Esprit des lois* more than 75 times in some 70 distinct articles.
27. "Crime," in *Encyclopédie, ou dictionnaire raisonné des sciences, des arts et des métiers*, ed. Denis Diderot and Jean le Rond D'Alembert. University of Chicago, IL: ARTFL Encyclopédie Projet (Winter 2008 Edition), Robert Morrissey ed., http://encyclopedie.uchicago.edu/. (4:466–7).
28. *Encyclopédie*, 5:116. As Edelstein points out, Diderot was not alone in calling for the enemy of society to be *etouffé*. Rousseau and Nicolas-Gabriel Clerc used nearly identical language. (Edelstein, *Terror of Natural Right*, 42, 205). On the concept of the enemy of the human race in general, see Edelstein, 26–42.
29. Jean-Jacques Rousseau, *Du Contrat social; ou principes du droit politique* (Amsterdam, 1762), 79–80 (chapter V).

30. Ibid, 81.
31. Lynn Hunt, *Inventing Human Rights: A History* (New York and London, 2007), 80.
32. Cesare Beccaria, *Traité des délits et des peines* (Philadelphia, PA, 1766), 91.
33. *Mémoires de l'abbé Morellet* (Paris, 1821), 1:157–8. See also Morellet's letter to Beccaria introducing himself and his intentions in Beccaria, *Des délits et des peines* (Paris, 1797), xxix–xxxix.
34. Beccaria, *Traité*, 60. This, and all subsequent parenthetical citations refer to the 1766 edition.
35. See Ibid, 93–4, where Beccaria compares and contrasts the punishment of the wheel to perpetual slavery.
36. "Preface to the First Edition [of A Fragment on Government]" (1776), in *The Works of Jeremy Bentham*, Part I (Edinburgh, 1838), 231.
37. Beccaria, *Dei delitti e delle pene* (Paris, 1786), 64.
38. From this perspective, Maximilien Robespierre's initial support of abolition, and his later change of heart, may have less to do with his views on the death penalty itself than with his changing perception of the dangers to public safety.
39. Letter from Morellet to Beccaria (February 1766) in Beccaria, *Des Délits et des peines* (Paris, 1797), xxxi.
40. In addition to Italian and French, there would be editions in Spanish, German, English, and Polish. See Marcello Maestro, *Cesare Beccaria and the Origins of Penal Reform* (Philadelphia, PA, 1973), 127–9. On Beccaria's influence on Jefferson and Catherine the Great, see pp. 68–70 and 141–2.
41. See Ibid, 55–9.
42. Cited in Piers Beirne, *Inventing Criminology: Essays on the Rise of "Homo Criminalis"* (Albany, NY, 1993), 49.
43. Quoted in Marcello T. Maestro, *Voltaire and Beccaria as Reformers of Criminal Law* (New York, 1942), 143. The translation is mine.
44. J.-P. Brissot de Warville, *Bibliothèque philosophique du législateur, du politique, du jurisconsulte* (Berlin and Paris, 1782–5), 10 vols.
45. Joseph-Michel-Antoine Servan, "Discours sur l'administration de la justice criminelle (prononcé au parlement de Grenoble en 1766)" *Oeuvres choisies de Servan* (Paris, 1825), 2:81.
46. *Bibliothèque philosophique*, 7:318.
47. Servan, *Oeuvres*, 2:83. See also Voltaire, "Le Prix de justice et d'humanité" (London, 1777), 11; "Peine," in *Répertoire universel et raisonné de jurisprudence civile, criminelle, canonique et bénéficiale*, ed. Guyot (Paris, 1781), 45:337; Jean-Paul Marat, *Plan de législation criminelle* (Paris, 1790), 30 (originally published in Brissot's *Bibliothèque*, vol. 5); Nicolas Pinel, "Dissertation sur la peine de mort," in *Bibliothèque philosophique*, 7:328.
48. Voltaire, "Le Prix," 7. See also J.-P. Brissot de Warville, *Les Moyens d'adoucir la rigueur des loix pénales en France, sans nuire à la sûreté publique…* (Châlons-sur-Marne, 1781), 80, and Servan, *Oeuvres*, 2:83–4.
49. See Brissot, *Les Moyens*, 60; *Discours de M. Bernardi* (bound with Brissot, *Les Moyens*), 73, and Marat, *Plan*, 30, 67.
50. Marat, *Plan*, 29.
51. Brissot, *Les Moyens*, 81.
52. Voltaire, "Le Prix," 11.
53. Voltaire, *Commentaire sur le livre Des Délits et des peines* (Geneva, 1767), 29. Although this appears to be the first time he made this observation, he repeated it in "L'Homme

au quarante écus," in *Nouveaux Mélanges philosophiques, historiques, critiques* (n.p, 1768), 6:162, and in "La Raison par alphabet" (1769), 2:26.
54. Voltaire, *Commentaire*, 29. See also [Augustin Rouillé d'Orfeuil], *L'Alambic des loix* (Hispaan, 1773), 403.
55. J.-P. Brissot de Warville, *Théorie des loix criminelles* (Neuchatel and Paris, 1781), 1:152.
56. Voltaire, "Le Prix," 13–14. See also "Notes sur le Traité des délits et des peines," in *Oeuvres complètes de Diderot* (Paris, 1875), 4:68; Brissot, *Théorie*, 154, and *Les Moyens*, 83–4. On the popularity of Beccaria's forced labor among subsequent penal reformers, see Robert Favre, *La Mort au siècle des lumières. Dans la littérature et la pensée françaises* (Lyon, 1978), 308–9. Favre's text is an indispensable guide to the texts of early modern penal reform, and was crucial to my understanding of the subject.
57. Voltaire, *Commentaire*, 29; Voltaire, "Le Prix," 14. Brissot, *Les Moyens*, 146; "Peine" in *Répertoire universel*, 336; Claude Emmanuel Joseph Pierre Pastoret, *Des Loix pénales* (Paris, 1790), vol. 1, part 2, 5-6.
58. Brissot, *Théorie*, 1:147. See also Brissot, *Les Moyens*, 83–4, and *Discours de M. Bernardi*, 72–3.
59. Brissot, *Théorie*, 1:154.
60. Ibid, 1:147–8.
61. [D'Orfeuil], *Alambic*, 403–4.
62. Brissot, *Théorie*, 1:149.
63. Ibid, 1:149–50.
64. Marat, *Plan*, 32. See also Voltaire, "Le Prix," 10, 13; Brissot, *Théorie*, 1:137; Brissot, *Les Moyens*, 85; and Pinel, "Dissertation," 330.
65. [Jean-Baptiste Claude Delisle de Sales], *De la Philosophie de la nature* [1770] (London, 1789), 2:117.
66. Ibid, 123–4.
67. Ibid, 125–6.
68. Muyart de Vouglans, *Réfutation des principes hasardés dans le Traité des délits et Peines...* (Lausanne, 1767), 4–5.
69. Ibid, 18, 22.
70. Ibid, 86–7.
71. Brissot, *Théorie*, 1:144.
72. *Discours de M. Bernardi*, 61.
73. Gabriel Bonnot de Mably, "De la Législation, ou Principes des lois," in *Oeuvres complètes de l'Abbé de Mably* (Lyon, 1796), 9:284–5.
74. Servan, *Discours*, 96.
75. De Sales, *De la Philosophie*, 121.
76. Voltaire, "Le Prix," 16–17. See also Diderot, who scribbled the following note in the margin of his copy of Beccaria's treatise: "As for the justice of this penalty [of death], it is founded on convention and on common utility. If it is necessary, it is just." ("Notes sur le Traité des délits et des peines," in *Oeuvres complètes de Diderot* [Paris, 1875], 4:67).
77. "Peine," in *Répertoire universel*, 45:335–7.
78. Brissot, *Théorie*, 1:146.
79. Brissot, *Les Moyens*, 55.
80. Pinel, "Dissertation," 7:329.
81. Servan, *Discours*, 21 2.
82. Mably, *De la Législation*, 285–6.
83. Marat, *Plan*, 32, 47, 56.

CHAPTER 9

1. Albert Desjardins, *Les Cahiers des États généraux en 1789 et la législation criminelle* (Paris, 1883), xix–xxvi.
2. Ibid, 52.
3. See for example, the *cahier* of Poitou, bailliage de Vouvans, art. 13, quoted in Ibid, 53.
4. Quoted in Ibid, 54.
5. Third Estate of Audun, art. 30, quoted in Ibid.
6. Maximilien de Robespierre, *Discours couronné par la société royale des arts et des sciences de Metz...* (Amsterdam, 1785), 15–16.
7. Desjardins, *Cahiers*, 56.
8. Quoted in Ibid, 54.
9. *Archives parlementaires de 1787 à 1860*, ed. M. J. Mavidal (Paris, 1862–), 9:350 (6 October 1789).
10. Ibid (9 October 1789), 9:393; according to the *Moniteur*, Guillotin presented these articles for consideration on the morning of the 10th (*Réimpression de l'ancien moniteur* (Paris, 1840–), 2:32).
11. *Archives parlementaires*, 9:393–4.
12. According to another source, he presented his proposals on 24 October as well. See *Journal Politique de Bruxelles*, 44 (31 October 1789), 387–8.
13. *Mercure de France*, 49 (5 December 1789), 143. See also the *Journal des débats et des décrets*, excerpted in Ludovic Pichon, *Code de la guillotine: Recueil complet de documents concernant l'application de la peine de mort en France et les exécuteurs des hautes oeuvres* (Paris, 1910), 11.
14. *Tableau des opérations de l'Assemblée Nationale, d'après le Journal de Paris* 2(3), 92. This journal reports that Guillotin's speech was given on 28 November 1789. See also "Account of the Proceedings of the National Assembly of France since the Revolution in that Kingdom, July 14, 1789," in *European Magazine and London Review*, 18 (1790), 303, which also records the date of the speech as 28 November.
15. *Journal des Etats Généraux* (Paris, 1789), 6, no. 15, 237.
16. Both of these statements are quoted in Daniel Arasse, *La Guillotine et l'imaginaire de la terreur* (Paris, 1987), 26, as well as throughout the secondary literature on the guillotine. Arasse provides no citation for his original source. The earliest source that I have found for the first statement is *Anecdotes du règne de Louis XVI* (Paris, 1791), 3:104–5. As for the second statement, this would appear to be attributed to Guillotin by nineteenth-century authors, the earliest of which I have come across being the apocryphal *Souvenirs de la marquise de Créquy, 1710 à 1802* (Paris, 1836), 5:385.
17. *Moniteur*, 2:280.
18. *Archives parlementaires*, 11:278 (21 January 1790). See also the *Moniteur*, 3:195.
19. *Révolutions de Paris*, no. XXIV, 8. Prudhomme, an abolitionist, thought it would be a good idea "to forget both [Guillotin's] motion as well as the song." See also *Chronique de Paris* (14 December 1789), cited in Eugène Hatin, *Histoire politique et littéraire de la presse en France* (Paris, 1861), 7:53.
20. The song begins with the verse: "Guillotin, Médecin, Politique, Imagine un beau matin; Que pendre est inhumain; Et peu Patriotique. Aussi-tôt; Il lui faut; Un supplice; Qui, sans corde ni poteau; Supprime de bourreau, L'office. And it ends with the following verse: Et sa main, Fait soudain, La machine, Qui simplement nous tuera. Et que l'on nommera, Guillotine." ("Guillotin—physician, politician—imagines one fine

morning that hanging is inhuman, and not very patriotic. Right away, he needs a punishment that, without cord or gibbet, gets rid of the hangman's job.... And he suddenly makes by hand a machine which will simply kill us. And that will be called Guillotine.") *Les Actes des Apôtres* (Paris, 1790), 1:156–7.
21. *Reimpression de l'ancien Moniteur* (18 December 1789), 2:410.
22. See chapter 3 (pp. 79–80).
23. For an account of these debates, see Paul Friedland, *Political Actors: Representative Bodies and Theatricality in the Age of the French Revolution* (Ithaca, NY, 2002), 3–6, 219–27.
24. *Révolutions de Paris*, 24, 3–5. See also Gorsas, *Le Courrier de Paris dans les provinces, & des provinces à Paris* 19, quoted in Maton de la Varenne, *Mémoire pour les exécuteurs des jugements criminels de toutes les villes du Royaume, Où l'on prouve la légitimité de leur état* (Paris, 1790), 24–5.
25. *Archives parlementaires*, 10:756 (23 December 1789).
26. "Pétition de l'exécuteur de la haute justice à Paris, le S. Sanson, en date du décembre 26, 1789...", A.N. C101, no. 165.
27. *Archives parlementaires*, 10:754.
28. Ibid. He apologized for using the word *bourreau*, or "hangman," preferring *exécuteurs*.
29. Ibid.
30. Ibid, 10:782.
31. Maton de la Varenne, *Mémoire pour les exécuteurs*, 17.
32. *Moniteur*, 8:533.
33. *Revolutions de Paris*, 8:322 (21–28 May 1791).
34. For useful discussions of these debates, see Michel Pertué, "La Révolution française et l'abolition de la peine de mort," *Annales historiques de la Révolution Française*, 55 (1983), 14–37; J. Goulet, "Robespierre: La peine de mort et la Terreur," *Annales historiques de la Révolution Française*, 53 (1981), 219–38; and Louis Masson, *La Révolution pénale en 1791* (Nancy, 1899), 112–22.
35. *Archives parlementaires*, 26:617. Subsequent parenthetical citations refer to the *Archives parlementaires*.
36. According to the *Archives parlementaires*, this speaker's name was Mercier, presumably Louis Nicolas Lemercier, or possibly Jean Mercier-Terreford, a supplementary delegate from Bordeaux. The *Moniteur* does not identify the speaker.
37. See chapter 2 (pp. 60–2).

CHAPTER 10

1. A.N. AA 55, dossier 1513. Digitized at www.criminocorpus.cnrs.fr by Jean-Claude Farcy and Marc Renneville (accessed 3 March 2011).
2. *Mémoire d'observation sur l'exécution de la tête tranchée, avec la nature des différens inconvéniens qu'elle présente, et dont elle sera vraiment susceptible*, in *Code de la guillotine: Recueil complet de documents concernant l'application de la peine de mort en France et les exécuteurs des hautes oeuvres*, ed. Ludovic Pichon (Paris, 1910), 75–7.
3. See the letters from Louis François Ferey, the executioner of Orléans, and Joseph Doublos, the executioner of Blois, to the Minister of Justice, A.N. BB³ 206.
4. Verrier, commissaire du Roi to Roederer (2 March 1792), in *Code*, 79.
5. Minister of Justice Duport to the National Assembly (3 March 1792), in Ibid, 80–1.
6. *Archives parlementaires* (3 March 1792), 39.350.
7. A.N. AA 55, dossier 1513. Digitized at www.criminocorpus.cnrs.fr by Jean-Claude Farcy and Marc Renneville (accessed 3 March 2011).

8. *Archives parlementaires*, 40:188.
9. Letter from Roederer to Guillotin (10 March 1792), in *Code*, 82–3.
10. *Archives parlementaires* (13 March 1792), 39:677, 685.
11. Ibid (20 March 1792), 40:188.
12. Letter from Moreau to Roederer (11 April 1792), in *Code*, 91. See also the correspondence between Roederer and the Minister of Public Contributions (23 March and 5 April 1792), 83–4 and 88–9.
13. Letter from Dr. Louis to Dr. Michel Cullerier, chief physician at the Château de Bicêtre (12 April 1792), in *Code*, 93.
14. Letter from Cullerier to Louis (12 April 1792), quoted in Jacques Delarue, *Le Métier de bourreau, du moyen âge à aujourd'hui* (Paris, 1989), 130.
15. On these conflicted emotions, see Daniel Arasse, *La Guillotine et l'imaginaire de la terreur* (Paris, 1987), 34.
16. Delarue, *Métier*, 131; see also Hector Fleischmann, *La Guillotine en 1793* (Paris, 1908), 44, and Alister Kershaw, *A History of the Guillotine* (London, 1958), 45.
17. Letter from Louis to Roederer (19 April 1792), reprinted in Fleischmann, *La Guillotine en 1793*, 44.
18. Cabanis, "Note…sur l'opinion de Messieurs Oelsner et Soemmering et du citoyen Sue, touchant le supplice de la guillotine," in *Magasin encyclopédique, ou Journal des sciences, des lettres et des arts* (Paris, 1795), 5:163.
19. Roederer to Lafayette (25 April 1792), in *Code*, 100.
20. *Chronique de Paris* (26 April 1792), no. 118, 468.
21. Joseph Duplain, *Supplement au Courrier Extraordinaire* (27 April 1792), 12. This report has been incorrectly cited throughout the secondary literature as Duplan, *Journal de France*.
22. For another account of spectators singing the refrain in disappointment, see *Journal de la Cour et de la Ville*, no. 61, 482 (30 April 1792). Yet another journal report, which is nearly omnipresent in the secondary literature, but whose authenticity I have been unable to verify, describes much the same reaction as Duplain reported: "The people, moreover, were not at all satisfied. They had seen nothing. They dispersed in disappointment, singing, to console themselves the following couplet: 'Give me back my wooden gallows. Give me back my gallows.'" This report was originally quoted in G. Lenotre, *La Guillotine et les exécuteurs des arrêts criminels pendant la revolution* (Paris, 1932), 235, and subsequently cited throughout the secondary literature. Although Lenotre is normally reliable, he cites the *Chronique de Paris* as his source for this quotation, but I have been unable to find it there. I suspect this quotation may be a paraphrase of Duplain's original account, which Lenotre eventually mistook for a direct quotation and then misattributed.
23. René-Georges Gastellier, *Que Penser enfin du supplice de la guillotine?* (Paris, year IV) quoted in Arasse, *La Guillotine*, 50–1.
24. Letter from the Attorney General of the Bas-Rhin (19 May 1792), in *Code*, 101. See also Edmond Seligman, *La Justice en France pendant la révolution, 1789–1792* (Paris, 1901), 1:463–4.
25. Letter from the Commissaire du Roi of Falaise to the Minister of Justice (8 June 1792), quoted in Seligman, *La Justice*, 464.
26. Lenotre, *La Guillotine*, 164.
27. See chapter 5 (pp. 120–4).
28. *Compte rendu aux sans-culottes de la République française, par très-haute, très-puissante, et très-expéditive Dame Guillotine…contenant le nom et surnom de ceux à qui elle a accordé des passe-ports pour l'autre monde…* (Paris, year II).

29. Arasse, *La Guillotine*, 76.
30. *Le Républicain, journal des hommes libres de tous les pays* (22 January 1793), excerpted in *Captivité et derniers moments de Louis XVI*, ed. Marquis de Beaucourt (Paris, 1892), 1:340–1.
31. *Révolutions de Paris* (no. 185, 19–26 January 1793), excerpted in Ibid, 1:358–68.
32. Arasse, *La Guillotine*, 50.
33. Fleischmann, *La Guillotine en 1793*, 63.
34. Questions were consistently raised as to whether the guillotine was so quick that the head was somehow still alive, thinking and feeling, after it had been separated from the body. See Cabanis, "Note," 153–74. See also Daniel Gerould, *Guillotine: Its Legend and Lore* (New York, 1992), 53–7.
35. Quoted in Fleischmann, *La Guillotine en 1793*, 129–30.
36. Ibid, 158.
37. Ibid, 253.
38. See Lenotre, *La Guillotine*, 244, 312.
39. Mona Ozouf, *Festivals and the French Revolution*, trans. Alan Sheridan (Cambridge, MA, 1991), 176–7.
40. Report of Dutard to Garat (19 June 1793), in Adolphe Schmidt, *Tableaux de la révolution française, publiés sur les papiers inédits du département et de la police secrète de Paris* (Leipzig, 1869), 2:75.
41. Ibid, 2:76–7. See also Lenotre, *La Guillotine*, 295–6.
42. See *La Guillotine dans la révolution: Exposition organisée par Valérie Rousseau-Lagarde et Daniel Arasse* (Chateau de Vizille, 1987), 124–5 and 130–1. See also Fleischmann, *La Guillotine en 1793*, 45.
43. On the cult of the guillotine in general, see Fleischman, *La Guillotine en 1793*, 221–31 and 263–72; Lenotre, *La Guillotine*, 295–312; and Gerould, *Guillotine*. For references to the "Sainte Guillotine" (some of the more colorful of which may be Thermidorian and Counter-Revolutionary fabrications) see Fleischmann, *La Guillotine en 1793*, 223, Lenotre, *La Guillotine*, 312, Maurice Dommanget, "La Déchristianisation à Beauvais, les pratiques culturelles, les miracles et le fanatisme révolutionnaire," in *Annales révolutionnaires*, 12:46, and Georges Duval, *Souvenirs de la terreur* (Paris, 1842), 4:226.
44. Barjavel, public prosecutor of the department of the Vaucluse to the public prosecutor of the Gard (30 Brumaire, year II), quoted in Lenotre, *La Guillotine*, 54.
45. On the king as the head of France's political and mystical body, or *corpus mysticum*, see Paul Friedland, *Political Actors: Representative Bodies and Theatricality in the Age of the French Revolution* (Ithaca, NY, 2002), chapter 1.
46. Report of Pourvoyeur (1 Ventôse, year II [19 February 1794] and 19 Ventôse, year II [9 March 1794]), excerpted in Charles-Aimé Dauban, *Paris en 1794 et en 1795: Histoire de la rue, du club, de la famine* (Paris, 1869), 66 and 196.
47. Report of Perrière (16 Ventôse, year II [6 March 1794]), in Ibid, 167.
48. Dorinda Outram, *The Body and the French Revolution: Sex, Class and Political Culture* (New Haven, CT, and London, 1989), 114–15.
49. "Exécution des dames de Noailles (1794), Récit de l'abbé Carrichon...," in *La Nouvelle Revue*, 50, 299–303. See also Lenotre, *La Guillotine*, 166–76.
50. Hébert, quoted in Lenotre, *La Guillotine*, 297.
51. *Mémoires de Fleury de la Comédie française (1757 à 1820)*, ed. Jean-Baptiste-Pierre Lafitte (Paris, 1836), 4:390–1. On the myth of the *tricoteuses*, see Dominique Godineau, "La 'tricoteuse': formation d'un mythe contre-révolutionnaire," in M. Vovelle,

ed., *L'Image de la Révolution française* (Paris, 1989), 3:2 278–85, as well as Dominique Godineau, "Histoire d'un mot: tricoteuse de la Révolution française à nos jours," in *Langages de la Révolution (1770–1815)* (Paris, 1995), 601–13.
52. P. J. B. Buchez and P. C. Roux, *Histoire parlementaire de la révolution française* (Paris, 1837), 34:488.
53. Charles Dickens, *A Tale of Two Cities* (chapter 15). Carlyle had portrayed the *tricoteuses* who "shriek or knit as the case needs" as fixtures of the Jacobin club, rather than the scaffold. Thomas Carlyle, *The French Revolution: A History*, vol. 3, "The Guillotine" (London, 1837), 123.
54. Report of Pourvoyeur (6 Pluviôse, year II [25 January 1794]), in Pierre Caron, *Paris pendant la terreur. Rapports des agents secrets du ministre de l'intérieur* (Paris, 1943–), 3:149.
55. Report of Pourvoyeur (26 Pluviôse, year II [14 February 1794]), in Ibid, 4:110.
56. See chapter 7.
57. Report of Perrière (17 Ventôse, year II [7 March 1794]), in Dauban, *Paris en 1794 et en 1795*, 175–6.
58. For other examples of women accused of having sympathetic feelings towards execution victims, see the reports of Perrière and Pourvoyeur in Ibid, 115–16 and 136–7.
59. Report of Perrière (18 Ventôse, year II [8 March 1794]), in Ibid, 183.
60. Extracts of reports by Dugas and Perrière (9 Ventôse, year II [27 February 1794]), in Ibid, 121.
61. Report of Beraud (5 Pluviôse, year II [24 January 1794]), in Caron, *Paris*, 3:120.
62. Cabanis, "Note," 171.
63. See Charles de Monseignat, *Un Chapitre de la Révolution française ou Histoire des journaux en France de 1789 à 1799* (Paris, 1853), 175.
64. Dauban, *Paris en 1794 et en 1795*, 261 and 267ff, and Caron, *Paris*, 6:100.
65. Report of Latour-Lamontagne (26 Ventôse, year II [16 March 1794]), in Caron, *Paris*, 5:345–6. See also the report the following day: "There is only one cry: that the punishment of the guillotine is too gentle for the conspirators who have just been arrested. People believe that it doesn't sufficiently frighten this sort of guilty person." Report of Dugas (27 Ventôse, year II [17 March 1794]), in Ibid, 5:363.
66. Report of Boucheseiche (25 Ventôse, year II [15 March 1794]), in Ibid, 5:315.
67. Report of Grivel (5 Germinal, year II [25 March 1794]), in Ibid, 6:100.
68. Report by Pourvoyeur (26 Ventôse, year II [16 March 1794]), in Ibid, 5:354.
69. Lenotre, *La Guillotine*, 265.
70. Report of Perrière (5 Germinal, year II [25 March 1794]), in Ibid, 6:112.
71. Ibid, 6:111.
72. A letter purportedly written by a member of the Committee of Public Safety urged that some festivity be added to executions by guillotine to compensate for their spectacular shortcomings: "I don't want you to have these fuckers [*bougres*] accompanied by a drum, but by a trumpet, something which would better announce the justice of the people. It is necessary to supplement [ie. compensate for] the speed of the guillotine in order to electrify the people, while their enemies are led to the scaffold. This must be a kind of spectacle for them. Songs, dancing must prove to the aristocrats that the people see only happiness in their punishment." Quoted in Louis Marie Prudhomme, *Histoire générale et impartiale des erreurs, des fautes et des crimes commis pendant la révolution française* (Paris, 1797), 6:128. See also the *Journal de l'anarchie, de la terreur et du despotisme*... (Paris, 1821), 3:1423 and M.-A. Madrolle, *De la Nécessité d'une translation en province de la chambre des députés*... (Paris, 1829), 31, which dates the letter as having been written on 27 December 1793.)

73. Arasse, *La Guillotine*, 168. Admittedly, figures 10 and 12 are drawn by the same artist, Villeneuve; nevertheless, there is little to distinguish the portrait of one head from the other.
74. See "Loi qui établit près des tribunaux criminels un exécuteur de leurs jugemens, et qui fixe le traitement de ces exécuteurs" (13 June 1793), in *Code*, 33–5.
75. "Tableau des exécuteurs éxistant dans le Royaume," A.N. BB³ 206.
76. There are many letters from executioners refusing commissions in the south, often preferring to cite health reasons, so that they would not seem to be flouting the authority of administrators. See A.N. BB³ 207.
77. Letters from Laurent Coquellin to several different officials, A.N. BB³ 206 (July 1795).
78. Quoted in Lenotre, *La Guillotine*, 345–7.
79. "Décret sur les exécuteurs des Hautes Oeuvres" (25 November 1870), in *Code*, 64–8.

EPILOGUE

1. *Révolutions de Paris* (27 April 1793), quoted in G. Lenotre, *La Guillotine et les exécuteurs des arrêts criminels pendant la révolution* (Paris, 1932), 258–9.
2. Letter from the Procureur général syndic to Citoyen Guidon (13 May 1793), in *Code de la guillotine: Recueil complet de documents concernant l'application de la peine de mort en France et les exécuteurs des hautes oeuvres*, ed. Ludovic Pichon (Paris, 1910), 118. Chaumette's views are summarized in this letter.
3. Procès-verbal of the meeting of the General Council of Gers, quoted in G. Brégail, *Les Bourreaux à Auch* (Auch, 1923), 39.
4. Order of J. Marie, 5 Brumaire, year III (26 October 1794). A.D., Côte d'Or, L1783.
5. The citizens who live near the Place du Morimont to Citizen Calère, representative of the people... (7 Nivôse, year III [27 December 1794]), A.D., Côte d'Or, L1783.
6. Séance du 27 Prairial, year VI (15 June 1798), quoted in Brégail, *Les Bourreaux*, 52.
7. Lenotre, *La Guillotine*, 271–8; *Code*, 40. Daniel Arasse, *La Guillotine et l'imaginaire de la terreur* (Paris, 1987), 133–41.
8. Decree of the Prefect of the Seine (20 January 1832), quoted in Jacques Delarue, *Le Métier de bourreau, du moyen âge à aujourd'hui* (Paris, 1989), 270–1.
9. See Laurence Guignard, "Les Supplices publics à Paris au xixe siècle: l'abstraction du corps," in *Le Corps violenté, du geste à la parole*, ed. Michel Porret (Geneva, 1998), 167. On the parallels between capital punishment and animal slaughter, see Paul Friedland, "Friends for Dinner: 'Humane Slaughter' and the Early Modern Roots of Modern Carnivorous Sensibilities," in *History of the Present: A Journal of Critical History*, 1:1 (Summer 2011), 84–112.
10. Victor Hugo, "Fragment sur la peine de mort," *Revue de Paris*, 36 (Paris, 1832), 181–2.
11. See Maxime du Camp, *Paris, ses organes, ses fonctions et sa vie dans la seconde moitié du XIXe siècle* (Paris, 1875), 3:259. See also Gordon Wright, *Between the Guillotine and Liberty: Two Centuries of the Crime Problem in France* (New York and Oxford, 1983), 70, and Delarue, *Le Métier*, 299–300.
12. Delarue, *Le Métier*, 299–300. The five granite slabs put in place at this location to support the weight of the guillotine are still visible at the intersection of the Rue de la Croix Faubin and the Rue de la Roquette.
13. Maxime du Camp, *Paris*, 3:260. This description was originally written in 1869, before the scaffold was eliminated, and was first published in *Revue des Deux Mondes*, 85 (January 1870).

14. De Camp, *Paris*, 3:299–300.
15. J. L. Ortolan, *Eléments de droit penal* (Paris, 1855), 901.
16. Babinet report (1864), quoted in Delarue, *Le Métier*, 304. See also the report of 1870 in *Code*, 121–4.
17. Jean-François Heidenreich, quoted in Delarue, *Le Métier*, 304.
18. "Décret sur les exécuteurs des Hautes Oeuvres" (25 November 1870), in *Code*, 64–8.
19. Chamber of Deputies, session of 20 March 1879 (Annexe no. 1,265), in *Journal officiel de la République Française* (3 April 1879), 2,868.
20. In 1877, the Minister of the Interior sent around a notice to all the prefects of France, forbidding the handing out of entry passes to journalists on the day of execution in order to prevent the publication of "accounts in which the public often found details designed to satisfy a misplaced curiosity." (*Circulaire du Ministre de l'Intérieur aux préfets au sujet des autorisations de pénétrer dans les prisons le jour où doivent avoir lieu des exécutions capitales* (15 January 1877), in *Code*, 69).
21. See chapter 7 (p. 191).
22. Chamber of Deputies, session of 20 March 1879 (Annexe no. 1,265) in *Journal officiel de la République Française*, 92 (3 April 1879), 2,868.
23. Ibid.
24. Ibid.
25. Emmanuel Taïeb, "Le Débat sur la publicité des exécutions capitales: Usages et enjeux du questionnaire de 1835," *Genèses*, 54 (March 2004), 137–9.
26. The Court of Appeals of Riom, quoted in Emmanuel Taïeb, "La Peine de mort en République, un 'faire mourir' souverain?," *Quaderni*, 62 (Winter 2006–7), 20.
27. The Court of Appeals of Douai, quoted in Ibid.
28. *Le Rappel* (10 December 1884), quoted in Ibid.
29. Pierre Lallier, "Publicité des exécutions capitales," *Revue pénitentiaire, Bulletin de la Société Générale des Prisons* (Paris and Melun, 1894), 18th Year, 924–6, and *Pandectes françaises: nouveau répertoire de doctrine, de législation et de jurisprudence*, ed. André Weiss and H. Frennelet (Paris, 1903), 44:805.
30. Ibid, 44:806. This objection recalls the suspicion of spectators at the execution of the veiled Madame de Lescombat in 1755. See chapter 7.
31. Delarue, *Le Métier*, 342–5.
32. *Circulaire* of the Minister of the Interior (11 January 1909), reproduced in A. Montagne, "Droit et libertés publiques: les actualités filmées ont enfanté la censure du cinéma français en 1905," *Les Cahiers de la Cinémathèque*, 66 (July 1997), 84–6.
33. See David Walker, "Literature, History and Factidiversiality," *Journal of European Studies*, 25 (March 1995), 35–50.
34. *Petit Parisien* (17 June 1939).
35. *Paris-Soir* (18 June 1939), quoted in Simon Grivet, "Executions and the Debate over Abolition in France and the United States," in *Is the Death Penalty Dying? European and American Perspectives*, eds. Austin Sarat and Jürgen Martschukat (Cambridge, 2011), 160.
36. Delarue, *Le Métier*, 356–8.
37. *L'Ouest-Eclair* (28 June 1939).
38. *Journal officiel* (25 June 1939), cited on http://www.ladocumentationfrancaise.fr/dossiers/abolition-peine-mort/decret-loi1939.shtml (accessed 1 March 2011).
39. Even today, spectators can view the execution of Weidmann on the internet.
40. *Paris-Municipal* (23 July 1939).

CONCLUSION

1. See the Introduction (p. 2).
2. (State of Georgia v. A Number of Dangerous Dogs. August 17, 2009)
3. The prosecution of human negligence is usually demanded in cases of animal homicide if there is any possible rationale that can justify it. In the well-known case of the homicidal Pitt Bulls in California, the dogs were euthanized, and in the subsequent trial, the two owners were respectively found guilty of second-degree murder and involuntary manslaughter. (People of the State of California v. Robert Noel and Marjorie Knoller [2002]). In a more recent case, in which a couple's pet python killed their daughter in the middle of the night, the parents were found guilty of third-degree murder, manslaughter, and child neglect (State of Florida v. Jaren Hare and Charles Darnell [2011]).

Index

Abbeville 60
Ableiges, Jacques d' 47, 64–5
Abelard, Peter 48
abortion 148
Actes des Apôtres 223
actors 76, 169, 224–6, 255
adultery 36–7, 55–6, 95, 135–6, 139, 197
Agen 46, 127
Alaric II, Visigothic king 27;
  see also *Breviary* of Alaric
amende honorable 96–9, 102, 108, 125–6, 147, 149, 176–7
  sèche 92, 96
Amiens 73, 79
anatomy theaters 130–1
animals
  compared to dangerous criminals 197, 203, 215
  liability of for damages or crimes committed by 41
  natural behavior and emotions of 161–2
  punishment of, 1–11, 17–19, 91, 106–7, 110–16, 280–3, 303 n.45
  restrictions on the keeping of 76, 78
  sexual relations with, *see* sodomy
  suffering of 151, 155, 162–3, 187
  theft of 29–30
  vivisection of 129–30
Angers 114
Anselm of Canterbury 36, 44, 98
Antwerp 124
Aquinas, Thomas 203, 290 n.77
Arasse, Daniel 249–50, 262
Aristocracy
  execution of during the Terror, 253
  penchant for watching executions among 144–50, 155–7, 165–7, 171, 179, 182–3, 188–90
  privileges of 75–6
  punishment of 63, 166, 172–3
Armstrong, David 12
Arras 65, 73–4, 77, 79, 87
arson 64, 220, 231, 236–7
assault 50, 54
Asemblée nationale, *see* National Assembly
assets, confiscation of 56, 58–9, 63, 90, 93, 109; see also civil death
Assizes of Jerusalem 55
atonement, *see* penance; *see also amende honorable*; redemption
Auch 268
audience
  compassion of 91, 101, 103–5, 119–20, 127, 136–43, 147–8, 164, 167, 184, 186, 206, 236, 252, 256, 302 n.41
  criticism of for watching penal spectacle 149–51, 155–8, 160–2, 164, 165–6, 170, 173, 176–83, 186–91, 266, 271
  horror expressed by 180–3, 186–91, 256–8;
    see also executions, horror of
  hostility expressed by 104, 106, 119, 126–7, 137–9, 142, 148, 164, 167, 177, 247, 254–6, 259–60
  large number of spectators in 110, 119, 124, 126, 138–40, 144, 147–8, 156–7, 165, 170, 172–4, 176–9, 186, 188, 254, 260, 274
  reaction of at odds with deterrent intent 16–17, 23, 91, 110–1, 131–2, 141–2, 149, 165–6, 173, 175, 190–91, 227, 231–2, 234, 238, 242, 258, 267, 270–2, 275, 279
  social composition of 142–3, 145, 147, 150, 164, 165–6, 183–4, 186, 189–91, 272, 274–5
  supposed disorderly nature of in 19th and 20th centuries 271–7
  supposed terror experienced by 12–14, 23, 91, 109–10, 177, 201, 273, 275, 279, 302 n.40
  voyeurism of 119–20, 127, 130–3, 136, 141–58, 164, 165–91, 252, 272, 274–275
  watching from windows, 120, 130–3, 140–2, 144, 147–50, 155–8, 164, 165–6, 172–3, 176–80, 182, 186, 188, 259–61, 276, 278; *see also* sympathy; guillotine, spectator reactions to; tricoteuses
Augsburg 73
Austria 75
Autopsy, *see* dissection
Avignon 46, 63, 73, 105
Ayrault, Pierre 114–16

Baasner, Frank 153–4, 160
Bachaumont, Louis Petit de 188
Back, family of executioners 75
Balleroy, Madeleine Charlotte Emilie, marquise de 166
banishment 56, 61, 65, 90–1, 94–5, 99–100, 108, 229, 284
  compared to death penalty 197, 203–4, 217, 230, 284
  see also executions, as casting out
barbarians, *see* Burgundians; Ripurian Franks; Salian Franks; Visigoths

Barbier, Edmond-Jean-François 168–70, 172, 174–7, 180, 200
Bardoux, Agénor 273
Barère (de Vieuzac), Bertrand 233
Barnwell, P. S. 25
Barthès, Pierre 168, 188
Basel 128–9
basses oeuvres, *see* executioners, works other than punishment performed by
Bastien, Pascal 13, 14, 104, 302 n.37
Bataille, Georges 103
Baudouin, François 114
Beaumanoir, Philippe de 46–7, 50–51, 54–55, 58–60, 63, 112–14
Beccaria, Cesare 195, 205–17, 226–28
Bée, Michel 14–15, 17, 103–4
beheading 63, 102, 129, 131, 133, 140, 156, 172–3, 186–7, 215
 as sole means of capital punishment 219–21, 235–7, 240–3; *see also* guillotine
Belgium 106, 111
Belleperche, Pierre de 51–2, 292 n.43
Benoist, Michel 87
Bentham, Jeremy 14, 202, 207–8
Bergues (Flanders) 55
Berman, Harold 30, 39, 43
Bernard, Pierre 92–5
Bernardi, Joseph Elzéar Dominique 214
Berquin, Louis 125–6
bestiality, *see* sodomy
Béthune, town of 274
Béziers, Abbé 3–6
Bicêtre, hospital of 246
 prison of 269
Binder, Guyora 49
Blanot, John de 55
blasphemy 57, 62, 77, 100, 125–6, 138, 166
Blois 73
Bodin, Jean 114–16
boiling 54, 59–60, 63, 151
Bologna, law school of 40
Bonnet, Charles 184
Bordeaux 46, 84
Bouches-du-Rhône 264
Boutillier, Jean 47, 53–4, 63
branding 90, 93–5, 100, 108, 126, 221, 235
Breviary of Alaric 27–8, 39
Brillat-Savarin, Jean Anthelme 232
Brillon, A. 4, 6
Brinvilliers, Marie Marguerite d'Aubray, marquise de 146–9, 155
Brissot de Warville, Jacques-Pierre 210–16
Britain, 35, 37, 40, 46, 52, 158–62 183, 197, 208, 272
Brittany 145–6
Brittany conspiracy 252
Britton 54
Brundage, James 16, 40, 44
Buchez, P. J. B. 255
Budé, Guillaume 113, 305 n.75

Burgundians 27, 29, 32
Burke, Edmund 184–6
Burlamaqui, Jean-Jacques 203, 216
burning, at the stake 2, 28, 57, 59–60, 63, 110–11, 125–8, 138–9, 147–9, 166
 of books, 125–6, 200
burying alive 57, 63
Buvat, Jean 168

Cabanis, Pierre Jean George 247–8, 258
cadavers, punishment of, *see* punishments, post-mortem; *see also* suicide; dissection
Caen 3, 107
Caesarius, bishop of Arles 34
Caillois, Roger 103
Calés, J. Marie 267
canards 135–7, 139
canon law 16, 38, 40–1, 44–5, 48–9, 214
Canu, Alexandre 126–7
capital punishment, original definition of 90, 94; *see* death penalty; executions
Caractères, Les 149
Carbasse, Jean 30, 56
Carlier, Jean Baptiste François 75
Carloman, king of the Franks 36
Carlyle, Thomas 255
Carrichon, abbé 254–5
Cartouche 169–72, 172, 179, 231–2
Cartouche, musical comedy 169–70
carts (transporting the condemned) 94, 101–2, 257–61, 266, 269–70
Casanova, Giacomo 182–3
Catherine the Great, 208, 210, 212, 215
Catholicism, *see* punishments, religious aspects of; *see also amende honorable*; Christ, Passion of; confession; penance; redemption; *Salve Regina*; sin
Caumartin de Boissy, brother of the marquise de Balleroy 166, 172
Caumont 55
Caux 73
censorship 272–4, 276–7, 323 n.20
Chabroud, Jean-Baptiste Charles 230, 235–6
Châlons-sur-Marne 74, 81
 competition of 210–1
Chalon-sur-Saône 85
Charlemagne 33–4, 36–8
Charles V, king of France 56
Charles VI, king of France 89
Charles VII, king of France 47
Charles the Bald 24
Charnage, Claude François Blondeau de 3–4
charrette, *see* cart
Chartres 77, 111
Chaulnes, Madame de 149
Chaumette, Pierre-Gaspard 267
Chesdeville, François 87
Chiffoleau, Jacques 63
Childebert, king 32
children, punishment of 63, 92

Index

sensitivity of 162, 181
chrenecruda 99
civil death 90, 108; *see also* assets, confiscation of
class, *see* audience, social composition of; *see also* aristocracy
Clermont 109
Clermont-Tonnerre, Stanislas de 224–6
Clovis, king of the Franks 29
Cohen, Esther 14–15, 17, 38, 47, 99, 101
Collé, Charles 180
Colombières, François de Bricqueville, sieur de 133
Comédie française 169
Comité de Constitution 226–38
Comité de Législation Criminelle 222, 226–38, 240, 242–3, 245
common law, as pan-regional customary law of France 66
   as romano-canonical law, or *ius commune* 41
   in England 49
compassion, *see* audience, compassion of; *see also* sympathy
compensation, *see* fines
Conciergerie 92, 123, 133, 155–6
condemned, *see* patient
confession 36, 89, 99, 101
confessors 93, 101–3, 133, 144, 148, 244, 249, 254, 266
confraternities 105–6
confrérie de la Misericorde 105
Conseil de Pierre de Fontaines 46, 49–50
Constantia, De 151–2
contumace, 108–9; *see also* effigies
Coquellin, Laurent 264
Corday, Charlotte 253
Corneille, Pierre 141, 149
Corneille, Thomas 149
Corpus Iuris Civilis 27, 38–46, 113–14
counterfeiting 53–4, 57, 59–60, 96, 211, 231, 292 n.35
Courrier Extraordinaire 247
Coutances 74
Coutume de Vermandois 47
Coutumes de l'Anjou 50
Coutumes du comté de Clermont en Beauvaisis, see Beaumanoir
Coutumes et stilles observez et gardez ès pays d'Anjou et du Maine 47
Crémieux, Adolphe 271
Crespin, Jean 126–7
crimes, public fascination with 135–42, 146–50, 168–72; *see*; *a*dultery; arson; assault; blasphemy; counterfeiting; heresy; incest; *lèse-majesté*; manslaughter; murder; parricide; poisoning; prostitution; rape; regicide; sodomy; theft; treachery; treason

crimen laesae majestatis see *lèse-majesté*
criminal ordinance of 1670, *see* royal ordinance, of 1670
crowd, *see* audience
Croÿ Solre, Emmanuel de 177, 179
Cullerier, Michel (Dr.) 246–7
Custine, Adam Philippe, comte de 233–4, 237–8, 265, 271
customals, drafting of 46–7
   editing of in 16th century 66
customary law 23–5, 46–67, 89, 113–16

D'Alembert, Jean le Rond 205
Dalembourg, family of executioners 75
Damiens, Robert-François 12–13, 137, 157, 165, 175–88, 191, 205, 209, 216, 256, 294 n.79
David, Jacques-Louis 260–1
death penalty (as concept, divorced from spectacle)
   debates in National Assembly on 219–38
   opposition to in pre-Revolutionary period 189, 196–200, 204, 207–9, 212, 214–16
   proposed methods for executing humanely 240–43
   support for in pre-Revolutionary period 195, 197, 199, 202–4, 207–9, 214–17, 218; *see also* executions (as public performance); guillotine
DeJean, Joan 153–4
Delisle de Sales, Jean-Baptiste-Claude 213, 215
Descartes, René 152–3, 159
desertion 60, 211, 218
Desjardins, Albert 218
Desmorest, family of executioners 74, 87
Desrues, Antoine François 97, 188
deterrence, general concept of 5
   in early modern theory and practice 104, 109–16, 139, 151, 165, 188, 197–8, 200–2, 205–7, 210–12, 214, 216–7, 219, 302 n.40
   in medieval theory and practice 33–4, 37, 44, 51, 56, 89, 91–2, 100, 109–13
   in modern penal thought 15, 266, 270, 272–5, 279, 282–4
   in Revolutionary theory and practice 227–38, 241–2, 244, 258
   in Roman law 43
   intent of, at odds with audience reactions 16–17, 23, 91, 110–1, 131–2, 141–2, 149, 165–6, 173, 175, 190–91, 227, 231–2, 234, 238, 242, 258, 267, 270–2, 275, 279
   retroactively imposed on customary penal practices 5, 11–12, 30, 112–16, 280
   see also punishments, spectacular
La Devineresse 149, 169–70

Dickens, Charles 255
Diderot, Denis 181, 204
Digest 38–9, 41–3, 50–1, 53, 292 n.35
Dijon 73, 76–82, 85, 87, 95, 267–8
Discipline and Punish 11–14, 71, 176
dissection 129–31
dismemberment, *see* mutilation
drawing, prior to execution of death sentence 57–9, 63–4, 109, 188, 215
Drew, Katherine Fischer 24
droit écrit, *see* Roman law
Dubos, Abbé Jean-Baptiste 162, 167–8, 185–6
Du Camp, Maxime 270, 272
Dufau, Antoine 234
Dufort de Cheverny, Jean Nicolas 182
Dülmen, Richard van 14
Du Moulin, Charles 66
Du Noyer, Anne-Marguerite 155–6, 278
Dupaty, Charles Marguerite Jean Baptiste Mercier, 209
Duplain, Joseph 247
Duport, Adrien 232
Duport-Dutertre, Louis-François 87, 242, 245
Durandus de St. Pourçain 44
Duret, Jean 114
Du Vair, Guillaume 152–3

échelle, *see* pillory
Edelstein, Dan 314 n.20, 314 n.28
edict of Pistes 24
effigies 13, 56, 91, 106–12, 114, 273, 280, 284, 303 n.45
Elias, Norbert 14, 142
Elizabeth, Tsarina of Russia 212
emotions, 151–64, 181; *see also* audience, compassion of; pity, tragic; sympathy; sensibility
Encyclopédie 204
England, *see* Britain
Erasmus, Desiderius 125
Esprit des lois 200–2, 204
Essarts, Pierre des 120
Estates General (of 1789) 218–19
Etablissements de Saint Louis 46, 62
Etampes 74
Euric, code of 27
Evans, E.P. 9, 111
Evans, Richard J. 14
eye for an eye, *see* talion, law of
example, *see* deterrence
executioners
  abolition of privileges of 85–7
  attacks against 81, 85, 106, 241
  civil status of debated in National Assembly 224–6
  clothing and patches worn by 72, 79–81, 223
  cry of 94, 300 n.10
  curative powers of 72
  emotion expressed by 139, 156
  family members of 73, 81–2, 85
  fees and salary paid to 83–6
  hereditary dynasties and endogamy among 72–5
  outcast status of 71–88, 95, 221, 223, 262–4
  in post-Revolutionary France 264–5, 271
  privileges of 72, 75–88, 262
  profane touch of 71–2, 78–9, 82, 86, 90–5, 99, 140, 219, 225, 243
  in Revolutionary France 87–8, 241, 262–4
  rise of the profession of 73–5
  works other than punishment performed by 76–8, 81; *see also* guillotine, effect of on executioners
executions (as public performance)
  accounts of prior to Reformation, 120–4
  accounts of during Reformation and wars of religion 124–35
  accounts of in Revolutionary period 248–60
  accounts of in 17th and 18th century 134–49, 155–83, 186–91
  as casting out 90–1, 95, 98–101
  cost of 83–6
  drawing prior to 57–9, 63–4, 109
  frequency of 120
  horror of 165, 167, 180–3, 186–91, 205–6, 209, 235–6, 240, 242–3, 256–8, 267–8, 271
  iconographic logic of 59
  location of 102, 236, 238, 244, 267–70, 302 n.40
  performed on animals 1–11, 17–19, 91, 106–7, 110–16
  performed on books 125
  performed on cadavers 91, 107, 109–11, 115–16
  performed on effigies 13, 56, 91, 106–12
  procession towards 101–2, 106, 108, 147, 249, 254, 256, 270
  religious aspects of 101–7
  ritual of in medieval Europe 57–65, 89
  shift from ritual to spectacle of 121, 124–42; *see also* audience; spectacular punishment; for specific types of execution *see* beheading; boiling; burning at the stake; burying alive; *fourches patibulaires*; guillotine; hanging; quartering; wheel
exemplary deterrence, *see* deterrence
extermination 197, 284; *see also* death penalty

Falaise, 1–11, 17–19, 84, 248
  Church of the Holy Trinity in 6, 18–19; *see also* Sow of Falaise
Fallières, Armand 274
Favre, Robert 316 n.56
Ferey, family of executioners 74–5
feudalism, bonds and loyalty in 55, 60

fiction, *see* novels
Fiering, Norman 158
Filarete 196–7, 227
Filles-Dieu 102
film, *see* motion pictures
fines
  collected by executioner 76–7
  in customary law 50–51, 55–6, 62
  in medieval and early modern periods 92
  in penitentials 35–6
  in Salic law 29–33
Flanders 84
Fléchier, Esprit 109
Fleury, actor 255
Fontaines, Pierre de 46, 49–50
forced labor 195–200, 204, 206–7, 210–16, 228, 235, 258; *see also* galleys
Foucault, Michel 11–16, 71, 176
fourches patibulaires 60–5, 89, 102, 109, 294–5 n.54
Fraher, Richard 43–4
Frangipani, comte de 145
Frankfurt 80
Franks, *see* Salian Franks or Ripurian Franks; *see also* Salic law
Frolo, Jean 108
furies, *see* tricoteuses

Galigai, Leonora 138
galleys 90, 93–5, 99–100, 108, 221
Gallo-Romans 27, 29
gallows speeches, *see* patients, speeches of
Gamaches, Étienne-Simon de 159–62, 164
gambling 50, 77, 135
Garat, Dominique 233–4
Garland, David 12
Garnot, Benoît 108
Gastellier, René-Georges 248
Gatrell, V.A.C. 286 n.29, 313 n.73
Gaudemet, Jean 25, 27, 28, 38, 49
Gaul, Roman province of 24–7, 38–9
Gauvard, Claude 14, 120–1
Gazette d'Amsterdam 176
Gazette de Paris 144
Geertz, Clifford 14
Geneva 108–9, 126
Georgia (United States), 281–3
Germany 27, 73, 75, 77, 79–80, 89, 111, 135, 145, 270, 272
Gers, department of 267
Gilbert, Nicolas-Joseph-Laurent 187
Girardet, citizen 240
gladiatorial combat 28
Glanvill 46
glossators 40
Gonthier, Nicole 14, 99
grace 94, 121–3, 136, 155
Grand Coutumier de France 47, 64–5
Grand Coutumier de Normandie 46
Gratian, canon lawyer 40

Gregory VII, pope 39, 43, 52
Grenoble 264
Grève, *see* Place de Grève
Grévy, Jules 271–3
Grignan, Françoise-Marguerite de Sévigné, comtesse de 145–49, 154
Grotius, Hugo 203, 216
Guémadeuc, Thomas de 139–40
Gueullette, Thomas-Simon 168–70, 172–3, 175–80, 248, 278
Guillaume, family of executioners 74–5, 83
Guillaume, Louis-Marie 220–1
Guillotin, Joseph-Ignace 219–25, 244–5, 247–9, 253
guillotine
  accounts of execution by 248–60
  as exemplification of industrial mass production 250–2, 260–5, 278–9
  effect of on profession of executioner 88, 223, 225, 262–5
  first use of 247–8
  idea of proposed to National Assembly 221–5
  invention and construction of 243–6
  location of 267–70
  popularity of 252–60
  relative invisibility of 247–8, 250, 258, 260–1, 265, 270
  spectator reactions to 183, 247–60
  speed of 247–8, 250, 258, 265, 270, 320 n.34.
  vanishing of 266–79

hanging 28–9, 57–60, 63–4, 133, 235
Hardy, Siméon-Prosper 168, 180, 182, 186, 188, 190, 248
Hausset, Nicole du 182
haute justice, *see* high justice
havage, *see* executioners, privileges of
Hébert, Jacques René (Père Duchesne) 253–4, 259–60
Henri II, king of France 133
Henri III, king of France 133
heresy 44–5, 51–2, 59, 64, 96, 108, 124–28, 131
high justice 58, 63–6, 76, 82; *see also* low justice
Histoire des Sevarambes 197–8
Histoires tragiques 136–42, 148, 187–8
Hobbes, Thomas 39, 158, 160, 162–3
Hoïm, comte d' 172
homicide, simple, *see* manslaughter; premeditated, *see* murder
homogenization of punishment
  in Europe, 37–41, 45
  in France 66–67, 89–90
homosexuality, *see* sodomy
honor 30–1, 36, 59, 201; see also *amende honorable*
Honorius III, pope 40

Horn, Antoine comte de 166, 172
horror, *see* executions, horror of
Hôtel de Ville, *see* Place de Grève
Hotman, François 113–14
Hugo, Victor 269–70
Huguenots, *see* Protestants
Hume, David 310 n.68
Hunt, Lynn 14, 150, 205
Hurel, J.-M. 18
Hutcheson, Francis 162, 181

Ibelin, Jean d' 55
incarceration, *see* prison
incest 32, 135–7, 139
Innocent III, pope 44, 52
inquisitorial system 37, 43, 66
insanity, as excusing culpability 50
insouciance, *see* audience, voyeurism of; *see also* sympathy
intentionality
  concept of in Roman law 30, 41–3, 48
  in customary law 48–56
  in medieval and early modern penal practice 112–16
  in modern period 282–3; *see also* malice aforethought
Ireland 35
Irnerius, scholar of Roman law 38–40, 289 n.57
Italy 38–40, 59, 105, 205, 208

Jars, Chevalier de 144
Jaucourt, Louis de 204
Jefferson, Thomas 208
Jews 72, 76, 80, 166, 224–5, 304 n.69
Joan of Arc 305 n.5
Joly de Fleury, Jean-François 86
Jouhanne, Nicolas 73
Journal des Etats Généraux 221
Journal d'un bourgeois de Paris (1405–1449) 120, 248
Journal d'un bourgeois de Paris (16th century) 122, 124–5
judgment, *see* sentence
judicial discretion 66
Justinian, emperor 27, 38; see also *Corpus Iuris Civilis*

Kantorowicz, Hermann 39
Kuttner, Stephan 39, 48–9

La Bruyère, Jean de 149–51, 155, 160, 164
Lachèze-Murel, Pierre Joseph 234
La Condamine, Charles Marie de 179
Lafayette, Gilbert du Motier, marquis de 247
Lally, Thomas Arthur, comte de 186–8, 240, 243
Lameth, Charles Malo François de 234
Langevin, P. G. 4–6, 10, 18

Laon 74
Lateran Council of 1215 36, 45
La Voisin, *see* Monvoisin, Catherine
law schools, rise of in the Middle Ages 40–1, 44, 46
Lefranc, Pierre 84
Legrand, Jérôme 233–5
Lenotre, G. 248–9, 260
Lepeletier de Saint Fargeau, Louis Michel 226–30, 233–6, 238
lepers 76–8, 80–1
Lescombat, madame de 174–5, 243, 272
lèse majesté, 44, 52–4, 63, 65, 123, 138, 292 n.35, 292 n.43
lèse-nation 228, 231
L'Estoile, Pierre de 132–36, 177
lethal injection 282–3
Leviathan 158
lex talionis, *see* talion, law of
liability, concept of in Roman law 41–3
Liancourt, François Alexandre Frédéric, duc de (la Rochefoucauld) 222
Life Magazine 277
liminality, *see* punishment, as casting out
Limoges 105–6
Lipsius, Justus 151–2
Livre de Jostice et de Plet 46, 49, 50, 54, 59–60, 62–3
Locke, John 203
Lombards 32
Louis the Pious 37
Louis IX, king of France 56
Louis XIV, king of France 155–6, 169
Louis XV, king of France 170
Louis XVI, king of France 74, 218–20, 249–51
Louis, Antoine (Dr.) 243, 245–7
low justice 58, 63–5, 76
Lupoi, Maurizio 30
Luther, Martin 125
Lutherans, executions of 124–27, 130; *see also* Protestants
Lyon 105

Mably, Gabriel Bonnot de 214, 231
Maistre, Joseph de 72
Malebranche, Nicolas de 158–60, 164
malice aforethought 30, 38, 48, 51, 56, 63–4, 113, 295 n.84
Mandeville, Bernard 159, 163
Mandrin, Louis 174
Mangin, Arthur 7–8
Mansfield, Mary 36
manslaughter 30–1, 48, 50, 56, 64, 112, 324 n.3
Marais, Mathieu 168–9
Marat, Jean-Paul 211, 213, 217
Marie-Antoinette 253–4, 260–1
Marillac, Louis de, Maréchal de France 144
Marivaux, Pierre de 167–8, 181

massarrer 129
Match 277
Maton de La Varenne, Pierre-Anne-Louis de 226
Maury, abbé 224, 231
Mauss, Marcel 103
Medici, Catherine de' 133
Medici, Marie de' 138
medicine, punishment conceived of as, 44, 202–4, 290 n.77
mens rea, *see* intentionality; *see also* malice aforethought
Mercier, Louis-Sébastien 72, 182, 188–90
Mercure 169, 221
Metz 210
middle justice 64
mines, *see* forced labor
Mirabeau, Honoré Gabriel Riqueti, comte de 220, 223
missi dominici 37
Moeglin, Jean-Marie 97–8
Les Moeurs 199–200
Moiria, 173
monetary fines, *see* fines
Monfaucon 102, 294 n.65
Mongommeri, Gabriel comte de 133
Moniteur 223
Montaigne, Michel de 150–1, 155, 161, 163, 196
Montaigu, Jean 121–2
Montesquieu, Charles-Louis de Secondat, Baron de 24, 195, 200–5, 207–8, 210, 215–16, 226
Montigny 102
Montpellier, city of 128–32
law school of 40
Monvoisin, Catherine 148–9, 155, 169–70
More, Thomas 196–9, 202
Morellet, abbé 205, 208, 215
motion pictures 260, 274–5, 277–9, 284
Mougins de Roquefort, Jean-Joseph 231
Muchembled, Robert 14
murder, premeditated 48, 50–1, 57–8, 64, 109, 137, 166, 215, 220, 228, 231, 236–7; *see also* manslaughter
Murray, Alexander 50
mutilation 57, 60, 62, 76, 90, 100–1, 125–6, 131, 138, 166, 176, 178–9, 233, 294 n.71
Muyart de Vouglans, Pierre-François 214

Nancy 262–3
Nantes 166
National Assembly 219–38
National Defense, government of 271
National Guard 247
natural law, 198, 200, 203–4, 209, 214
Netherlands 2, 75, 89, 124, 183
Nicholls, David 127
Noailles, Anne D'Arpajon, Maréchale de 254

nobility, *see* aristocracy
Normandy 46, 73
Normans 37
novels 150, 284; *see also* pity, tragic
nuda cogitatio 51; *see also* intentionality

L'Ouest-Eclair 276
On the Laws and Customs of England 46
Orléans, city of 74
Orléans, Elizabeth Charlotte, Princess Palatine, duchesse d' 172
Orléans, Philippe II, duc d', regent of France 169
Ortolan, Joseph Louis 24, 270
Outram, Dorinda 254
Outredebanque, Pierre Joseph 87
Ozouf, Mona 251

Pactus legis Salicae, *see* Salic law
Papin, Léger 222–3
pardon, *see grace*
Paris-Municipal
Paris-Soir 276
parricide 28, 57–9, 100–1, 134, 176, 198, 233, 236–7.
Pas-de-Calais 274
Passion of Christ 15, 101–2
passions, *see* emotions
Passions de l'âme, Les 152
patients
active participation of in penal ritual 98, 119, 123–4, 129, 133
definition of 94
post-mortem punishment and/or display of 89, 91, 104, 106–7, 109–10, 115–16, 129, 133, 131, 138, 151, 176, 188
reintegration of at death 99, 101–7, 109
remorse expressed by 90, 101–5, 119, 123–5, 134, 136–40, 156, 166, 178
speeches of 123, 126–7, 129, 133–8, 140, 249
strange behavior of 120–1, 124;
unrepentant attitude of 124–6, 133–4, 137–8, 149
pays de coutumes, *see* customary law
pays de droit écrit, *see* Roman law
Pelletier, Nicolas-Jacques 247, 253
Penal Code (of 1791) 226–38
penal reform 195–216
penal servitude, *see* forced labor
penance, public 33–8, 97–9; *see also amende honorable*; confession
penitents, *see* confraternities
pénitents noirs 106
pénitents pourpres 106
Perpignan 106
Pennington, Ken 44
Pennsylvania, Constitution of 210
Père Duchesne, *see* Hébert, Jacques René
Pétion de Villeneuve, Jérôme 231–2

Petit Parisien 275–6, 278
photography 277, 283; *see also* motion pictures
Picardie 86
pillory 60–3, 65, 76, 90, 95–6, 98–99, 102, 107, 126, 234
Pinel, Nicolas 216
Pippin, king of the Franks 36
Pirot, Edme 148
pity, tragic 137–43, 148, 155–7, 161, 164, 184; *see also* sympathy; audience, compassion of
Place de la Bastille 268
Place de Grève 103, 122–3, 126, 133–4, 139, 144, 148–9, 155, 165–6, 170, 173–9, 182, 186, 188–9, 268–9
Place de la Liberté (Dijon) 268
Place de la Révolution 249, 256, 258–60, 268–9
Place du Morimont (Dijon) 268
Place du Trône-Renversé 268
Platter, Felix 128–32, 143, 248
poisoning 96, 146–9, 188, 220, 228, 231, 236–7
Poitiers 83–5
Pontcallec, Clément-Chrysogone de Guer, marquis de 166
Pontoise 75
Porret, Michel 14, 108–9
Pourvoyeur, police observer 255–6
Prairial, uprising of 269
Préandeau, madame (de) 180–2, 187, 190, 278
prison, 12, 51, 125–6, 196, 198, 212, 217, 221, 227–32, 234, 269–70, 272, 276–7, 279, 284
  compared to death penalty, 234, 278
private settlement of disputes 30
procession toward the scaffold, *see* executions, procession towards; *see also* carts
prostitutes 61, 63, 76–8, 80–1
Protestants 108, 124–28, 131–35
Prudhomme, Louis-Marie 223–4, 229, 250, 266
Prugnon, Louis-Pierre-Joseph 230–1
public safety, as rationale for death penalty 202–4, 208, 215, 231–2, 246, 258, 283; *see also* self-defense, death penalty as form of societal
Pugachev rebellion 215

quartering 63, 129, 131, 146, 151, 165, 176, 178–9, 215, 294 n.79
question préalable and *préparatoire*, *see* torture
Quebec 75

Radding, Charles 39
rape 29, 58, 64, 134, 137
Le Rappel 273
Ravaillac, François 13, 176–7, 216, 294 n.79

Ravel, Jeffrey 309 n.45
reason, contrasted to passion 151–5, 159, 163
Réaux, Gédéon Tallemant, Sieur des 144
redemption, communal 13, 44, 91, 104–5, 119, 141
reform, *see* penal reform
regicide 12–13, 52–54, 100, 165, 176–9, 216; *see also* Damiens, Ravaillac
religion, *see* punishments, religious aspects of; see also *amende honorable;* confession; confraternities; Passion of Christ; penance; redemption; *Salve Regina;* sin
remorse, *see* patients, remorse expressed by
Rennes 146
Rétif de la Bretonne, Nicolas-Edme 188–91, 256
Revolution of 1830 269
Revolution of 1848 270
Révolutions de Paris 223–4, 229, 250, 266
Richardson, Samuel 150
Richelieu, Cardinal 144
Richelieu, Louis François Armand Du Plessis, duc de 182
Ripurian Franks 29, 32
Robespierre, Maximilien de 210, 219, 231, 238, 315 n.38
Roederer, Pierre-Louis 209, 241, 243–5, 247
Roman law, after fall of Rome 23–9; 38–9
  in 11th–13th centuries, 38–41, 44
  infiltration into customary law, 47–66
  influence on modern law 283
  reevaluation of in 16th century, 113–16; see also *Corpus Iuris Civilis*; *Digest*; intentionality, liability, malice aforethought, *Theodosian Code*
Roquette, prison of 270
Rosset, François de 136–42, 148, 187–8, 284
Rouen 73–4, 81, 83
Rousseau, Jean-Jacques 150, 161–3, 181, 183–4, 204, 208, 215–16, 231
Roux, P.C. 255
royal ordinance
  of 1396, 89–91, 101
  of 1670 (Criminal Ordinance), 66, 108
  of Blois, 66
  of Villers-Cotterêts, 66
Ruff, Julius 108
Russia 208, 212, 215

St. Andrew's cross 129
Saint Cyprian 115
Saint-Honoré, rue 259–61; *see also* carts
Saint-Jacques, faubourg of 269
Saint-Omer, town of 60, 73, 82, 294 n.79
Saint-Pierre, prison of 275
Saint-Pol, Louis de Luxembourg, comte de 119, 123–4, 133
Saint-Simon, Louis de Rouvroy, duc de 156–7, 160, 164, 167
Salcède, Nicolas 133

Salian Franks 24–9
Salic law 24, 29–32, 36–7, 41–3, 47, 99, 112, 202
Salve Regina 103–5
Sanch, confraternity of the 106
Sanson, Charles 74, 83
Sanson, Charles Gabriel 87–8
Sanson Charles Henri 74, 88, 178, 224, 241–2, 247–8
Savigny, Friedrich Carl von 24
Sayre, Francis Bowes 49
Scarron, Paul 144
Schaub, chevalier de 172
Scotland 35
Scudéry, Madeleine de 152–4, 160
self defense, death penalty as form of societal 203–4, 208, 216, 229
Semblançay, Jacques de Beaune, sieur de 102
sensibility 142–3, 150–64, 181; *see also* sympathy
sentence, reading of 92, 94–5, 99, 101
Serpillon, François 292 n.43
Servan, Joseph-Michel-Antoine 209–10, 215–16
Sévigné, Marie de Rabutin-Chantal, marquise de 144–49, 154–5, 166, 248, 278
sexual offences 36, 45; *see also* sodomy, adultery, rape
Shaftesbury, Anthony Ashley Cooper, the third Earl of 160–3, 181, 183, 314 n.18
shame, rituals of 56, 90–8
Sharpe, J. A. 307 n.43
simony 43, 52
sin 33–7, 43, 48–9, 101; *see also* penance
slander 31
slavery, as punishment 31, 211
    forced labor as replacement for, 212
slaves, punishment of 31–2, 112
Smail, Daniel Lord 293 n.49
Smith, Adam 185–6, 188
smuggling 174, 211
social class, *see* audience, social composition of; *see also* aristocracy
sodomy, as general category 59–60, 64, 100, 110–11
    as relations between human beings and animals, 2, 110–11
    as same-sex relations, 28, 60, 110, 172
Somme rural 47, 53–4, 63
sorcery 28, 37, 95, 138, 148
Sourches, François-Louis Du Bouchet, marquis de 156–7, 160, 164
sovereign majesty, punishment as the exercise of 11–14, 28
Sow of Falaise, 1–11, 17–19, 111, 280–1; *see also* animals, punishment of
Spain 35, 40, 105–6
spectacular punishment, concept of, 16, 43–4, 48–9, 56–7, 95, 111–16, 175, 191
    calls for restoration of 258–60
    criticism of 151, 181, 191, 205–6, 209–11
    decline of and limitations on 173, 175, 188, 203, 217, 225, 233, 264, 266–79
    as pure spectacle (without violence) 198, 212–13, 228–9, 234, 240
    Revolutionary debates on the abolition of 219–38
    rise of, in medieval Europe 57–65, 89
    as sign of high justice 58, 76; *see also* audience; deterrence; executions; mutilation; patients; pillory; whipping
spectators, *see* audience
speeches, *see* patients, speeches of
Spierenburg, Pieter 14, 17, 310 n.7, 313 n.73
Spirkel, family of executioners 75
squeamishness, *see* executions, horror of
Stein, Peter 40
stoicism 151–55, 160, 163
Strasbourg 77
Stuart, Kathy 80
Suard, Jean-Baptiste-Antoine 191, 272
suffering, *see* patients
suicide 107, 109, 188, 211, 292 n.43
Sully, Madame de 149
Summa Theologica 203
surgery, death penalty compared to 203–4, 219
Sweden 272
Switzerland 2, 14, 75, 108–9, 111, 126, 128–9, 135
sympathy
    affective circle of 146, 155–60, 162–4
    as natural human instinct 142–4, 151, 154–55, 158–64, 165–7, 173, 181, 183–5, 257, 275, 279
    as peculiar trait of individuals 150–1, 153–4, 163, 256–7
    as voyeurism and self-interest 184–6, 188
    see also audience, compassion of; sensibility; women, sensitivity of

Taïeb, Emmanuel 273
Tale of Two Cities 255
talion, law of 6, 9, 62, 200, 202–3
Tellenbach, Gerd 43
The Terror 183, 252–61, 266–9
Theodosian Code 27–8, 32, 39, 53
theater 169, 181, 184, 206; *see also* actors
theatricality, *see* pity, tragic
theft, in Salic law 29, 32
    in customary law 50–52, 57–8, 62
    in medieval and early modern periods, 100, 196, 200, 202, 211, 215
Thermidor 254, 258, 267–9
Thomas, citizen 242–4
Ticquet, Angélique-Nicole Carlier de 155–8, 160, 167
Tocqueville, Alexis de 145–6, 150, 154
tombereau, *see* cart

torture (inquisitorial) 92–3, 155, 170, 195, 214
Toulouse, city of 138, 168, 188
  customal of 46
  law school of 40
Touraine 66
Tournai 56, 62
Toussaint, François-Vincent 199–200
tragic pity, *see* pity, tragic
treachery 50, 53–5
treason 28, 53, 96, 186, 216; *see also* treachery
Très Ancien Coutumier 46, 58, 112
tricoteuses 183, 255, 257, 276, 278
Troyes 77, 82, 144
Troyes, Jean de 123
Tuault de la Bouverie, Joseph Golven 235–6
tumbrel, *see* carts
Turgot, Anne–Robert–Jacques 85–6
Turgot, Michel-Etienne 173
Turner, Victor 15, 99
Tyssot de Patot, Simon 198–99

undoing, punishment as a form of 31
United States 271–2, 280–4
Utopia 196–8, 202

Vacarius, legal scholar 40
Vairasse, Denis 197–9, 207, 212

Valence 174
Versailles 219, 275–6
Vienna 145
Villars, Marie (Gigault de Bellefonds), marquise de 145
Viollet, Paul 25, 50
Visigoths 24, 26–8, 35
Vogel, Cyrille 34, 35
Voltaire 182, 208, 210–12, 215
voyeurism, *see* audience, voyeurism of

Weidmann, Eugène 275–9
wergeld 29–30, 32–3, 35–6, 99
wheel, punishment of 63–4, 129, 133, 144–6, 166, 170, 172–4, 184, 188–90, 201, 227
whipping 62, 63, 76, 90, 92–5, 98–99, 108, 221
windows, *see* audience, watching from windows
witchcraft, *see* sorcery
Wollaston, William 162
women
  criticism of for watching executions 156–7, 165, 179–83, 190–1, 255–6, 276, 278
  punishment of as distinct from men 57, 59–60, 63, 100
  sensitivity of 157, 162, 181–2, 190–1, 256–7

The manufacturer's authorised representative in the EU for product safety is
Oxford University Press España S.A. of el Parque Empresarial San Fernando de
Henares, Avenida de Castilla, 2 – 28830 Madrid (www.oup.es/en or product.
safety@oup.com). OUP España S.A. also acts as importer into Spain of products
made by the manufacturer.

www.ingramcontent.com/pod-product-compliance
Ingram Content Group UK Ltd.
Pitfield, Milton Keynes, MK11 3LW, UK
UKHW022230230426
12048UKWH00016BA/1169